5/01

CUCKOOS, COWBIRDS AND OTHER CHEATS

CUCKOOS, COWBIRDS AND OTHER CHEATS

N. B. Davies

Illustrated by
David Quinn

T & A D POYSER

London

First published in 2000 by T & A D Poyser Ltd
Harcourt Place, 32 Jamestown Road, London NW1 7BY, UK
http://www.academicpress.com

ISBN 0-85661-135-2

A catalogue record for this book is available from the British Library

Typeset by Phoenix Photosetting, Chatham, Kent, UK
Printed by The Bath Press, Bath, Avon, UK

00 01 02 03 04 05 BP 9 8 7 6 5 4 3 2 1

Contents

The colour plate section can be found between pages 150 and 151.

For Jan, Hannah and Alice

Acknowledgements

Many people have helped with this book. My studies of cuckoos and their hosts have been done together with Michael Brooke, Stuart Butchart, Lisle Gibbs, Ian Hartley, Alex Kacelnik, Rebecca Kilner, Susan McRae and David Noble. It is a pleasure to thank them, and the Natural Environment Research Council and The Royal Society for funding our work. Several of my PhD students at Cambridge have studied brood parasites and have given me the privilege of writing about their discoveries, including: William Duckworth and Christopher Kelly (Common Cuckoos), Gabriela Lichtenstein (cowbirds), Anna Lindholm (Common and Diederik Cuckoos), David Noble (cuckoos in Namibia) and Susan McRae (moorhens). My ideas have also been influenced by discussions with Arnon Lotem, Karen Marchetti, Arne Moksnes, Hiroshi Nakamura, Robert Payne, Tomas Redondo, Eivin Røskaft, Stephen Rothstein and Fugo Takasu.

I thank my colleagues at Pembroke College, Antony Hopkins and Colin Wilcockson, for advice about cuckoos in history and literature, and Audrey Meaney, for translating a cuckoo riddle from the Old English. I am very grateful to the following, who helped me by providing information and commenting on the various chapters: Michael Brooke, Lesley Brooker, Michael Brooker, Stuart Butchart, Jeremy Field, Tibor Fuisz, Rebecca Kilner, Naomi Langmore, Gabriela Lichtenstein, Bruce Lyon, Susan McRae, Ben Mines, David Noble, Val Nolan Jr., Robert Payne, Juan Carlos Reboreda, Scott Robinson, Stephen Rothstein, Paul Sherman, Jamie Smith, Juan José Soler, Manolo Soler, Michael Sorenson and Michael Taborsky. Several colleagues have generously allowed me to use their colour photographs, which are acknowledged in the Plates.

Once again, it has been an honour to team up with David Quinn. His brilliant drawings illuminate the evolutionary questions and, at the same time, convey the thrill of watching these astonishing birds in the wild. For help in providing study specimens for the drawings, David thanks Clemency Fisher, Malcolm Largen and Tony Parker from the Liverpool Museum, and Mark Adams and Frank Steinheimer from the British Museum at Tring. We both thank Andrew Richford, from Academic Press, for his enthusiastic and expert advice and for seeing our project through to publication.

Finally, a special thank you to Ann Jeffrey, without whom I would still be floundering with chapter 1. She not only helped with all the correspondence, but also put two ink pots'-worth of my hand-written script onto a disc, with incredible speed and good humour, and enabled an academic dinosaur to stagger into the next century.

I dedicate this book to my wife Jan, and to my daughters, Hannah and Alice.

Nicholas Davies
Cambridge, June 1999

CHAPTER 1

A monstrous outrage on maternal affection

We begin on Wicken Fen, just north of Cambridge in the east of England. It is early June, and the city throngs with students celebrating the end of the University year and with the first crowds of summer tourists. But out in the fens, there is a different world – a vast, flat landscape where the horizon is bounded by waving reeds and where nature provides other summer visitors, with dramas more extraordinary than any dreamt by human kind.

It is late afternoon, and we sit quietly on the bank of a dyke to witness a miracle of evolution. Hidden deep in the reeds and woven around three newly sprouting stems, just one metre above the water surface, is the nest of a Reed Warbler. It is a deep cup, built entirely from the old, pale yellow stems and seed heads of last year's reeds. The female laid her final egg this morning, an hour after dawn, and now she sits on a clutch of four. The eggs are pale green in colour, speckled with olive, grey and darker green, and they fit snugly into the nest as the reeds sway in the wind. The incubating bird seems nervous. Though she may briefly close her eyes and settle deep into the nest cup, the slightest sound alerts her. She peers over the edge when a Pike splashes in the water below or as a Moorhen swims past, and every few minutes she stands to poke into the nest or to turn the eggs with her bill. The male begins to sing his jaunty, scratchy song on the other side of the dyke and the female slips quietly away to join him, flitting between the reeds and catching a damselfly from the water surface as she leaves.

All seems quiet, until a faint rustle of a branch in the hawthorn tree behind leads us to turn and catch a glimpse of a large grey bird gliding straight towards the nest. She lands on the rim and bows into the cup. A few seconds later she lifts her head and, carefully holding one of the warbler's eggs in her bill, she moves forward to sit on the nest. We can see her yellow eye and pale underparts, barred with grey like a hawk (**Plate 1a**). Her abdomen moves down slightly as she lays her own egg. Then, without even a single glance into the nest, she flies off, still carrying the warbler's egg in her bill. She lands in the bushes some 30 m away, swallows the egg whole, and then utters a strange, liquid bubbling cry as if in triumph. She is immediately answered in the distance by the more familiar two-note call of a male, a loud ringing 'cuck-oo', and then she flies off, low between the bushes, with rapid shallow beats of her pointed wings.

The Cuckoo's visit to the Reed Warbler's nest lasted no more than 10 seconds. It is hard to believe she could have laid in such a short time. But we wade out to the nest and, sure enough, she has succeeded. There is still a clutch of four, but now one egg is a little larger, more rounded and glossy than the others, though it is an impressive match of the warbler's eggs both in ground colour and spotting (**Plate 1b**).

We retreat to our sitting place on the bank. A minute later the female Reed Warbler returns. She peers briefly into the nest. All appears to be well. She shuffles down to resume incubation. We watch a Marsh Harrier sail overhead, and the Reed Warbler also tilts her head to watch it pass. Fifteen minutes later her mate arrives with a large yellow and black hoverfly in his bill. He passes it gently to her and she then leaves. The male looks at the clutch, pecks briefly at the bottom of the nest, and then he settles down on the eggs to keep them warm while the female feeds nearby.

Eleven days pass. The reeds have grown and the nest is now well concealed among the new green leaves. In the early morning we wade out into the dyke once more. There are still three warbler eggs, but the cuckoo egg has just hatched. There, among the fragments of its empty egg shell, lies the cuckoo chick, naked, pink and blind. We retreat to continue our vigil. The female warbler arrives, picks up the broken shells and flies off. A few seconds later she is back on the nest.

Later that day we return to observe one of the most extraordinary events in the natural world. The cuckoo chick is just a few hours old but it has become more active and wriggles about in the bottom of the nest. It has an unusually broad back, with a shallow depression, and when, by chance, one of the warbler's eggs touches this spot, it springs into action. Balancing the egg in the hollow of its back, it braces its legs against the sides of the nest. With its head held down, it slowly works the egg up to the nest rim, its wings outspread to help keep the egg in place (**Plate 1c**). The cuckoo weighs 3 g and the warbler's egg is just under 1 g, so the task is not easy. Short bouts of effort alternate with spells of rest, where the cuckoo holds its position, braced against the side. Eventually the cuckoo backs the egg up to the edge of the nest. Clasping the rim with its wing tips, it gives a final push and jerks its load over the top. The egg plops into the water below and the cuckoo collapses back into the bottom of the nest, panting from exhaustion. The whole exercise took four minutes. And there are still two eggs to go.

The Reed Warblers return to their reduced clutch and continue to take turns on the nest. An hour later, the second ejection begins while one of the parents is brooding. It shuffles and tries to keep its position while beneath it the cuckoo chick climbs up the nest. Eventually the warbler is pushed right off. It stands aside to watch and does nothing to interfere as its egg is heaved overboard. The last egg meets the same fate, but this time the cuckoo needs three attempts to accomplish its task because the egg keeps rolling back into the nest cup. But by dusk, the work is done and the cuckoo has become the sole occupant of the nest.

Apparently oblivious to the destruction of their own chances of reproduction, the pair of warblers then slave away to feed the imposter. By 10 days of age it completely fills the nest but the warblers continue to bring food from dawn to dusk, even as the chick grows to eight times their own body weight (**Plate 2a**). By the time the cuckoo fledges, at 20 days of age, the nest has disappeared beneath it and has become flattened into a precarious platform. The cuckoo then leaves the reeds and flies to the bushes nearby, where it is fed for a further two weeks until it becomes independent. During the final stages, the warblers sometimes have to perch on the cuckoo's back in order to feed it and they seem to risk being devoured themselves as they bow deep into the enormous gape with food (**Plate 2b**).

A BLIGHT ON CREATION

Naturalists have marvelled at these interactions between the Common Cuckoo *Cuculus canorus* and its hosts at least since the time of Aristotle (384–322 BC), writing some 2,300 years ago:

> it lays its eggs in the nest of smaller birds after devouring these birds' eggs.[1]

> they . . . do not sit, nor hatch, nor bring up their young, but when the young bird is born it casts out of the nest those with whom it has so far lived.[2]

A few years earlier, the playwright Aristophanes (414 BC) used the name 'Nephelococcygia', which means cloud cuckoo land, for his imaginary city with a community free from all cares and duties, which suggests that he also knew about the cuckoo's parasitic habits.

In England, too, the cuckoo makes frequent appearances in the oldest writings. This bird riddle, translated from Old English, appears in *The Exeter Book*, a manuscript dating from AD 950–1000, and surely refers to the cuckoo being raised by foster parents:[3]

> In these days my father and mother gave me up as dead; nor was there a spirit for me as yet, a life within. Then a certain very faithful kinswoman began to cover me with garments, kept me and protected me, wrapped me in a sheltering robe as honourably as her own children, until I, under the garment, as my fate was, grew up, an unrelated stranger. The gracious kinswoman fed me afterwards until I became adult, could set out further on my travels.

The young Cuckoo is often quoted as a symbol of greed. In Chaucer's poem, *The Parlement of Foules* (*c.* 1382), the Merlin chastises the Cuckoo (line 612):

> Thow rewtheless glotoun!

In another fourteenth-century poem, *The Boke of Cupide* by Sir John Clanvowe (heavily reliant on Chaucer), the Cuckoo's lack of parental care comes to represent a life with no love at all. An opposition is set up between the Cuckoo and the Nightingale. The Cuckoo says love is nonsense and only brings unhappiness. The Nightingale argues that love is mainspring of 'al goodnesse, al honour and al gentilnesse . . . perfyt joy'. The birds decide to have a 'parlement', with an eagle in charge, so that a judgement will be given on the debate. The event will be on Valentine's Day, 'Before the chambre wyndow of the quene'. The reader is left to imagine the result, but there is little doubt that the Cuckoo will become an outcast.

The adult Cuckoo's habit of abandoning all care of its eggs and young to other, host, species has also inspired country superstitions. In the southwest of England, in the county of Somerset, young children were told to run their fastest if they ever heard a Cuckoo, so as to ward off any infections of laziness.

The Cuckoo's cheating of its hosts might be supposed to have given rise to the word cuckold, a husband cheated in love by an unfaithful wife. However, 'cuckold' may have a separate derivation and no original association with the bird. Nevertheless, frequent links are made between the two in English literature. Shakespeare often plays on the word cuckoo when alluding to adultery. In *Love's Labours Lost*, for example, there is the song:

> When daisies pied and violets blue
> And lady-smocks, all silver white,
> And cuckoo-buds of yellow hue
> Do paint the meadows with delight,
> The cuckoo then on every tree
> Mocks married men, for thus sings he
> Cuckoo!

One of the most crazy of all cuckoo theories was inspired by a direct link between the two words. Acworth (1946) suggested that the host male really is a cuckold because the Cuckoo chick is in fact a hybrid offspring of the male Cuckoo and the female host species! Equally strange were the ideas of the Russian biologist Lysenko who, in the late 1940s, formulated a new theory of species formation. He suggested that many species of plants and animals could transform spontaneously into other, quite different species. As an example, he asserted that warblers could give birth to cuckoos.[4] These are mad ideas, of course, and easily refuted by our visit to the fens where we observed the female Cuckoo lay in the host nest. Nevertheless, perhaps we should reserve some sympathy for even the wildest of theories because the behaviour of the Cuckoo is indeed both abhorrent to the layperson and a puzzle to the professional biologist.

Why does the Cuckoo readily abandon its eggs and offspring to the care of others? We are so familiar with our own strong parental urges and with our observations of birds defending their nests and feeding their young that we may suppose that these instincts should be part of the normal behaviour of all species whose offspring require nurture and protection. The Cuckoo's behaviour seems both cruel and unnatural. It is not surprising, therefore, that early writers sought for explanations based on abnormalities in cuckoo design. A common view was that the Cuckoo had defective parental instincts and so its parasitic habits were bestowed by a benevolent Creator. In *The Fowles of Heauen* (1614), Edward Topsell admired 'that naturall discretion with which the Grand Creator hath bestowed upon this siely fowle for the propagation of her oune kinde … it understandeth her oune frigiditie, or coldnes of nature, utterly disablinge it to hatche her oune kinde. Nature beinge defective in one part is wont to supply by another … want of streingth is recompenced with witt … the worke of God is wonderfull, and his mercy to his Creature magnificent.'

Others thought that the Cuckoo's defect laid not so much in its parental behaviour but rather in its anatomy. In 1752 the French anatomist Herissant proposed that the Cuckoo's strange gut prevented it from incubation. He noted that its stomach was large and protruded low into the belly, and suggested that were the Cuckoo to sit on her eggs she would surely smash them.[5] In his *Natural History of Selborne* (1789), the British naturalist Gilbert White also regarded the Cuckoo's parasitic habits as unnatural and 'a monstrous outrage on maternal affection, one of the first great dictates of nature'. He dissected a Cuckoo and concurred with Herissant that 'the crop placed just upon the bowels must, especially when full, be in a very uneasy situation during the business of incubation'. However, he went on to show that other species, including the Nightjar, Swift and Hen Harrier, which do care for their own eggs and young, also had similar internal anatomy and concluded that 'Monsieur Herissant's conjecture, that cuckoos are incapable of incubation from the disposition of their intestines, seems to fall to the ground: and we are still at a loss for the cause of that strange and singular peculiarity in the instance of the cuculus canorus'.[5]

Edward Jenner (1788) agreed that 'the principal matter that has agitated the mind of the naturalist respecting the Cuckoo [is] why it should not build a nest, incubate its eggs and rear its own young'. He tested Herissant's idea directly by experiment. He placed two partly incubated eggs of the Pied Wagtail under a two-week-old Cuckoo nestling that was being raised in the nest of a Hedge Sparrow (= Dunnock). After a week, the wagtail eggs hatched so Jenner concluded that if the young Cuckoo was capable of incubating a clutch then surely the adult could do so too. Instead, he suggested that the reason the Cuckoo does not raise its own young is the fact that it spends such a short time on the breeding grounds. In the Cambridgeshire fens, for example, most Cuckoos lay their first eggs in early June and they depart for African winter quarters in the second week of July. This six-week breeding period would, Jenner argued, hardly be sufficient to enable the Cuckoo to look after its own eggs. The Cuckoo lays at two-day intervals, so even a modest clutch of three, for example, would take five days to complete. To this we need to add, say, a week to build a nest, 11 days' incubation, 20 days to feed the nestlings and another two weeks' care after fledging, a total of at least eight weeks for a single brood. Jenner's idea was that the Cuckoo's habit of laying at two-day intervals, coupled with its early migration, compelled it to be a parasite.

This is a fascinating argument, but it seems odd to today's naturalists who are familiar with the idea of evolution. Jenner's assumption that the Cuckoo is stuck with an immutable habit of early migration seems unlikely, given the variable migratory patterns within many species. Instead, it seems obvious that Jenner has got his argument back to front – the Cuckoo chooses to depart early precisely because it is a parasite and has no need to stay longer. In fact the adult Cuckoos' departure in the second week of July coincides with the time that the Reed Warblers cease to start new clutches and so marks the end of the season's opportunities for parasitism.

In 1824, John Blackwall was one of the first to appreciate that the various instincts of the Cuckoo, including the early migration of the adults and the ejection behaviour of the newly hatched nestling, made good sense in relation to its parasitic lifestyle and concluded that 'the history of the Cuckoo, by the evident marks of design which it displays in the admirable adoption of means to ends, affords a most convincing proof of the existence of a Great First Cause, the mysterious source of all that is good and beautiful in nature'. But it was Charles Darwin who showed how such beautiful design could come about; far from being unnatural, the Cuckoo's parasitic habits could have evolved from a non-parasitic ancestor as adaptations to increase its own selfish reproductive output.

NATURAL SELECTION

Darwin's revolutionary idea in *The Origin of Species* (1859) was the theory of natural selection. The idea is so simple that, on first hearing it, Darwin's friend T.H. Huxley remarked 'How extremely stupid of me not to have thought of that myself!' But its far-reaching implications for how we expect animals to be designed are still keeping biologists busy today. There are five steps to the argument and we can illustrate them by considering the Reed Warbler, which we saw playing host to the Cuckoo on Wicken Fen.

- Individuals within a species differ in their morphology, physiology and behaviour (**variation**). For example, some Reed Warblers are slightly larger than others, or have more pointed wings, or darker plumage, or their eggs differ in ground colour or spotting patterns. There is also variation in their behaviour; for example, some are bold and exploratory when confronted with new situations or a predator near the nest while others are more nervous.
- Some of this variation is **heritable** so offspring will tend to be like their parents. As shown for other bird species, it is likely that many aspects of Reed Warbler morphology and behaviour are influenced by genes, including body size, egg colour, boldness, and so on.
- Organisms have a huge capacity for increase in numbers. A pair of Reed Warblers has time for two broods per year, each of four chicks. In captivity, small birds may live for 10 years or more. If, in the wild, the parents and all their offspring survived, then in the following year the population would have increased five-fold and after 10 years it would be several million times as large! Clearly this does not happen. Numbers do vary between years but in the long term, provided the habitat available does not change, many populations remain more or less steady in numbers. This means that in nature there must be heavy mortality. In the Reed Warbler, only half of the nests produce fledged young. The rest fail through predation, parasitism by Cuckoos and occasional destruction in heavy wind and rain. Thus each pair raises, on average, four young to the fledging stage. About half the adults die between breeding seasons, so if the population remains constant then three out of four young fledged per year must die before they have the chance to breed. Darwin concluded that there must be a struggle for existence with strong **competition** for scarce resources, such as food and places to live.
- Some of the mortality may occur simply through bad luck. A particularly ferocious storm may destroy all the Reed Warbler nests, for example. But sometimes mortality will vary depending on the characteristics of the individual and some variants will leave more surviving offspring than others. The offspring

will inherit the characteristics of their successful parents and so, by the inevitable process of **natural selection**, organisms will become **adapted** to their environment. The individuals that are selected by nature will be those with characteristics which best enable them to survive and reproduce.

- If the environment changes, then new variants may win the competitive struggle. So natural selection can give rise to **evolutionary change** between generations. Populations may gradually evolve different characteristics (behaviour or structure) over time. Darwin's argument was a verbal one but has now been modelled mathematically. For example, if there are two variants in a large population which differ by just 1% in their chance of surviving to breed, then this small difference will be sufficient to cause the more successful variant to increase from 1% of the population to 99% in under two thousand generations, a mere blink of an eye in the aeons of evolutionary time.[6]

Darwin assumed that evolution by natural selection would proceed so slowly that we would not be able to observe the changes ourselves. Indeed, *The Origin* does not document a single case of natural selection in action, and in a famous passage Darwin wrote, 'natural selection is daily and hourly scrutinising, throughout the world, the slightest variations; rejecting those that are bad, preserving and adding up all that are good . . . [but] we see nothing of these slow changes in progress, until the hand of time has marked the lapse of ages'.

However, there are now several examples of variants having such a strong selective advantage in nature that evolutionary change takes place even within a few years. Two recent studies of wild bird populations provide wonderful cases of evolution in action. The first comes from a study of the Medium Ground Finch on the island of Daphne Major in the Galapagos. Darwin spent just three weeks in the Galapagos, but Peter and Rosemary Grant and their co-workers from Princeton University have been there for the past 25 years, carefully measuring the beaks of the finches and the sizes of the seeds available. Some individuals in the Medium Ground Finch population have small beaks and they prefer small seeds, while others have larger beaks and prefer larger seeds. In 1977 there was a terrible drought, the plants withered and 85% of the finch population starved to death. Peter Boag and Peter Grant found that it was the small-beaked birds which suffered the greatest mortality because the small seeds became especially scarce. The larger-beaked individuals survived better because they were more efficient at dealing with the larger seeds. This differential mortality was a dramatic demonstration of Darwin's principle of natural selection. The result was a greater proportion of large-billed birds in the breeding population. Their offspring inherited their parents' large bills and so the average beak size of the population increased over the following generation. The magnitude of this evolutionary change, observable over just a few years, was exactly that predicted from detailed measurements of the feeding efficiency of different beak sizes and their heritability from parent to offspring.[7]

A second example comes from the remarkable studies of bird migration by Peter Berthold, from the Max-Planck Institute at Radolfzell, Germany. The Blackcap is a small warbler which breeds in Europe and migrates to Africa for the winter. Over the last 30 years or so, with warmer winters, there have been more and more records of Blackcaps spending the winter in Britain. At first it was assumed that these were

British breeders which had stayed on, instead of migrating. But ringing recoveries showed that the winter birds came from central Europe, and had adopted the new migration route of going northwest to Britain in the autumn instead of south to Africa. Berthold was able to study the migration direction of the Blackcaps in the laboratory, by keeping birds in cages where they could see the star patterns of the night sky, which they use as a means of navigation. During the migration period the birds fluttered against one side of the cage, indicating the direction they wanted to fly. He showed that migration direction is genetically controlled, with offspring from parents which migrate northwest inheriting the preference for the new migration direction.[8] This is a fascinating example of a recent evolutionary change in behaviour likely to have been favoured as a result of global warming.

DARWIN ON CUCKOOS

Darwin's theory of natural selection showed, for the first time, how adaptation and complex design could come about without a Creator. In chapter 8 of *The Origin of Species* he used his theory to explain the parasitic behaviour of the Common Cuckoo. His argument involved comparing its habits with those of the 'American cuckoo', which makes its own nest and rears its own young. It is not clear exactly to which species Darwin is referring here, but it was probably the two North American cuckoos in the genus *Coccyzus*, the Yellow-billed Cuckoo and the Black-billed Cuckoo, which are similar in size and appearance and have the same nesting habits. Although they are classified in a different genus to the parasitic Common Cuckoo, they are placed in the same family, the Cuculidae, and so are close relatives. Darwin learnt from his correspondents that the American cuckoos occasionally laid eggs in the nests of other species, which later studies have confirmed. He then suggested the following evolutionary sequence:

> Now let us suppose that the ancient progenitor of our European cuckoo had the habits of the American cuckoo, and that she occasionally laid an egg in another bird's nest. If the old bird profited by this occasional habit through being enabled to migrate earlier or through any other cause; or if the young were made more vigorous by advantage being taken of the mistaken instinct of another species than when reared by their own mother, encumbered as she could hardly fail to be by having eggs and young of different ages at the same time; then the old birds or the fostered young would gain an advantage. And analogy would lead us to believe, that the young thus reared would be apt to follow by inheritance the occasional and aberrant habit of their mother, and in their turn would be apt to lay their eggs in other birds' nests, and thus be more successful in rearing their young. By a continued process of this nature, I believe that the strange instinct of our cuckoo has been generated.

Darwin packs more good ideas into these four sentences than all previous commentators on the Cuckoo since Aristotle, so it is worth going over his argument more slowly. He raises three questions, and these form the basis for much of this book. First, he points out the positive advantages of parasitism. Not only is the adult relieved of all parental duties, so it can migrate earlier and, we might add, has the potential to lay more eggs, the young may also gain a benefit. They are raised alone in the host nest and escape competition for food, so may gain better nurture than they would if reared in a brood by their own parents. Put this way, the worries of Jenner and his contemporaries 70 years earlier can be turned on their heads – why are there not lots of species of cuckoo in Britain, instead of just one, to take advantage of the work force offered by all the honest parental species?

Second, Darwin suggests that the host's acceptance of the cuckoo egg and chick is the working of a 'mistaken instinct'. The Reed Warblers are designed by selection to be efficient at raising their own offspring. They sometimes raise a Cuckoo simply because they are tricked into doing so. This interpretation seems so obvious now that it is difficult to appreciate the revolution brought about by Darwin's ideas. But consider the following explanation of the host's response to a cuckoo, offered by Bechstein in pre-Darwinian days.[9]

> It is wonderful to observe what great apparent delight the birds show when they see a female Cuckoo approach their abode. Instead of leaving their eggs, as they do when disturbed by the approach of other animals, they seem quite beside themselves for joy. The little Wren, for example, when brooding over its own eggs, immediately quits its nest on the approach of the Cuckoo, as though to make room to enable her to lay her egg more commodiously. Meanwhile she hops round her with such expressions of delight that her husband at length joins her, and both seem lavish in their thanks for the honour which the great bird confers upon them by selecting their nest for its own use.

Here, the hosts are assumed to behave for the good of all Creation and their alarm calls are mistaken for glee. But there is no room for such generosity in Darwin's world. Any hosts which preferred to raise cuckoos rather than their own young would, of course, fail to pass on their generous instincts to future generations. Their habits would soon be weeded out by natural selection. As Darwin himself wrote,[10] 'If it could be proved that any part of the structure of any one species had been formed for the exclusive good of another species, it would annihilate my theory, for such could not have been produced through natural selection.'

However, all the evidence, from both theory and observations, points to a world full of organisms pursuing their own selfish interests. We don't have to look far to realize that hosts are not designed for the good of cuckoos. For example, the neat, domed nest of the Wren is a perfect fit for a brood of their own young, but the young Cuckoo becomes so enormous that it has to burst through the roof. Reed Warbler nests have a deep cup to keep their brood safe and snug as the reeds sway in the wind, but the young Cuckoo soon outgrows this home and the nest sometimes disintegrates beneath its bulk, with the result that it falls into the water below and drowns. Clearly, the Cuckoo has had to adapt its life as best it can given host adaptations that have evolved for the good of the hosts themselves. As we shall discover, this includes beating defences that hosts evolve to thwart the Cuckoo. The result is 'an evolutionary arms race' in which each party is selected to outwit the other.[11] One of the main aims of this book is to explore the consequences of this battle. Why, for example, don't Reed Warblers evolve instincts that are not susceptible to the mistake of accepting a cuckoo chick?

The third suggestion made by Darwin is that the parasitic habits of the Common Cuckoo evolved gradually from a parental ancestor. In fact, we now know that only 40% of the world's cuckoo species are parasitic (57 out of the 140 species in the family Cuculidae), so the majority of cuckoos raise their own young. Darwin went on to discuss possible examples of the gradual perfection of parasitic instincts in birds, but field studies of bird behaviour were still in their infancy during Darwin's time and he had little information to support his conjectures. However, during the last 30 years, field workers have produced a wealth of new observations on the extent of brood parasitism in birds. Furthermore, new methods for studying the evolutionary relationships of bird species now offer the possibility of testing ideas for how parasitism may have evolved.

Our field trip to Wicken Fen to watch the Common Cuckoo and its Reed Warbler hosts has provoked some fascinating questions. Before we tackle them, however, we need to widen our scope and look at other species that are also brood parasites.

CHAPTER 2
One hundred brood parasites and some puzzles

According to the latest taxonomy, there are 9672 species of birds.[1] Of these, one hundred, or about one per cent, are obligate brood parasites. That is to say, they never raise their own young but, like the Common Cuckoo, rely entirely on other host species to do all the work of nest building, incubation and chick rearing. The hundred species and their hosts are listed in the Appendix. The parasites come from six families or subfamilies, which are likely to reflect six different evolutionary origins of the parasitic habit in birds (see chapter 15). The aim of this chapter is to provide a brief introduction to the six groups. We need to know who they are, and what they do before we consider the details of how they make their living from tricking other species. The map below shows how they are distributed around the world.

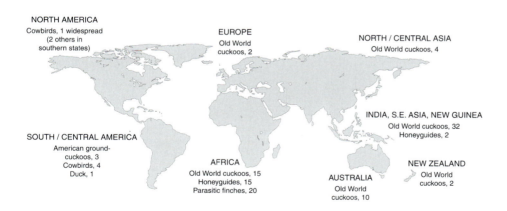

Figure 2.1 Distribution of parasitic birds around the world. The numbers indicate the number of species of each parasitic group in different regions. Some species occur in more than one region.

THE CUCKOOS

Traditional taxonomy, based on anatomy, suggests that the cuckoos are most closely related to the turacos and combines these two families in the order Cuculiformes. However, recent studies of similarities in DNA indicate that the cuckoos have no close living relatives, which suggests that they should, perhaps, be placed in an order of their own. There is also disagreement over classification within the cuckoos because information based on similarities in anatomy and DNA sometimes conflicts. Here, we follow the recent treatment by Robert Payne of the University of Michigan.[2] The cuckoos are placed in one family, Cuculidae, with six subfamilies, three in the Old World and three in the New World. The parasitic cuckoos are in bold.

- OLD WORLD CUCKOOS
  Cuculinae: Old World parasitic cuckoos (54 species)
  Phaenicophaeinae: malkohas (16 species)
                      couas (10 species)
  Centropodinae: coucals   (28 species)

- NEW WORLD CUCKOOS
  Coccyzinae: American cuckoos (18 species)
  Crotophaginae: anis and Guira Cuckoo (4 species)
  Neomorphinae: non-parasitic American ground-cuckoos (7 species)
                      parasitic American ground-cuckoos (3 species)

The parasitic cuckoos occur in just two of the subfamilies. All 54 species of the Old World Cuculinae are parasitic, while three of the 10 species of the New World Neomorphinae are parasitic. All the other cuckoos are non-parasitic – they build nests and rear their own young, just like most other birds. According to this classification, the Old World and New World cuckoos evolved their parasitic habits independently from nesting cuckoo ancestors (chapter 15).

Old World cuckoos

There are just two species in Europe; most live in Africa, Asia and Australasia. They are arboreal birds, with a slim elongated body, long tails and long pointed wings. With their swift and direct flight they often look like birds of prey as they dash past with rapid wing beats. The legs are short and, like all the cuckoos, they have zygodactyl feet, with the middle two toes pointing forwards and the other two (the inner first and outer fourth) pointing backwards. The bills are stout, usually with a hooked tip.

The 54 species are easier to remember if we divide them into groups.

- The genus *Cuculus* contains 14 species; eight breed in Asia, three in Africa, one in Madagascar, one in Australia and one, the Common Cuckoo, breeds throughout the Palaearctic. Most of them are similar in appearance, with greyish or brownish upperparts and paler, heavily barred underparts. They vary in size from the Lesser Cuckoo (25 cm length from bill to tail tip; 52 g) to the Large Hawk-Cuckoo (40 cm; 150 g).

- The genus *Cacomantis*, which includes eight species, has smaller birds (18–26 cm; 22–44 g) again with greyish upperparts but mostly plain brown or rufous underparts. Five occur in southern Asia and three in New Guinea and Australia.
- The genus *Chrysococcyx*, with 15 species, has the smallest cuckoos of all (15–20 cm; 17–35 g). They are known as the glossy or bronze-cuckoos and are often iridescent metallic green or bronze above and plain or barred below. Most of them (11 species) occur in southeast Asia and Australasia with the other four species in Africa.
- The koels, *Eudynamys*, (two species in Asia and two in Australasia) are large cuckoos (38–46 cm; 120–320 g), some glossy black in plumage and others brown and barred.
- The three species of long-tailed cuckoos, *Cercococcyx*, all live in Africa. They are medium-sized (31–34 cm; 55–65 g) and look like long-tailed versions of the *Cuculus* cuckoos.
- The four *Clamator* species are large cuckoos (34–46 cm; 70–125 g) and their scientific name refers to their loud chattering calls. The Levaillant's Cuckoo is restricted to Africa while the Jacobin, or Pied, Cuckoo has a disjunct range, including Africa and the Indian sub-continent. Both these species occur in two morphs; a black and white morph (glossy black above and mainly white below) and an all-black morph (with a white wing patch). The two other *Clamator* cuckoos have longer and more pointed wings, and they lack the black morph. The Chestnut-winged Cuckoo lives in Asia while the Great Spotted Cuckoo ranges from southern Europe to Iran and throughout much of Africa.
- The six other cuckoo species are thought to be sufficiently distinct that they each command their own separate genus. One lives in Africa, the Thick-billed Cuckoo (36 cm; 115 g). One lives in southeast Asia, the Drongo Cuckoo (25 cm; 35 g). Three are from New Guinea: the Long-billed Cuckoo (18 cm; 31 g), the White-crowned Koel (33 cm; 117 g) and the Dwarf Koel (20 cm; 43 g). Last, and by far the largest of all the parasitic cuckoos, is the Channel-billed Cuckoo of Australia (60 cm; 620 g), a huge grey bird with an enormous bill.

The koels and the Channel-billed Cuckoo eat a lot of fruit but most species favour invertebrates, especially the larvae of moths and butterflies, including hairy caterpillars, which other birds find noxious and avoid. Many caterpillars have guts filled with toxins from the leaves they have eaten. Cuckoos extract these contents by the neat trick of snipping off one end and then passing the caterpillar back and forth through the bill to squeeze out the insides before they swallow it. Alternatively, they may remove the gut contents by bashing the caterpillar repeatedly against a branch. The hairs of hairy caterpillars form a mat in the stomach of the cuckoo and are then regurgitated as a pellet.

Cuckoos are solitary and shy, more often heard than seen. Their vernacular names are often derived from the monotonous calls of the males, such as 'cuck-oo', 'ko-el' and 'dee dee dee diederik'. In his poem, addressed to the Common Cuckoo, the English poet William Wordsworth gently complained:

selection's ability to pick out those sounds which are most distinctive against the background noise. In support of Lack's suggestion, playback experiments show that each cuckoo responds only to its own species' call. For example, the African Cuckoo, which looks very similar to the Common Cuckoo but differs in bill colour and details of its plumage, gives the same two-note call but with emphasis on the second note, cuck-oó, and with the second note rising, rather than falling, in pitch. This subtle change makes all the difference; the African Cuckoo responds, by counter-calling and approach, only to its own species' song.[2]

The earliest known records of brood parasitism have been collated by Herbert Friedmann.[4] The oldest reference is to the Asian Koel, in ancient Vedic writings from India around 2000 BC, some four thousand years ago. The bird was given the name 'anya-vapa', which means 'reared by another', so its parasitic habits were known, though no further details are given. The first reference to its hosts are in Sanskrit literature (*c.* AD 375) where koels are described being raised by crows, now known to be the major hosts of this cuckoo. The earliest definite reference to the Common Cuckoo as a parasite is in Aristotle (384–322 BC), quoted in the last chapter. We then wait nearly two thousand years before another brood parasite is mentioned by Jehangir (1605–1627), a Moghul emperor of India, who referred to the Pied Cuckoo using babblers as hosts. In 1806, Levaillant recorded the parasitic habits of some African cuckoos (the Black, African and Diederik). In 1853, Brehm presented the first evidence that the Great Spotted Cuckoo was a parasite in North Africa and in 1879 Meyer reported that Channel-billed Cuckoos in Sulawesi parasitized crows.

The genus *Pachycoccyx* (the Thick-billed Cuckoo) was not known to be parasitic until Townley observed it in 1936. In 1939 Moreau and Moreau suggested for the first time that the long-tailed cuckoos *Cercococcyx* were also likely to be parasitic.[5] They saw a Barred Long-tailed Cuckoo sitting briefly on the nest of an akelat but the cuckoo then returned and apparently destroyed the clutch. Later, the Moreaus caged an injured cuckoo of this species and it laid an egg which closely resembled that of the akelat. Another egg of this type was also observed in the nest of a broadbill, which later contained only a young cuckoo, of unknown species. Bit by bit, therefore, the jigsaw of observations was put together to glimpse a picture of another parasite. But even today, for none of the long-tailed cuckoos are the hosts well known. Indeed a question mark appears in the host column of the Appendix for no fewer than 15 of the 54 Old World cuckoos. There is plenty of bird watching still to be done.

Nevertheless, we now know enough to make some general conclusions. Most hosts are song birds smaller than the cuckoo itself, usually insectivorous species of moderate size (e.g. babblers and shrikes) or of small size (e.g. warblers, chats, sunbirds). In most of the species, just like the Common Cuckoo, the female lays one egg per host nest and then the newly hatched cuckoo chick ejects the host eggs or young and so it is raised alone. This applies to all the *Cuculus*, *Cacomantis* and *Chrysococcyx* cuckoos that have been studied, as well as to *Pachycoccyx*, *Cercococcyx*, *Surniculus* and two of the koels (the Australian Koel and the Long-tailed Koel). However, the Asian Koel does not eject, nor does the Channel-billed Cuckoo. Both these cuckoos parasitize crows of a similar size to themselves. It would be interesting to know whether in these cases the young cuckoo attempts to eject, but soon gives up because the host eggs and chicks are too large, or whether it simply does not try in the first place. Nestlings of the *Clamator* cuckoos likewise do not eject, and apparently never try to do so. They also parasitize largish hosts, including crows and large babblers. Even so, although these non-ejecting cuckoos are sometimes raised alongside the host young, they often outcompete them for food with the result that the host chicks are crushed or starve to death. In species where the cuckoo is raised with the host chicks, the female cuckoo may sometimes lay more than one egg per nest.

Cuckoos are often cited as an example of how natural selection produces perfection in trickery, because the cuckoo egg is such a close match of the host egg. In some cases, the match is indeed wonderful. Many of the cuckoos that parasitize babblers lay plain blue eggs so like those of their hosts, in both size and colour, that the only sure way of identifying the cuckoo egg is by its heavier shell. In other cases the match in colour and spotting is impressive, but the cuckoo egg is obvious to the human observer because it is larger and more rounded in shape. This applies to Common Cuckoo eggs in Reed Warbler nests, for example. But in many cases the cuckoo egg looks strikingly different from the host egg. There may be a rough match in colour, but the spotting pattern is clearly different, or there may be no match at all. For example, in South Africa Jacobin Cuckoos lay plain white eggs, quite unlike the spotted eggs of their bulbul hosts, and Red-chested Cuckoos lay uniform dark brown eggs which look nothing like the pale and spotted eggs of their main host, the Cape Robin. This variation is one of the puzzles we will address later on.

Many of the parasitic Old World cuckoos are migrants. Populations of the two species that breed in Europe spend the winter in Africa, south of the Sahara. An early ringing recovery of the Common Cuckoo was reported in a British national newspaper, *The Observer*, on 5 November 1933: 'A cuckoo ringed in a Pied Wagtail's nest near Eton, Buckinghamshire, met its end in a jungle clearing of the French Cameroons, via the arrow of a native.' Many Asian cuckoos migrate south to winter in southeast Asia and the Malay archipelago, while Australian species move north to New Guinea and the Pacific islands. Within Africa, there are often local movements. For example, cuckoos that breed in South Africa may move north to equatorial regions in the non-breeding season.

These regular movements have led to tropical cuckoos being known as 'rain birds', because they arrive on the breeding grounds and sing at the onset of the rains when most host species begin to breed. In Europe, the Common Cuckoo has long been regarded as a harbinger of spring.[6] The oldest secular lyric in English, dating from *c.* 1250, is the cuckoo song:

> Sumer is icumen in,
> Lhude sing cuccu,
> Groweth sed, and bloweth med,
> And springth the winde nu-sing cuccu!

And Edmund Spenser, sometime undergraduate of my College in Cambridge, Pembroke, also linked the cuckoo's arrival to the coming of spring in his sonnet sequence 'Amoretti' (1595).

> The merry Cuckow, messenger of Spring,
> His trompet shrill hath thrise already sounded.

A traditional rhyme from Norfolk, eastern England, refers to the summer months by the cuckoo's behaviour:

> In April come he will;
> In May he sings all day;
> In June he changes his tune;
> In July he prepares to fly;
> In August, go he must.

Indeed, so regular is the cuckoo in its activities that it was looked upon as a reliable forecaster of future events. Traditions dating back to Roman times advise lovers, on hearing the first cuckoo in spring, to search under their feet for a hair, for it will be the colour of the hair of their future spouse. The number of calls heard was also said to predict the number of children a couple would have, or how long you would live, or how long you would remain unmarried, and so on. In some parts, it was thought unlucky to hear a cuckoo before breakfast, and hearing the first cuckoo in bed was a sure sign of illness or death. However, good fortune would come if one was heard while out walking, and a child born on the first day a cuckoo calls in spring could expect good luck throughout its life.[6]

In Danish folklore, the cuckoo is said not to have time to build a nest simply because it is kept so busy answering all these questions!

New World Cuckoos

The three parasitic ground-cuckoos from the New World are long-legged and long-tailed birds with brown plumage and short, rufous crests. The Striped Cuckoo (28 cm; 52 g) inhabits scrub, forest edge and open country with scattered trees, and it feeds on insects on the ground and in the vegetation. It was first recorded as parasitic in 1909. The hosts are small passerines with domed nests. The cuckoo's eggs are white, bluish-white or bluish-green. Many of the hosts lay eggs of these colours, so there is likely to be egg mimicry. It may be difficult for the young cuckoo to eject the host eggs from a domed nest. Instead, it has another trick. It is equipped with sharp bill hooks and kills the host young. In 1979, Eugene Morton and Susan Farabaugh first described how a three- to four-day-old cuckoo chick stretched up with its gape open and made biting and twisting movements at anything that touched it. As a result, its nestmates (newly hatched wren chicks) became covered in scars, died from their wounds and were then removed by the host parents.

The two *Dromococcyx* cuckoos were not known to be parasitic until 1914 (Pheasant Cuckoo 36 cm; 80 g) and 1949 (Pavonine Cuckoo 28 cm; 48 g). They are forest birds which feed mainly on the ground on insects and lizards. The hosts are small passerines with either open or domed nests. Neither of these cuckoos' eggs are well known. There are reports of host young disappearing soon after the cuckoo hatches but it is not known how this happens. All these species need further study.

Striped Cuckoo (left) with one of its favourite hosts, the Rufous-and-white Wren.

THE COWBIRDS

Two hundred years ago, it was discovered that cuckoos are not the only parasitic birds.[4] In his book *American Ornithology* (1810), Alexander Wilson described observations of a female Brown-headed Cowbird sitting on the nest of a Red-eyed Vireo. On later inspection, the clutch was found to contain an egg quite unlike those of the vireo. Eight years earlier, in 1802, Don Felix de Azara wrote of the parasitic habits of the Shiny Cowbird in Paraguay and Argentina. The Bronzed Cowbird of central America was added to the list of parasites in 1861.

Then, in 1874, W.H. Hudson's observations in Argentina showed that the Screaming Cowbird was a parasite of the Bay-winged Cowbird. Hudson was so thrilled with this finding that he wrote: 'Today I have made a discovery, and am as pleased with it as if I had found a new planet in the sky. The mystery of the bay-wing's nest . . . found containing over the usual complement of eggs is cleared up.' The discovery was a triumph of careful observation because although the parasite and host young are raised together, the eggs are more or less identical, and the nestlings and fledglings are also almost impossible to tell apart, even though the adults of the two species are so different (**Plate 6d**). Only when Hudson saw some of the fledglings apparently 'undergoing the process of transmutation into another species' did he realize what was going on. He concluded: 'It seems impossible for mimicry to go further than this.'[7] Finally, in 1894 the Giant Cowbird was recorded as a parasite to produce a final total of five parasites out of the six cowbird species.

Female Brown-headed Cowbird (left) and one of its many hosts, the Red-eyed Vireo.

The cowbirds are members of the family Icteridae, the New World blackbirds, which includes 96 species. Apart from five cowbirds, all the rest raise their own young. The icterids are among the dominant species in savannahs, grasslands and marshes of North and South America. Many species have adapted to land modified by humans, especially farmland and pastures with cattle. As a result, some of the cowbirds, in particular, have spread dramatically in the last few hundred years. Icterids often feed by probing their bills into the ground, vegetation or crevices, and gaping to expose food under the surface. They are mainly insectivorous, but also eat fruit and seeds. They may gather in large mixed-species flocks in the non-breeding season. Many icterids, including the parasitic cowbirds, have glossy black plumage (**Plates 5a, 6a**). Females are often less glossy or brown.

Two of the parasitic cowbirds are specialist parasites of other icterids. The Screaming Cowbird (18–21 cm; 50–60 g) is highly specific and almost always only parasitizes the Bay-wing Cowbird (18 cm; 45 g). The Giant Cowbird (31–34 cm; 162–219 g) parasitizes just oropendolas and caciques. The other three cowbirds are generalists, parasitizing a variety of passerine species but including other icterids among their favourite hosts. The Brown-headed Cowbird (16–18 cm; 40–50 g) exploits more than two hundred hosts in North America and the Shiny Cowbird (18–21 cm; 45–55 g) also exploits more than two hundred hosts in South America. The Bronzed Cowbird (19–21 cm; 57–67 g) in central America has more than 70 hosts.[8]

The female cowbird often punctures or removes some host eggs before laying, and usually lays just one egg per host nest, though she may lay two or more and some host nests are parasitized by more than one female. The eggs of the Screaming Cowbird are very like those of their host and those of the Giant Cowbird are often a good match of the oropendolas' and caciques' eggs. By contrast, the eggs of the three generalist cowbirds are usually quite unlike those of their hosts (**Plates 5b, c and 6c**).

THE HONEYGUIDES

The honeyguides comprise seventeen species in a separate family, the Indicatoridae. Their closest relatives are the woodpeckers (Picidae). Fifteen species of honeyguide are confined to Africa, south of the Sahara, while the other two are Asian. They are small, inconspicuous birds of forest and open woodland, with olive, grey or brown plumage. They vary in length from 10 to 20 cm and in weight from 10 to 55 g. The bill is short and stout in most species but the three *Prodotiscus* are flycatcher-like and have fine, pointed bills. All the species feed on insects but the characteristic peculiarity of the family is that they also eat wax, taken from active or abandoned bees' nests or from the exudate of other insects. The wax is digested with the help of special bacteria that live in the bird's gut.[9]

In Africa, two species (the Greater and Scaly-throated Honeyguides) guide large mammals to bees' nests and this is the source of the family name. The followers are usually Honey Badgers or Man, but baboons may also be involved. The bird sits nearby while the mammal breaks open the nest, and then it feeds on any comb that remains. Honeyguides eat both bee larvae and the wax, but not the honey itself. This is a remarkable example of cooperation between the honeyguide, which can find the bees' nests but cannot break them open, and mammals, which can gain access to the nests but have difficulty in locating them.

Honey gathering by humans is depicted in rock paintings made 20,000 years ago, so the relationship between honeyguides and Man may well be an ancient one. It has been particularly well studied in Kenya, where the Boran people find honey by following the Greater Honeyguide.[10] Both parties benefit: the average time for a Boran to find a new bees' nest is nine hours if he searches alone, but just three hours with the bird's help, while 96% of bees' nests are accessible to the birds only after humans have opened them with tools. The humans' use of smokey fire to calm the bees' aggression reduces the chance that the birds get stung too.

The Boran and honeyguides have developed a remarkable way of signalling to each other.[10] The Boran whistle (**Plate 7b**), and if there's a honeyguide nearby that knows the whereabouts of a bees' nest, it approaches and flies about restlessly, emitting a persistent call 'tirr-tirr'. It then disappears in the direction of the nest, probably to check its position, and after a while it returns. The time of this 'first disappearance' tells the Boran how far away the nest is – the shorter the time, the closer the nest. The bird then makes short flights towards the nest, waiting to make sure that the Boran are following. The Boran whistle to tell the bird that they are on the trail, and as soon as they catch up to within 5–15 m, the bird flies off again, calling and spreading its white outer-tail feathers, which make it more conspicuous. As bird and humans approach their quarry, the bird makes shorter and shorter flights, and when they arrive it changes its call and circles the nest. The Boran claim that when nests are very far away (more than 2 km) the birds encourage them to follow with deceptively short flights which indicate 'there's not far to go!'. This wonderful interaction with Man, once common in many parts of Africa, is now disappearing because of cultural changes in tribespeople, especially the use of alternative sources of sugar and the loss of local knowledge and skills.

The first discovery of brood parasitism in honeyguides was in 1867 and all of the

Lesser Honeyguide (left) and one of its hosts, the Black-collared Barbet.

11 species whose breeding habits are known are parasitic.[4] The main hosts are hole-nesting species, especially other members of the Order Piciformes, the woodpeckers and barbets, together with hoopoes, woodhoopoes, kingfishers, bee-eaters and starlings. However, the *Prodotiscus* honeyguides parasitize open-nesting hosts, such as flycatchers, warblers and white-eyes.

The female honeyguide lays one egg per host nest, sometimes after she has punctured or removed one or more host eggs. The eggs are white, like those of their hole-nesting hosts (**Plate 7a**). This is likely to reflect the honeyguides' own ancestry as hole-nesters, rather than a newly evolved adaptation for tricking their hosts. In the *Indicator* honeyguides, the young parasite has sharp bill hooks with which it

Figure 2.2 Parasitic chicks with lethal weapons.
Left: The bill hooks of a nestling Lesser Honeyguide (photo by Robert B. Payne).
Right: Bill hooks of a nestling Striped Cuckoo (from Morton & Farabaugh 1979).

lacerates and kills the host nestlings, which are then either trampled into the nest lining or removed by the host parents. It is remarkable that this same weapon has evolved independently in honeyguides and New-World ground-cuckoos. Young *Prodotiscus* honeyguides are also apparently raised alone, but it is not known how the host young die.

The Parasitic Finches

The African parasitic finches include all nineteen species in the genus *Vidua* plus one odd bird, the Cuckoo Finch. The *Vidua* finches are usually classified as grassfinches, Estrildidae, which includes 130 other species, none of which are parasitic. The Cuckoo Finch is traditionally assumed to be more closely related to the weavers, Ploceidae. However, recent genetic studies show that the Cuckoo Finch and the *Vidua* finches are each other's closest relatives, and that they form a distinct group most closely related to the Estrildidae. These results suggest that brood parasitism evolved just once in the African finches, from an ancient estrildid-like ancestor.[11]

The *Vidua* finches are birds of grassland and open woodland and they feed on small seeds of annual grasses that have dropped to the ground. In the non-breeding season they gather in large flocks. Their parasitic habits were first discovered in 1907.[4] They all parasitize other estrildid finches, smaller than themselves, and most specialize on just one host species. Three groups of *Vidua* can be distinguished.[12] In all three groups, the females and non-breeding males are sparrow-like in plumage.

- The indigobirds (10 species) are all similar in size (11 cm; 13–16 g) and appearance. Breeding males are black. The species vary in the colour of their gloss, which may be green, blue or purple, and in the colour of their bill and feet. Their hosts are firefinches and twinspots.
- The paradise whydahs (five species) are larger (15 cm; 19–22 g) and breeding males appear larger still because they have an enormous tail that adds an extra 15–22 cm to their length. The tail is formed through elongation of the central tail feathers, which are flattened and twisted vertically. The breeding males have black upperparts with a yellow collar and belly and a chestnut breast. Their hosts are pytilias.
- The waxbill whydahs (four species) are intermediate in size (12 cm), and the breeding males also have long tails, which adds an extra 20–22 cm to their length, but the tails are narrower. They parasitize waxbills.

All *Vidua* finches lay white eggs, like those of their hosts (**Plate 7c**). This is unlikely to be evolved mimicry but rather a reflection of shared ancestry, because all estrildids have white eggs. The female parasite apparently does not remove any host eggs, and usually lays just one egg per host nest. Unlike most cuckoos and the honeyguides, the young parasite does not kill or eject the host young. Instead, they are all raised together and the parasite chick shows remarkable mimicry of the mouth colour and gape spots of the chicks of its particular host species (**Plate 7d**).

Male and female Shaft-tailed Whydah and their host, the Violet-eared Waxbill.

As we shall see in chapter 13, this is a case of evolved mimicry because parasites and hosts have speciated independently.

The Cuckoo Finch (13 cm; 21 g) differs from the Vidua finches, both in appearance and parasitic habits. The male is bright yellow and the female is streaky brown. It inhabits open grassland, especially near damp areas. It was discovered to be a parasite in 1917.[4] It is not tied to one host but parasitizes various species of small *Prinia* and *Cisticola* warblers. The Cuckoo Finch egg tends to mimic the host eggs, being pale bluish-white with red speckles. Assuming the parasite's ancestor was an estrildid-like bird with white eggs, this is likely to reflect evolved mimicry. The laying of a parasitic egg is usually accompanied by the disappearance of one or more host eggs, so the female Cuckoo Finch probably removes a host egg or two, though this has not been observed directly. Also in contrast to the *Vidua* finches, the Cuckoo Finch chick is strikingly different from the host chicks and there is no mimicry of gape colour. The parasite chick does not evict the host young, but it outcompetes them for food and usually no host young survive to fledge.[13]

A PARASITIC DUCK

The final specialist brood parasite is a duck from South America, the Black-headed Duck, which breeds on freshwater marshes and parasitizes another duck, the Rosy-billed Pochard, two species of coots, and several other hosts too, including gulls and ibises. Its parasitic habits were first discovered in 1918.[4] However, many other species of ducks are occasionally parasitic (chapter 14), and it was only recently that Weller (1968) confirmed that the Black-headed Duck never cares for its own eggs or chicks, so it is the only obligate parasite among some 150 species in the family Anatidae.

The eggs are whitish to buff in colour and unmarked, similar to those of the Rosy-billed Pochard but unlike the coots' eggs, which are spotted. Most host nests have just one parasitic egg. There is only one observation of egg laying, from captivity, where the parasite waited for the Rosy-billed Pochard host to leave its nest and then laid within a visit of eight minutes, simply adding her egg to the clutch without damaging any host eggs.[14] In the wild, there is no evidence that the pochard hosts reject the parasite eggs, but the coots sometimes do so, by burying them under the nest lining.

The parasite egg usually hatches before the host eggs and the duckling is extraordinarily precocial, not only able to feed itself soon after hatching (like other ducks) but also able to keep itself warm within a day or two. Two captive ducklings became independent of the host parent and its brood mates within two days of birth.[15]

Black-headed Duck and one of its hosts, the Red-gartered Coot.

SOME PUZZLES

Our survey of the hundred species of brood parasites is a tribute to generations of naturalists, who have slowly pieced together these fascinating pictures of exploitation, often from fragmented observations. The many missing pieces from the jigsaws also remind us of how little we still know about the natural world. Nevertheless, we already have a host of questions:

- Why are there only one hundred species of brood parasites?
- Why are they restricted to these six groups?
- Why do they usually choose host species smaller than themselves?

- Why are some parasites specialists, while others use many different host species?
- Why are some parasites raised alongside the host young, while others kill them or eject the host eggs?
- Why in some cases does the parasite egg mimic the host egg, while in others it is clearly different?
- Why do parasitic chicks sometimes mimic the host chicks, whereas in other cases they are nothing like them?

Needless to say, we will not be able to provide complete answers to all of these questions. But we can make a start and point to what we need to know in the future. Our starting point will be to return to the Common Cuckoo. This is the best known brood parasite in the Old World, and its wonderful trickery and the counter-defences of its hosts provide clear evidence of an evolutionary arms race. Studies of these interactions may help us to understand why some of the other brood parasites, the generalist cowbirds in particular, are not so refined in their parasitic behaviour.

CHAPTER 3

The Common Cuckoo and its hosts

The Common Cuckoo is an ashy-grey bird, with white underparts barred with brownish-black. In this chapter, I shall refer to it simply as the 'Cuckoo'. The sexes are similar, but some females are distinguishable by buff on the breast and there is also a rare female morph which has rufous upperparts barred with black. Usually, however, it is impossible to tell the sexes apart unless the male gives his 'cuck-oo' call or the female utters her strange bubbling cry. The size is similar to a Collared Dove, though the Cuckoo's long pointed wings and longer tail gives it the appearance of a bird of prey. It breeds throughout Europe, from northern Scandinavia south to the Mediterranean (including the northern shores of Africa) and Turkey, then east through Siberia to Japan and south to the Himalayas and China. Birds from the western Palaearctic winter in Africa, south of the Sahara, while those from east Asia winter in the Indian sub-continent, southeast Asia and the Philippines.[1]

Most Cuckoos arrive in Britain towards the end of April, the males first, followed a week or so later by the females. Their main food supply, caterpillars, does not become abundant until May. This probably explains why females delay laying until the first two weeks of May, so that they can find enough food to form eggs.[2] As a consequence, the Cuckoo misses the chance to parasitize many first clutches of host species resident in Britain, which begin to breed in April (Dunnocks, Robins, Meadow Pipits, Pied Wagtails). However, the Cuckoo arrives in time to victimize Reed Warblers throughout their breeding season as this host is also a summer visitor, and does not start to nest until late May or early June. Adult Cuckoos leave Britain in early July, as soon as the hosts have finished starting new clutches. Some of them may have reached their African winter quarters while their young are still being cared for by the hosts back in Britain, 5000 km away. The last young Cuckoos may not leave Britain until mid-September.

FAVOURITE HOSTS

For the past 60 years, thousands of bird watchers have completed nest record cards for the scheme administered by the British Trust for Ornithology, combining the fun of finding nests with a valuable contribution to knowledge of our avifauna. Largely because of their efforts, we have a good picture of host use by the Cuckoo in Britain. During the period 1939 to 1982, a total of 1145 parasitized nests was recorded. There were five main host species, which accounted for 90% of the parasitized nests; the Reed Warbler in marshland, the Meadow Pipit in moorland and heathland, the Dunnock and Robin in woodland and farmland, and the Pied Wagtail in open country. More than 50 other species have been recorded as occasional hosts if we include observations outside this scheme.[3]

We do not have such detailed information for most other parts of Europe, though these five species continue to be favourite hosts, alongside some others. For example, here are the major hosts in studies from seven other countries:[4]

- *Finland.* Redstart, White Wagtail, Brambling, Willow Warbler and Chiffchaff which together comprised 60% of the 369 parasitized nests).

Four favourite hosts of the Common Cuckoo in Britain: the Reed Warbler in marshland (top left), the Dunnock in woodland and farmland (top right), the Meadow Pipit in moorland (bottom left) and the Pied Wagtail in open country (bottom right). Individual female Cuckoos tend to specialize on one particular host species.

- *Sweden.* White Wagtail, Meadow Pipit, Tree Pipit, Whitethroat and Redstart. (64% of the 222 parasitized nests).
- *Norway.* Meadow Pipit. (89% of the 27 parasitized nests).
- *France.* White Wagtail, Robin, Dunnock, Wren and Reed Warbler. (76% of the 46 parasitized nests).
- *Germany.* Red-backed Shrike, White Wagtail, Wren, Garden Warbler and Barred Warbler. (88% of the 925 parasitized nests).
- *Czechoslovakia.* Robin, Redstart and White Wagtail. (70% of the 1870 parasitized nests).
- *Russia.* White Wagtail, Redstart, Robin and Great Reed Warbler. (53% of the 477 parasitized nests).

The egg collecting habits of previous generations provide another valuable source of information. Arne Moksnes and Eivin Røskaft, from the University of Trondheim, visited museums and private collections throughout Europe and the U.S.A. and found over 12,000 clutches of European passerines containing eggs of the Common Cuckoo.[5] This included 108 host species. Of these, 58 species had fewer than 10 parasitized clutches and another 21 species had between 10 and 50. This leaves 29 species with more than 50 parasitized clutches, which includes all the major hosts identified from the field studies above, together with a few others. Combining data from nest watching and egg collecting, we can now summarize the main hosts in Europe as follows:

- *Marshland.* Reed Warbler, Great Reed Warbler, Sedge Warbler, Marsh Warbler, Reed Bunting.
- *Moorland and heathland.* Meadow Pipit, Tree Pipit, Whinchat.
- *Open farmland and pastures.* Pied/White Wagtail, Yellow Wagtail, Yellowhammer.
- *Woodland, scrub, parkland, hedgerows.* Red-backed Shrike, Dunnock, Wren, Robin, Redstart, Spotted Flycatcher, Linnet, Greenfinch, Chaffinch, Brambling, Garden Warbler, Whitethroat, Blackcap, Lesser Whitethroat, Barred Warbler, Willow Warbler, Chiffchaff, Wood Warbler.

These host species vary in size from just 11 cm in body length and 8 g in weight (Chiffchaff) up to 17–19 cm and 32 g (Red-backed Shrike and Great Reed Warbler), so they are all much smaller than the Cuckoo itself (33 cm, 110 g). Almost all of the hosts have open nests in low vegetation or on the ground, with the exception of the Redstart and White/Pied Wagtail, which nest in crevices. Almost all feed their young on invertebrate food, especially insects. There are two exceptions. The Linnet feeds its young on seeds, and although it is regularly parasitized, in Britain at least it has never been recorded rearing a young Cuckoo to fledging.[3] It is probably parasitized as a last resort by Cuckoos that fail to find a suitable Dunnock nest. The Greenfinch feeds its young on a mixture of seeds and invertebrates, and can sometimes raise young Cuckoos successfully,[6] though it is probably not an ideal host.

The Cuckoo is not a common bird, so the overall average frequency of parasitism of even the favourite hosts is not high and it is always a thrill to find a Cuckoo egg or chick in a host nest. Over the whole of Britain, the parasitism rates from the nest record scheme were 5% for Reed Warblers (out of 6927 nests recorded), 2% for Dunnocks (23,352 nests), 3% for Meadow Pipits (5331 nests), and less than 0.5% for Robins (12,917 nests) and Pied Wagtails (4945 nests).[3] These figures, combined with population estimates for the main hosts, suggest that there are currently about 21,000 female Cuckoos breeding in Britain each summer.[7]

On a local scale, however, parasitism rates can be much higher because although Cuckoos are widely distributed they are commoner in some areas than others. In Britain, for example, Reed Warbler populations in south Wales are largely unparasitized whereas those in the heart of the fens of eastern England may have 20% parasitism.[8] Keen cuckoo watchers have understandably concentrated their efforts in these good areas. For example, in Lorraine, north east France, Blaise (1965) recorded 21% parasitism of 1099 Reed Warbler nests in marshland and 17% parasitism of 116 Robin nests in woodland. In southern Finland, Lagerström (1983) found 44% parasitism for 430 Redstart nests monitored between 1975 and 1983. Molnar (1944) recorded 43% parasitism for 504 Great Reed Warbler nests along a 20 km stretch of the Old Körös river in Hungary, from 1935 to 1944. Varga (1994) found an impressive total of 2073 Robin's nests between 1965 and 1991 in the woodland around Salgótarján, Hungary, and 32% were parasitized.

VARIATION IN CUCKOO EGGS

The eggs of the Common Cuckoo are astonishingly variable (**Plate 2c**). In Europe, the background colour varies from pale whitish-grey to green or brown. Most have spots, but these vary too from sparse speckles to dense speckles through to heavy splodges of various colours, or even scribbles. Some have no markings at all, usually an immaculate pale blue in colour but sometimes plain white.

The similarity between the eggs of the Cuckoo and the host clutch have been known at least since 1767, when it was noted by Salerne.[9] In Britain, for example, Cuckoo eggs in Meadow Pipit nests tend to be brownish and spotted, matching the Pipit's own eggs. In Reed Warbler nests, the Cuckoo egg is greenish and spotted like those of the Reed Warbler. In Pied Wagtail nests, the Cuckoo egg is much paler with sparse speckles, again mimicking the host eggs. In other parts of Europe, Cuckoo eggs in Redstart nests are immaculate pale blue, a perfect match for the host, and in Great Reed Warbler nests they are of greenish background with heavy grey and brown spots which copy, almost to perfection, the spotting on the Warbler's eggs.[10]

Could a female Cuckoo vary the colour of her egg depending on which host she chose? This seemed most unlikely, given that individual females of other species were known to always lay eggs of a constant type. By collecting a series of eggs from what they presumed to be the same individual Cuckoos, because each laid in a restricted territory, Baldamus (1892) and Rey (1892) showed that, just like other birds, each female always laid exactly the same type of egg though the colour and spotting varied between females. They assumed, therefore, that each female Cuckoo somehow managed to specialize on the host species for which her egg was a good match. The alternative was that Cuckoos simply laid at random and only good-matching eggs survived for the egg collectors to record. It was already known that birds often rejected foreign eggs placed in their nests. Leverkühn (1891) surveyed the results of early experiments and later Baker (1913) in India, and Swynnerton (1918) in Africa, showed that many cuckoo hosts discriminated particularly against eggs unlike their own. However, random laying followed by host rejection seemed an unlikely explanation for the match between cuckoo and host eggs because many cuckoo eggs were collected soon after they were laid and, in any case, random laying would be extremely wasteful from the cuckoo's point of view. Furthermore, the observations of Baldamus and Rey on individual female cuckoos suggested that they each favoured one particular host species.

THE PIONEERING WORK OF EDGAR CHANCE

The brilliant field study by Edgar Chance on a Worcestershire common, central England, from 1918 to 1925, provided conclusive evidence for these conjectures as well as many more discoveries. Chance's daily observations enabled him to follow individual female Cuckoos throughout a whole summer and to record every egg they laid. He was even able to predict where the next laying would be and captured the whole sequence on cine-film for the first time. With no false modesty, he entitled his first book (1922) *The Cuckoo's Secret* and the sequel (1940) *The Truth About the Cuckoo*.

By profession, Chance was a businessman, director of a company of glass manufacturers in Birmingham. But his passion was egg collecting. He had heard that Eugene Rey had collected a series of 20 eggs in one season from a female Cuckoo in Germany and was determined to beat this record. (In fact Chance had been misinformed; Rey's series was of 17 eggs.) Together with his assistants, the two Simmonds (a local coal miner and his son), O.R. Owen and P.B. Smyth, Chance began a daily routine of searching for host nests and Cuckoo eggs. The Common was about four hundred by six hundred metres and bounded on three sides by woodland. The main potential hosts were ground-nesting species, Meadow and Tree Pipits, Skylarks, Yellowhammers and Stonechats, with Linnets nesting in the scrub. In the first summer, 1918, they collected eggs from two female Cuckoos, distinguishable by their distinctive markings. One, Cuckoo A, laid 10 eggs in the nests of Meadow Pipits and one in that of a Skylark. The other, Cuckoo B, laid just four eggs, all in Meadow Pipit nests. Chance noted that the Cuckoo eggs appeared during the host laying period, usually before the clutch was complete and incubation had begun. As each host nest was suitable for parasitism for such a short time, three to five days only, Chance realized that the Cuckoo must watch her victims carefully to get her timing right. He determined to watch Cuckoos as well as search for nests.

The next season was eagerly awaited. Meadow Pipits appeared to be the favoured host but there were only about 10 pairs nesting on the Common, so Chance decided to give the Cuckoos a helping hand. In mid-May, just before the Cuckoos were due to arrive, he collected all the Pipit clutches that were already underway. These pairs immediately began to build new nests, so the result was more Pipits at the right stage for the early Cuckoo eggs. To the watchers' delight, the same two females returned, recognizable by their characteristic eggs laid in exactly the same territories as the year before. During the 1919 summer, 18 eggs were collected from Cuckoo A and just two from Cuckoo B (both after Cuckoo A had finished laying). All were from

Meadow Pipit nests, even though 'there were many Skylarks, Tree Pipits and other small birds nesting in the area'. The sequence from Cuckoo A, which Chance was sure represented all the eggs she laid that summer, showed conclusively that she laid on alternate days. The first five were laid in this regular sequence from 18 to 26 May. Then the next 13 were laid, again on alternate days, from 30 May to 23 June.

Chance had, in fact, beaten Rey's record by one, but his misinformation led him to believe that he was still three eggs short. In 1920, he decided to increase the availability of Pipit nests still further by farming them throughout the season so as to make sure there would be a nest ready for the Cuckoo whenever she needed one, namely on alternate days. If the Pipits had empty nests on these days, Chance added an egg or two, either from a Pipit or a Skylark's nest, to make the nest appear as if laying had begun. To his relief, Cuckoo A returned once more. This time, with Chance's help, she laid a total of 21 eggs, 20 in Meadow Pipit nests and one in the nest of a Tree Pipit, and the 'world record' was secure.

This third season had revealed yet more about the Cuckoo's behaviour. Chance spent the non-laying days checking host nests, so he could predict which one would be laid in next. He soon realized that the Cuckoo was doing exactly the same thing herself, and so the easiest way to find nests was simply to watch her. Often she would visit the nest that she would use the next day, apparently to check its progress. As Chance noted: 'by enlisting the Cuckoo as a member of our band of observers, we could make her do much of the donkey work'.

Chance was especially keen to observe the details of laying. At first he 'laboured under the delusion that the Cuckoo, like most birds, laid early in the morning.' He stayed out on the Common all night, to make sure he was by the host nest at dawn, but was surprised to find that the Cuckoo had always already laid. One cold and misty morning, he awoke at 3.45am to find a new Cuckoo egg alongside a Pipit egg, both cold and damp and clearly unattended during the night. He realized that the Cuckoo must have laid the previous afternoon. The team of observers now focused their attention on the female Cuckoos every afternoon, and were able to watch laying, usually between 1200 and 2000 GMT, with a peak around 1500 to 1800. Before laying, the female remained motionless on a branch, hidden in a tree up to a hundred metres from the host nest. Then, after a period of 30 minutes to two and a half hours, she glided down to the nest, remained there for just 10 seconds or less, and left. It was during this extremely short visit that she laid her egg. But still no-one had seen exactly how she did it.

Cuckoo A returned again in 1921. This time, Chance and his team put hides up around the Common, made from wood and covered with heather. By now he was so confident of predicting when the Cuckoo would lay and which host nest she would choose that he hired a cameraman to film the event. While the cameraman was in the hide, Chance stood by watching as the female sat quietly on her observation perch. As soon as she commenced her glide towards the host nest, Chance blew a whistle to alert the photographer.

During the summer they obtained wonderful pictures that showed, for the first time, exactly how laying took place. As soon as she landed by the host nest, the female removed a host egg. Then, holding this in her bill, she sat briefly on the nest to lay her own. She then backed off and flew away, carrying the host egg with her. Previous observers had often seen Cuckoos carrying eggs like this and had assumed

Asian Koel (left) with one of its main hosts, the House Crow.

Oh Cuckoo! Shall I call thee Bird
Or but a wandering Voice?

Others have taken more drastic action. The persistent calls of several species have led to them being known as 'brain-fever' birds; this includes the Pallid Cuckoo of Australia, the Common Hawk-Cuckoo, Plaintive Cuckoo and Brush Cuckoo of Asia and the Black Cuckoo of Africa. The mournful notes of the Black Cuckoo, 'whoo-whoo-wee', rendered as 'I'm so sad' or 'No more rain', may go on for hours, often through the night, and some people have found the persistent calling so unendurable that they have called the offender over, by mimicking its whistle, and have then promptly shot it!

David Lack was succinct with his explanation for these loud, simple and distinctive calls:[3] 'The song is loud presumably because the birds are rather scarce, so it has to carry far, it is simple presumably because the young cannot learn it from their parents, so it is entirely inherited, and it is distinctive presumably to assist specific recognition, especially where several species of cuckoos breed in the same area.'

Thus, throughout its range, the Common Cuckoo gives the same familiar call, with the emphasis on the first note, and its common name hardly changes as we move from its western limits (Cuckoo in Britain, Coucou in France, Koekoek in Holland), east through Germany (Kuckuck) to Japan (Kak-ko). In Japan, the call is used to alert humans at pedestrian crossings in big cities, a tribute to natural

*Figure 3.1 Edgar Chance getting into his hide to watch a Common Cuckoo lay her egg.
His assistants are the two Simmondses, father and son. (From Chance 1940.)*

that the female must first lay on the ground and then carry her egg to the host nest in her bill. However, Chance showed conclusively that the carried eggs were host eggs and that the Cuckoo laid her own egg directly into the host nest within a 10-second visit. His observations also refuted an alternative previous belief that the Cuckoo carried her egg in her oesophagus and regurgitated it into the host nest. We now know that direct laying is the normal procedure for the Common Cuckoo with all its hosts, including those with domed nests, like Wrens, or those that nest in crevices or holes, such as Redstarts. The female simply clings to the nest, places her cloaca against the nest hole, and squirts the egg in.[11]

In mid-June 1921, Chance deliberately stopped collecting completed host clutches and, as expected, without his help Cuckoo A laid fewer eggs that season. The total was just 15, 14 in Meadow Pipits' nests and one in a Tree Pipit nest. This showed that the number of eggs laid was limited by the availability of host nests.

Cuckoo A's fifth and final season in 1922 was, as Chance described it, 'an outstanding and historic performance'. With human help restored, to make available as many host nests as possible, and including the additional trick of putting out extra, artificial nests next to occupied ones, she achieved a total of 25 eggs, all collected by Chance. These were all laid in Meadow Pipits' nests and involved just 11 pairs of hosts. In fact both Chance and Cuckoo A were lucky to make the total of 25. Just before the laying of number twenty, a local villager mistook the Cuckoo for a hawk and was about to shoot her before Chance interrupted, just in time. During this last season, guests were invited to watch the egg-laying performance and Chance was accompanied by up to 10 visitors on some days. Not all shared Chance's enthusiasm or patience, sometimes nodding off in the warmth of the hide during the crucial 10 seconds!

Figure 3.2 Cuckoo A parasitizing a Meadow Pipit nest in 1922. First, she picks out one of the host eggs. Holding it in her bill, she then lays her own egg directly into the nest, turns (top), and flies off (bottom). Her laying visit lasts less than 10 seconds. (Photos by Oliver G. Pike. From Chance 1940.)

Chance was proud of his season's record from Cuckoo A, though he admitted that it was achieved largely as a result of his help through the constant collection of clutches to re-start the Pipits. He believed that nature, unguided, could never provide so many laying opportunities and claimed that the record would 'never be equalled so long as cuckoos continue to lay'. However, Chance under-estimated the Cuckoo's cunning. He knew that Cuckoos would sometimes depredate whole clutches of host eggs that were too advanced for parasitism, but subsequent studies have shown that this is a regular strategy used by female Cuckoos to re-start the hosts. Unwittingly, Chance had simply been doing what the Cuckoos normally do themselves. In a study near Hamburg, Germany, Karsten Gärtner (1981) found that

30% of Marsh Warbler nests containing completed clutches or young chicks were depredated by female Cuckoos.[12] In another study of Reed Warblers, Gehringer (1979) discovered that the Cuckoo laid more than a quarter of her eggs in the replacement nests that followed such predation. Only female Cuckoos, not males, plunder the host nests, so it is a strategy to increase host nest availability, not simply a hungry Cuckoo looking for an easy meal. In 1988, a Cuckoo studied by Mike Bayliss in Oxfordshire, central England, equalled Chance's record without human help. She parasitized a population of 36 pairs of Reed Warblers, laying 25 eggs in the season and parasitizing 24 of the pairs, one pair twice.[13]

Over the five seasons, Cuckoo A had laid 90 eggs, apparently all collected by Chance except for the few that hatched before he found them. Eighty-seven had been laid in Meadow Pipit nests, two in Tree Pipit nests and one in a Skylark nest. He also collected series of eggs from five other Cuckoos which showed strong preferences for Meadow Pipits, as follows:[14]

Cuckoo	Years	Number of eggs laid in nests of						Total
		Meadow Pipit	Tree Pipit	Skylark	Yellow-hammer	Willow Warbler	Linnet	
Successor to A	1924–5	11	2	–	2	1	–	16
S	1921	13	1	–	–	–	–	14
N	1922–4	18	1	–	–	–	1	20
PGa	1928–32	19	4	1	1	–	–	25
PGb	1928–30	10	–	–	1	–	–	11

Other observers found similar specializations by individual Cuckoos for other hosts. These included series collected within a season of 16, 17, 17, 18 and 19 eggs all in Reed Warbler nests, 10 all in Sedge Warbler nests, 11 all in Dunnock nests and 14 all in Pied Wagtail nests.[14] It could be objected that these suffer from observer bias, namely the collector concentrating on nests of what was believed to be the female Cuckoo's primary hosts. However Chance also reported series of eggs from unusual hosts; 9 all in the nests of Spotted Flycatchers and 14 all in Yellowhammer nests.[14] Neither of these species is particularly common compared with other small passerines in the same habitat and Yellowhammer nests, in particular, are not easy to find. All the evidence pointed to a remarkable degree of host specialization, with different females favouring different hosts. The occasional parasitism of other species occurred simply when a suitable nest of the preferred host was not available.

It is difficult to assess the average number of eggs laid by a female Cuckoo during a season. The most prolific females may lay 15 to 25 eggs over a period of four to seven weeks. Others may lay just one or two eggs in a particular area, because they are excluded by more dominant females. It is possible that they may wander more widely and lay other eggs elsewhere, but for some this meagre total may be all they can manage for the summer.

The most detailed data so far are provided by Ian Wyllie's study of Reed Warbler-Cuckoos in Cambridgeshire, eastern England.[15] By observing marked individuals, or through identifying females indirectly through their distinctive eggs, his six-year study (1974–1979) followed 19 females that laid at least two eggs on his site in a given season. The average number laid per season was eight (range 2–15).

HOST-SPECIFIC CUCKOO GENTES

Baldamus, Rey and Chance had uncovered many of the Cuckoo's secrets, but one big puzzle remained. It was clear that the Common Cuckoo must be divided into several host-specific races. Alfred Newton called these races 'gentes' ('gens' for the singular), a Latin word denoting a clan of families descended from a common ancestor.[16] (Incidentally, Newton worked in the Zoology Department at Cambridge, and I have the privilege of writing this book on the same old desk he used to write his Cuckoo article, almost exactly one hundred years ago.) Each Cuckoo gens seems to specialize on a particular host species, and lays distinctive eggs that tend to match its host's eggs: brown and spotted for Meadow Pipit specialist Cuckoos, green and spotted for Reed Warbler specialists, plain blue for Redstart specialists, and so on (**Plate 2c**). The puzzle is: how do these races, or gentes, remain distinct?

The following solution was suggested. It was assumed that a daughter Cuckoo laid the same egg type as her mother and then chose to parasitize the same host species that raised her, perhaps by learning the host's characteristics through imprinting when she was a nestling or fledgling.[14] Thus, for example, a young female Cuckoo raised by Meadow Pipits would, when adult, choose to parasitize Meadow Pipits. If she laid a brown spotted egg, like her mother, then the match between Cuckoo and host eggs would be maintained across the generations.

There is one final twist. In domestic chickens and Spottedbacked Weaverbirds, two species in which the inheritance of egg colour has been studied most intensively, both the father's and mother's genes determine the egg colour laid by their daughter.[17] If this were the case for Cuckoos, not only would a female Cuckoo have to remain faithful to the host species that reared her, but male Cuckoos too would have to restrict their matings to female Cuckoos raised by the same host, otherwise the mimicry would break down in the next generation. In this scenario, the different races of the Common Cuckoo would be genetically isolated and so would, in fact, be different species. How would a male restrict his matings to females of his own gens? He would either have to recognize them directly, for example through some subtle difference in plumage or voice, or perhaps he could also imprint on the hosts or the habitat in which he was raised, so he would be most likely to encounter females raised by the same host. In 1954, H.N. Southern from the University of Oxford, suggested that this was a likely possibility because egg mimicry seemed to be best in large tracts of uniform habitat, for example Hungarian reed beds (the Great Reed Warbler gens) or Scandinavian forests (the Redstart gens). In cultivated England, by contrast, egg mimicry is poorer or absent altogether (the Dunnock gens). Southern supposed that this was because the habitat was broken up into such small patches that males often encountered females of other gentes and interbreeding disrupted the egg mimicry.

The other possibility is that in Cuckoos only the mother's genes influence her daughter's egg type.[18] This is, at least in theory, a possibility in birds because of their method of sex determination. Remember that in mammals, like ourselves, the sex of the offspring is determined by the father, who produces sperm with one of two kinds of sex chromosomes (Y sperm produce sons, X sperm produce daughters). In birds, however, the sex of the offspring is determined by the mother, who produces ova with one of two kinds of sex chromosomes (W ova produce daughters, Z ova produce sons). If the genes for egg colour were located on the W chromosome, unique to females, then the mother alone would determine her daughter's egg type. In this second scenario, only the females need imprint on their hosts. Males would be free to mate with females from all the races without disrupting the maintenance of their daughters' egg mimicry. This interbreeding would maintain the Common Cuckoo as the one species, and the gentes would be restricted to the female sex.

These ideas have been discussed for more than 60 years, yet we still do not have a complete answer to the puzzle. There is still no information on the inheritance of egg colour in Cuckoos. We also have no evidence that Cuckoos imprint on their hosts. Chance himself tried to determine whether a female Cuckoo victimized the same species of host that raised her as a youngster. He collected 17 Cuckoo eggs or newly hatched Cuckoo chicks and placed them into the nests of Meadow Pipits, Stonechats or Skylarks. He ringed the Cuckoos in the hope that they would return to his Common to breed, but none were seen again.[14] Wyllie (1981) also ringed a large number of Reed Warbler Cuckoos as nestlings, but none returned to his study site to breed. Michael Brooke and I tried a different technique, raising Cuckoos in captivity with either Robins or Reed Warblers as hosts.[19] When we tested them as adults, we could find no strong host preferences. However, none of the captive Cuckoos laid eggs so the artificial conditions in our aviaries may have prevented them from behaving normally.

In another captive study, Yvonne Teuschl and Barbara and Michael Taborsky, from the University of Vienna, hand-raised Cuckoos in one of five different habitats (these were cages containing objects of different colours and shapes). When they tested the Cuckoos as adults, a year or two later, both males and females preferred their familiar habitat when given a choice. This suggests that habitat imprinting might be one mechanism by which Cuckoos come to choose their hosts.[20]

Teuschl and the Taborskys think that host choice may involve a sequence of decisions.[20] First, young Cuckoos are known to return to the general area where they were born. Considering birds ringed as nestlings and then recovered as adults during subsequent breeding seasons, two thirds of them were found within 20 km of their natal site.[21] This 'homing' would not be sufficient to ensure host specificity in today's fragmented habitat. Second, the Cuckoo may then search for the habitat on which it imprinted as a nestling. This would increase the chance that it encounters the species of host that raised it. Finally, host imprinting may enable it to seek out the characteristics of one host species (sight, song, nest type). Further experiments are needed to test whether this actually occurs. My guess is that host imprinting will turn out to be the key, as has been shown for host choice by parasitic finches (chapter 13).

Despite our lack of knowledge on how Cuckoos come to choose their hosts, some progress has been made since Chance's day. New genetic techniques developed in the last fifteen years have allowed us to study the Cuckoo's mating system for the first time, and to analyse differences between the gentes. This has thrown new light on how the various host races remain distinct.

TERRITORIES AND MATING

In one of his letters in *The Natural History of Selborne*, Gilbert White wrote: 'A neighbour of mine, who is said to have a nice ear, remarks that . . . the note of the Cuckoo . . . varies in different individuals; for about Selborne wood, he found they were mostly in D: he heard two sing together, the one in D, the other in D sharp . . . and about Wolmer-forest some [sing] in C.' Based on recognition of their distinctive calls, some males have been thought to return to the same breeding range for up to 10 years, while females, identified through their egg characteristics, have been reported laying at the same site for up to seven years.[11] However, if we want to follow individuals in detail we need to mark them.

Most studies of bird behaviour use colour ringing to identify individuals, but because Cuckoos are so shy and difficult to observe the only sure way of following them is by radio-tracking. A small transmitter is glued to the feathers on the bird's back and the signal can then be picked up with an antenna from up to 3 km away. The transmitter usually lasts for just a couple of months at most, which is sufficient to follow the Cuckoo for a whole breeding season. At the end of the summer, when the bird moults, it falls off.

The first study was by Ian Wyllie (1981), who radio-tracked two males and a female at a reed bed site in Cambridgeshire, eastern England, where the hosts were Reed Warblers. Other Cuckoos were individually recognizable through coloured wing tags. At the breeding site, males had song ranges of *c.* 30 ha each (one hectare is 100×100 m) which overlapped extensively the singing areas of up to four other males. Each female had a distinct breeding range, also of *c.* 30 ha, within which she laid her eggs. Sometimes this was largely exclusive and appeared to be defended as a territory, but sometimes two to four females had overlapping breeding ranges. When there was overlap, one female appeared to be dominant and laid more eggs than the others. The radio-tracked female's breeding range was overlapped by six different males during the breeding season and several males were often seen together following her around. She laid 15 eggs during the summer, the first in a Sedge Warbler nest and the next 14 all in Reed Warbler nests. Both males and females often left their breeding ranges to feed in orchards up to 4 km away, where there were plenty of caterpillars.

Lutz Dröscher (1988) tracked four males and five females near Hamburg, Germany, where the main hosts were Marsh Warblers and Reed Warblers. He found similar results to Wyllie's study. Birds had separate breeding and feeding areas, commuting up to 23 km from the breeding sites to feed in woodland patches. At the breeding sites, male singing areas often overlapped, while female breeding ranges could be largely exclusive or could overlap those of other females. The results, together with previous observations at this site by Gärtner (1981) suggested that there were three types of female. Dominant females defended egg laying territories, to which they returned in successive years. Subordinate females had ranges that overlapped the range of one or more dominants, and they laid fewer eggs. They inherited the breeding territory when the dominant female disappeared. Finally, nomadic females were non-territorial and roamed over larger areas, perhaps laying just one egg in a dominant female's territory. One radio-tracked female laid in two Reed Warbler nests 2 km apart.

The most detailed study of Common Cuckoo social systems and egg-laying behaviour is that of Hiroshi Nakamura and his colleagues from Shinshu University, who followed Cuckoos for 10 years (1984–1993) along the Chikuma river, in the suburbs of Nagano City, central Japan.[22] Their remarkable field work has set new standards of excellence for Cuckoo watchers, just as Edgar Chance did for a previous generation 70 years ago. There are three main hosts in their study area: the Great Reed Warbler, which breeds in reed beds along the river; the Bull-headed Shrike, which breeds in bushes, and the Azure-winged Magpie, which breeds in the trees of acacia groves and orchards. During a decade of research, Nakamura and his team caught more than three hundred Cuckoos in mist nets and marked them individually with coloured wing ribbons. Eighteen males and 22 females were radio-tracked for periods of 10 days or more to provide the most complete record yet of how the Cuckoo spends its summer.[23]

Each year, there were between 22 and 28 adult male and 21 to 26 adult female Cuckoos resident on the study site, an area of approximately 7 km². As in the earlier studies, the Cuckoos had breeding ranges centred on areas with host nests but they rarely fed there, leaving to feed in other woodland areas up to 5 km away where hairy caterpillars were abundant. They never called in these feeding areas; all the calling and mating took place in the vicinity of the host nests. Individuals spent about nine hours each day in their breeding ranges (60% of the daylight time). Males tended to arrive at dawn and then left for their feeding areas in the late morning, sometimes returning for an hour or so in the early evening. Females arrived at the breeding site later and were more likely to stay on into the afternoon, especially on egg-laying days.[23]

A female's breeding range averaged 64 ha in area (range 21 to 168 ha) and often included the nests of two or even all three host species. Nevertheless, females specialized on just one host. Of 21 females followed in detail, 11 were Great Reed Warbler specialists, eight specialized on Azure-winged Magpies and two did so on Bull-headed Shrikes. Magpie specialist cuckoos had larger ranges than those of warbler specialists, reflecting the wider dispersion of their host nests. Female breeding ranges overlapped the ranges of other females, both those specializing on the same host and those specializing on different hosts.[23]

Male song areas were on average 40 ha (range 3 to 96 ha) and overlapped each other extensively. There was a lot of chasing among the males and access to females seemed to be secured by dominant males. In another study area, the Kayanodaira heights, where host nests were not so dense, some males defended exclusive territories, successfully evicting all other males. When they left their territories to feed, however, subordinate males intruded and sometimes sang until the owners returned to evict them. Therefore, the extensive overlap of male ranges along the Chikuma river was likely to result from the greater density of host nests, which attracted so many males that territory defence became impossible.[23]

What can we conclude from these studies? There are, in fact, some simple themes underlying the apparently complex social system. First, a female Cuckoo competes for areas with a good supply of host nests. This makes good sense; the more host nests available to her, the more eggs she can lay. In some small areas where host

Three main hosts of the Common Cuckoo in Japan: the Great Reed Warbler (top), the Bull-headed Shrike (left), and the Azure-winged Magpie (bottom).

nests are not too dense, one female may be able to defend an exclusive egg-laying territory. In larger sites with abundant nests, however, so many females are attracted to the area that territory defence is impossible and females have overlapping ranges in which a dominant bird lays most of the eggs. Competition for host nests is indicated by the fact that subordinates take over the breeding range when the dominant female dies, and by the fact that some host nests get parasitized by more than one female Cuckoo. For example, in our study of Reed Warbler-Cuckoos on Wicken Fen, Michael Brooke and I found that 14% of parasitized nests were later parasitized by a second Cuckoo,[24] whereas in Molnar's study of Great Reed Warbler-Cuckoos in Hungary this occurred at 45% of parasitized nests.[25] This competition may seem odd given that over a large area, the whole of Britain for example, only 1–5% of host nests are parasitized. Surely then, there should be plenty of host nests to go round? However, not all host nests are suitable for Cuckoos. For example, females prefer to parasitize nests near bushes and trees, probably because they are easier to find and monitor from closer vantage points.[26] Competition for these accessible nests can be intense.

Second, males clearly compete for females. They call and chase each other at the egg-laying sites and also chase after the females. This also makes good sense. Males play no part in egg laying, so their success depends simply on the number of females they can mate with and their ability to keep other males at bay, so they can ensure their paternity. So while female Cuckoos focus on host nests, male Cuckoos focus on female Cuckoos. Sometimes a male may be able to monopolize a female's breeding range and gain exclusive access to her. However, at rich sites for host nests there are so many females with overlapping ranges that many males are competing for matings. The result of the intense intruder pressure is several males overlapping several females.

Third, the best places for host nests are not always the best places for caterpillars, so cuckoos have to leave their breeding ranges from time to time in order to feed. This makes it even harder for a female Cuckoo to maintain exclusive access to the host nests in her breeding area, and likewise harder for a male to monopolize females.

These recent radio-tracking studies have confirmed the remarkable host specificity of female Cuckoos. They strongly suggest that females imprint on the hosts that raised them. They have also shown that both males and females have access to several partners during the breeding season. The key question now is: who mates with whom? If we could answer this question then we could determine whether the host races of the Common Cuckoo are restricted to the females or whether the races are completely isolated and hence separate species.

GENTES RESTRICTED TO THE FEMALE LINE

Paternity will always remain uncertain for animals with internal fertilization, unless a male stays with his mate continuously, to ensure that no other males mate with her. In *The Merchant of Venice*, Old Gobbo, who is 'sand-blind', fails to recognize the voice of his son, who comments:

> if you had your eyes, you might fail of the knowing me:
> It is a wise father that knows his own child.

Shakespeare's assertion applies especially well to birds. Since 1985, new and powerful molecular techniques have been developed which allow, for the first time, precise determination of paternity and maternity.[27] They are based on the discovery that parts of the DNA are extremely variable between individuals, so much so that they can be used as unique 'genetic fingerprints'. Half of an offspring's genetic fingerprint is inherited from its mother, half from its father. Therefore its parents can be determined simply by matching its genetic profile to those of potential mothers and sires. The easiest way to collect a DNA sample from a bird is from a small drop of blood, which can be taken harmlessly from a superficial vein in the wing or leg, without causing undue stress. Bird red blood cells have nuclei, from which the DNA can be extracted. These new methods have revealed many surprises, even in some species where casual observations had suggested that a male and female bred as a faithful monogamous pair. Often up to 50% of the offspring are sired by other males, either because the female accepts copulations from intruders, or because she actively seeks extra-pair suitors through forays onto neighbouring territories.[28] If even supposedly monogamous species are producing broods with multiple paternity, then we clearly cannot rely on bird watching alone to work out what is happening in Cuckoos, where both sexes interact with many potential partners.

Hiroshi Nakamura and his team managed to catch and take blood samples from about three-quarters of the adult Cuckoos in their breeding population along the Chikuma river. There was sometimes heavy predation on clutches, so to make sure that all the nestling Cuckoos were sampled, they collected the Cuckoo eggs as soon as they were laid and incubated them in the safety of the laboratory. Soon after hatching, they were returned to their nests. The blood samples were then taken to McMaster University in Canada, where Karen Marchetti and Lisle Gibbs analysed them to produce genetic profiles.[29] Of a total of 136 nestlings, they could identify both parents for 84 of them, the male parent only for 16, and the female parent only for 14. The genetic profiles of the other 22 chicks did not match those of any of the sampled adults, so their parents must have evaded capture.

The first interesting conclusion was that 65% of the males and 50% of the females did not produce any offspring. This supports the behavioural observations that there is intense competition among females for host nests and among males for matings with females. Some individuals are very successful while others are excluded. Second, within any one season, although some individuals have just one mate, some males and females mate with multiple partners; 17% of the females had offspring sired by two or three different males while nearly 50% of the males had offspring with two or more (maximum four) females. This again confirms what may have been expected from the behavioural observations of several males overlapping the breeding ranges of several females. The third, and the most exciting result, one that certainly could not have easily been deduced from bird watching alone, was that whereas females were highly host specific, males often sired offspring in the nests of more than one host species. The genetic profiles showed that only 8% of females had offspring in more than one host species nest while 37% of the males did so.[29]

The conclusion is that, at least in this Japanese population of Cuckoos, males often mate with females that have been raised by a different host species. This means that the gentes are restricted to female lines, with cross mating by males maintaining the Cuckoo as the one species. This accords with the fact that, at least to our eyes, Cuckoos specializing on different hosts all look exactly the same.

Recent analysis of genetic differences between the Cuckoo gentes also supports the idea that just female Cuckoos are divided into distinct host races. The analysis involves considering the two kinds of DNA that a young bird inherits from its parents.

- *Nuclear DNA.* This is a random mixture, half from its father and half from its mother, brought together when a sperm fertilizes an egg. There is one exception to this random mixing of nuclear DNA, namely the sex chromosomes. Recall that female birds produce two types of eggs, those with a W chromosome which, on fertilization, will produce daughters and those with a Z chromosome which, when fertilized, will produce sons. (All sperm have Z chromosomes). Therefore W chromosomes only get passed on from mother to daughter.

- *Mitochondrial DNA.* This is the small amount of DNA that is present in mitochondria, small organelles in the cytoplasm of cells that are involved with energy metabolism. A sperm is a naked nucleus containing only nuclear DNA, while an egg cell has cytoplasm and contains both nuclear DNA and mitochondria. This means that all an individual's mitochondrial DNA comes from its mother.

How would we expect these two kinds of DNA to differ between the gentes? Any mutations in the mitochondrial DNA, or in the DNA of the W chromosomes, will get passed on through the female line only. Over time, we would expect each gens to have 'clocked up' increasing differences in this female-specific DNA, simply because of its isolation from the other gentes. In principle, the degree of difference could be used to measure the time for which a gens has been isolated, if we knew the rate at which mutations occurred each generation. The greater the difference between two gentes, the longer their separation must have been.

What about the rest of the nuclear DNA (excluding that on the female-specific W chromosome)? If males, too, are divided into separate host races (because they restrict their matings to females of one gens), then the nuclear DNA should also differ between the gentes, because they would be isolated genetically. However, if males mated across the gentes, to maintain the one Cuckoo species, then the nuclear DNA would not differ because it would become scrambled across the generations. Any nuclear DNA passed on from mother to son, would be transferred to another gens if the son mated with a female raised by a different host species.

The first comparison of DNA between Cuckoo gentes revealed no differences,[30] but a closer look has now found that both British gentes and Japanese gentes differ in mitochondrial DNA sequences, but not in their nuclear DNA.[31] This is exactly what we would have predicted from the mating results from the Japanese Cuckoos, namely female-specific host races within one Cuckoo species.

There are two implications of these results. The first is that egg colour is determined by genes on the W chromosome, so that daughters will lay the same type of egg as their mother irrespective of whether their father was raised by the same host as her or by a different host. Second, the results suggest that only females imprint on the host species that raises them, subsequently seeking out that same species for parasitism. However, neither of these is known for sure. To confirm them we need information comparing egg type and host choice between mothers and daughters. Until this is done, the Cuckoo will still keep two of its best secrets.

CHAPTER 4

Co-evolution of host defences and Common Cuckoo trickery

Hosts of the Common Cuckoo gain no reproductive rewards from a successfully parasitized nest. The Cuckoo chick sees to that by ejecting the host's own eggs and young. In theory then, natural selection should favour host defences. This, in turn, will select for more sophisticated trickery by the Cuckoo. The result should be an evolutionary 'arms race', leading to intricate adaptations and counter-adaptations by either side.[1] This cycle of evolutionary change, where each party responds to selection pressure imposed by the other, is known as co-evolution. We can represent it by the following diagram:

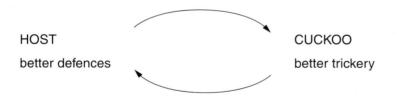

How can we test whether this actually goes on in nature? At first sight this seems an impossible task. With morphology, we can study the fossil record for evidence of changes during evolution. For behaviour, however, fossils would be of little use. Even if we had a perfect fossil record of cuckoos and their hosts, we could never reconstruct the evolutionary changes in how hosts defend their nests by chasing cuckoos or rejecting badly matching eggs, for example. Nevertheless, our proposed co-evolutionary cycle is not doomed to remain only as a theoretical conjecture. There are ways of testing it by simple field experiments and by comparing the behaviour of different host species to the threat of parasitism.

First, let us consider the top arrow of our diagram. Have cuckoos evolved in response to selection pressure from the hosts? We would have evidence for this if we could show that the cuckoo's egg-laying tactics are specifically designed to circumvent host defences. To test this we can behave as cuckoos ourselves and parasitize host nests with model eggs. Let us return to Wicken Fen once again to study how Reed Warblers defend themselves against Common Cuckoos (often referred to in this chapter as 'the Cuckoo', for short).

EGG MIMICRY

During 1985 and 1986, Michael Brooke and I monitored a total of 274 Reed Warbler nests daily during egg laying. Of these, 44 (16%) were parasitized by Common Cuckoos. Two of these clutches were destroyed by predators soon after laying. At eight of the remaining 42 nests (19%), the Reed Warblers rejected the Cuckoo egg, four by desertion and four by ejecting it from the nest. Thus, although the hosts sometimes rebelled, at the majority of the nests (81%) the Cuckoo egg was accepted. How does the Cuckoo ensure such a high success rate? The aim of our experiments was to vary each part of the Cuckoo's egg-laying procedure in turn, to see whether it aided deception of the hosts and, if so, how.[2]

The Common Cuckoo's tactics for parasitizing a host nest, in this case a Reed Warbler. She times her parasitism to coincide with the host laying period. Her laying visit is in the afternoon and lasts just 10 seconds. She picks out a host egg, lays her own in its place, and flies off with the host egg. Field experiments have tested the significance of each part of this laying procedure.

We first considered why the Cuckoo lays a mimetic egg. We copied the procedure of real Cuckoos by removing a host egg (under licence) from the Reed Warbler nest one afternoon during the laying period and substituting a model Cuckoo egg. The models, of the exact size and weight of real Cuckoo eggs, were made of resin and painted to resemble the different eggs laid by various gentes (**Plate 2c**). They looked very realistic, so much so that Bruce Campbell, one of Britain's most experienced ornithologists, came across one of our experimental nests and recorded it as parasitized by a real Cuckoo!

The warblers accepted almost all the model eggs that resembled their own eggs in colour and spotting (painted green, like the Reed Warbler gens of Cuckoo). However, they rejected two-thirds of the models that clearly differed from their own, for example brown, spotted eggs typical of the Meadow Pipit gens, whitish-grey, spotted eggs of the Pied Wagtail gens or immaculate, pale blue eggs of the Redstart gens. The rejections occurred mainly by ejection (some model eggs were found under the nest), or by desertion, often following a bout of pecking at the model.[2] Most of these rejections occurred either as soon as the warblers completed their clutch, or a day or two later. Very few occurred before clutch completion. This delay may make good sense, because it would be easier to spot an odd egg once the whole clutch was completed. In Reed Warblers, both sexes incubate and it was clear from watching their pecking at the models that both showed rejection behaviour.[2] However, the pair did not always make the same decision. At one nest, the female deserted while the male still continued to incubate. She began to take the nest to bits, using the material to build a new nest nearby. This was very amusing to watch – every time the female pulled out a beakful of nest material, the male peered over the nest rim and I imagined him thinking, 'My wife has gone quite mad!' After several hours, during which the nest was almost completely dismantled beneath him, the male was forced to agree to the move!

Although deserting warblers usually built a new nest somewhere nearby, some built their new nest on top of the clutch containing the model.[2] This method of rejection also occurs sometimes in response to real cuckoo eggs.[3] The result is a two-storey nest, with the old, deserted clutch on the bottom floor and the new clutch above. Why do Reed Warblers sometimes build on top of the old nest rather than at a new site? It's unlikely that there is a shortage of suitable sites in the reeds. An entertaining idea is that it might reduce the chance of further parasitism. If female Cuckoos remember the sites where they have already laid, and leave these nests free from further interference, then it would pay the warblers to build their new nest on top of the old one. The female Cuckoo might then be fooled into regarding this as a nest she has already parasitized and so would leave it alone. Perhaps a nest in a new site would be more readily noticed as a new nest?

Clearly, these results show that discrimination by hosts selects for a mimetic egg on the part of the Cuckoo. Baker (1913) was the first to describe how this would occur during evolution: 'The process of perfect adaptation is attained by the slow but sure elimination by the foster parents of those eggs which contrast most distinctively with their own ... by this means those strains of cuckoos which lay the most ill-adapted eggs gradually die out, whilst those that lay eggs most like those of the fosterer are enabled to persist.'[4]

This may seem such an obvious and expected result that our experiment was hardly worth doing. However, there are at least two alternative hypotheses for how the mimicry might evolve. Alfred Russel Wallace (1889), Darwin's contemporary and co-discoverer of the principle of natural selection, interpreted bird egg colours as an example of protective coloration. He suggested that cuckoo eggs have come to resemble host eggs so that the clutch is not made conspicuous to predators: 'if each bird's eggs are to some extent protected by their harmony of colour with their surroundings, the presence of a larger and very differently coloured egg in the nest might be dangerous and lead to the destruction of the whole set. Those cuckoos, therefore, which most frequently placed their eggs among the kinds which they resembled would in the long run leave most progeny, and thus the very frequent accord in colour might have been brought about.' Therefore, even in the complete absence of any host discrimination, cuckoo egg mimicry could still evolve through selective predation.[5]

We could test Wallace's hypothesis by examining predation of the Reed Warbler nests in which we placed model eggs. However, there was no tendency for nests with non-mimetic model eggs to be more heavily depredated than those with mimetic models.[2] Another experiment, in which I painted quail eggs and put them into old Blackbird nests, also showed that clutches with an odd egg did not suffer greater predation.[6] So there is, at present, no support for Wallace's idea.[7]

Another hypothesis for the evolution of egg mimicry stems from the observation that a proportion of parasitized nests is later parasitized again, by a second Cuckoo. This occurred at six out of our 44 parasitized nests on Wicken Fen, and was a consequence of the overlapping egg-laying ranges of female Cuckoos.[2] Now there is only room for one young Cuckoo per nest; if two hatch out, then there is a struggle in which one will eventually evict the other. This was first described in 1788 by Edward Jenner, who found two young Cuckoos in a Dunnock nest:

> Two cuckoos were hatched in the same nest this morning. In a few hours after, a contest began between the cuckoos for the possession of the nest, which continued undetermined till the next afternoon; when one of them, which was somewhat superior in size, turned out the other. This contest was very remarkable. The combatants alternately appeared to have the advantage, as each carried the other several times nearly to the top of the nest, and then sunk down again, oppressed by the weight of its burden; till at length, after various efforts, the strongest prevailed.

As discovered by Edgar Chance, the female Cuckoo first removes an egg before she lays her own. If the nest has already been parasitized, it would clearly pay the second Cuckoo to pick out the first Cuckoo's egg for removal, especially as her egg is likely to hatch later and so her chick will lose the battle for possession of the nest. Host egg mimicry may evolve, therefore, because it reduces the chance that second Cuckoos will be able to discriminate, and remove, a Cuckoo egg from the clutch.[2]

We could test this hypothesis too, because sometimes a Cuckoo visited a nest in which we had placed a model egg. There was indeed a tendency for the Cuckoo to remove the model egg, rather than one of the Reed Warbler eggs, but there was no hint that the model was more likely to be removed if it was different from the host eggs in coloration. Therefore there is no strong support from our study for the idea that Cuckoo egg replacement selects for host egg mimicry.[2,8] Even if Cuckoos did discriminate, and picked out odd eggs for removal, the selective pressure would be less than that from host discrimination. Only 14% of our naturally parasitized Reed Warbler nests were visited by a second Cuckoo, whereas host rejection of non-mimetic eggs occurred at 69% of host nests. In other words, a badly matching Cuckoo egg has at most a 14% chance of being removed by other Cuckoos compared with a 69% chance of being removed by Reed Warblers. Nevertheless, it would be interesting to test the hypothesis on other study sites, and with other cuckoo-host systems, because there are hints that cuckoo egg removal may sometimes be a strong selection pressure (chapter 7). As far as is known, all *Cuculus* and *Chrysococcyx* cuckoos remove a host egg before they lay. However, neither Jacobin nor Great Spotted Cuckoos do so, so at least for these two species, host egg mimicry could not evolve through cuckoo egg replacement.

SPEED AND TIMING

The Common Cuckoo clearly needs a mimetic egg to beat host defences. What about the other parts of its egg-laying behaviour? To test whether these were important components of Cuckoo deception, we did further experiments with Reed Warblers using mimetic model eggs (painted to resemble the eggs of the Reed Warbler gens) but varying each part of the Cuckoo's strategy in turn.[2]

When models were placed in nests before the hosts themselves began to lay, even mimetic eggs were all rejected. Thus the hosts, very sensibly, seemed to adopt the rule: 'any egg appearing in the nest before I start to lay cannot be mine, so reject it'. This explains why Cuckoos wait until hosts begin to lay before they parasitize a nest. Once the host began its clutch, the number of host eggs had no effect on rejection frequency. Nevertheless, real Cuckoos prefer to lay early on in the host laying period. There are fewer Reed Warbler nests parasitized at the four-egg stage, or later, than expected from the proportion of nests that are vulnerable at this stage. Why is this so? Most Reed Warblers have clutches of four eggs, but because incubation usually begins at the three- or even the two-egg stage, Cuckoos that laid at the four-egg stage would be at a disadvantage because their chicks would be less likely to hatch before the host chicks, and host chicks are probably more difficult to eject than host eggs. Thus selection has favoured Cuckoos which parasitize host nests not too early, but not too late.[2]

Most passerine birds lay in the early morning. On Wicken Fen, Reed Warblers usually laid within an hour of sunrise, from 0500–0600 hours. Cuckoos, by contrast, lay in the afternoon, mainly between 1400 hours and dusk.[9] Why? Cuckoos often parasitize host nests at the one-egg stage. In order to make use of these nests, they must clearly lay after the hosts, so this would explain why they lay later in the day though not necessarily why laying was late in the afternoon rather than mid-morning. Another possibility is that hosts are less attentive to their nests in the afternoons and so more likely to accept a Cuckoo egg. We tested this by placing mimetic model eggs into Reed Warbler nests at dawn, and found that they were more likely to be rejected than an experimental parasitism in the afternoon. Afternoon laying is therefore an important part of the Cuckoo's trickery, perhaps because later in the day the warblers are less likely to be in attendance at the nest.[2] Nevertheless, afternoon laying is not characteristic of all brood parasites; Brown-headed Cowbirds and Jacobin Cuckoos lay at dawn.

What about the remarkable speed of laying? Most birds spend between twenty minutes and an hour on the nest when laying an egg. By contrast, the female Cuckoo lays with amazing speed. Chance's cuckoo 'A' spent an average of 8.8 seconds on the pipit's nest; of eight layings that were timed accurately, seven were 10 seconds or less (the fastest was just 4 seconds) and the maximum was 16 seconds.[9] Reed Warbler-Cuckoos also usually lay within 10 seconds.[3] Rapid laying may reduce the chance that other Cuckoos, or predators, are attracted to the nest. It may also reduce damage from host attacks. Great Reed Warblers have been seen to knock laying Cuckoos from the nest into the water below, where they sometimes drown.[10] Even smaller hosts, like Meadow Pipits and Reed Warblers, may damage the Cuckoo's plumage by striking it with their bills and feet. However the secretive behaviour of the female Cuckoo prior to laying also gives the impression that she is decreasing the chance of alerting the hosts. Rapid laying may be favoured by selection because the sight of a Cuckoo on their nest alerts them to reject the Cuckoo egg.

We tested this idea by placing a stuffed Cuckoo on the host nest one afternoon during the laying period, and allowing the hosts to observe it for a period of five minutes. At all nests the Reed Warblers mobbed the Cuckoo, flitting about within a metre or two, snapping their mandibles, giving 'churr' calls and occasionally attacking it. We then removed the Cuckoo and placed a mimetic Cuckoo egg in the nest. These models were significantly more likely to be rejected than those placed in nests without the stuffed Cuckoo presentation.[2] This response may, in part, have been a result of the warblers' increased general excitement, which made them more aware of their nest and eggs, rather than a specific reaction to the Cuckoo itself, because presentation of a stuffed Jackdaw (a nest predator) also stimulated increased rejection of model eggs. However, there was a tendency for the stuffed Cuckoo to have a stronger effect.[2] Of course, even if the increased rejection resulted from a generalized response to any nest intruder, it would still select for rapid laying by the Cuckoo. Similar experiments have shown that the sight of a Cuckoo on the nest also stimulates increased rejection of model eggs by Meadow Pipits.[11]

Studies in the Czech Republic by Ingar Øien and his colleagues have shown that Reed Warbler nests are more likely to be parasitized the nearer they are to trees.[12] Fernando Alvarez found the same for Rufous Bush Chat hosts in southern Spain.[13] Proximity to trees may increase hosts' vulnerability in two ways. First, it must make it easier for the Cuckoo to watch the hosts from a secret look-out, so she is more likely to find the nest and time her parasitism correctly. Second, it provides cover for the laying visit, and so may decrease the chance that the Cuckoo alerts the hosts to reject her egg.

Cuculus cuckoos look rather like *Accipiter* hawks, both in their plumage (grey upperparts, barred underparts, long tails) and in their direct, dashing flight. This may reflect convergent evolution on the same design but for different purposes; the hawk needs to be both camouflaged and swift in order to surprise and kill its prey, while the cuckoo may need these attributes to avoid being noticed while it searches for and exploits host nests. However, it has been suggested that the resemblance could reflect mimicry. Perhaps it pays cuckoos to look like dangerous birds to protect themselves from predation. This may be especially important for pipit-cuckoos, for example, which have to spend time out in the open looking for host nests. Alternatively, a raptor-like appearance might induce host mobbing and so make it easier for the cuckoo to find the host nests.[14] These ideas still need to be tested. The one suggestion we can reject is that raptor resemblance reduces host attacks. Many attacks on cuckoos involve actual blows, whereas both real and stuffed Sparrowhawks are mobbed only from a safe distance.[15]

EGG SIZE AND STRENGTH

We now return to the cuckoo egg itself. Parasitic cuckoos lay much smaller eggs than non-parasitic cuckoos of the same size.[16] The egg of the Common Cuckoo weighs only 3.4 g on average, about the size of a Skylark's egg, whereas a non-parasitic cuckoo of the same body weight (100 g) would be expected to lay a 10 g egg, like that of a Mistle Thrush. Such a large egg may be impossible for a small host to incubate, but our experiments showed that hosts also discriminate against these large eggs.[2] When we placed model 10 g eggs in Reed Warbler nests, they were more likely to be rejected than the normal-sized Cuckoo eggs. Nevertheless, Common Cuckoo eggs are still larger than those of most of its regular hosts. Would an even smaller egg be more likely to be accepted? Surprisingly, the answer is no, at least for Reed Warbler hosts. Mimetic model eggs the same size as the Reed Warbler's own eggs were no more likely to be accepted than those the size of Common Cuckoo eggs.[17] Therefore, hosts discriminate against giant eggs but they tolerate eggs slightly larger than their own. This means that although the Cuckoo egg has to be a good match in colour and spotting, it does not have to match the host eggs exactly for size. In fact, it may pay the Cuckoo to lay a larger egg than that of its hosts to give the cuckoo hatchling sufficient strength to eject the host eggs.

The eggs of parasitic cuckoos have another peculiarity, namely unusually strong shells. If we compare parasitic cuckoo eggs with those of the same size laid either by non-parasitic cuckoos, or by other non-passerine species, then we can see that their unusual strength is achieved in two ways. The eggs of *Clamator* cuckoos have much thicker shells than expected.[18] Those of *Cuculus*, *Cacomantis* and *Chrysococcyx* cuckoos do not have unusually thick shells,[18] but they have shells of higher density, and so are of greater mass than normal egg shells.[19] Why should parasitic cuckoos have stronger-shelled eggs? One possibility is that it makes it harder for hosts to eject them. At least some Common Cuckoo eggs are ejected whole, because undamaged Cuckoo eggs have been found under host nests. They must have either been grasped and ejected, or rolled out. Others, however, are punctured first, which makes it easier to pick them up and eject them. A thicker shell would make puncture-ejection harder, and may cause some hosts to accept the parasitic egg if their motivation for rejection was weak.[20] Alternatively, a strong shell may reduce damage during laying. This may be especially advantageous if the cuckoo is in a hurry, or if it has to squirt the egg through a narrow nest entrance, where there will be a short drop into the nest cup.[21] Finally, a stronger egg in *Clamator* cuckoos may enable them to resist damage when other parasitic eggs are laid in the nest;[18] in these cuckoos multiple parasitism is regular, either by the same or different female cuckoos, and host eggs are often cracked during laying (see chapter 8).

THE NESTLING CUCKOO

The eggs of parasitic cuckoos usually hatch a day or so before the host eggs. For cuckoos that are raised together with the host young, this gives the cuckoo chick an early start in its growth and so improves its competitive ability in the brood. For cuckoos that eject, early hatching enables them to eject the host eggs, likely to be an easier task then ejecting host chicks.

Although Aristotle briefly mentioned that the young cuckoo 'casts out of the nest those with whom it has so far lived', the credit for the first detailed description of the extraordinary performance goes to Edward Jenner, the celebrated discoverer of vaccination. Prior to his famous work on smallpox, in 1788 he published a paper on Cuckoos, which led to his election to the Royal Society in the following year. Here he describes the events in a Dunnock nest on 18 June 1787, where 'to my astonishment [I] saw the young cuckoo, though so newly hatched, in the act of turning out the young hedge sparrow [= dunnock]. ... The little animal ... contrived to get the bird upon its back and ... clambered backwards with it up the side of the nest till it reached the top, where, resting for a moment, it threw off its load with a jerk ... I afterwards put in an egg, and this, by a similar process, was conveyed to the edge of the nest and thrown out.'

These observations were met with widespread disbelief, and perhaps Sir Joseph Banks, the President of The Royal Society, also had his doubts because Jenner's paper was initially rejected with the comment, 'Council thought it best to give you full scope for altering it.' However, Jenner stuck to his story and he was subsequently vindicated by other respected ornithologists of the day, including Blackwall (1824) and Montagu (1831), though even a hundred years later some persisted in the belief that it was the female Cuckoo who returned to the host nest to do the evicting. For example, in his otherwise admirable account, Baldamus (1892) wrote: 'The female cuckoo removes and hides the eggs of the nurse after the young parasite is hatched.' However, there is no evidence that female Cuckoos ever do this. Incredible as it may seem, the blind and naked Cuckoo chick does all the work.

The newly hatched Cuckoo usually begins its ejection of the host eggs between eight and ten hours after hatching, though it may begin sooner, when the chick is just three hours old. In the nests of small hosts, like warblers and pipits, it may take as little as 20 seconds to eject the egg once the Cuckoo has the egg on its back, but the average is three to four minutes.[22] The chick rests between each load, so it may take three to four hours to evict the whole clutch, and sometimes as much as one to three days, especially if the Cuckoo is ejecting large host young. There is one report of an unusually late hatching Cuckoo in a Dunnock nest, where the two-day old

Newly hatched Common Cuckoo chick ejecting an egg from a Reed Warbler nest. It has already ejected a host chick, which is slowly dying, wedged against the outside of the nest by a supporting reed stem. The host parents do nothing to interfere as they witness the destruction of their own reproductive success.

Cuckoo chick successfully evicted a seven-day old host chick.[22] Perhaps the cuckoo chick has to delay its ejection when it is in the nests of larger hosts, in order to build up its strength. For example, when Indian Cuckoos (which are about the same size as Common Cuckoos) parasitize Brown Shrikes, the cuckoo chick hatches about two days before the host eggs but ejection usually does not occur until the cuckoo is three to four days of age, and so the cuckoo often has to eject young host chicks.[23] By contrast, with small hosts, Common Cuckoos usually eject host eggs within a day of hatching. The cuckoo's performance is not without its own hazards; in two out of 114 cases observed by Ian Wyllie in Reed Warbler nests, the Common Cuckoo chick fell out of the nest in the process![3]

The urge to eject disappears by four days of age. By this time, the Cuckoo has usually gained sole command of the nest and any host young that still remain are likely to get crushed to death, or will simply starve, unnoticed by their parents under the rapidly growing cuckoo. Very occasionally some host young do survive.[22] This has been reported for the Great Grey Shrike, a large host, where Cuckoos have been raised together with up to four host young. In one remarkable case, a Cuckoo chick hatched a day after a brood of four Robins and after spending a whole day trying to evict them, it gave up. The Cuckoo left the nest after 20 days, a normal nestling period while, amazingly, the slow-growing Robins underneath survived too and fledged at 23 days of age, 10 days later than usual.[36]

These observations show that the earlier the Cuckoo chick hatches, the easier it will be to clear the nest. The Cuckoo's unusually small egg certainly reduces incubation time, but the egg is still often a little larger than the host eggs, and because the Cuckoo lays during the host laying period it receives the same incubation time as the host eggs. How, then, does it usually manage to hatch out first? We now encounter yet another amazing Cuckoo trick. Newly laid Cuckoo eggs already have partly developed embryos.[24] When Claudon (1955) found this, he wrongly interpreted it as evidence that the Cuckoo could move its partly incubated egg from a deserted nest, and place it in another host nest. In fact the early development occurs inside the female Cuckoo's oviduct. Female Cuckoos lay on alternate days, but it takes just 24 hours for an egg to be fully formed, from ovulation to the laying down of the shell. So the female carries a hard egg in her oviduct for about a day before it is laid, and this internal incubation gives the Cuckoo chick a head start, enabling it to hatch before the host eggs.[25]

The habit of parasitic cuckoos to lay on alternate days has not evolved specifically to allow internal incubation, because many non-parasitic cuckoos also lay every other day. Nevertheless, an ancestral habit of laying on alternate days could set the stage for the evolution of internal incubation. Laying on alternate days could have other advantages too, for example increasing the time available to form energy reserves for eggs and, for parasitic cuckoos, allowing more time to find suitable host nests.

EGG REMOVAL AT LAYING

All the various aspects of the Common Cuckoo's laying tactics that we have examined so far, namely egg mimicry, timing, speed and egg size, have involved adaptations to increase the chances that the host will accept the parasitic egg. One feature, however, apparently has nothing to do with host defences, namely the Cuckoo's habit of removing an egg before she lays. Female Common Cuckoos usually remove one host egg, occasionally two, and very rarely three host eggs. This normally takes place immediately prior to laying, during their ten-second visit to the nest. If one egg is removed, the female holds it in her bill while she lays her own egg and then she flies off with it. If two or more are removed, then the first eggs are swallowed, with a backward toss of the head, while the female is at the nest, and the last is held in the bill while she lays. Occasionally, female Cuckoos will remove one or two host eggs a day or two before laying, and then may remove another during the laying visit itself.[26]

One might think that it is important for Cuckoos to remove a host egg because the hosts can count, and would easily notice an extra egg in their nest. However, experiments with both Reed Warbler and Meadow Pipit hosts have shown that most mimetic model eggs are accepted, and non-mimetic model eggs have the same chance of rejection, regardless of whether a host egg is removed or not.[2,11] Why, then, do Cuckoos remove an egg? One possibility is that they are searching to remove other Cuckoo eggs, by picking out the largest or oddest egg for example. Our data from visits by Cuckoos to Reed Warbler nests where we had previously placed model eggs provided a little support for this idea, but not strong support (see above). Alternatively, egg removal might ensure more efficient incubation of the Cuckoo egg. Our experiments suggest this is so, because unhatched Reed Warbler eggs were more usual in nests where we did not remove a host egg to make room for a model, than at nests where we did remove a host egg, implying that there is a limit to the number of eggs the host can hatch.[2,37]

Finally, egg removal may be advantageous simply because it gives the female Cuckoo a free meal while she is laying. Why, then, does she not remove all the host eggs? Our experiments show that host responses again provide the answer.[2] When we reduced the warbler's final clutch size to three eggs, they never deserted, but a reduction to two eggs sometimes caused desertion and a reduction to one egg nearly always did so. Most Reed Warblers lay a clutch of four, though clutches of three and five are also common. Therefore the maximum the Cuckoo can safely take from a clutch of three is one (she replaces this with her own egg, so the final clutch is three), and from a clutch of four the maximum is two (two removed then her own egg added to give a clutch of three). This argument predicts quite well the observed behaviour of Cuckoos, which is to remove usually one, sometimes two host eggs, rarely more. An additional cost of removing more than one egg, of course, is that it entails a longer stay at the nest and so a greater chance that the hosts will be alerted.

Although Reed Warblers nearly always desert a single egg, they never desert a single chick (either their own or a Cuckoo). This explains very neatly why it is the Cuckoo chick which takes on the task of ejecting the remainder of the nest contents, rather than its mother earlier on during the egg stage. While there is a limit to the number of eggs the laying female can remove, later on the Cuckoo chick can safely eject the entire nest contents without penalty.

GOOD AND POOR EGG MIMICRY IN DIFFERENT CUCKOO GENTES

Our conclusion from these experiments is that much of the Cuckoo's egg-laying procedure, from the design of the egg to the details of how it is laid, is beautifully adapted to circumvent host defences. This is the first piece of evidence that the Cuckoo has indeed responded to selective pressure from its hosts, as proposed by the top arrow of our co-evolutionary cycle. The second piece of evidence comes from comparing the degree of egg mimicry shown by the different Cuckoo gentes in Europe.[27] Our experiments with Meadow Pipits and Pied Wagtails revealed that, like Reed Warblers, they tended to reject model eggs unlike their own but were more likely to accept a well-matching model, representing the mimetic egg type laid by their own Cuckoo gentes. Great Reed Warblers also show strong rejection of badly matching eggs,[28] and again their gens of Cuckoo has evolved excellent egg mimicry. Experiments and observations with other major hosts of Common Cuckoos,[29] and other *Cuculus* cuckoos that lay mimetic eggs,[30] have also revealed strong host rejection.

The glaring exception to egg mimicry among the main hosts of the Common Cuckoo is the Dunnock (**Plate 2c**). Dunnock eggs are plain turquoise-blue. Cuckoo eggs in Dunnock nests, however, are greyish-white and heavily spotted with reddish-brown. As Gilbert White (1789) remarked: 'you wonder, with good reason, that the hedge sparrows [= dunnock] can be induced at all to sit on the egg of the cuckoo without being scandalised at the vast disproportioned size of the supposititious egg; but the brute creation, I suppose, have very little idea of size, colour or number.' No-one has yet radio-tracked Dunnock-Cuckoos to confirm that this is a distinct gens, but it seems most likely to be so. The most extensive study of nests parasitized in farmland and woodland was by Owen (1933), who recorded 509 parasitized nests in the Felsted district, Essex, between 1912 and 1933. Of these, the Dunnock was easily the most frequent victim, with 302 parasitized nests, and it seems certain that many of the Cuckoos must have specialized on this host. Furthermore, although the Cuckoo egg in Dunnock nests is clearly not mimetic – not only is it the wrong colour, it has spots – the egg is of a distinctive type, intermediate in darkness between those of the pipit gens and wagtail gens, and no more variable than those of these other gentes.[27]

Why does the Dunnock-Cuckoo, alone among the European gentes at least, show no egg mimicry? The answer is clear. It is because Dunnocks, alone among the major European hosts, show no egg discrimination. Our experiments show that they will accept model eggs of any colour, or spotting pattern.[27] We wondered if Dunnocks simply had poor colour vision, or found it difficult to discern egg colour in their nests, which are built in dense cover. Perhaps in the dark nest their own blue eggs and the various models would all appear a similar shade of grey. We therefore did further experiments with white or black model eggs, which should have been easily detected as different in shade, but again these were accepted. Even presentation of a stuffed Cuckoo failed to elicit rejection. Moreover Dunnocks accepted whole clutches of model eggs unlike their own, and then accepted their own eggs back again later, so their acceptance of a single model egg was not simply because they regarded it as a harmless lump of resin![31]

In conclusion, the degree of egg mimicry exhibited by the various Cuckoo gentes in Europe reflects the degree of discrimination shown by their respective hosts, indicating that Cuckoo eggs clearly evolve in response to selection from hosts. A Cuckoo gens in eastern Europe lays an immaculate blue egg for its host the Redstart, whose eggs are blue like those of the Dunnock.[32] Thus Cuckoos certainly have the potential to mimic Dunnock eggs; they haven't bothered, simply because Dunnocks have not required them to do so. This still leaves unresolved the problem of why the Dunnock-Cuckoo nevertheless lays a distinctive egg-type, different in darkness from the other gentes and no more variable. One possibility is that secondary hosts have selected for this Cuckoo egg-type; many woodland and farmland passerines have pale mottled eggs, and so the Dunnock-Cuckoo egg may be a generalized match for a variety of hosts. Alternatively, the Dunnock-Cuckoo egg may be cryptic, blending in with the nest lining, which may reduce the chance of removal by second Cuckoos, as suggested by Michael and Lesley Brooker for some Australian cuckoos, which lay a specific cryptic egg-type despite the complete absence of any host discrimination (chapter 7).

UNSUITABLE HOSTS

Both Cuckoo egg colour and Cuckoo laying tactics have clearly evolved in relation to host defences, so we now have good evidence for the top arrow of the co-evolutionary cycle. What about the bottom arrow? Have hosts, in turn, responded to selection from Cuckoos? We can test this experimentally too. If the rejection of eggs shown by hosts of the various mimicked Common Cuckoo gentes has evolved specifically in response to cuckoo parasitism, then species that have never interacted with Common Cuckoos should show no rejection of eggs unlike their own. There are two groups of such birds. The first group comprises seed-eaters (e.g. some species of finches, Fringillidae), which are unsuitable as hosts because the young Cuckoo needs an invertebrate diet for successful rearing. The second group has a suitable diet, but nests in small holes, inaccessible to the laying female Cuckoo (tits, Pied Flycatcher, Wheatear, Starling, House Sparrow, Swift). To this list can be added the Barn Swallow, which feeds its young by regurgitation (all Common Cuckoo hosts feed their young from the bill).

Experiments both in Britain[31] and in Norway[33] have revealed that these two groups of 'unsuitable' hosts have little or no rejection of eggs unlike their own, in sharp contrast to the rejection shown by 'suitable' hosts, namely passerine birds with open nests and which feed their young on invertebrates. It could be argued that demonstrating that hole nesters are accepters is trivial, because they cannot see their eggs anyway. However, the model Cuckoo eggs also differed from the host eggs in size, and at least two 'dark-nesting' hosts of other brood parasites have sensitive size discrimination,[34] so in principle it seems as if hole nesters could evolve counter-adaptations to Cuckoo eggs if they became hosts.

Some comparisons between the responses of closely related species are particularly interesting. Thus, the Spotted Flycatcher, whose open nest is accessible to female Cuckoos, shows strong rejection of eggs unlike its own whereas the Pied Flycatcher, which nests in holes and so is inaccessible, shows no rejection at all. In the finch family, the two species that feed their young predominantly on invertebrates, and are therefore suitable as cuckoo hosts, namely the Chaffinch and the Brambling, show strong rejection, while four species that feed their young mostly on seeds show little or no rejection (Greenfinch, Linnet, Redpoll, Bullfinch). These comparisons suggest that rejection behaviour is not strongly constrained by taxonomy.[35] Rather, it evolves as a defence only when a species is exploited by Cuckoos.

It is, perhaps, surprising to find such a clear difference in egg rejection between suitable and unsuitable Cuckoo hosts. As we shall see in chapter 14, many species suffer parasitism by conspecifics, including some in the 'unsuitable Cuckoo host' list above (Starlings and Barn Swallows). Shouldn't conspecific parasitism also select for rejection of odd-looking eggs? However, the majority of species, including Starlings and Barn Swallows, will accept a conspecific egg placed among their own clutch (chapter 14). Another female's egg is so like their own that it would probably be impossible to reject without costly discrimination errors (chapter 5). Therefore, most unsuitable Cuckoo hosts have never been confronted with eggs very unlike their own, and so they have not evolved defences to reject them. However, there are exceptions. In a few species, egg differences are so marked that females are able to pick out a foreign conspecific egg, and it is likely that both their distinctive egg variation, and their rejection behaviour, have evolved in response to conspecific parasitism alone, or to joint pressure from conspecifics and cuckoos (chapter 14).

UNPARASITIZED PIPITS AND WAGTAILS IN ICELAND

These comparisons suggest that in the distant past, before Cuckoos began to parasitize Meadow Pipits, White Wagtails and other current favourite hosts, these species would have shown no rejection of eggs unlike their own. We cannot go back in time, of course, but we can do the next best experiment. Common Cuckoos breed from western Europe to Japan but not in Iceland, which does however have isolated populations of both Meadow Pipits and White Wagtails. In 1987, Michael Brooke and I took our model eggs to Iceland to become that country's only cuckoos for that summer. On our arrival at the airport, the customs officer opened my suitcase and was confronted by hundreds of coloured eggs. 'What lovely sweets!' she said and, with a smile, let us through.

We searched for nests in the moorland around Myvatn, a lake in the north rich in bird life. Myvatn means 'midge lake' and is aptly named. The swarms that danced over the lake and surrounding countryside were so dense that any deep breath could lead to a midge-mouthful. Often the ground became so littered with their bodies that our bicycles skidded on the tracks and every so often we had to stop to unclog the wheels and chains before we could continue. This vast and seething insect mass provided a wonderful food supply for the birds. Every day we would find dozens of nests of shorebirds, including Red-necked Phalaropes, Whimbrel, Dunlin and Golden Plover. But the densities of Meadow Pipits and White Wagtails were very low, and even on a good day we might find just two or three nests at a suitable stage for experimental parasitism. It was often hard to keep one's concentration on the search for their nests, while Gyr Falcons chased Ptarmigan and ducks overhead, and

Great Northern Divers wailed and yodelled from the lake nearby. A local fisherman did not share our delight in the divers, and complained that of all the birds he had caught, this species was by far the hardest to strangle!

After a month's hard searching, we had found enough pipit and wagtail nests to test our prediction.[31] As expected, the Icelandic populations, isolated from Cuckoos, were much less discriminating against odd eggs than their counterparts in Britain, which are parasitized. In Iceland, all the Meadow Pipits accepted 'Pied Wagtail-Cuckoo' model eggs, which are greyish-white and much paler than their own brown eggs. Similarly, all the Icelandic wagtails accepted 'Meadow Pipit-Cuckoo' model eggs, even though their dark brown colour contrasted markedly with the wagtail's own pale eggs (**Plate 2d**). By contrast, the parasitized pipit and wagtail populations in Britain show strong rejection of these non-mimetic eggs. However, we also found an unexpected result. The Icelandic birds rejected some pure blue eggs of the Redstart-Cuckoo gens, though at a lower frequency than the British populations. This model type is the one most strongly rejected by British wagtails and pipits, and so is apparently regarded by the birds as the one most unlike their own eggs.[31]

Why do the Icelandic birds not behave like the unsuitable host species which, untainted by Cuckoos, accept all non-mimetic eggs? The Icelandic pipits and wagtails must have colonized after the last Ice Age, perhaps some 9000 years ago. If they are derived from the parasitized populations in other parts of Europe, then they may still have a legacy of their ancestors' egg discrimination. Or maybe there used to be Cuckoos breeding in Iceland, before the arrival of the Vikings and their livestock in AD 874 led to the devastation of the birch forest and, perhaps, a depleted avifauna.[31] We don't know whether the greater acceptance by Icelandic birds is caused by genetic differences, or whether it represents flexibility in individual behaviour. Perhaps hosts are simply less likely to reject if they assess parasitism to be absent, for example because they don't encounter Cuckoos (see chapter 5). Either way, the results suggest that host egg rejection is a specific counter-adaptation against Cuckoos.

AGGRESSION AGAINST ADULT CUCKOOS

Egg rejection is not the only host defence that has evolved as a specific adaptation against cuckoo parasitism. Arne Moksnes, Eivin Røskaft and their co-workers from the University of Trondheim, have shown that unsuitable host species, such as the hole-nesting titmice and the Pied Flycatcher, and the seed-eating Greenfinch, also show less aggression to model adult Cuckoos than do suitable hosts.[33]

William Duckworth's study, on Wicken Fen, of how Reed Warblers mob Cuckoos in comparison with other predators also supports the view that hosts have specific aggressive responses suited to the threat of parasitism.[15] Cuckoos are a threat to the nest contents but not to the host parents themselves and adult Reed Warblers will readily attack a Cuckoo near their nest, pulling feathers from it whether it is a live bird or a stuffed mount. Indeed, speedy intervention is often necessary to prevent a stuffed Cuckoo's destruction! By contrast, Reed Warblers are less ready to approach a Jay and even less likely to approach a Sparrowhawk; the former is a danger not only to the nest but also to the adult, while the latter is a danger to the adults only. Further evidence of adaptive responses to Cuckoos is the fact that reactions to a Cuckoo more or less cease once the young fledge (the Cuckoo is no threat to fledglings) whereas alarm to a Jay or Sparrowhawk continues (both are capable of killing fledglings). Clearly the host's different responses to these three predators is adapted to their respective dangers to the nest and the adults themselves.

*   *   *

These experiments have provided strong evidence for both arrows of the co-evolutionary cycle that we proposed at the beginning of the chapter. The next question is: what is the outcome of these reciprocal interactions? Does the cycle simply continue for ever, with each party evolving more and more refined tricks and counter-adaptations? Or could the interaction reach a stable conclusion? Perhaps the Cuckoo evolves such good trickery that the host is doomed always to accept parasitic eggs and chicks? Alternatively, perhaps the host evolves such good defences that the Cuckoo is forced to seek new victims? In this case, maybe different hosts of the Cuckoo are at different stages of the arms race – could the Dunnock's blind acceptance of non-mimetic eggs reflect the fact that it is a new victim of the Cuckoo, and simply has not had the time to evolve defences?

These are fascinating questions, but before we tackle them we need to look more carefully at how hosts defend themselves against Cuckoos. Defence entails costs, and these costs have an important influence on how the arms race proceeds.

CHAPTER 5
How to spot a cuckoo egg

In our own lives, we are familiar with the idea that defences are costly. For nations, investment in armed forces is at the expense of other public services, such as schools and hospitals. For individuals, it is expensive to buy padlocks and alarm systems to protect personal property. The defence costs escalate as one's opponents, other nations or burglars, invest in better weapons. Given these costs, it is not surprising that we vary our levels of defence in relation to the risks of attack. In country villages we may not even bother to lock our doors, while in some towns it may be necessary to have not only heavy locks but even armed guards.

For animals too, defences against enemies are costly. Towards the end of the 1980s, Sparrowhawks re-colonized the Cambridge area as a result of reductions in the use of pesticides in the surrounding farmland.[1] This has had a profound effect on the behaviour of small birds. They are now much less likely to feed out in the open, where they would be vulnerable to surprise attacks, and they are more nervous than before. For example, they often dart into the bushes whenever a large bird flies overhead, even if it's a harmless dove. Before the Sparrowhawks returned, the doves were ignored. This change in behaviour makes good sense, of course. An extra few seconds to check whether the approaching bird is a hawk or a dove could save valuable feeding time, but it could also tempt instant death, a crushing beneath powerful talons. It is better to be safe than sorry, despite the cost of false alarms.

Defences against cuckoos are also likely to be costly for the hosts. Even a little extra time looking out for cuckoos or cuckoo eggs is likely to be at the expense of other vital activities such as foraging or incubation. There could also be the problem of false alarms; the odd egg in the nest might not be a cuckoo egg but rather one of the host's own eggs. Perhaps this is why the Icelandic pipits and wagtails, isolated from cuckoos, have reduced rejection of non-mimetic eggs, and why species unsuitable as hosts, and so completely untainted by interactions with cuckoos, have no rejection at all. There is no such thing as a free adaptation. Nature is ruthless in her economy and only equips animals to deal with circumstances that are important for their daily survival and reproduction. If we could measure the costs of host defences, then we could calculate the parasitism rates at which it would pay hosts to defend themselves. To do this, we need to take a closer look at exactly how a host could discriminate against cuckoo eggs and cuckoo chicks.

LEARNING TO RECOGNIZE YOUR OWN EGGS

In the last chapter, we saw that cuckoo hosts often reject eggs that are unlike their own. The ways in which hosts discriminate against foreign eggs has been particularly well studied in two species. In Africa, a common host of the Diederik Cuckoo is the Spottedbacked (or Village) Weaver (chapter 7). Individual females of this host lay eggs of a constant type, but there is considerable variation between females. The ground colour may be white, pale blue-green or dark blue-green, and the eggs may be either plain or spotted (**Plate 3b**). In experiments where one host egg was removed and replaced with an egg of another female, J.K. Victoria, from the University of California, Los Angeles, found that the greater the difference between the foreign egg and the host eggs, the more likely it was to be rejected.[2] For example, females with plain eggs rejected most of the spotted eggs, and were only likely to accept a plain egg if it was the same colour as their own. Conversely, females with spotted eggs rejected most of the plain eggs, and were more likely to accept spotted eggs if they had the same background colour as their own eggs. Rejected eggs were pecked open and then carried off, usually within 24 hours of experimental parasitism, but sometimes within a few minutes.

One rule the weavers could adopt is, 'reject an odd-looking egg from my clutch'. However, females were just as likely to reject a foreign egg from a clutch of two, with just one egg of their own. Furthermore, if they were given two foreign eggs plus one of their own, so that their own egg was now the odd one out, they rejected both the foreign eggs. Remarkably, they even rejected a whole clutch of foreign eggs, with none of their own for comparison.[2] These experiments suggest that the weavers know what their own eggs look like.

A major host of the Common Cuckoo is the Great Reed Warbler, which has pale eggs, heavily spotted with brown and grey (**Plate 2c**). In a study of their discrimination behaviour in central Japan, Arnon Lotem, Hiroshi Nakamura and Amotz Zahavi placed painted conspecific eggs into their nests.[3] In Great Reed Warblers, only the females incubate and so only the females make decisions concerning egg rejection. Dark brown eggs were rejected at 94% of the nests, usually within a day. They were first punctured, some of their contents were drunk, and then they were picked up through the puncture hole and carried off. An egg painted light brown, not so different in shade from the warbler's own eggs, was rejected at only 78% of nests and rejection took, on average, a day longer. Just like the weaverbirds, the warblers did not simply reject the oddest egg, because if they were given a whole clutch of brown painted eggs they often rejected them all. Interestingly, in this case they did not save time by deserting straight away. Rather, they carefully pecked and removed each egg until the nest was empty, then they deserted. Natural selection has designed them to respond appropriately for parasitism by one, perhaps two, Cuckoo eggs and the sensible procedure would, indeed, be to remove each foreign egg in turn. We would not expect the warblers to necessarily reject in the best way with a whole clutch of foreign eggs, a situation they would never meet naturally.

These experiments show that the hosts know their own eggs. The most likely way they could do this is by learning what their eggs look like the first time they breed.

The obvious experiment to test for learning is to replace each egg of a first-time breeder, as soon as it is laid, with a foreign egg. This should trick the bird into learning the wrong type of egg. Perhaps it would then even reject one of its own eggs? The first person to try this was Rensch (1924, 1925). In one experiment he replaced the first three eggs in a Garden Warbler nest with eggs of a Lesser Whitethroat, which are paler in colour. The Garden Warblers laid a fourth egg and then promptly rejected it! Rensch interpreted this as 'rejecting the odd one out', but it is also possible that the Garden Warblers had learned the Lesser Whitethroat egg patterns as their own and then saw their own fourth egg as foreign. However, the age of the birds was not known and none of Rensch's experiments was replicated.

Stephen Rothstein, from the University of Santa Barbara, was the first to do controlled experiments of this type, using Grey Catbirds, a host of the Brown-headed Cowbird in North America.[4] The catbirds have plain blue-green eggs, clearly different from the cowbird's whitish, spotted and slightly smaller egg. Like the Great Reed Warblers and Spottedbacked Weavers, the catbirds know what their own eggs look like. If, at the end of laying, they are given cowbird eggs, then they reject them

A Great Reed Warbler ejecting an egg of a Common Cuckoo. Experiments show that these hosts learn what their eggs look like during the laying of their first clutch. They then reject eggs that differ from this learnt set.

all, but not their own eggs, whether the cowbird eggs are in the minority, the majority or even the only egg type present. However, Rothstein found that foreign eggs were more likely to be accepted if they were introduced early on during laying. If the first-laid egg was quickly replaced with a cowbird egg, but the remainder of the clutch left in the nest, the birds sometimes accepted the cowbird egg along with their own, apparently learning both types as part of their own set. By contrast, in one experiment where the entire clutch was replaced with cowbird eggs, the catbirds learned only the cowbird eggs as their own and they then rejected one of their own eggs.

These experiments support the learning hypothesis, but the age of the catbirds was not known, so we are still left with the question of whether learning occurs just once, the first time a female breeds, or whether it continues over several successive clutches. The Great Reed Warbler study provides evidence that it occurs during a female's first breeding attempt, and that the female can thereafter remember her egg type.[3] Some young females could be recognized for certain because they retained juvenile tail feathers. Compared with other birds, these known first-time breeders were more likely to accept a non-mimetic egg placed in their nests during laying, but they were just as likely to reject if given it once their clutch was complete. This suggests that learning occurs during the laying of the first clutch. Furthermore, if a young female's exposure to her first clutch was minimized, by replacing each of her eggs, soon after laying, with a dark brown painted egg, then she would accept the foreign eggs. Most old females, however, were not tricked by this procedure and rejected the clutch of brown eggs, showing that they could remember their own eggs from previous breeding attempts. Interestingly, a few old females did accept the brown clutch, but if they were then given a single egg of their own this seemed to jog their memory and they then immediately rejected all the brown eggs.

The young female Great Reed Warbler 'imprints' on the first clutch of eggs in her nest, rather like the imprinting shown by some young birds and mammals when they follow the first conspicuous object they see and treat it as their mother. However, Lotem, Nakamura and Zahavi were not able to get the young warblers to reject one of their own eggs after they had imprinted on a clutch of brown-painted eggs. One possibility is that the birds had some brief but sufficient experience of their own eggs before they were replaced with the brown eggs. Alternatively, they may have some innate preference to learn egg types similar to their own and so are prepared to accept their own eggs even at a later stage.[3]

Why should birds have to learn their eggs at all? The most likely explanation is that egg patterns are usually so complex that it would be difficult, perhaps impossible, for there to be a completely innate program for egg recognition. In another context where complex patterns have to be acquired, namely bird song, learning is also involved though there may be an innate 'template' which predisposes individuals to be more likely to learn their own species' songs.[5]

A cost of having to learn your own eggs is that of mis-imprinting on the wrong type. This occurred in the experiments, but it will also happen in nature whenever a cuckoo parasitizes a first-time breeder, which will be tricked into learning even a non-mimetic egg as one of her own. The implication is that the bird would then be doomed to accept that foreign egg type for the rest of her life. Arnon Lotem suggests that this may explain why experimenters often find some low level of acceptance in nature, even of very non-mimetic eggs.[3] An obvious way of avoiding the cost of mis-imprinting would be to imprint only on the first-laid egg. This would ensure that the host learned what its egg looked like before the parasite had a chance to lay. This would work beautifully if there were no variation in the host's own eggs, because the first egg would provide a perfect picture of what all the other eggs look like. If a female's eggs were variable, however, then she would need to prolong learning to make sure that she got to know the various shades or spotting patterns of her own eggs. In fact, like many species, Great Reed Warblers do have some variation in the appearance of their own eggs. This may be why they imprint on a whole clutch rather than just their first egg.[3]

Another way of overcoming the problem of variation within your own eggs would be to imprint on the first egg, but to accept a range of eggs around this type. This would be an excellent defence against a parasite that laid eggs of a very different appearance from your own set, because it would avoid the cost of mis-imprinting. Perhaps it is the mechanism used by some cowbird hosts, where the parasite egg is often completely unlike the host eggs and where hosts may achieve 100% rejection, which implies that they do not have a mis-imprinting problem (chapter 10). However, Lotem points out that this would be no good for most cuckoo hosts, where the parasite egg is highly mimetic.[3] For example, in both Reed Warblers and Great Reed Warblers some of the host's own eggs look just as different from the rest of the clutch as a cuckoo egg. Any generalizations from the host's first egg would be likely to include the cuckoo's egg type. Hosts would certainly make many mistakes if they tried to recognize their eggs from the appearance of their first one. The best compromise may be simply to prolong learning until the host has been exposed to a range of its own eggs, despite the occasional cost of mis-imprinting if the bird is unlucky and gets parasitized during the learning period.[3,23]

EGG SIGNATURES

Given all these recognition problems caused by variation in their own eggs, we might wonder why cuckoo hosts don't make all their eggs look exactly the same. This would be easiest for plain-coloured eggs. The problem is that it is then simple for the cuckoo to evolve a perfect match. This occurs, for example, in the Common Cuckoo gens that parasitizes Redstarts, and in several *Cuculus* and *Clamator* cuckoos that parasitize babblers, where cuckoos and hosts both lay plain blue eggs. With perfect mimicry, imprinting on the first egg would not help the hosts to avoid parasitism.

Most hosts, however, have spotted eggs and with such complex markings it might simply be impossible to make them all the same. Spotting may help camouflage the clutch in species with open nests. In a remarkable early paper, C.F.M. Swynnerton (1918) suggested another explanation:

With the growth of discrimination on the part of the species most victimized . . . , would come mimicry. I doubt whether this would be the end of the matter, for, when a cuckoo's egg became indistinguishable from its hosts, variation in the latter would still afford some means of distinguishing it from the cuckoo's

... it is even imaginable that a race may ... have taken place between the host's eggs and those of the cuckoo. High distinctiveness might sometimes have been the result. In other cases, sheer variability would help much to baffle the cuckoo ... and the influence of parasitic birds has thus contributed much, in the course of ages, towards the production of that quality of diversity that today so characterises passerine eggs.

Swynnerton's idea is that the spotting patterns evolve as signatures. In effect, the hosts write on their eggs, 'this is my egg'. The cuckoo then has to copy the signature, by writing 'and so is this'. An evolutionary arms race ensues leading to more complex signatures, as the hosts try to escape the forgeries of the cuckoos. This is an exact analogy of the human battle between bankers and cheats, which has led to the complicated patterns on our banknotes and credit cards. The signature hypothesis predicts that cuckoo hosts should evolve less variation within their own clutches (to make it easier to pick out a cuckoo egg), and more variation between clutches of different females within a species (with more distinctive individual signatures, it will be harder for the cuckoo to evolve a good match).[6]

The evidence for these predictions is equivocal. When suitable hosts of the Common Cuckoo are compared with unsuitable hosts (species untainted by Cuckoos), then there is no tendency for the suitable hosts to have less variation within clutches, at least as scored by human observers.[7] So the variation may simply be something that the hosts have to put up with, as a consequence of having a complex pattern on their eggs. In the same way, we find it impossible to produce an identical signature every time we write our own name. Comparing variation between clutches, there was indeed a tendency for suitable hosts to have more variation between females within a species, but this was simply because there were so many hole nesters in the unsuitable host category. Hole nesters tend to have plainer and less variable eggs, often pure white (probably so the hosts can see them more easily in their dark nests). When hole nesters were removed from the comparison, there was no difference between suitable and unsuitable hosts.[7] Another complication is that parasitism by conspecifics may also influence the evolution of egg signatures (see chapter 14).

Nevertheless, although there is still some uncertainty about whether egg patterns evolve under selection from cuckoos, it is clear that they influence the ease with which hosts discriminate model eggs. Host species with less variation in their own clutch, and more variation between the clutches of different females, show stronger rejection of model cuckoo eggs.[8] It is apparently easier to spot a foreign egg in a more uniform clutch, and where an individual female's egg signatures are more distinctive.[24]

ATTRACTIVE CUCKOO EGGS?

When animals 'imprint' on an object, by learning its characteristics, they often prefer not something that looks exactly like the object but rather an extreme form of it, a so-called 'super-normal' stimulus. For example, male Japanese Quail prefer as mates females that are even more spotted than the spotting patterns they learnt from their companions as young birds.[9] It is possible that the same phenomenon occurs with imprinting on eggs. Gerard Baerends and Rudi Drent, from the University of Groningen, were able to make a model egg that Herring Gulls found to be more attractive than one of their own eggs. They tested gulls by placing two eggs on the edge of their nest, a painted wooden model and one of the gull's own eggs, and looked to see which one the gulls chose to roll back into the nest first. A super-normal egg, one preferred to the gull's own, was a little larger and more finely speckled than the gull's eggs.[10] This raises the possibility that perfect mimicry may not be the only outcome of a cuckoo-host arms race. Perhaps some cuckoos evolve super-normal eggs. Indeed, some cuckoo eggs do tend to look more speckled than the host eggs, as well as often being a little larger.

Even eggs which look completely different from the host eggs may provide attractive stimuli which induce hosts to accept them. In southern Spain, there is a gens of Common Cuckoo that parasitizes the Rufous Bush Chat. This host has greyish-white eggs with dense brown spots. In experiments with model eggs, Fernando Alvarez showed that eggs were much more likely to be accepted if they were painted to mimic the host eggs exactly rather than just roughly, for example through less dense spotting. However, plain white eggs, or white eggs with highly contrasting black spots, were just as likely to be accepted as the highly mimetic eggs. It is interesting to note that the eggs of the Cuckoo gens which specializes on this host tends to have darker spots than those on the host eggs. Perhaps this is a supernormal feature that increases acceptance.[11]

REJECTION DECISIONS

Discriminating cuckoo eggs is a two-stage process. So far, we have discussed the first stage, namely how the hosts recognize a foreign egg. The answer is that they learn about their own eggs, so that they can recognize eggs that are different. The next stage is the rejection decision. Imagine that the hosts notice an egg slightly different from their learnt set. Should they reject it? It could be a cuckoo egg, but it could be one of their own eggs, perhaps a rare type that they have not seen before or one that got a bit muddy, or soiled by faeces, in the nest lining. A sensible host should take account not only of the appearance of the egg, but also of the probability of parasitism. Just as we carry umbrellas only when there is a good chance of rain, so hosts should vary their rejection threshold depending on their assessment of cuckoo abundance.

We have already encountered evidence for such host flexibility in the previous chapter. Reed Warblers on Wicken Fen accept most mimetic eggs, whether they are real Common Cuckoo eggs or model eggs. However, the presentation of a stuffed Cuckoo causes them to increase their rejection. If they can reject mimetic eggs when alerted by a Cuckoo, why don't they always reject them? Their flexible response would make good sense if there were a cost to rejection, a cost that would be worth incurring only if the host had good reason to believe that a Cuckoo really had laid in its nest. Are there rejection costs?

Our experiments with model eggs revealed that hosts of Common Cuckoos face two costs when they decide to reject.[12] First, they sometimes crack their own eggs when trying to eject the Cuckoo egg. Larger-billed hosts may avoid this cost completely; they find it easy to pick the Cuckoo egg up by grasping it between their mandibles, and simply throw it out. Smaller-billed hosts, unable to grasp the parasite egg, may have to puncture it first, to get a hold. In doing so, the Cuckoo egg may roll against their own eggs and crack them. The smallest hosts of all may not even be able to puncture the Cuckoo egg, because of its unusually strong shell. They may try to roll it out, a precarious procedure in which the Cuckoo egg could fall back into the nest and crack other eggs. Perhaps this is why smaller-billed hosts are more likely to reject non-mimetic model eggs by deserting the clutch altogether.[13,14] Although our model eggs were solid, and so could not be punctured, Reed Warblers showed the same ejection cost for them as for real Cuckoo eggs, namely half an egg lost per ejection.[12]

The second rejection cost is that of recognition errors. Sometimes hosts reject the wrong egg. When there was a mimetic Cuckoo egg in their nest, either a real one or a model, the Reed Warblers made a mistake in 30% of their ejections, throwing out one of their own eggs rather than the Cuckoo egg. We should, perhaps, not be surprised at this, because sometimes one of the warbler's own eggs looked more different from the rest of the clutch than did the Cuckoo egg. Strong evidence that these are indeed recognition errors comes from the fact that the Reed Warblers never rejected only their own eggs when there was a non-mimetic model egg in their nest, and hence easily distinguishable from the rest.[12] A comparison of two studies of Great Reed Warblers reveals the same result. In Hungary, where the Common Cuckoo egg is a good mimic, the Great Reed Warblers made recognition errors in 28% of the cases that they ejected eggs from parasitized nests.[15] By contrast, in Japan, where the Cuckoo egg is not a good match, the warblers very rarely made such ejection errors (less than 1% cases).[3] Recognition errors have also been reported for other hosts.[16]

Even when a nest is unparasitized, hosts apparently sometimes throw out one of their own eggs. In a study of Yellow-browed Leaf Warblers in Kashmir, Karen Marchetti found that single eggs disappeared from 5% of unparasitized nests, and some of these were found intact, outside the nest, just like ejected experimental eggs.[16] In our Reed Warbler study, the presentation of a stuffed Cuckoo sometimes led the warblers to reject eggs, even if there was no model Cuckoo egg in the nest.[12]

Now we know the costs of rejection for the Reed Warblers on Wicken Fen, let us return to the problem faced by the hosts who find a 'mimetic' egg in their nest, say one that is only slightly different from their learnt set.[17] Should they accept or reject? If the nest is unparasitized, it will contain on average four host eggs (the average clutch size for Reed Warblers). If it has been parasitized, then it has three host eggs and a Cuckoo egg (remember that the Cuckoo replaces one host egg with her own). Let's assume that the host decides to accept. If it is lucky, and is not parasitized, then it gets the reproductive success from four eggs. If it is parasitized, however, it gets nothing because the Cuckoo chick will eject all the host eggs.

Now let's see what the host would gain from rejection. If it is parasitized, it makes recognition errors in 30% of the cases and throws out one or more of its own eggs (in fact, the average is 1.2 own eggs lost). In these cases, of course, the Cuckoo egg remains in the nest so the host's reproductive payoff is zero. In the other 70% cases it correctly ejects the Cuckoo egg, along with an average of 0.5 of its own three eggs (the ejection cost), so it is left with 2.5 of its own eggs in the nest. Its average payoff is therefore $(0.3 \times 0) + (0.7 \times 2.5) = 1.75$. In the absence of parasitism, we assume that a rejector host makes the same frequency of rejection errors. In other words, in 30% of the cases its own eggs look sufficiently strange to stimulate ejection and it ejects 1.2 of them, while in the other 70% of cases it leaves all four eggs in the nest. The average payoff is therefore $(0.3 \times 2.8) + (0.7 \times 4) = 3.6$. This last calculation is the most uncertain, because we need more information on the frequency of rejection errors in unparasitized nests.

We can summarize these calculations as follows. The numbers refer to the number of Reed Warbler eggs in the nest resulting from the four outcomes.

Host decision	Nest	
	not parasitized (four host eggs)	parasitized (three host + one cuckoo egg)
Accept	4	0
Reject	3.6	1.75

What should the warblers do? If they are not parasitized, it is clearly better to accept. If they are parasitized, however, then rejection is best. The critical parasitism frequency above which rejection is better than acceptance is 19%. Below this threshold, it is not worth incurring the costs of rejection and the best thing to do is to accept.[17]

These calculations help to explain why Reed Warblers vary their response to mimetic model Cuckoo eggs.[17] If they do not see a Cuckoo at their nest, then their best estimate of parasitism is simply the average rate for the population. In most years on Wicken Fen this falls well below 19%, which fits with our finding that most real Cuckoo eggs (81%) and most mimetic model eggs (97%) were accepted. However, when we placed a stuffed Cuckoo on the nest, the warblers changed their behaviour and were much more likely to reject. If the sight of a Cuckoo on the nest were a certain predictor of parasitism, then the warblers should have always rejected. In fact they did so in only 56% of the stuffed Cuckoo presentations. Perhaps this is because a Cuckoo visit is not always followed by parasitism; as found by Edgar Chance, sometimes Cuckoos visit nests to inspect them rather than to lay. In addition, because Reed Warbler eggs are variable between clutches, our mimetic model eggs were a better match (at least to our eyes) for some clutches than for others. When we asked colleagues to rank, from photographs, how well the model matched each clutch, the cases where the warblers rejected the model were ranked as poorer matches. The sight of a Cuckoo, therefore, seems to stimulate the warblers to reject an egg that looks different from their own set.[12]

FLEXIBLE HOST DEFENCES

Needless to say, we are not suggesting that the Reed Warblers themselves do all these calculations. Just as they can evolve cryptic plumage or spotting patterns on their eggs without being aware of how these work to improve their survival and reproductive success, so they can evolve adaptive behaviour patterns without any awareness of the outcomes or the underlying costs and benefits. Our conclusion is simply that in unparasitized populations, 'acceptor' hosts will do best because they don't incur wasted rejection errors. So natural selection will favour acceptors over rejectors. Only above a certain threshold parasitism rate will rejectors gain an advantage.[3,6]

Nevertheless, the flexible behaviour of the Reed Warblers shows that they are not genetically fixed as either rejectors or acceptors, but can vary their decision adaptively in relation to the perceived threat of parasitism. Flexible individual behaviour makes good sense, because local parasitism rates vary widely over time and between nearby sites.[18] This is particularly true for small patches of habitat, where changes in the parasitism rate are determined by the chance death or dispersal of just one or two female Cuckoos. For example, on the island of Bardsey, off the tip of the North Wales peninsular, there are about 50 pairs of Meadow Pipits. Parasitism varied unpredictably between 1955 and 1968; in nine years there were no Cuckoos, in three years there was just one female and in two years there were two.[19] Similarly, at a reed bed in the southwest of England, Chew Valley Lake, the frequency of parasitism of Reed Warblers varied widely between 1970 and 1995; there were 15 years with no Cuckoos, interspersed unpredictably with parasitism in the other 11 years varying from 2 to 16%. Therefore adult Reed Warblers returning to breed at a particular site will encounter variable parasitism rates during their lifetime. Furthermore, although many of their offspring may return to breed at the same site, some may disperse to breed up to 200 km away (the average natal dispersal distance is 50 km), so are likely to encounter different parasitism rates from those experienced by their parents. For these reasons we would expect flexible individual rejection behaviour rather than fixed responses.[18]

Recent studies have shown that egg rejection by Reed Warblers does indeed vary between sites and between years in relation to changes in parasitism frequency. Anna Lindholm and Robert Thomas, from Cambridge University, studied two reed beds in South Wales where Reed Warblers have never been known to be parasitized. Their experiments showed that these populations had much less rejection of non-mimetic model eggs, and also less aggressive responses to stuffed Cuckoos, compared with the parasitized population on Wicken Fen, some 250 km away.[20] Given the wide natal dispersal of Reed Warblers, the South Wales populations are unlikely to be genetically isolated from the nearest parasitized populations, just 80 km away. To test whether individuals would change their behaviour under reduced parasitism, 35 adults were caught at the start of the summer on Wicken Fen and transported to one of the unparasitized Welsh sites. Unfortunately, only two were found breeding in their new home but both accepted non-mimetic model eggs.[20]

Observations on Wicken Fen show how there may be dramatic changes at a site even within a few years.[21] Cuckoo parasitism plummeted from 16% in 1985–86 to just 2–6% in 1995–97, owing to a decline in Cuckoos. Our experiments with model eggs showed that over this twelve-year period there was a marked decline in host rejection of non-mimetic eggs, from rejection at 75% of Reed Warbler nests in 1985–86 to 25% of nests in 1997. Calculations suggest that this decline in host defences is too rapid to reflect only genetic change, and so is more likely to be the outcome of individual flexibility. One other result also showed flexibility in host responses. There was a strong seasonal decline in parasitism, and this too was accompanied by a strong seasonal decline in rejection.[21] In Spain, Fernando Alvarez also found less rejection by Rufous Bush Chats when Cuckoos left the study site later in the season. By testing the same host individuals at different stages of the summer, he showed that this was due to individuals changing their responses.[22]

How do hosts assess parasitism rate? The most likely mechanism is that they do this by their encounter rate with Cuckoos, either by sight or by sound. Lindholm and Thomas tried to increase the rejection of the Welsh Reed Warblers by daily presentations of stuffed Cuckoos, accompanied by Cuckoo calls. Their failure to induce a response could simply reflect the fact that the Reed Warblers demand more realistic evidence of Cuckoos.[20] On Wicken Fen, we expected to find stronger rejection at host nests in the close vicinity of naturally parasitized nests, where Cuckoos would be more frequently encountered, but we found no such effect. Nevertheless, at a small unparasitized population just 11 km away, where there were no Cuckoos, the Reed Warblers did not reject any of our model Cuckoo eggs.[21] This suggests strongly that the hosts must be monitoring Cuckoo activity in their local area.

CHAPTER 6

Driving parents cuckoo

The experiments on egg learning and egg rejection described in the last chapter, have revealed remarkably sophisticated defences by hosts. Now we come to one of the biggest puzzles of all. Given such finely tuned discrimination at the egg stage, why do hosts of the Common Cuckoo show such blind acceptance of the Cuckoo chick? The newly hatched Cuckoo is bright pink and the gape is orange without any markings. The Reed Warbler's own young have black skin and their gapes are yellow, with two conspicuous black spots on the tongue. These are the kind of differences that the hosts can discriminate with ease at the egg stage. Yet there is no evidence that Reed Warblers, or any other host of the Common Cuckoo, ever reject the Cuckoo chick. This is an extraordinary state of affairs.

One possibility is that the hosts are prevented from discrimination simply because the Cuckoo chick hatches first and ejects their eggs before they have the chance to make a comparison with their own young. In 1787, Edward Jenner tied a young Cuckoo down in the nest so it could not eject the eggs of its host, a pair of Dunnocks. The main aim of his experiment was to confirm that it was the young Cuckoo who did all the ejecting, never the adult female Cuckoo. As expected, the young Dunnocks hatched and Jenner found that the 'old birds fed the whole alike, and appeared in every respect to pay the same attention to their own young as to the young cuckoo.'[1]

Michael Brooke and I enabled Reed Warblers to compare their own young with a Cuckoo by using a different technique. We tied a second nest next to their own, supporting it with a bamboo cane. Pairs that were feeding their own young were given a young Cuckoo in the nest alongside, while pairs that were feeding a Cuckoo were given young Reed Warblers. We watched the hosts for an hour and then exchanged the contents of the two nests and watched for another hour, to test whether any preferences were due to a preference for a particular nest rather than for its contents. When the Reed Warblers returned with food, they perched above the nests and peered down at the two sets of chicks. After a quick inspection, they began to deliver the food. There was no strong preference for either nest or either type of chick. We got the impression that the adults simply fed whichever chicks were begging the most.[2] These experiments show that hosts will feed a Cuckoo even when they have their own chicks alongside for comparison.

Richard Dawkins and John Krebs have suggested that whereas the Cuckoo relies on deception to get its egg accepted, it relies on a different trick at the chick stage, namely that of manipulation.[3] They proposed that the hosts may not be able to resist a Cuckoo chick any more 'than the junkie can resist his fix'. However, we found that hosts of the Common Cuckoo would accept chicks of other species too, raising them as their own despite their odd appearance. For example, Reed Warblers accepted among their own brood a single Dunnock chick, which has pink skin and an orange gape, contrasting with the black skin and yellow gapes of their own young.[2] Similarly, Reed Buntings will accept a single Reed Warbler in their brood, Chaffinches will accept a Dunnock chick and Dunnocks will accept a Chaffinch chick.[4] In these cases too, the foreign chick looks very different from the host's own young. These experiments allow us to reject the drug analogy. The Cuckoo chick does not need to possess any special super-stimuli to induce acceptance. The hosts simply fail to discriminate at the chick stage and will feed any begging mouth in their nest.

PROBLEMS FOR HOSTS OF RECOGNIZING FOREIGN CHICKS

Why do Common Cuckoo hosts reject odd eggs but not odd chicks? One possibility is that there is stronger selection for rejection of Cuckoo eggs because the earlier the hosts spot the parasitism the better. They are then more likely to save their current brood, but even if they are unable to do this (for example because they reject by desertion), early rejection, at the egg stage, is more likely to give them the chance to raise a replacement brood that year. By the time the chicks hatch, it may be too late for this. A second consideration is that discrimination of strange chicks may be a more difficult task than discrimination of strange eggs. An egg looks exactly the same throughout incubation, whereas a chick changes dramatically as it grows. One day it may be naked and black, two days later it is feathered and brown. Furthermore, because host chicks often hatch over a period of a day or two, there will be young of different ages in the nest and so considerable variation in appearance even within the host's own brood. To spot a Cuckoo chick amongst this variability may not be easy.[2] Nevertheless, neither of these arguments is wholly convincing. There are still some simple rules that hosts could use. For example, any Reed Warbler that only fed chicks with tongue spots would never be fooled into raising a young Cuckoo.

Arnon Lotem, from the University of Tel-Aviv, has suggested another, ingenious solution.[5] How would hosts come to recognize their young? The answer is likely to involve learning, just as with egg recognition. We have already seen that learning works well at the egg stage. Occasionally the host is unlucky and is parasitized during its first clutch, in which case it learns both its own eggs and the foreign egg as part of its own set. But this cost of mis-imprinting is not too bad; although in future these individuals will be fooled into accepting the foreign egg, in many cases they will not be parasitized and so can happily raise their own young. However, Common Cuckoo hosts that adopted this learning procedure for chicks would incur a much larger cost of mis-imprinting. If they were parasitized in their first attempt, they would imprint only on the Cuckoo chick. They would then reject all of their own young in future, unparasitized attempts. It turns out in this case that it would be better not to learn at all, but rather to accept any chick in the nest. And that is exactly what hosts of Common Cuckoos, and other ejector cuckoos, seem to do. So there is no selection for chick mimicry, and these cuckoos, and other parasites that are raised alone, can get away with chicks that are completely unlike the host chicks.

What about cases where the parasite chick is raised alongside the host young? In these cases it would pay the hosts to learn their own young because the situation is just like that at the egg stage. Unlucky hosts, parasitized in their first attempt, imprint on both their own chicks and the foreign chick. They will then accept both types in future. Most hosts, however, will imprint only on their own young, so they will recognize non-mimetic chicks as foreign. Just as with eggs, selection will therefore favour chick mimicry when parasite and host young are raised together.

As predicted by Lotem's argument, there is indeed often mimicry by parasite chicks in cases where they are raised alongside the host young.[2] The most remarkable examples come from the African parasitic finches (chapter 13). Each *Vidua* parasite specializes on one species of estrildid finch host. The host young have intricate gape markings, which differ between species, and the parasite nestling mimics the pattern of its particular host species (**Plate 7d**). By contrast, the Cuckoo Finch, which is raised alone in the host nest, does not mimic the host young.

The koels provide a similar comparison. Asian Koels parasitize crows, and the young parasite is raised alongside the crow host young. The feathered young koel is black all over just like a young crow. No-one has yet done experiments to test whether the crows would reject non-mimetic young. The best evidence that this resemblance is due to mimicry comes from the contrast with the Australian Koel, which some regard simply as a subspecies of the Asian Koel. The Australian Koel parasitizes smaller host species, and the young koel ejects the host eggs and so is raised alone. In this case the feathered parasite chick is not black, but brownish and barred, and it does not mimic the host young.[6]

A final impressive example of chick mimicry comes from the Screaming Cowbird, which specializes on Bay-winged Cowbirds as hosts. The young parasite is almost indistinguishable from the host young with which it is reared, both as a nestling and as a fledgling (**Plate 6d**; chapter 12). This match is certainly evolved mimicry, not similarity through common descent, because these two species of cowbirds are not each other's closest relatives. The mimicry seems to be important at least at the fledgling stage, because the hosts refuse to feed young which look different from their own.[7]

This comparison between non-mimetic parasite chicks raised alone, and mimetic parasite chicks raised together with host young, certainly supports Lotem's hypothesis. But it would also be good to have direct experimental evidence that hosts really do imprint on the young in their nest, in cases where parasites are raised alongside host chicks. The hosts of *Vidua* finches would provide an excellent opportunity to test this, because they are easy to breed in captivity.

CHARMING ALIENS?

All these examples of impressive host chick mimicry come from parasites that specialize on one host species. Tomas Redondo, from the Biological Station at

Doñana, southern Spain, has pointed out that they are also cases where the parasite might find it easy to evolve mimicry.[8] The *Vidua* parasite finches and their hosts come from the same family, as does the Screaming Cowbird and its Baywing host. With such similar genetic makeup, it should be relatively easy to copy host chick gape markings or plumage. Koels are not close relatives of the crows, but the adult koel has black plumage (the male is all black, while females are variable, sometimes brown, sometimes with various amounts of black), so once again the parasite is 'pre-adapted' to evolve chick mimicry, perhaps by some simple developmental change in the expression of adult coloration.

In some cases, however, the parasite may find it impossible to evolve a good match between its chick and the host chick.[8] For example, two other non-evicting cuckoos that parasitize crows (Great Spotted Cuckoos in Europe and Africa, and Channel-billed Cuckoos in Australia), both have adult plumage very different from that of crows and have failed to evolve close chick mimicry. In generalist brood parasites, where individual females exploit a range of host species, it is clearly impossible for the parasite chick to be a perfect match every time, because the chicks of different hosts vary considerably in appearance. This applies to the generalist cowbirds (chapters 10–12), where the parasite chick often looks very different from the host chicks with which it shares the nest.

If the parasite chick does not mimic the host young in some of the cases where they are raised together, how does it avoid being rejected? One possibility is that these hosts don't learn what their own chicks look like, and so accept odd-looking chicks. Perhaps, for reasons we do not yet understand, the learning rule is not always advantageous at the chick stage for hosts of non-evicting parasites. Tomas Redondo suggests a second possibility.[8] Perhaps the parasite chick adopts another trick to induce acceptance. Rather than deceiving the hosts through mimicry, it may become a 'charming alien', compensating for its odd appearance by exaggerating features the host parents find attractive in their own young. In effect, it becomes like ET in Steven Spielberg's marvellous film. We know it's an alien, but the sweet voice and large eyes charm us because they are, in exaggerated form, what we find attractive in our own children. This is like the argument of Dawkins and Krebs[3] – the parasite manipulates the foster parents with attractive stimuli that they cannot resist.

One example of an attractive parasite feature is simply large size. Hosts might prefer to feed the largest chick in their brood. In most cases they are not parasitized and this preference makes good sense. The largest chick in the nest is one of their own, and it's the one most likely to survive. Only in the rare cases of parasitism does the preference mis-fire, resulting in the acceptance of a parasite chick. It may simply be difficult to reverse a parental preference that works so well most of the time. Loud begging calls may also be stimulating and help make up for a parasite's odd appearance. Although Great Spotted Cuckoo chicks do not look like their corvid host young, they do mimic the host begging calls and furthermore, they call more loudly that the host chicks. Redondo suggests this may be essential if they are to avoid rejection.[8] The other possibility, of course, is that they are simply being more selfish because they have no genetic interest in the survival of their brood mates. We shall consider these alternatives when we discuss the Great Spotted Cuckoo (chapter 8) and cowbirds (chapter 12) in more detail.

PERSUADING HOSTS TO BRING ENOUGH FOOD

We now return to the Common Cuckoo chick once more. Like other parasites that are raised alone, it apparently doesn't have to use mimicry or charm to fool the hosts into accepting it, because the hosts adopt the rule 'accept any chick in my nest'. However, the Cuckoo's problems are not over. It cannot simply sit back and expect the hosts to slave away to feed it. Our studies show that the young Cuckoo needs persuasion and trickery if it is to get enough to eat.

On Wicken Fen, we found that nestling Cuckoos were fed the same diet as the Reed Warblers brought to their own brood.[9] This was mainly billfuls of small flies or single larger items, such as caterpillars, moths and butterflies, damselflies, hoverflies and dungflies. The Cuckoo was also fed at about the same rate as for an average brood (four) of the Reed Warbler's own young,[9] though the Cuckoo is dependent for longer (17 days in the nest plus 16 days after fledging, compared with 11 days as nestling plus 12 days as fledgling for the host young). Other studies have also found that single cuckoo chicks do not command unusually high provisioning rates.[10]

It is well known that parent birds work harder for older chicks and larger broods. How, then, does a single Cuckoo chick get the Reed Warbler foster parents to work as hard as they would for a whole brood of their own young? Rebecca Kilner, David Noble and I tested this by experiment.[11] At first we thought the Cuckoo chick's large size alone might be sufficient to stimulate the hosts. If so, then similar-sized chicks of other species should be provisioned at the same rate. We tested this by temporarily replacing a Reed Warbler brood with a single Blackbird or Song Thrush chick. These crouched when the Reed Warbler nest swayed in the wind (their own nests, in bushes, are much more stable), but once we tied the supporting reeds to an anchored bamboo cane, they begged normally and the Reed Warblers worked away to feed them. However, these chicks were fed at a much lower rate than a Cuckoo chick of the same weight. Simply the presence of a large and hungry chick is not a sufficient stimulus to persuade the hosts to raise their feeding rate.[11]

Next, we wondered whether the Cuckoo's vivid orange-red gape might be the key stimulus (**Plate 2a**). Previous work by Rebecca Kilner had shown that in some seed-eating finches, nestlings signal their hunger with a flush of blood to the mouth, which causes their gapes to become bright red. The hungrier the chick, the redder the mouth. Experiments, in which chick mouths were painted with dyes, revealed that parents preferred to feed chicks with redder gapes. This flushing may be an honest signal of hunger, because chicks that have already been fed would put their blood to better use in absorbing the nutrients from their meal. Hungry chicks, with nothing to digest, could more easily afford to divert blood to the gape to produce the signal.[12]

Cuckoos chicks do not have such a flush. Instead their mouth is made red by pigment. Could they be cheating the system by giving a permanent signal of 'I'm hungry', which spurs the hosts to greater effort? We tested the responses of three major hosts of the Common Cuckoo, the Robin, the Dunnock and the Reed Warbler, but found no evidence that they preferred chicks whose mouths had been artificially dyed red. Nor did they work harder if the mouths of the whole brood were made red.[13] Unlike the seed-eating finches, none of their chicks showed a red flush to the gape when hungry, so perhaps it is not surprising that their parents ignored redder gapes. Clearly the red-flush is not a universal signal of hunger,[14] and the Cuckoo's red gape is apparently not a super-stimulus, at least for these hosts. Non-parasitic cuckoos also have red gapes, so the Cuckoo's gape colour may reflect its ancestry rather than a special adaptation for exploiting hosts.[15]

We concluded that the Cuckoo chick must provide stimuli other than size or gape colour, to elicit adequate host care. Another obvious candidate is the begging call. The Cuckoo nestling's call is very strange, a continuous and rapid 'si, si, si, si ...', quite unlike that of a single host chick's much slower 'tsip ... tsip ...'. In fact the Cuckoo didn't sound to our ears at all like a single chick; it sounded like a whole brood of hungry chicks! We compared calls under standard conditions of hunger, by temporarily removing chicks from their nests and keeping them in artificial nests in the laboratory. Their parents were meanwhile given some chicks from other nests to keep them from deserting until their own brood was returned. We fed the chicks to satiation with a special mix of egg, honey and ground seed. Then, an hour later we stimulated them to beg and recorded their calls. At seven days of age, the young Cuckoo called at the rate of five calls per second, far faster than a single Reed Warbler chick of the same age (0.4 calls per second) but closely matching the rate of a brood of four reed warblers. If the Cuckoo's begging call is the key to stimulate

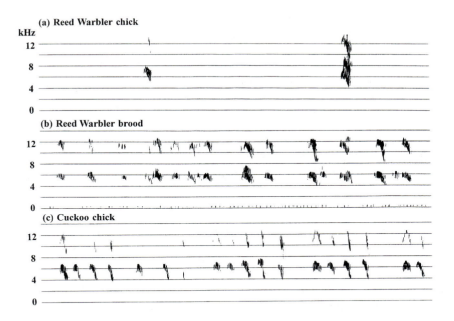

Figure 6.1 Sonograms (each 2.5 seconds long) of the begging calls of 6-day old chicks, recorded in the laboratory one hour after they had been fed to satiation. The Common Cuckoo chick (c) calls at a much faster rate than a single Reed Warbler chick (a), and sounds more like a brood of four Reed Warbler chicks (b). Older Cuckoos call even faster, much more than a Reed Warbler brood. (From Davies et al 1998.)

the hosts, then broadcasts of Cuckoo begging calls next to the single Blackbird or Thrush chick should increase the host provisioning level to that of a Cuckoo. Furthermore, if mimicry of a brood is involved, Cuckoo vocalizations should be as effective as those of a brood of Reed Warblers.

We tested these predictions by again temporarily replacing a Reed Warbler brood with a single Blackbird or Thrush chick, but this time it was accompanied by a little loudspeaker next to the nest. We sat quietly, some 6 m away, and watched through binoculars for three successive hours, one where we broadcast Cuckoo begging calls every time the chick begged, one where we broadcast the calls of a brood of four Reed Warblers, and one control hour with no broadcast. We did the experiment at 10 nests, varying the sequence at successive nests, and using recordings of different chicks at each nest. The Reed Warblers seemed unperturbed by the experimental set-up. Indeed they often perched on the speaker and when leaving the nest sometimes flew straight over our heads, dropping faecal sacs on us as they passed by! The results were clear; both Cuckoo and brood playbacks caused similar and marked increases in the work rate of the host parents, just as we would predict if the Cuckoo calls mimicked those of a begging brood. The hosts reacted quickly to the broadcasts and became noticeably more active in their foraging, as if they regarded the chick as more hungry. Furthermore, their provisioning rate to the Blackbird/Thrush was now elevated to that for a Cuckoo chick, showing that the rapid call was indeed the key.[11]

Figure 6.2 A Blackbird chick in a Reed Warbler nest, with speaker in position for broadcasting various begging calls.

TUNING INTO THE HOST PARENT-OFFSPRING COMMUNICATION SYSTEM

Why does the Common Cuckoo need such vocal trickery? Our idea was that perhaps the hosts calibrated their provisioning rate both by what they saw and what they heard. Perhaps the Cuckoo needs an unusually rapid begging call to compensate for the fact that it presents a visual stimulus of just one gape. To test this we needed to know exactly how the Reed Warblers integrated visual and vocal cues from their own brood. Then we could try to understand how the Cuckoo chick plugged in to the system. So we went back to Wicken Fen once more for another two summers' experiments.

First, we investigated how a brood of four Reed Warblers signalled their hunger. We kept broods in artificial nests, fed them to satiation, and then stimulated them to beg every 10 minutes. With increasing hunger, more of the brood opened their gapes and individual chicks called more rapidly. The two signals together gave more information about the brood's need than did either signal alone.[16] For example, after a certain time the number of gapes on display reached a plateau (all four chicks always begged) but calling rate continued to increase. At the end of our recordings, the chicks were fed again and returned to their nest. We ensured that the hunger levels reached in this experiment did not exceed those encountered naturally in the wild, so that the birds were not unduly stressed.

Next, we needed to know exactly how the parents responded to these two signals. To tease their effects apart, we manipulated brood sizes, by temporarily swapping chicks between nests, so that the adults were confronted by broods of between one and eight chicks. The largest natural broods were of five, and we could not fit more chicks than this into a nest. So to give the birds larger broods, we placed an old Blackbird nest over the top of the Reed Warbler's own nest and put the chicks in that for the duration of the experiment. Once again, the Reed Warblers were remarkably tolerant and hardly seemed to notice the change, settling down to feed the brood straight away. They are probably used to natural changes in the vicinity of their nests, as the reeds grow rapidly during the season and strong winds often cause gaps to appear in the reed beds. Our temporary manipulations were apparently regarded as nothing out of the ordinary.

The parents quickly adjusted their provisioning rate in relation to the number of chicks. They would bring just 10 feeds per hour to a single chick but 50 for a brood of eight. Interestingly, the work rate for this largest brood exceeded that to a Cuckoo chick, so the Cuckoo does not work the hosts to their maximum capacity. These various brood sizes were sometimes accompanied by playbacks, either the calls of a single Reed Warbler chick or of a brood of four chicks. These playbacks showed that increased vocal signals also spurred the hosts to greater effort. A single chick call broadcast through the speaker increased work rate a little, four chicks' calls increased it still more. However, visual cues were clearly important too. For example, the parents brought more food to a brood of eight (eight chicks seen and eight heard) than they did to a brood of four accompanied by playbacks of four begging chicks (four chicks seen and eight heard). By making a range of comparisons across all brood sizes, with and without playbacks, we were able to describe exactly how the parents integrated the two signals, and varied their provisioning rate in response to what they saw (total gape area displayed) and what they heard (rate of calling).[16]

The final question was, how does the Cuckoo exploit this communication system between host young and their parents? The answer was fascinating. The Cuckoo's visual stimulus is subnormal compared with that of a brood of four Reed Warblers. It has just one gape, but even though this is larger than that of a single Reed Warbler, it can never match the total area displayed by a whole brood. Furthermore, as it gets older, the Cuckoo's visual stimulus becomes increasingly disadvantaged compared with a host brood of the same age. Assuming the host parents integrated the two begging signals in exactly the same way as they did for their own chicks, we could now predict how rapidly the Cuckoo would need to call to make up for its poorer gape area, in order to be provisioned at the rates we observed in the wild. The predictions were an impressive match of the observed calling rate.[16] Week-old Cuckoos could elicit adequate host care if they simply mimicked the calling rate of a brood of four Reed Warblers. However, as the Cuckoo chick got older it had to call at increasingly supernormal rates to compensate for its increasingly subnormal gape stimulus. In the oldest Cuckoo nestlings, these begging rates far exceeded those of a normal host brood, and they sounded more like eight host chicks! But, far from whipping up the hosts into a feeding frenzy, these extraordinarily rapid begging calls reflected the poor Cuckoo's struggle to compensate for its single gape and persuade the hosts to work at their normal rate. We found that the combined visual and vocal display of the Cuckoo functioned entirely to solicit food, so there was no hint that some of the exaggerated calling was to 'charm' the hosts and combat rejection.[17]

SELFISH BEGGARS?

In theory, a chick's selfishness in the nest should reflect a balance between its own needs and those of its relatives. Even a host chick should be a bit selfish, and try to grab more than its fair share of food. However, natural selection will temper its greed because of the harm this does to its siblings.[18] First, there are the siblings with which it now shares the nest – the more food it grabs the less they will get to eat. Second, there are its potential future siblings – the more it demands from its parents, the less likely they are to survive to produce future broods. In the selfish gene language of Richard Dawkins, any gene that programmed a host chick to be too selfish would lose out from the reduced survival of the chick's brothers and sisters, which means that fewer copies of that gene would get through to future generations.[19] So in general, although host chicks do compete with each other for food, there is a limit to their selfishness; once an individual has had a reasonable amount to eat, it stops begging. The best evidence that chick selfishness is constrained by the needs of relatives comes from studies of bird species where a female mates with several males. In these cases, the chicks in the nest are less closely related because they often have different fathers, so they are half-sibs rather than full-sibs. As predicted, they have more exuberant begging displays.[20]

Now consider a Cuckoo chick. It has no kinship with the hosts, so a gene that programmed the Cuckoo to be so selfish that it caused the death of the host chicks, would not suffer any cost; the gene has no copies in the bodies of those host chicks. That's why the Cuckoo ejects the host eggs and young, so it can command all the food. According to theory, it should then demand more food than the host chicks, because it has no genetic stake in the host parents' future reproductive success.[21]

Rebecca Kilner and I compared how much a single Cuckoo chick and broods of four Reed Warbler young demanded, through their begging displays, in relation to various measures of need. We found some evidence that the Cuckoo was being a little more selfish in its food demands, but the difference from the host brood was not marked.[17] Perhaps the Cuckoo chick has to match its demands to that of an average brood of host young, simply because it is unable to provide signals which would get the hosts to work any harder. Alternatively, it may be risky for the Cuckoo to over-work the hosts, because they may be incapable of sustaining a rate beyond their usual efforts for the whole of the Cuckoo's period of dependence, which is already 10 days longer than for the host's own young.

DIFFERENT CUCKOOS – DIFFERENT BEGGING CALLS?

These results have revealed an interesting trade-off. By ejecting or killing the host chicks, a parasite gains the advantage of avoiding competition once food arrives, but this is at the expense of having to do all the work of stimulating the hosts to collect it. Parasitic honeyguide chicks, which use mandibular hooks to kill the host nestlings, have also been reported to sound like several young,[22] so rapid begging calls may be widespread in parasitic chicks that are raised alone.

Parasites that are raised alongside the host young have the opposite problem. They have help from their brood-mates in providing the begging stimuli to get the hosts to go off and collect food, but they have to compete once the food arrives. Great Spotted Cuckoo chicks have special gape stimuli and exaggerated begging calls that increase the chance that they are fed (chapter 8), while some cowbird chicks also gain more than their fair share of food through more selfish begging behaviour (chapter 12).

It will be interesting to discover whether the Common Cuckoo chick's call is different in the various gentes. We might expect this, because different host species have different parent-offspring communication systems. For example, Meadow Pipit chicks are much less vocal than Reed Warbler chicks, perhaps because their ground nests are particularly vulnerable to predation. On the other hand, Dunnock chicks call much more rapidly. Female Dunnocks often mate with two males,[23] which means that their chicks often share the nest with half-sibs, rather than full-sibs. This may cause them to be more selfish, and to call more rapidly.[20] Therefore, Cuckoo chicks may have to tune into different signalling systems in different host nests. In the Diederik Cuckoo, which also has gentes (chapter 7), begging calls do indeed differ between chicks raised by different hosts.[24] If gentes are restricted to female lines of cuckoos (chapter 3), then any gens differences in begging displays would probably arise through learning. Remarkably, in two New Zealand cuckoos, the Long-tailed Koel and the Shining Bronze-Cuckoo, which also eject host eggs or chicks, the young cuckoo mimics the structure of the begging calls of the host young.[25] They do not have the opportunity to copy the host chick calls, so the cuckoo calls must either be programmed entirely genetically, or develop through the cuckoo trying out a range of calls at first, and then homing in on the ones which are most effective in stimulating host care, namely those like the host young.

CUCKOO NESTLING DEFENCES

Most nestlings crouch low when a predator approaches, in the hope that they will not be noticed. By contrast, the Common Cuckoo nestling has some remarkable defences from about a week of age. If you put your hand towards it, it erects its head feathers, opens its red gape and stretches its neck. Then it suddenly snaps its head back. This is a shock even for someone who is familiar with the performance, and must surely be an effective deterrent against predators. Jenner (1788) provided a good description: 'Long before it leaves the nest, it frequently, when irritated, assumes the manner of a bird of prey, looks ferocious, throws itself back, and pecks at anything presented to it with great vehemence, often at the same time making a chuckling noise like a young hawk. Sometimes, when disturbed in a smaller degree, it makes a kind of hissing noise, accompanied by a heaving motion of the whole body.' Perhaps the Cuckoo's red gape makes the display even more effective. In addition, if touched, the Cuckoo produces foul-smelling brown liquid faeces. These are quite unlike the normal faeces, which are white and contained in a gelatinous sac to make it easier for the host parents to carry them away.

Why has the Cuckoo evolved these defences? There may be two reasons. First, the Cuckoo's conspicuous begging calls are likely to attract predators to the nest. Certainly, the calls often led us to discover parasitized nests that we had missed at the egg stage. Second, the Cuckoo's unusually long nestling period may also increase the chance that predators will find it in the nest. Young Reed Warblers leave well before they can fly, clambering up the reeds. This suggests that the nest is a vulnerable place to be, and should be escaped as soon as possible. But the Cuckoo has to stay for longer simply because it takes more time to grow to the size where it can fledge.

CUCKOO FLEDGLINGS

Once the young cuckoo leaves the nest, it looks rather like an adult cuckoo. Why, then, do the hosts continue to feed it? Some observations suggest that fledgling cuckoos may be attacked or mobbed by their foster parents when they fly, but then are fed as soon as they sit quietly on a perch and beg! Perhaps this is why they usually remain perched in one place, to avoid being mistaken for an adult.[8] There are several reports of parasite fledglings being fed by extra birds, sometimes different species from the foster parents. For example, Common Cuckoo fledglings may beg from any small bird that passes close by. In a seventy minute observation of one Cuckoo fledgling, it was fed not only by the two Pied Wagtail foster parents, but also by a pair of Redstarts, a Meadow Pipit and a Dunnock! These other birds may have been primed to feed the Cuckoo because they were collecting food for their own

A Pied Wagtail feeding a Common Cuckoo fledgling. Sometimes other birds, in addition to the hosts, are attracted to feed the young Cuckoo.

young nearby. The Redstarts had a nest with young in the vicinity, and there were also fledgling Meadow Pipits in the area.[26] Sometimes even nestling Cuckoos will attract attention from other birds. In one report, a pair of Dunnocks was feeding a nestling Cuckoo, and a Wren, with a brood of its own nearby, often passed the Cuckoo on its way back to its own nest and sometimes stopped off to feed it.[27]

These examples are simply mistakes by parents preparing to feed their own young. They may occasionally feed the young of other species too. For example, a colleague has seen Robins provisioning young Song Thrush fledglings immediately after their own young had been depredated. However, Tomas Redondo has suggested that parasite fledglings may be particularly attractive because of their exaggerated begging signals.[8] Most of our knowledge of the fledglings is anecdotal and more systematic observations would probably produce some surprises. Maybe the cuckoo fledgling has to adopt new and more charming begging tricks as it grows, simply to prevent the hosts from treating it as an adult cuckoo.

CHAPTER 7

Bronze-cuckoos in Africa and Australia

Once more, we are sitting on a river bank fringed with reeds. But this time the chirping songs come from dazzling, bright red birds with black faces and breasts. These are male Red Bishops defending their nesting territories. There are perhaps 20 in view and each male displays over his little patch, cruising on rapid wing beats like an enormous bee, with his back feathers puffed out to show off his brilliant red. The brown females are busy lining the domed nests which their males have weaved from strips of grass leaves, suspended from the reed stems. In the spiny trees on the bank, there is another blaze of colour; gold and yellow male weaverbirds are showing off their globe-shaped nests, which are suspended from the tips of the branches, so that the trees seem to be covered in strange fruits. The males hang below their nests, fanning their wings and producing rasping songs. There is a loud barking from the opposite bank; a baboon troop makes its way to the water's edge to drink. A crocodile drifts slowly past. This is Africa, another world where other cuckoos are at work.

From the tree above us, a small bronze bird flies fast into the reeds. It is just half the length of a Common Cuckoo but similar in shape, with a long tail and pointed wings. A few seconds later, it returns to its perch carrying a blue egg in its bill, and it then swallows the egg whole. Once again, we wade out into the reeds and this time we find a bishop's nest. Peering through the side entrance hole we can see three turquoise blue eggs, all identical in appearance. But one of these will produce not a young Bishop, but a young Diederik Cuckoo, which will eject the other eggs out of the nest. Nearby, we hear one of the most characteristic sounds of the African bush, the male cuckoo's plaintive whistle 'dee dee dee dee – diederik'.

THE DIEDERIK CUCKOO

The Diederik Cuckoo is the commonest cuckoo in Africa. It occurs throughout the continent south of the Sahara and apart from dense forest, which it avoids, it is widespread in a variety of habitats, including woodland, savannah, the edges of marshes, parks and gardens.[1] It is 18 cm in length and weighs 32 g, a little larger than its main hosts, the weavers *Ploceus*, bishops *Euplectes* and sparrows *Passer*

(13–17 cm; 21–28 g). The adult male Diederik is a striking glossy bronze-green above and white below, with green bars on the flanks. It has a white eye stripe and a bright red eye (**Plate 3a**). The female is duller, greenish-brown above and with a buff throat and a brown eye.

It is resident in equatorial Africa, and a breeding visitor to southern Africa and the northern tropics, arriving in the rainy season when the hosts are nesting.[2] Many of the favourite hosts are colonial nesters. In some sites, a male Diederik apparently defends a host colony as a territory, chasing off rival males and singing from favourite song posts. In many areas, however, the large size of the host colony attracts so many Diederiks that territoriality breaks down. In one colony of Spottedbacked Weavers in Ghana,[3] there were five male cuckoos singing at once from the adjacent trees, and although there were frequent chases all the males remained in the area. Three females laid eggs in the colony and sometimes a female was pursued by all five males together. So far there have been no radio-tracking studies, which would be necessary to work out the details of the social system. But some females probably restrict their egg laying to one or two adjacent host colonies. Females deposit just one egg per host nest and lay on alternate days, just like Common Cuckoos. Examination of the ovaries of dissected birds suggests that they may lay some 16 to 21 eggs in a 10-week breeding season.[1]

Like Common Cuckoos, Diederiks occur in various gentes, each of which lays a distinctive egg that matches its favoured host. The eggs of the different gentes are identical in size and also similar in size to the host eggs. In southern Africa, where the Diederik has been best studied, there appear to be at least five main gentes, which parasitize the following hosts:[1]

- *Red Bishops*, which breed communally in reed beds and lay plain, turquoise-blue eggs. The Diederik's egg is an excellent match, either plain blue or sometimes with faint dark green spots. Experiments by Mike Lawes and Steven Kirkman, from the University of Natal, have shown that these hosts reject non-mimetic eggs, including those that are plain dark-blue and those that are spotted, but they nearly always accept mimetic plain, pale-blue eggs.[4] Even so, despite their near-perfect mimicry, some real cuckoo eggs are still rejected. In one colony near Pietermaritzburg, Lawes and Kirkman recorded rejection at five out of 16 naturally parasitized nests. In one case the cuckoo egg was ejected, while in four cases the bishops deserted. When mimicry is so good that the hosts cannot pick out the cuckoo's egg then, if they know they have been parasitized, the best response may simply be to desert and start again.
- *Cape Weavers*, which also nest colonially in reed beds and nearby trees, and also lay plain blue eggs. The Diederik Cuckoo egg is again a perfect match, plain blue. It is not known whether individual female Diederiks favour either Red Bishops or Cape Weavers, or if they parasitize both. The same cuckoo egg would be a good match for either host. If a female cuckoo imprints on the host species that rears her, then these two gentes are likely to be distinct even though they lay the same egg type. However, females of the two gentes could successfully parasitize the other's host as a secondary host, so there may be considerable mixing of the two gentes in areas where both hosts occur together.
- *Cape Sparrows*, which breed in trees, bushes and crevices, sometimes colonially,

and which lay whitish to greenish, heavily spotted eggs. The Diederik's egg is variable in background colour and spotting density, but is a reasonable match of the host eggs.

- *Lesser Masked Weavers*, which nest colonially in trees or bushes, sometimes near water, and lay plain white eggs. The Diederik's egg is also plain white. Anna Lindholm, from the University of Cambridge, found evidence for host specificity from a study of a mixed-species colony of weavers at a small dam near Pietermaritzburg.[5] In one season, all 16 Diederik Cuckoo eggs were laid in Lesser Masked Weaver nests (19% of their 86 nests were parasitized), while none of 48 Yellow Weaver nests, none of 13 Thick-billed Weaver nests and none of five Spottedbacked Weaver nests were parasitized. Twelve of the eggs were laid by one female cuckoo that was resident at the dam and seen every day, while four were laid by another female who made occasional visits to the site. Experiments showed that Lesser Masked Weavers tended to reject non-mimetic eggs, either spotted eggs or those with a different background colour from their own pure white eggs.[5]

- *Masked, Spottedbacked* and *Yellow Weavers*, all of which have remarkably variable eggs. We know from studies of captive birds that individual females lay eggs of a constant type; the variation within each species comes about because of differences between females.[6] The background colour varies from white, pink, buff, green or blue and the eggs may be plain, sparsely spotted or heavily spotted (**Plate 3b**). The Diederik Cuckoo eggs in the nests of these three host species are also just as variable, with the same astonishing range of background colours and spotting as in the host eggs. Jensen and Vernon (1970) suggest that rather than three host-specific gentes, this may represent one gens of cuckoo which specializes on all three hosts and perhaps others that lay similar, variable eggs. They point out that the female weavers are rather similar in appearance (though the males are distinctive), their nests are similar, and they may nest in mixed-species colonies.

However, Anna Lindholm's observations show that Diederik females can still be host-specific even in mixed colonies.[5] And in another study, Reed found three gentes laying eggs in one small 20 ha site near Johannesburg, exploiting Red Bishops, Cape Sparrows and Masked Weavers respectively.[7] Clearly, more detailed studies are needed to determine the degree of female host specificity. Perhaps, like Common Cuckoos, individual female Diederiks favour one particular host, but lay in other species' nests if their favourite host is in short supply. We also need to discover whether individual male Diederiks mate with several female gentes, like Common Cuckoos, and so maintain the Diederik as one species.

The remarkably variable host eggs of Masked, Spottedbacked and Yellow Weavers seem to be an excellent defence against cuckoos. In all three of these weaver species, experiments have shown that a female will reject conspecific eggs that differ from her own, either in background colour or spotting pattern.[5,6,8] The cuckoo is therefore faced with two options. She could lay eggs at random, in which case she will often suffer host rejection, whenever her egg is a poor match. Alternatively, she could get to know her own egg type and then target those individual hosts in the colony whose eggs are like her own. This last option would clearly be better, and it would be fascinating if cuckoos turned out to have this ability. However, mismatching cuckoo eggs seem to be quite common for weaver hosts with variable eggs, so the cuckoos may have to put up with the first option and suffer a high rejection rate.

The South African nest record scheme shows an average parasitism rate of 2–8% for these various weaver and bishop hosts[9] but, as we found for Common Cuckoos, local rates may be much higher (up to 65% nests parasitized) and there is also marked variation at sites between years.[1] For Red Bishops, colony size seems to have an important influence on parasitism.[4] Smaller colonies, with fewer than 50 active nests, suffer a much higher percentage parasitism than the larger colonies. A large host colony may simply swamp the cuckoos, providing more nests than they could ever lay in, but larger colonies may also be better able to defend their nests by mass attacks which drive the female cuckoos away. Either way, it will pay the hosts to nest together to gain safety in numbers. Another factor is distance from cover; female cuckoos need trees or bushes from which they can observe the hosts to assess which nests are suitable for parasitism. Colonies further from cover seem to have lower parasitism, perhaps because the cuckoos find these harder to watch.

WEAVERBIRD NEST ENTRANCES – A DEFENCE AGAINST CUCKOOS?

A weaverbird's nest is one of the wonders of the bird world. Its construction has been particularly well studied for Spottedbacked Weavers by Nicholas and Elsie Collias, of the University of California at Los Angeles.[10] The woven structure is built entirely by the male, using his bill to weave the outer shell from some three hundred strips of fresh green leaves, which he tears from grasses or from palm fronds. The nest is suspended from a hanging fork in the branches of a tree or bush. First the male weaves the strips around the sides of the fork and then he joins them below to form a vertical ring. This is extended to form a roof above and an egg chamber below, leaving a hole for the entrance. The walls of the nest are made by threading strips alternately over and under other strips, just as humans do to make a basket. The bird may loop the ends of a strip back on itself to form a tidy knot. The outer shell can be completed within a day, after which the male sings to display his work to passing females. Like human weavers, male Spottedbacked Weaverbirds improve with practice, so females often choose to pair with older, more experienced males that have built the better nests. Once she accepts a nest, the female lines the egg chamber with soft grass heads and feathers, and then egg laying can begin.

The details of the nest vary from species to species. Some, like Red Bishops, have a domed nest with a simple hole entrance at the top on one side. Others, like the Spottedbacked and Masked Weavers, hang from the branches and they have an entrance below. In some species, the male adds an entrance tube once the female has lined the nest. The tube may be just 2 cm long, but in some species it can be 30 cm or more, hanging down from the nest like an enormous spout.

Could these entrance tubes help keep out cuckoos? In her study of a Lesser Masked Weaver colony, Anna Lindholm once watched a host pair pecking at a Diederik Cuckoo which was stuck for 30 seconds, half inside the tube. Eventually the

male weaver pulled the cuckoo out and both tumbled down into the water below, before parting and flying off to safety! There is one other report of a female Diederik which became trapped in the entrance of a Lesser Masked Weaver nest and died inside the tunnel. In most cases, however, the cuckoo is able to squeeze through the tunnel because the loose weave allows some expansion.

Nevertheless, an entrance tube could still act as a deterrent because it makes it more difficult for the cuckoo to enter the nest and might give the hosts more time to launch attacks. In a comparative survey of 34 species of *Ploceus* weavers in Africa,[11] Scott Freeman of the University of Washington at Seattle, found that only four of 13 species (31%) with nest tubes were regularly parasitized by cuckoos, compared with 13 out of 21 species (62%) whose nests had no tube. This suggests that an entrance tube might help as a defence, though it is clearly not perfect; both Lesser Masked and Spectacled Weavers have long nest tubes and are still regular victims of Diederik Cuckoos.

Scott Freeman also considered why some weaver species have monomorphic eggs (little or no variation between females, as in the plain blue eggs of the Cape Weaver) while others are polymorphic (high variation within a species, as in Yellow, Spottedbacked and Masked Weavers). His analysis showed that species without nest tubes are more likely to have variable eggs (67% of 21 species) than those with nest tubes (15% of 13 species). The simplest explanation is that a nest tube makes the inside of the nest darker, so distinctive individual signatures would be of little use; the female would not be able to see what she had 'written'. But the difference could also reflect the two alternative weaver defences against cuckoos; either have variable eggs, or have a nest tube (in which case variable eggs are not needed so much).

A complication with the interpretation of these results is that both defences may have other advantages too. Nest tubes may help to keep out predators, while individually distinct egg signatures may also act as a defence against parasitic laying by other members of your own species (chapter 14). If just the weaverbirds without nest tubes are considered, then the ones with the most variable eggs tend to be those that nest in denser colonies. This would increase the opportunities for cuckoo parasitism and parasitism by your own species.[11] It may be difficult to tease apart the importance of these two selection pressures, which are both likely to be important.

DIEDERIK CUCKOO PARASITIC BEHAVIOUR

Weaverbirds lay just two or three eggs per clutch, a typical clutch size for tropical birds and only half that of most temperate song birds. This means that tropical cuckoos have a much shorter window of time for parasitism. Nevertheless, they still manage to lay during the host laying period. For example, in her Lesser Masked Weaver colony, Anna Lindholm found that 15 out of 18 Diederik eggs were laid either during the two or three days that the hosts laid, or a day or two afterwards.[5] How does the female cuckoo get her timing right, given that the nest contents are

A male Lesser Masked Weaver attacking a female Diederik Cuckoo, which is stuck in the nest entrance tube (drawing based on a photograph by Anna Lindholm).

hidden in a domed nest? One possibility is that she uses host behaviour as a cue; nest lining and copulation commence a couple of days before the first egg is laid. Alternatively, she may be able to gauge the onset of laying by seeing the eggs through the bottom of the nest, which human observers can sometimes do. Or perhaps she goes right inside the nest on pre-laying visits to check on its progress?

The female Diederik's laying procedure is just like that of the Common Cuckoo.[5] She watches quietly from a nearby perch, perhaps for an hour or so, and times her parasitism to coincide with the period that the hosts are most likely to be away from the colony feeding, namely late morning or afternoon. She flies rapidly to the host nest, usually removes a host egg and then, holding this in her bill, she lays directly into the nest, and leaves, usually a stay of just 5–10 seconds. With large host nests, the cuckoo goes right inside and turns around, emerging head first with the host egg. With smaller host nests, the female's tail and wing tips may stick out while she lays and she then has to back out. If the hosts catch her at their nest, then they attack. In experiments with stuffed cuckoos at host colonies in Namibia, David Noble of Cambridge University found that both Masked Weavers and Red Bishops would readily strike mounts of Diederik Cuckoos placed near their nests, but they only gave mild alarms at mounts of other cuckoo species which did not target them as hosts.[8] This shows that these hosts recognize their own specific cuckoo as an enemy.

The Diederik's egg hatches out after 11–12 days incubation, usually one to three days before the host eggs. Unlike Common Cuckoo chicks, which often eject within a day of hatching, the Diederik chick waits until it is two or three days old.[1] Common Cuckoos are from three to 12 times the adult body weight of their hosts, while the Diederik Cuckoo is only 15–50% heavier than its hosts, so the newly hatched Diederik is likely to need to put on weight first, so that it has the strength to eject the host eggs or small chicks. Perhaps ejection from a domed nest is also more difficult, unless the young cuckoo can direct its load towards the entrance hole.

The cuckoo chick is in the nest for about 20 days and after fledging it is fed for a further three to four weeks. Most weaver hosts feed their young on insects, which they bring in the bill. However, Red Bishops regurgitate food loads to their chicks from the crop and bring mainly seeds, together with some insects. The Diederik Cuckoo chick seems to do equally well on both diets and with both methods of host feeding, because it grows just as well in bishop nests as with the other foster parents.[5] The begging calls of the young cuckoo are very loud and rapid.[1] Perhaps, like Common Cuckoo chicks, the Diederik chick needs exaggerated calls to stimulate sufficient care (chapter 6). There are also reports that the Diederik Cuckoo chick's begging cries are different in different host nests.[7] It would be fascinating to discover the importance of host-specific begging calls and to find out how they develop.

There are no convincing records of Common Cuckoos feeding their young, so it is remarkable to find several reports of Diederik Cuckoos feeding 'fledgling' Diederiks.[1] In all cases the provisioning bird was a male, so this suggests two possible explanations for these curious observations. First, it could be a male courtship feeding a female (which frequently occurs) and the observer has mistaken the female for a young bird. Female Diederiks are quite variable in appearance and some are dull-brown like the juveniles. Alternatively, male Diederiks may be so keen to provide food for their females, that they are occasionally fooled into feeding a begging fledgling cuckoo, which provides a similar stimulus.

TWO BRONZE-CUCKOOS IN AUSTRALIA

We now leave the African sun for the equally fierce sun of western Australia. We are on Gooseberry Hill, an area of heathland with low shrubs one or two metres high, part of the Darling escarpment, some 30 km east of the city of Perth. Here, Ian Rowley and Eleanor Russell of the CSIRO Division of Wildlife and Ecology have studied a colour-ringed population of Splendid Fairy-wrens since 1973. These tiny birds, just 10 g in weight, are stunning. The males are a brilliant purplish-blue all over, while the females are brown with a blue tail. They live in groups of two to eight individuals which defend permanent territories throughout the year. The group comprises a breeding pair plus their previous offspring, which remain at home as 'helpers', sometimes for several years, until they either inherit the territory or obtain a breeding vacancy nearby. These helpers join in defence of the family territory and help to feed and guard their parents' subsequent broods. Each year, Rowley and Russell have studied up to 34 groups of birds on Gooseberry Hill.[12]

The breeding season lasts from late August to early January, some 20 weeks and double that of a typical north temperate song bird such as the Reed Warbler. The Splendid Fairy-wren's nest is an untidy dome of grass, leaves and bark, well hidden in a low bush. It has a large hole as a side entrance and so it is well illuminated and easy to check for eggs. The usual clutch is three, with eggs laid at daily intervals in the early morning. When the chicks hatch they are fed by the whole group for ten to 12 days as nestlings and then for another month as fledglings.

In 1984, Michael and Lesley Brooker, also of CSIRO, started a detailed study of cuckoo behaviour on Gooseberry Hill.[13] The Splendid Fairy-wrens are parasitized by the Horsfield's Bronze-Cuckoo, which arrives in June, two to three months before their hosts begin to lay. After breeding, towards the end of January, they disperse north, 'wintering' across northern Australia, with some moving as far north as Indonesia and New Guinea. These cuckoos are even smaller than Diederik Cuckoos, just 17 cm in body length and weighing 23 g, similar in size to a sparrow, though with the typical long pointed wings and long tail of a cuckoo. They are brownish-bronze above and whitish below, with bronze bars on the breast and flanks. They are found throughout most of Australia, preferring drier and more open country and avoiding forests. The main hosts are various species of fairy-wrens, with thornbills as another important host.[14]

On Gooseberry Hill, during the period 1973 to 1987, from 0 to 44% of the Splendid Fairy-wren nests were parasitized each year, an average of 20%. The female cuckoo lays between one and three hours after sunrise, shortly after the hosts have laid their egg for the day. She enters the nest, leaving her tail and wing tips sticking out of the entrance hole, lays directly into the nest cup and then emerges backwards, carrying a host egg in her bill. Her stay at the nest is just five seconds.[15] Although the nest is domed and the cuckoo is more than double the weight of the fairy-wrens, it doesn't damage the nest. The entrance, woven from grass and cobwebs, soon springs back into shape.

If the fairy-wrens find an adult cuckoo at their nest, the whole group may mob it and occasionally they are successful in driving it away. Experiments with stuffed cuckoos show that both the adult pair and their helpers will strike the cuckoo, pecking at its head and pulling feathers out.[16] Attacks are just as vigorous at the incubation and nestling stage as during laying, because, like Common Cuckoos, the Horsfield's Bronze-Cuckoo will eat partly incubated clutches or young broods, perhaps to force the hosts to re-lay. However, group defence does not seem to reduce the risk of parasitism because the nests of larger groups were just as likely to be parasitized as those of pairs or smaller groups.[23]

The fairy-wren's eggs are pinkish-white and finely speckled with reddish-brown. The cuckoo's egg is an excellent match both in colour and size, sometimes so good that the Brookers themselves did not know that there was a cuckoo egg in the nest until it hatched (**Plate 3c**). The cuckoo egg hatches after 12 days' incubation, compared with 13–14 days for the host eggs, so most hatch well before the host eggs.[13] Cuckoos that hatch more than four days after the host chicks do not survive. This means that the laying cuckoo has a window of about seven days in which to lay her egg, namely three days of host laying plus the first four days of incubation. But the later she lays, the more difficult it will be for her chick to eject the nest contents, because they are more likely to be large host chicks rather than host eggs. Like hosts of the Common Cuckoo, fairy-wrens reject cuckoo eggs that appear in their nest before they begin to lay themselves. These early cuckoo eggs get buried in the nest lining.[14]

The young cuckoo usually evicts the nest contents when it is between one and two days old.[17] As with Diederik Cuckoos, the delay may be necessary to give it time to gain strength for the task. Common Cuckoo chicks eject at one day of age or less, when they are 3 g in weight and the host eggs are each about 1 g. Horsfield's Bronze-Cuckoos weigh about 1.4 g at hatching and are also confronted with host eggs a little over 1 g in weight. By two days of age, they are 2–3 g, a comparable size advantage to that of the Common Cuckoo when it ejects. Even so, some older Horsfield's Bronze-Cuckoos are capable of quite prodigious feats, evicting wren nestlings more than twice their size.[17] Robert and Laura Payne[18] suggest that the cuckoo is more active than the host young at lower temperatures, and often does its ejecting in the early morning, when any host chicks are still sluggish, and less likely to struggle as the cuckoo balances them on its back, one by one, and heaves them through the entrance hole.

So far, the system appears to be remarkably like that of the Common and Diederik Cuckoos and their hosts. But now we come to a big surprise. When the Brookers tested for host rejection, by placing model eggs into Splendid Fairy-wrens' nests, they found total acceptance, even of non-mimetic models painted plain blue or blue with large polka dots, and clearly very different from the wrens' own white, finely speckled eggs. In 24 experiments, not a single odd-looking model egg was rejected.[13] The lack of rejection in the experiments is supported by observational evidence. In

A female Splendid Fairy-wren (left) has just come off her nest, having just laid an egg. She is now being distracted by the presentation of a flower-petal from a neighbouring male, who wants to copulate with her. Meanwhile, a female Horsfield's Bronze-Cuckoo has entered her nest to lay – a visit of just five seconds. The Cuckoo is about to fly off, with the Fairy-wren's egg in her bill (drawing based on video films by Lesley and Michael Brooker).

more than 150 nests parasitized by real cuckoos, not a single cuckoo egg was rejected, nor was there any reduction in clutch size, such as might be expected if cuckoos parasitized nests and then the wrens rejected the cuckoo eggs before the Brookers found them.[17]

So here we have a cuckoo laying a beautifully mimetic egg even though the hosts show no discrimination! This is an extraordinary contrast to the strong rejection of non-mimetic eggs shown by most hosts of Common and Diederik Cuckoos. Before we consider this puzzle, let's look at the other bronze-cuckoo that lives on Gooseberry Hill.

Shining Bronze-Cuckoos are the same size as the Horsfield's and similar in appearance too, though they are greener above with a copper-coloured cap. They breed in eastern and southwestern Australia, avoiding the arid interior, and prefer the eucalypt forests and woodlands of the coastal and mountain areas. After breeding, they migrate north, 'wintering' in the Lesser Sundas, New Guinea and the Bismark Archipelago.[14] Their main hosts throughout Australia are various species of thornbills, tiny brown or yellowish birds (7–10 g) which build domed nests, hidden in low vegetation, or among the hanging foliage of taller trees or in small crevices in trees and under exfoliating bark. These nests have small side entrances and are very dark inside, much darker than those of the fairy-wrens. To check a thornbill nest you need a strong torch and a little mirror to see inside. Another difference from the fairy-wrens is that thornbills lay at two-day intervals, which is unusual for song birds. This means that though the clutch size is small, just three to four eggs, the cuckoo has a longer time to coincide its laying with the host laying period. In addition, thornbills have a long incubation period (17–19 days), which increases still further the suitable period for parasitism, because the Shining Bronze-Cuckoo's egg needs just 13–14 days to hatch.[13]

On Gooseberry Hill, the two bronze-cuckoos overlap completely in their home ranges and time of breeding.[19] Nevertheless, they stick to different main hosts. Shining Bronze-Cuckoos never parasitize the Splendid Fairy-wrens; instead they target Yellow-rumped Thornbills, with an average of 32% of the nests being parasitized each year from 1984–1991.[17] It would be interesting to discover how the two cuckoos come to specialize, even though both frequently encounter each other's host. Imprinting by young cuckoos seems a likely mechanism.[19] This could be tested by swapping young cuckoos between host nests, but there would still then be the problems of finding those same cuckoos when they become adult, and of following their host choice, no easy task! The Brookers have colour-ringed all the nestlings during their study, but they have never found one back on their site as a breeding adult.

Although the two species of bronze-cuckoo on Gooseberry Hill each go for a different main host, they overlap in their choice of a secondary host and both occasionally parasitize the Western Thornbill.[13] During 1984 to 1987, 21% of the Horsfield's eggs and 34% of the Shining Bronze-Cuckoo's eggs were laid in the nests of this host. It is not yet known whether these layings were by individual female cuckoos who could not find a suitable nest of their primary host, or whether a few cuckoos of both species favour Western Thornbills as their main host (which could arise if young cuckoos choose their hosts through imprinting). Use of secondary hosts could, of course, arise through both routes.

Yellow-rumped Thornbills lay pure white eggs, typical for species which have dark nests. White eggs must be easier to see, which will help the hosts to turn them during incubation, to check for signs of hatching, and to remove empty shells from the nest. By sharp contrast, the Shining Bronze-Cuckoo's egg is plain olive-brown, nothing like the host eggs.[14] Its dark colour makes it very hard to see inside the thornbill's nest (**Plate 3c**). Even the Brookers, who were looking out for cuckoo eggs, sometimes missed one and only realized that a nest was parasitized when they felt an extra egg in the clutch with their fingertips.

Stephen Marchant suggested that these dark cuckoo eggs may have evolved so that the hosts too would be less likely to notice them in their dimly lit nests.[20] Rather than hiding by mimicking the host eggs, the cuckoo egg could hide by being difficult to see against the dark nest lining. The Brookers tested this idea by putting model eggs into thornbill nests, but once again they found no evidence for host rejection. The plain blue or blue spotted model eggs were accepted in all 21 thornbill nests, showing that the cuckoo's egg need not be dark to avoid host rejection.[13]

MIMETIC AND CRYPTIC CUCKOO EGGS

We have an intriguing puzzle. The Horsfield's Bronze-Cuckoo lays a beautifully mimetic egg for the fairy-wrens and the Shining Bronze-Cuckoo lays a beautifully cryptic egg for the thornbills, yet neither host seems at all bothered by odd-looking eggs in its nest. Perhaps something else has selected for these types of cuckoo egg?

In chapter 4 we considered whether cuckoos themselves could be an important selection pressure on cuckoo eggs, through their habit of removing an egg before they lay. If a nest has already been parasitized, the second cuckoo would benefit by removing the first cuckoo's egg, otherwise its own egg might get ejected. However, on Wicken Fen we found little evidence that Common Cuckoos were more likely to pick out an egg which differed from the rest of the clutch. Even if they did so, their selection pressure would be lower than that from host rejection because only a small percentage of parasitized nests were visited by a second cuckoo. Furthermore, *Clamator* cuckoos do not remove an egg before they lay (chapter 8), so their lovely host egg mimicry cannot result from selection during egg replacement by cuckoos. Nevertheless, one of the lessons biologists learn early in their careers is that it is unwise to generalize from one or two studies. Nature is wonderfully varied and somewhere in the world there is likely to be a species which provides evidence for even the weirdest idea that we can dream up! Given the apparent complete lack of discrimination by fairy-wrens and thornbills, the Brookers suggest that egg replacement by cuckoos themselves is the most important pressure favouring the egg type laid by their bronze-cuckoos.[13]

We now need evidence that bronze-cuckoos are selective when they remove an egg. If it turns out that they are, why would this lead to a mimetic egg in one cuckoo and a cryptic egg in the other? The Brookers provide a nice explanation.[21] Imagine a female Horsfield's Bronze-Cuckoo who arrives at a fairy-wren's nest to lay. She has just a few seconds to decide which egg to remove. The nest is well lit, so any previous cuckoo egg could not easily hide against the nest lining. The best solution would be to mimic the host eggs. In this case, the next cuckoo would simply pick an egg at random. So, for example, in a clutch of two the cuckoo egg has a 50% chance of being removed and from a clutch of three the chance is 33%.

Now imagine what would happen in the dark nest of a thornbill. The female Shining Bronze-Cuckoo arrives and has to make a snap decision. If the previous cuckoo's egg is mimetic, white like the host eggs, then the chance that it is selected for removal is again 50% from two and 33% from three. But if it is dark-coloured and difficult to see, it could escape detection altogether. So in a dark nest, a cryptic egg would be an even better defence against other cuckoos. In fact, the Brookers report two cases where a Shining Bronze-Cuckoo visited a thornbill nest that had already been parasitized with a dark egg, and in neither case did it remove the first cuckoo's egg.[13]

Several other bronze-cuckoos lay dark-coloured eggs. A race of the Shining Bronze-Cuckoo breeds in New Zealand, arriving in October from wintering grounds in the Solomon Islands, some 3000 km to the north. It parasitizes Grey Warblers (= Grey Gerygone), which are in the same family as the thornbills (Acanthizidae) and have similar domed, dark nests with whitish eggs laid at two-day intervals. In a study on South Island, near Kaikoura,[22] Brian Gill from the University of Canterbury found that the hosts had usually completed their first broods of the season by the time the cuckoos arrived, so only the later nests were parasitized. Of the warbler nests built after the cuckoo's arrival, parasitism was heavy at 55%. Like the Australian race, the New Zealand Shining Bronze-Cuckoo lays dark olive-brown eggs and there is no evidence for host rejection at naturally parasitized nests. The Grey Warbler is the only known host in New Zealand, and the only song bird on the mainland there to have an enclosed nest. It would be interesting to test whether open-nesting species that are potential hosts would reject the cuckoo's dark egg.

In Australia, two other cuckoos lay dark eggs.[14] The Little Bronze-Cuckoo parasitizes *Gerygone* warblers, which have domed nests and white eggs, so the dark cuckoo egg could be cryptic. The Black-eared Cuckoo parasitizes two *Sericornis* warblers, which build domed-nests on the ground, the Speckled Warbler and the Redthroat (again in the family Acanthizidae). However, in this case the hosts lay dark brown eggs too, so the cuckoo egg is often a wonderful mimic, the best of any Australian cuckoo. Some match the host eggs so well that the only way to identify the cuckoo egg is to scratch the surface, which removes the brown pigment. The brown of the warblers' own eggs is incorporated into the shell and doesn't rub off. Perhaps these dark nesting hosts lay dark, rather than white, eggs because white eggs would be conspicuous in a ground nest, and would increase predation.[17] If so, the cuckoo's dark egg would be both cryptic and mimetic.

WHY DO FAIRY-WRENS AND THORNBILLS ACCEPT ODD EGGS?

Michael and Lesley Brooker's experiments show that neither the fairy-wrens nor the thornbills on Gooseberry Hill reject odd eggs, even though they suffer just as high cuckoo parasitism as the rejecting hosts of Diederik and Common Cuckoos. Why don't these Australian hosts also reject as a defence against cuckoos?

The Brookers suggest that two factors reduce the costs of parasitism for the Australian hosts, compared with those of Common Cuckoos.[23] The first is that it actually takes less time and effort to raise a bronze-cuckoo chick than a brood of the hosts' own young, the opposite of what we found for Common Cuckoo hosts. For the fairy-wrens, their own young are fed for 11 days in the nest and then 31 days after fledging, a total of 42 days. It takes six days less to raise a cuckoo chick, namely 17 days as a nestling plus 19 days as a fledgling. Furthermore, a cuckoo needs less food than a whole brood of host young. In the 11 days they are in the nest, a brood of three fairy-wrens increases in weight by 24 g compared with 18 g for a Horsfield's Bronze-Cuckoo over the same period. Similarly, over 16 days in the nest, a brood of three Yellow-rumped Thornbills increases by 26 g, while a Shining Bronze-Cuckoo does so by just 19 g.[13] The same results were found in Brian Gill's study in New Zealand, where the Shining Bronze-Cuckoo nestling was provisioned at a lower rate than a brood of four Grey Warblers (the average host brood) and it put on weight equivalent to a brood of just two or three host young.[24] By contrast, a Common Cuckoo chick demands the same effort from its Reed Warbler hosts as a full brood of their own young, and is also dependent for 10 days longer (chapter 6).

Secondly, the unusually long breeding season in Australia, some 20 weeks, gives the hosts plenty of time to raise their own young, even if they get lumbered with a cuckoo chick. One large group of Splendid Fairy-wrens studied by Ian Rowley had four successful nests in a single season, raising two cuckoos and two broods of their own young! This would be impossible for a European host, where the breeding season is perhaps just 10 weeks long. If a pair of Reed Warblers is parasitized in their first nest, they won't have time for another brood that year.

There is another important difference. Pairs of Splendid Fairy-wrens that have already raised their own young, are less likely to breed again that season than those that have raised a cuckoo. The reason is that the young fairy-wrens all remain at home, at least until the following year, and there is an annual limit to the number of young that can be accommodated on the territory. So although a pair of wrens that accepts a cuckoo egg will raise none of their own young from that nest, they will have plenty of time to catch up and raise as many of their own young over the whole season as pairs that escaped the cuckoo.[23]

We can summarize the Brookers' argument in the following diagram (see page 96), which compares Reed Warblers in Europe and Splendid Fairy-wrens in Australia. A lucky pair of Reed Warblers might just squeeze in two successful broods, a total of eight young. An unlucky pair, parasitized in their first nest, would take so long to raise a Common Cuckoo chick that there would be no time to raise any of their own young that year. A lucky pair of fairy-wrens might raise two broods of three young, which would be the limit for their territory that year, so they then stop breeding. An unlucky pair raises a cuckoo chick, which takes less time and effort than a host brood, so this, coupled with the long season, still allows them time to raise the annual quota of their own young from another nest or two. Over the season, they've done just as well as the unparasitized pair.

REED WARBLER (Europe)   :   10-week season

Unparasitized   __4__   __4__

Parasitized   __cuckoo_____ ------

SPLENDID FAIRY-WREN (Australia) :   20-week season

Unparasitized   __3_____   __3_____ ------------

Parasitized   __cuckoo__   __3_____   __3_____

The conclusion is that parasitism is much more costly for a Reed Warbler than for a Splendid Fairy-wren. If Fairy-wrens face the same kinds of ejection and recognition costs when rejecting cuckoo eggs as those incurred by Reed Warblers (chapter 5), then their lower costs of parasitism would favour acceptance rather than rejection.[23] So in this host-parasite system, the main driving force for the evolution of cuckoo eggs could be egg replacement by competing cuckoos, rather than host discrimination.[21] We shall discuss this further in chapter 9.

BRONZE-CUCKOO CHICKS

Just as with the Diederik Cuckoo, the begging calls of the Horsfield's Bronze-Cuckoo are different in different host nests. Robert and Laura Payne of the University of Michigan found that the differences emerged later on in the nestling period. By two weeks of age young cuckoos raised by Splendid Fairy-wrens sounded like young fairy-wrens whereas those raised by Western Thornbills sounded like young thornbills.[18]

In New Zealand, Ian McLean and Gillian Rhodes of the University of Canterbury have shown that the nestling Shining Bronze-Cuckoo also mimics the begging calls of its Grey Warbler host. However, despite the mimicry the warbler adults can still distinguish the cuckoo's call from a call of one of their own chicks. When experiments were performed with two loud-speakers, one broadcasting the begging calls of a cuckoo chick and the other the calls of a Grey Warbler chick, almost all the adults approached the calls of the warbler chick, irrespective of whether they were feeding a young cuckoo or a brood of their own young.[25] Further study of these begging calls would be fascinating.

There is yet another extraordinary and unexplained observation concerning Shining Bronze-Cuckoo chicks. In his study in New Zealand, Brian Gill noted that the newly hatched cuckoo looks remarkably like a Grey Warbler chick.[22] Both have the same skin colour, grey-pink, and both are covered in white down. They even have the same grey bill and the same yellowish-white flanges round the gape. Is this simply a coincidence? Or is it mimicry? Perhaps the delayed ejection of the nest contents by the bronze-cuckoos means that the hosts often have a day or two with both their own young and the cuckoo in the nest, sufficient time to favour the learning mechanism proposed by Arnon Lotem (chapter 6). In this case, the newly hatched cuckoo may have to mimic the host chicks to avoid rejection. Alternatively, perhaps chick colour is important for detection in the dimly lit nest; cuckoo and warbler chicks may have independently evolved the same best colours to make themselves conspicuous targets for food.[26]

CHAPTER 8

The non-evicting cuckoos: manipulative nestlings and Mafia tactics

Most cuckoo species favour hosts much smaller than themselves, the female cuckoo lays one egg per host nest and the newly hatched cuckoo nestling then ejects the host eggs or chicks. In six species, however, the cuckoo parasitizes large hosts and the cuckoo chick does not evict its nest mates. These six are the four *Clamator* cuckoos, the Channel-billed Cuckoo and the Asian Koel.

Two of the *Clamator* cuckoos (the Levaillant's and the Chestnut-Winged) favour babblers or laughing thrushes (Timaliidae), hosts of a similar size to themselves. The Jacobin (= Pied) Cuckoo also parasitizes babblers through most of its range (Asia, central and east Africa) but in South Africa it parasitizes smaller hosts, namely bulbuls and Fiscal Shrikes. The other *Clamator* cuckoo, the Great Spotted Cuckoo, favours members of the crow family, as does the Asian Koel. In both cases the hosts are usually larger than the parasite. The Channel-billed Cuckoo also includes crows among its main hosts, but this cuckoo is so enormous that it either matches its host for size or is larger.

Why in these six species does the cuckoo nestling not eject the host eggs or young? One possibility is that their hosts would find it unprofitable to raise a brood with just one chick, and so would abandon a single cuckoo. We can reject this idea because in some cases the cuckoo soon outcompetes the host chicks, which starve to death, leaving the cuckoo as the sole occupant, yet it continues to be tended.

Another explanation could be that the cuckoo nestling simply finds it impossible to eject such large host eggs or chicks. This may be true where the host is much larger than the cuckoo. It would be particularly interesting to know whether the young Asian Koel at first tries to eject the crow's eggs and then gives up, because the closely related Australian Koel, which parasitizes small hosts, does show ejection behaviour. However, in at least three of the *Clamator* cuckoos (the Great Spotted, the Levaillant's and the Jacobin) the cuckoo chick never attempts to eject, even when the host young are similar in size to itself. It is unlikely that ejection would be completely impossible, because Common Cuckoo nestlings eject eggs and host chicks of the Azure-winged Magpie, a host of similar size. However, Common Cuckoos usually parasitize small hosts, so their chicks may be programmed to 'always eject' and follow their blind routine even for occasional larger hosts. For *Clamator* cuckoos, which habitually parasitize larger hosts, selection may have favoured non-evicting nestlings because ejection of larger host eggs or chicks is so costly. It may be cheaper, energetically, to outcompete the host chicks in the nest rather than evict them.

There is a third hypothesis for why these cuckoo chicks do not evict. With large hosts, there is plenty of room in the nest for more than one cuckoo chick and in many cases the female cuckoo returns to the same host nest to lay a second egg. This means that an ejector cuckoo would eject not only the host eggs, in which it has no genetic interest, but also any eggs containing its own siblings, with which it has half its genes in common. Provided there is a good chance that the hosts could raise both cuckoo chicks, it would pay a cuckoo to tolerate its sibling in the nest. This could have favoured non-eviction as the best strategy to maximize a cuckoo's genetic contribution to future generations, including its personal success and the indirect success it will enjoy through the survival of its sibs.

Whether the reason for non-eviction is the difficulty of ejecting large host eggs and chicks, or the benefit of tolerating cuckoo siblings, the result is that the cuckoo chick ends up sharing the nest with host young. This sets the stage for the evolution of two behaviour patterns that we never encountered with the evicting cuckoos discussed in previous chapters. The first is obvious. A non-evicting cuckoo chick has to compete for food, unlike the ejector cuckoo chicks which are sure of getting every meal brought back to the nest. This competition results in some extraordinary cuckoo begging behaviour.

The second is an exciting idea first proposed by Amotz Zahavi, of the University of Tel-Aviv.[1] When the hosts have some of their own young in the nest, there is a strong incentive to continue to care for the current brood. In theory, the cuckoo could then adopt Mafia-like tactics and force the hosts to accept the parasite egg or chick as well, by destroying the broods of any hosts that dared to reject. Accepting a cuckoo chick is costly for the hosts but, if there is the threat of punishment, rejection could be even worse.

Finally, there is a further problem for cuckoos that parasitize large hosts, because they are powerful defenders of their nests. Crows have strong beaks which can inflict serious damage on a female cuckoo. Babblers are not so large, but they breed in cooperative groups, where the previous offspring remain behind on their parents' territory and help to raise subsequent broods. With perhaps 10 or more attendants at the nest, the cuckoo is again faced with formidable host defences. How, then, can the female cuckoo lay her egg?

We shall discuss these general problems by focusing on the non-evicting cuckoo that has been studied in the most detail, namely the Great Spotted Cuckoo.

GREAT SPOTTED CUCKOOS AND THEIR HOSTS

The Great Spotted Cuckoo breeds in the Mediterranean region of southern Europe, the Middle East and in Africa. During the last 50 years it has spread and increased in abundance in Spain, France and Italy. It is slightly larger (*c.* 140 g) than the Common Cuckoo (*c.* 110 g). The sexes look alike, with dusky brown upperparts spotted with white, creamy white underparts with a pale orange wash on the lower face and throat, and they are capped with a blue-grey crest (**Plate 4a**). In southern

Europe it inhabits semi-arid regions with trees and shrubs and its main host is the Magpie, with the Carrion Crow a regular secondary host. In Africa, it lives in open wooded country and mainly parasitizes various species of crows. In southern Africa, however, it also parasitizes open and hole-nesting starlings. The southern African Great Spotted Cuckoos are smaller and one wonders whether this increases the effectiveness with which they can exploit the starlings, which are much smaller than their normal corvid hosts.[2]

The Cuckoo's eggs are greenish-blue with brown spots. Although there is some variation, it is nothing like that in the Common Cuckoo and no-one has yet suggested that there are distinct host races with different egg types. Instead, the Great Spotted Cuckoo's egg is a generalized match for many of its main hosts. In Europe, it matches the appearance of both the Magpie (**Plate 4b**) and Carrion Crow eggs, and it is of similar size to Magpie eggs though 50% smaller by volume than Carrion Crow eggs. In Africa, it matches quite well the greenish spotted eggs of the Pied Crow, a common host throughout the continent, though again the Cuckoo egg is much smaller. However, the Black Crow, a common host in southern Africa, has pinkish eggs. For starlings, the Cuckoo egg is only a rough match though of similar size to the host eggs, which are greenish-blue, but immaculate or only sparsely spotted.[2]

In South Africa, the proportion of host nests parasitized, as measured by the Nest Record Scheme, is 13% for Pied Crows, 10% for Black Crows and 5% for Pied Starlings.[3] In southern Spain, during a 10-year period, Manuel Soler recorded 43% parasitism for Magpies and 8% for Carrion Crows, with low rates of parasitism for two other corvids, namely 2% for Jackdaws and 5% for Choughs.[4]

Great Spotted Cuckoos are most often seen in pairs during the breeding season, and the males in particular are very noisy, with loud chattering calls. In some areas, pairs defend territories containing host nests. For example, in southern Spain territories vary in size from 1 to 3.7 km² and may encompass up to 40 pairs of Magpies.[5] However, there is often overlap with neighbours and in areas with high Cuckoo density the territories break down so there is a good deal of overlap in breeding ranges.[6] As in Common Cuckoos, birds may feed well away from the breeding area, seeking out areas rich in hairy caterpillars.

GREAT SPOTTED CUCKOOS AND MAGPIES IN SOUTHERN SPAIN

The breeding behaviour of Great Spotted Cuckoos parasitizing Magpies has been particularly well studied near Granada, southern Spain, by Manuel Soler, Juan José Soler, Juan Gabriel Martínez, Anders Møller and their colleagues from the University of Granada. Their main study site, Hoya de Guadix, is a high plateau near the spectacular peaks of the Sierra Nevada mountains. The plateau is cultivated with cereal fields and groves of almond trees, where the Magpies build their nests. The study began in 1982 and requires a large team effort; more than 200 nests are monitored each year, with 25 km between the most distant territories. During the field season the research team live in a cave, a perfect retreat for an afternoon siesta after cuckoo watching in the Spanish heat.

Magpies have long been regarded as vermin by farmers because they steal fruit and eat the eggs and chicks of poultry and gamebirds. One of the researchers' main problems was to persuade the locals not to destroy all the Magpie nests. They did this by telling all the farmers that the Magpies were mainly raising Cuckoo chicks, not Magpies, and the more Cuckoos there were the harder life would be for the Magpie population. On learning of the Cuckoo's parasitic behaviour, one of the farmers said, 'Those birds are just like the priest in my village. He too has lots of children, all raised by other families!'

About a third of the parasitized Magpie nests had one Great Spotted Cuckoo egg, a third had two and a third had three or more (maximum of five). On the basis of egg characteristics, about 50% of the multiply-parasitized nests had eggs laid by the same female while the others were parasitized by two or three female Cuckoos.[4] A female Cuckoo lays up to 18 eggs per season, usually in three series with a week or so between them. Within each series, eggs are laid on alternate days.[7] This means that when a female lays a second egg in a particular host nest, it is usually laid two days after the first one. Most eggs (71%) were deposited during the host laying period, the rest after the hosts had completed their clutch. The Cuckoo eggs require less incubation (12–14 days) than the Magpie eggs (18–22 days). Therefore Cuckoo eggs laid during the host laying period hatch several days ahead of the host eggs, and even Cuckoo eggs laid at the start of incubation can still hatch out first.

The Great Spotted Cuckoos did not lay eggs in all the available Magpie nests but rather targeted the high quality hosts. When non-parasitized nests were experimentally given Cuckoo chicks and Magpie chicks, they were less well fed than chicks in parasitized nests. Older Magpies, which occupied better territories, built larger nests and nest size may have been one of the cues that Cuckoos used to assess host quality because parasitized nests tended to be the larger ones.[8] Two factors reduced parasitism. Magpies that laid in synchrony with their neighbours were less likely to be parasitized because this flooded the market, producing more suitable nests than the Cuckoos could use at once. In addition nearer neighbours reduced parasitism, perhaps because it allowed group defence against the laying female Cuckoos.[9]

The male Great Spotted Cuckoo courtship feeds the female throughout her egg-laying period, bringing large caterpillars or other insects. Presentation of a meal also usually precedes copulation. The male approaches with the food and, if the female is receptive, she jerks her body rhythmically up and down. The male then mounts and passes the food to her. However, he is reluctant to relinquish the prey until copulation occurs, and sometimes both birds maintain a grip on it, holding one end each until copulation is over, whereupon the male lets go and the female swallows the food.[7]

The female searches for suitable host nests by watching the hosts, often from a concealed perch. Although she may work alone during laying, male and female Great Spotted Cuckoos often cooperate as a team, so the female can overcome the powerful defences of the large hosts.[7] Another difference from Common Cuckoos is that laying can take place either in the early morning[10] or in the afternoon.[11] When the female Great Spotted Cuckoo is ready to lay, she may call the male over with a special vocalization. The pair then move towards the host nest, the male perching conspicuously on the tree tops and drawing attention to himself by calling, while the female remains silent and makes a low, concealed approach through the vegetation. As soon as the hosts fly over to mob the male, the female slips onto the host nest to lay. Laying is extraordinarily quick. Magpies have domed nests and the female may go right inside but she is usually in and out within 10 seconds. Such rapid laying is important to escape host attacks. If she was caught inside the nest, the Magpies could inflict serious injury. Sometimes she may simply sit at the entrance hole and squirt her egg inside, which takes less time.[11] With open-nesting hosts, like crows, the female may be even quicker, perching on the nest rim and dropping her egg into the host nest, a stay of just three seconds.[7] Crows are larger still and attacks would be very dangerous.

A pair of Great Spotted Cuckoos cooperating to parasitize a Magpie nest. The male Cuckoo has lured the Magpies away, which allows the female to slip into the nest to lay.

In 1993, the Spanish team of researchers took blood samples from the adult Cuckoos and from 73 nestling Cuckoos so they could use genetic markers to assign parentage.[12] There were seven cases of monogamy, where a pair of Cuckoos produced between two and 10 chicks during the season. There were also three cases of polygamy, where a male had mated with two females or a female had mated with two males. The genetic analysis confirmed that in some nests with two Cuckoo eggs the same female had laid both eggs, while in others two females were involved, in which case they had usually been fertilized by different males. The analysis also showed that one female used two hosts during the season. She laid her first two eggs in the nests of Carrion Crows, the next six in Magpie nests, and the final two again in Crow nests. The parasitism of Crows early and late in the season was when there were very few Magpie nests available, so this female apparently preferred Magpies and used the Crows only as secondary hosts.

Why do Great Spotted Cuckoos usually consort in pairs? The genetic analysis shows that in many cases the pair remain together throughout the season. In part this may reflect the fact that a male needs to follow a female around in order to protect his paternity. However, observations of the laying procedure itself suggests that a female also often needs a male's help in order to lay her egg. If a male demands paternity assurance before he is prepared to help her, then it may pay the female to be faithful to one partner.

Unlike Common Cuckoos, female Great Spotted Cuckoos do not remove any host eggs before they lay.[4] If they did so, they might risk removing one of their own eggs that they had laid earlier. However, this does not explain why they don't remove an egg or two during their first laying visit. Another explanation is that egg removal would extend the stay at the nest and lead to an unacceptable risk of host attack.

Although no host eggs are removed, two-thirds of parasitized Magpie nests have damaged host eggs, usually from one to three but sometimes more (**Plate 4b**).[13] Some are cracked or crushed and these are removed by the hosts. Others have tiny peck holes and are left in the nest, but the embryos do not develop. There was no such damage in unparasitized nests, nor in nests that were experimentally parasitized by the researchers. This shows that the Magpies do not damage their eggs, for example while attempting to reject the Cuckoo egg. Instead, the female Cuckoo herself must be responsible. Part of the damage may be caused as she drops her egg into the nest, but she may also quickly peck some host eggs, or crack some with her feet. Any Cuckoo eggs in the nest escape damage on account of their thicker shells, so the female Cuckoo avoids destroying any of her own eggs that she laid earlier.

The Great Spotted Cuckoo benefits in two ways from this damage to host eggs.[13] First, it reduces the number of host chicks with which her chick has to compete for food. On average, only one or two Magpie chicks hatch out in parasitized nests, compared with five in unparasitized nests. Second, it increases the chance that a late-laid Cuckoo egg will hatch. Magpies begin incubation before their clutch is complete, so their chicks hatch out over a period of several days. However, the female often ceases incubation within five days of the hatching of the first chick. By inflicting tiny pecks in the eggs, so the host leaves them in the nest even though they will not hatch, the Cuckoo increases the chance that the hosts will continue incubation to give a late Cuckoo egg time to hatch.

MANIPULATIVE GREAT SPOTTED CUCKOO CHICKS

In parasitized nests, Magpies have very poor reproductive success. Considering nests where at least one chick fledged (either Cuckoo or Magpie), three-quarters of the parasitized nests failed to produce any Magpie young and the average was just 0.6 Magpies fledged per nest. This compares with 3.5 Magpie chicks fledged per successful unparasitized nest.[14] Part of the reduced success is due to the female Cuckoo's egg destruction, but Magpie success is then reduced still further because the Cuckoo chick outcompetes the Magpie young for food. This is remarkable, given that the Magpies are larger than the Cuckoo. Healthy young Magpies fledge at a weight of about 175 g while young Great Spotted Cuckoos do so at 135 g. How can a smaller Cuckoo win the battle for food? It does so by three tricks.

The first is to hatch out early, usually several days before the Magpie chicks. The result is that the Cuckoo chick has a few days to grow before the host chicks hatch. Early hatching may partly result from a head start in development, just as in Common Cuckoos (chapter 4). In two other *Clamator* cuckoos, the Jacobin and the Levaillant's, the newly laid cuckoo egg already has a partly grown embryo because it develops inside the female cuckoo's oviduct for a day before it is laid, a consequence of the fact that she lays on alternate days.[15] The same might be true for Great Spotted Cuckoos, though this has yet to be investigated. With larger corvid hosts, such as Pied Crows, the cuckoo gains the additional advantage of hatching from a relatively small egg, which needs less incubation than the larger host eggs.

The second trick is that the Cuckoo chick grows very fast.[16] This enables it to maintain its size advantage against the slower growing host young. Magpies that hatch three to four days after the Cuckoo are unlikely to survive, not only because the Cuckoo can stretch up further to intercept the food but also because it often smothers and tramples on the host chicks, spreading its wings over the top of them and preventing them from begging normally.[17] Older Cuckoos may also be aggressive towards their nest mates, tugging at them and pecking hard at their heads. If there is more than one Cuckoo chick in the nest, the one that hatches first is more likely to fledge, but even so younger Cuckoos are better able to compete with it and often two Cuckoos are raised successfully together, especially if the second egg is laid just two days after the first. With longer intervals, the second Cuckoo is unlikely to survive. The young Cuckoo fledges at around 15–16 days of age, compared with the 21–27 day nestling period for Magpies and 30–40 days for Crows.[16]

The third trick is that the Cuckoo chick presents stimuli that the host parents find so attractive they prefer to feed the Cuckoo rather than their own young! The Magpie or Crow young have plain red gapes while the Great Spotted Cuckoo's gape is orange-yellow, with conspicuous white papillae on the palate (the roof of the mouth; **Plate 4c**). By placing temporary collars around the necks of nestlings, to prevent them from swallowing the food brought by the parents, Manuel Soler and his colleagues were able to measure the amount of food given to Magpie and Cuckoo young. They found that with a choice between a Cuckoo chick and a Magpie chick of about the same size, the hosts gave the Cuckoo more food. However, when the Cuckoo's gape was painted with red dye, so that the white papillae were masked and the gape looked like that of the Magpie chick, the Cuckoo was no longer preferred. Therefore the white papillae seem to act as a super-normal stimulus that encourages the hosts to feed the Cuckoo.[18]

The young Great Spotted Cuckoo also provides attractive vocal stimuli. Peter Mundy, now Chief Ornithologist of Zimbabwe National Parks, was the first to show that its begging calls mimic those of the host young, so that in Magpie nests the young Cuckoo sounds like a young Magpie while in Crow nests it sounds like a young Crow.[19] This mimicry is most likely to develop by the Cuckoo copying the begging calls of its nest mates. To test this idea, the best thing to do would be to cross foster young Cuckoos into the nests of various host species. Indirect evidence for copying comes from the fact that younger Cuckoo chicks do not mimic the host nestling calls so well. Furthermore there is a less striking resemblance between Cuckoo and Magpie calls compared with Cuckoo and Crow calls, perhaps because the host chicks are more likely to starve to death in Magpie nests.[20]

However, Tomas Redondo and Jesus Zuñiga, working at the Biology Station at the Doñana Reserve in southwestern Spain, have shown that the Great Spotted Cuckoo chick does more than simply mimic the calls of the host chicks. It exaggerates its hunger by giving calls that sound like those of a particularly hungry host chick.[17] In laboratory experiments chicks were fed to satiation and then their begging calls were measured at regular intervals. A well-fed Magpie chick gradually increased its begging intensity as it got hungrier, giving calls at a greater rate and for longer.[21] By contrast, a Cuckoo chick called at maximum intensity even within half an hour of being stuffed full of food. Its persistent gaping and continuous stream of calls far exceeded the performance of a Magpie chick that had not been fed for three hours. By enhancing the host begging call, the Cuckoo sounded not just hungry but 'super-hungry'. More remarkably, when offered food the Cuckoo simply spat it out because its gut was completely full, yet having thrown the food aside it continued to beg as though it was famished! These intense hunger cries were so disturbing for a visitor to Redondo's laboratory that she insisted he fed the 'starving' Cuckoos every few minutes until she realized that she was being deceived.

The Cuckoo's extraordinary performance is very effective in the host nest. Redondo and Zuñiga temporarily removed Magpie chicks from their nests and replaced them with just two chicks, a Cuckoo and a Magpie, both carefully weighed before the experiment. After three hours, the two chicks were weighed again to see which had been fed the most. If the Cuckoo was larger or the same size as the Magpie, it invariably got more food. Even when it was only half the mass of the Magpie, it managed to get fed just as much as its companion. By contrast, with two Magpie chicks in the nest, the larger one always got the most food and if the smaller Magpie was half the mass of the larger one, it rarely got fed at all. These experiments show that Magpies normally prefer to feed the largest chick, but small Cuckoos can beat the system through their exaggerated begging.[17] In most cases, of course, the cuckoo has the double advantage of being the largest chick in the nest and of sounding the most hungry. No wonder the host chicks usually starve to death!

Why should host parents favour large and hungry chicks? In fact this preference makes good sense in normal circumstances, when the nest is not parasitized. Magpies adjust their brood size in relation to the food available by allowing the smallest nestlings to die if food is scarce. They feed the largest nestling first and only when this is satiated does the next largest get fed. If food is in short supply, the smallest chicks quickly die and the Magpies raise a few healthy young. This is much better than spreading scarce food out evenly, in which case they may end up with a large brood of weedy chicks, none of whom would survive. Magne Husby, from the University of Trondheim in Norway, showed that brood reduction was in the parents' best interests by a neat experiment. In some nests where chicks had died from starvation, he replaced them with young chicks from other broods. The result was that these parents had more nestlings than where brood reduction had been allowed to take its natural course, but they ended up with fewer surviving fledglings because there wasn't enough food to raise the whole brood.[22]

The Great Spotted Cuckoo's exuberant begging exploits this system, which works so well for the host parents in unparasitized nests. Faced with a stimulus of a large chick that never seems to be satiated, Magpie hosts are tricked into diverting most of their hard won food to the Cuckoo and their own chicks usually starve to death.

ARE GREAT SPOTTED CUCKOO CHICKS SELFISH OR CHARMING?

As we saw in chapter 6, in theory we would expect cuckoo chicks to behave more selfishly because they have no kinship with their hosts. The only factor that might reduce the Great Spotted Cuckoo's self interest a little, is the occasional sharing of the nest with a sibling (because its mother might lay two eggs in the same host nest). Even so, it should still be more selfish than the host chicks. Whereas the hosts always have siblings in the nest, the Cuckoos only sometimes do so. Furthermore, unlike the host chicks, the Cuckoo has no genetic interest in the host parents' future reproduction.

The lack of kinship argument is compelling, but why does the Great Spotted Cuckoo continue to beg so vigorously even when it is completely full? One answer could be that the degree of satiation in the laboratory feeding experiments far exceeds that which would occur in nature. The Cuckoo's crazy begging when its mouth is stuffed with food may be like the behaviour of a fox in a hen house, which kills a hundred chickens even though it could only eat one or two. In nature, neither Cuckoos nor foxes would normally encounter such an excess. Their behaviour of 'beg whenever food is offered' or 'kill when you can', is a sensible recipe for success in nature, where food is usually limited. A hint that food may still be limiting for a Cuckoo, despite the fact that it often gets every meal brought back to the nest, comes from the observation that only two-thirds of fledgling Cuckoos raised by Magpies survive to independence. The survivors are those that are heavier as nestlings.[23] Furthermore, life for a Great Spotted Cuckoo may be even harder in other host nests. Crow nestlings are three times the mass of a Magpie nestling and three and a half times the mass of a Cuckoo nestling. Even with the head start from early hatching, the Cuckoo may often need its exaggerated begging to compete for food with such large nest companions.

Tomas Redondo suggests another explanation for exaggerated begging.[17] At hatching, the Great Spotted Cuckoo chick looks quite like a newly hatched host chick, though its gape is not so red as those of the corvid young (**Plate 4c**). However, as it grows it looks increasingly different from the host chicks. The feathered Cuckoo nestling has a black top to the head and nape, which some claim represents mimicry of the host young in the parts of the body that will be most conspicuous to the host parents. Nevertheless, the Cuckoo chick's mimicry is nowhere near as striking as in some other brood parasites that are raised alongside the host young. Its dusky-brown back with small white spots is nothing like the pure black of young crows, nor the bold black and white plumage of the young Magpies. As we argued in chapter 6, it might pay the hosts of non-evicting brood parasites to learn the characteristics of the chicks in their nest the first time they breed, and then to reject young that differ from this learnt set. Any hosts that are unparasitized in their first brood will 'imprint' only on their own young and would therefore reject a chick of a different appearance. This has apparently selected for excellent mimicry of host chicks in some parasites. In others, like the Great Spotted Cuckoo, where the mimicry is less good, Redondo suggests that the parasite uses exaggerated begging to charm the hosts, and so counteract rejection.

If exaggerated begging is the key to induce acceptance, then foreign chicks of other species should be rejected because they will lack the Cuckoo's extraordinary begging performance. Fernando Alvarez, Luis Arias de Reyna and Myriam Segura, also working at the Doñana Reserve, introduced single young (naked) chicks of other species into Magpie broods. All four Jackdaws were accepted and raised to fledging. Of six Spotless Starling chicks, four were raised to fledging while two were ejected after being fed for a week. Of four House Sparrows, two were raised to fledging and two disappeared after eight days. Finally, of eight Swallows, three were ejected 'immediately' and five were raised to fledging.[24]

At first sight, these results suggest that Magpies might indeed reject some foreign chicks. It is especially interesting that many rejections occurred when the chicks were about a week old, which is the time they would become feathered and take on a different appearance from the Magpie's own young. However, we need to know whether these chicks really are recognized as foreign and rejected alive. The other possibility is that they died from lack of food and were then removed, the same treatment that the Magpies would give to their own dead young. In another experiment, the head of one young Magpie per brood was painted grey, red, green or yellow, so it clearly differed from the normal black head of its nest mates. These odd-looking chicks were nevertheless fed normally.[24] This result calls into question the idea that the Great Spotted Cuckoo chick has evolved a mimetic black head. It also suggests that Magpies might not discriminate against odd chicks after all.

In another experiment, Manuel Soler and his team investigated whether Magpies would ever reject Cuckoo chicks.[25] They took single Cuckoo chicks and put them into other Magpie nests. Naked, young Cuckoos introduced into unparasitized nests with young Magpie chicks were all accepted. However, at a later stage, when the Magpies had large feathered nestlings and the introduced Cuckoo too was feathered, some of the host parents attacked the Cuckoo and ejected it from the nest. By contrast, Magpies that were already feeding a large young Cuckoo in their brood accepted another feathered Cuckoo. These results suggest that the Magpies learn the characteristics of the young in their nest at the late nestling stage, and then reject young that look different. Parasitized Magpies will learn the appearance of both Cuckoo and Magpie young, and so will accept another Cuckoo. Unparasitized Magpies, on the other hand, will learn only Magpie young and so will reject a feathered Cuckoo as foreign. This last result suggests that the Cuckoo's super-normal begging does not guarantee acceptance.

How do we reconcile the results from the Soler team's experiment with the fact that under natural conditions the Cuckoo chick is never rejected? If Magpies imprinted on the chicks in their nest the first time they bred, then those that were lucky and were unparasitized should subsequently be able to reject Great Spotted Cuckoo chicks, at least at the feathered stage when they become clearly different from the Magpie's own young. According to the imprinting theory, therefore, we should see a percentage of Cuckoos rejected that reflects the percentage of host pairs that are unparasitized in their first nest, and thus able to recognize the Cuckoo as a foreigner. But there is no evidence that Cuckoo chicks are ever rejected from naturally parasitized nests.

The Soler team's results could reflect a different sort of learning, which is well known from other birds, particularly those that nest in colonies like swallows and seabirds.[26] These species treat any chick in their nest as 'their own', and so will accept foreign nestlings at an early stage, just like the Magpies. However, just before the chicks leave the nest the parents learn their characteristics, in particular the details of their calls, which act as signatures to distinguish them from other broods. They might also learn plumage features too. Once the young leave the nest, their parents can then pick them out, even from a large crowd of fledglings, and so ensure that they direct their care to their own brood not someone else's. This learning is likely to occur afresh each time a bird breeds, so in the next brood the bird once again starts off with the rule 'any chick in the nest is mine' and then learns the signatures all over again just before the young leave the nest.

If this kind of learning occurs in Magpies, then the results of the various experiments begin to make some sense. If Magpies begin each brood by accepting any chick in their nest, this would explain why Cuckoo chicks are always accepted in naturally parasitized nests, where the Cuckoo would either hatch out before or alongside the host chicks. Other foreign chicks would be accepted too. But at the late nestling stage, the Magpies learn the characteristics of their brood so they can distinguish them after fledging, when they might intermingle with chicks from other broods. Cuckoo chicks introduced experimentally at this late stage into unparasitized nests are therefore rejected as foreign. Further experiments are clearly needed, especially to test whether Magpies will accept any foreign chick early on. If it turns out that they do, then the Great Spotted Cuckoo's exaggerated begging might not be necessary to counteract discrimination. Instead, it is likely to aid competition for food in the nest and to reflect the fact that its greed is less constrained by kinship (see also chapter 12).

EGG REJECTION BY MAGPIES

We now return to the egg stage. The egg of the Great Spotted Cuckoo is a good match for the Magpie's eggs and also a reasonable match for those of many crows.

Alvarez, Arias de Reyna and Segura placed model eggs in Magpie nests in southern Spain and found rejection of non-mimetic models but greater acceptance of mimetic eggs.[24] Clearly, host discrimination has selected for egg mimicry. Manuel Soler and Anders Møller then compared rejection of model eggs in three Magpie populations.[27] In an unparasitized Magpie population in Sweden (where there are no Great Spotted Cuckoos) all model eggs were accepted, even those that were non-mimetic. This shows that the rejection in southern Spain is a definite response to Cuckoos. Magpies have considerable variation within their own clutch and in the absence of parasitism it may be best to accept to avoid wasted recognition errors (chapter 5).

However, within southern Spain Soler and Møller also found fascinating differences between two parasitized host populations. In 1989 at Santa Fe, where Magpies have apparently been parasitized for many years, they rejected 100% of the non-mimetic models, 78% of the mimetic models and 33% of real Cuckoo eggs at naturally parasitized nests. By contrast, in Hoya de Guadix, just 60 km away, where local reports suggest that Cuckoos have colonized the area only since the 1960s, there was much less Magpie rejection; only 71% of non-mimetic eggs, 14% of mimetic eggs and no rejection at all at naturally parasitized nests. Furthermore, observations at Guadix over a decade showed an increase in Cuckoo parasitism from 31–41% in 1982–84 (20% Magpie nests had more than one Cuckoo egg) to 61% in 1990–92 (36% nests had more than one Cuckoo egg). During this period, the Magpies steadily increased their rejection behaviour from 61% to 89% of non-mimetic models, from 14% to 33% of mimetic models and from 0% to 10% of real Cuckoo eggs in naturally parasitized nests.[28]

Soler and his colleagues suggested that this increase in rejection might reflect a genetic change in the Guadix host population as it evolves stronger rejection in response to increased parasitism. They argued that the Santa Fe Magpies have long been exposed to parasitism and so have had plenty of time to evolve rejection. The Guadix population, by contrast, is still evolving defences in response to the new arrival of Cuckoos and so provides an example of evolution in action, just like the beak changes in Darwin's finches and the migration changes in Blackcaps that we discussed in chapter 1.

The alternative explanation for both the difference between Santa Fe and Guadix, and the recent increase in rejection at Guadix, is that these reflect flexibility in individual host behaviour.[29] In chapter 5 we saw that such individual flexibility could explain similar differences in rejection between Reed Warbler populations and also changes within a population over time. Perhaps individual Magpies also vary their rejection response in relation to parasitism pressure. This would explain how differences could occur between sites just 60 km apart, which are unlikely to be isolated genetically. Nevertheless, against this view is the fact that Cuckoos are now even more abundant at Guadix than at Santa Fe, yet the Guadix Magpie population has still not reached the Santa Fe rejection levels. Of course, the variation in host rejection could reflect both genetic differences and flexible individual responses. It might be difficult to tease these causes apart without breeding experiments and careful studies of the heritability of host rejection behaviour.

ASIAN KOELS, LEVAILLANT'S CUCKOOS AND JACOBIN CUCKOOS

We now have a quick look at some other non-evicting cuckoos. Their behaviour is similar to that of the Great Spotted Cuckoo.

Asian Koels

In India, the Asian Koel parasitizes House Crows as a favourite host. The male and female Koel sometimes cooperate during egg laying. B.S. Lamba describes how the male Koel flies up to the host nest and induces the Crows to attack it. It then retreats, luring the Crows away from the nest. While they are away, the female Koel, who has remained hidden nearby, sneaks onto the nest to lay very quickly.[30] If she is caught on the nest then she is attacked and may be injured.

Nests are usually parasitized during the host laying period. There is often just one Koel egg per Crow nest, but there may commonly be two or three and sometimes more (the record is 11!). It is not known whether multiple parasitism is the work of one female or several but variation in eggs suggests that several females are often involved.[30] Koel eggs are like the Crow's eggs, with a green ground colour and spots of red or brown, but they are smaller. Dewar doubted that the Crows ever rejected the Koel eggs because they accepted chicken eggs, heron eggs and even golf balls![31] The Koel egg hatches first, after just 13 days' incubation compared with 16–17 days for the Crow's eggs. As a naked nestling, it looks just like a Crow chick and there are claims that the feathered nestlings are mimetic too, with black or dark plumage, though some have reddish-brown barred feathers and are unlike the black Crow nestlings. Because of its head start and more vigorous begging compared with the host chicks it often outcompetes them and usually only one or two host chicks survive (out of a clutch of four or five eggs).

Levaillant's Cuckoo

The Levaillant's Cuckoo from Africa specializes on *Turdoides* babblers. In southern Africa it has been studied by Peter Steyn, where the only known host is the Arrowmarked Babbler.[32] The Cuckoo's egg is plain blue and a perfect match for the host egg both in colour and size. The Cuckoo pair cooperate in laying, with the male luring the hosts away while the female nips onto the nest and deposits her egg in about five seconds. Sometimes several attempts are made before the female can gain access to the nest because the babbler group (breeding pair plus helpers) is alert to intrusions and may attack her. In one report, the female was forced to the ground screaming while the babblers pecked at her head and back. The female doesn't remove any host eggs, but some may be damaged during laying. The begging calls of the Cuckoo nestling and fledgling are 'identical' to those of the babbler young and after fledging the Cuckoo huddles with the host young while the adults bring food. In Zimbabwe, nest records show that 8% of the babbler nests are parasitized. Often the hosts raise some of their own young as well as the Cuckoo, perhaps because the brood is fed by a group rather than just a pair of hosts.

Jacobin (= Pied) Cuckoo

The Jacobin or Pied Cuckoo breeds in the Indian sub-continent and Africa. Three subspecies are recognized:

Clamator jacobinus jacobinus breeds in southern India and Sri Lanka.
Clamator j. pica breeds in northern India, Pakistan, and tropical Africa.
Clamator j. serratus breeds in southern Africa.

The first two subspecies are pied in colour (*pica* is larger) and they both parasitize *Turdoides* babblers, laying highly mimetic plain blue eggs. The third occurs in two colour forms, pied and black (which interbreed), the pied being commoner in the interior of southern Africa and the black form on the coast. Perhaps because of competition with the Levaillant's Cuckoo, it does not parasitize babblers but rather bulbuls and Fiscal Shrikes. Furthermore, it lays pure white eggs, which look nothing like the coloured and speckled eggs of its hosts. There have been two detailed studies of Jacobin Cuckoos.

In the north Indian plains, near Delhi, Tony Gaston from the University of Oxford studied three species of babblers.[33] There were 40 babbler groups on his study site. Each group contained from three to 20 birds, with just one pair of breeders and the others acting as helpers at the nest. Gaston estimated that there were three pairs of Jacobin Cuckoos on his study site each year. Over a three-year period (1971–73) the percentage of nests parasitized was 71% for the Jungle Babblers, 42% for the Common Babblers and 29% for the Large Grey Babblers. Most parasitized nests (62%) had just one Cuckoo egg, some (33%) had two and rarely (5%) there were three or four. In some cases of multiple parasitism, the same female Cuckoo was probably involved because the eggs looked identical and appeared at two-day intervals. In other cases the eggs were of different shape and two females may have parasitized the same nest.

The Cuckoos hatched first, after 11–12 days' incubation, compared with 14–16 days for the babblers. They also developed faster and came to dominate the nest. The hosts never rejected them even though they looked clearly different from the babbler chicks both as naked nestlings, when the Cuckoo has blacker skin, and as feathered young, when the Cuckoo is black and white while the babblers are brown. In Jungle Babblers the average number of babbler young fledged from an unparasitized nest was 2.5, compared with 1.1 if parasitized. The host losses included eggs cracked when the Cuckoo laid its egg and young starving in competition with the more vigorous Cuckoo chick.[33]

In South Africa, Richard Liversidge studied Jacobin Cuckoos near Port Elizabeth over a four-year period (1959–62).[34] There were up to three females on his study site per year and all 50 Cuckoo eggs he found were in the nests of Cape Bulbuls, even though there were other potential hosts available, including Fiscal Shrikes and Sombre Bulbuls. In another area just 3 km away the Sombre Bulbul was the main host, while in drier areas where bulbuls were scarcer the Fiscal Shrike was parasitized. It would be nice to know whether individual female Cuckoos specialize, in which case there could be gentes even though all lay similar white eggs. On Liversidge's study area the parasitism rate of the Cape Bulbuls varied from 12–72%

per year though the number of host pairs remained fairly constant at 13–19 pairs. Over the whole of South Africa the nest record cards show parasitism rates of 16% for the Cape Bulbul, 13% for the Sombre Bulbul and 12% for the Black-Eyed Bulbul. Most nests have just one Cuckoo egg (78%), occasionally two, rarely more.[3]

The female Cuckoo watches the bulbuls build and may inspect nests, especially during the afternoon when the hosts are absent. Liversidge found that most layings were in the early morning (0700–0900), within one to three hours of dawn (0600). The laying procedure is exactly like that of the Great Spotted and Levaillant's Cuckoos and the Asian Koel, with the female often relying on the male to lure the hosts away, so she can slip on the nest to lay within 10 seconds or so. In India, Gaston saw a female lay within five seconds; she simply perched above the host nest and dropped her egg in. As with other cuckoos, eggs are laid on alternate days. From dissection of females to examine their ovaries, Robert Payne estimated that they could lay up to 25 eggs in a 10-week season.[35] Neither Gaston nor Liversidge found any evidence for host egg removal by laying female Cuckoos, though host eggs sometimes got cracked. In contrast to babblers, the bulbuls rarely fledged any young from a parasitized nest. Their chicks are smaller than the babblers and so more likely to be outcompeted by a Cuckoo.

The big surprise about the southern African subspecies of Jacobin Cuckoo is its non-mimetic white egg.[2] This becomes even more of a puzzle when we discover that bulbuls seem to reject non-mimetic eggs, though the evidence is limited to only a few experiments. In 1918, Swynnerton tested three pairs of Black-Eyed Bulbuls; two of them rejected foreign eggs, including the white eggs of mousebirds or coucals, while the third pair accepted them. More recently, David Noble (1995) placed various non-mimetic plaster eggs into host nests in Namibia and found that two out of three pairs of Red-Eyed Bulbuls rejected them. Why then is the Jacobin Cuckoo's egg white and apparently so different from the bulbul's coloured and spotted eggs?

Given that the main hosts elsewhere are babblers, for whom the Jacobin Cuckoo lays a beautifully mimetic blue egg, it is tempting to suggest that the Jacobin Cuckoo has only recently invaded southern Africa and, facing competition for babblers from the Levaillant's Cuckoo, it has turned to bulbuls as new hosts. Perhaps there simply hasn't been time to evolve egg mimicry? This argument seems unlikely, given that southern African Jacobin Cuckoos have had time to evolve into a separate subspecies and to evolve a different egg colour.

A more likely possibility is that the Cuckoo's white egg is somehow advantageous. Perhaps it is mimetic after all? It has been discovered recently that birds have good vision in the ultra-violet wavelengths, to which humans are blind.[36] It would be nice to know whether the 'white' Cuckoo egg and 'coloured' host egg, which look so different to our eyes, in fact look similar to the hosts, at least in the ultra-violet part of the spectrum. Or perhaps the white Cuckoo egg is a super-normal stimulus, which the host's find particularly attractive (chapter 5)?

There is one more possibility. The Cuckoo egg may be non-mimetic, but the Cuckoo could force the hosts to accept it through adopting Mafia-like tactics, namely punishing hosts that dared to reject.

MAFIA TACTICS

The Mafia hypothesis was originally suggested by Amotz Zahavi, whose explanations of animal behaviour are often inspired by analogies with human behaviour.[1] This can provide a useful source of ideas; we too are animals and have evolved adaptations to help us survive and reproduce in a competitive environment. Knowing how we cope with particular problems can sometimes help us to understand how animals behave under similar circumstances.

In our own lives, we often submit to control by others who are more powerful than ourselves. We tend to obey parents, teachers and bosses at work, even in cases where we would prefer to do otherwise, simply because it would be worse to disobey. In the same way, Zahavi argues that hosts might submit to control by cuckoos. Even if they can easily detect a non-mimetic cuckoo egg or chick, they may decide to accept it because if they rejected the cuckoos would punish them by destroying their clutch or brood. This 'Mafia hypothesis' could explain why hosts as intelligent as crows, which are able to recognize different foods, enemies and even individual people, nevertheless accept an odd-looking egg in their nest.

It is easy to see that this argument would be unlikely to work for hosts of the Common Cuckoo, and other parasites which eject or kill all the host eggs or young.[37] These hosts gain nothing from accepting the parasite egg, except in the rare cases that the cuckoo egg fails to hatch; instead they endure six weeks' hard work for no genetic reward. Any host that was sure it was parasitized would do best to reject, even if this meant abandoning the clutch altogether. Next time there must at least be a chance of escaping the cuckoo. Evidence from field work also suggests that Common Cuckoos do not adopt Mafia-like tactics. Hiroshi Nakamura's detailed radio-tracking in Japan shows that females never re-visit nests after parasitism to check on the progress of their eggs or chicks.[38] Furthermore, in the Japanese study site, when Cuckoo eggs were either rejected naturally or removed by the researchers, the Great Reed Warbler hosts did not suffer increased clutch or brood destruction.[39] Instead they enjoyed good reproductive success, their only loss being the one egg that the female Cuckoo had removed during laying.[40]

However, the Mafia idea could work for non-evicting parasites, where the hosts gain some reproductive reward from a parasitized nest. In theory the hosts might accept the parasite egg or chick as the price they must pay for the opportunity to raise a few of their own young alongside. Rejection could bring even lower host success, provided the adult parasite was able to detect and punish rejectors by destroying their clutch or brood.

This is a fascinating and plausible theory but could it work in practice? From the parasite's point of view there are two difficulties. First, it has to gain regular access to the host nests to check for rejection. This will not be easy for any of the cuckoos discussed in this chapter. Once incubation begins the hosts will be in constant attendance and even with male help to lure the hosts away, a female cuckoo is unlikely to be able to check nests without considerable time and effort.

Second, once she is at the nest she needs to distinguish her own eggs or chicks from those of the host, to determine whether rejection has occurred. Let's first consider problems of checking at the egg stage. In all the cases in this chapter, except one, the cuckoo's egg is either a perfect mimic (blue for babbler hosts) or at least a reasonable match (spotted for corvid hosts). Once there is mimicry, there is the problem of recognition errors by cuckoos as well as hosts. For example, in chapter 4 we saw that Common Cuckoos often failed to remove a previous Cuckoo egg. Recognition errors may be a particular problem in corvid clutches because the host eggs are remarkably variable. On top of this, there may also be parasitic eggs from other female cuckoos in the clutch. Indeed, if the cuckoo could control hosts through Mafia-like tactics one wonders why it then makes life difficult for itself by evolving egg mimicry. Surely a non-mimetic egg would be best? For these reasons, the most likely candidate for a Mafia system is perhaps the South African Jacobin Cuckoo, with its apparently non-mimetic white egg. Even if the background turns out to have ultra-violet mimicry of the host eggs, it should still be distinctive through its lack of spots.

What if a Mafia-cuckoo delayed checks until the chick stage? Again, there is the problem of distinguishing her chicks from the host young. However, apart from the Asian Koel, which is sometimes mimetic, this should be easy for the other five non-evicting cuckoos, especially when their chicks grow feathers and begin to look very different from the host young. Checking might therefore be easier with chicks rather than with eggs.

There may also be difficulties with the Mafia idea from the host's point of view. In many of the cases we have discussed in this chapter, the host chicks fare poorly in competition with the parasite chicks. If the nest is parasitized, bulbuls rarely raise any of their own young and Magpies raise just 0.6 Magpie young on average. To make acceptance of cuckoo eggs the best option for hosts, despite these miserable rewards, the cuckoo needs strong control of the host's reproductive opportunities.

In summary, Mafia-like control will be facilitated if the parasite can easily visit host nests and detect whether rejection has occurred. Hosts will be more likely to submit if they raise more of their own young from a parasitized nest or have fewer opportunities for other, unparasitized broods. This means that the Mafia hypothesis will be more likely for some parasite-host systems than for others.

A TEST OF THE MAFIA HYPOTHESIS

So far, there has been just one experimental test of the Mafia hypothesis, by Manuel Soler and his colleagues studying Great Spotted Cuckoos and their Magpie hosts in southern Spain.[41] The experiments were done from 1990 to 1992 in Guadix, when rejection rates of Cuckoo eggs at naturally parasitized nests were around 10%. There was a hint from these naturally parasitized nests that something interesting was going on. In most cases where the Cuckoo egg was accepted the nest was successful, but in the few cases that the hosts rejected, the clutch was often then destroyed. Could this reflect punishment by the Cuckoo? The alternative, of course, is that a predator was responsible, perhaps a crow. But predation at nests where Magpies rejected was higher than at unparasitized nests, which is not easy to explain by the predator theory.

Manuel Soler and his team decided to test the Mafia hypothesis experimentally. The experiment involved allocating naturally parasitized nests at random to one of two treatments, namely 'experimental', where the researchers removed the Cuckoo egg (to simulate a Magpie that rejected), and 'control', where they visited the nest but did not interfere with the clutch (in retrospect, a better control would have been to remove a Magpie egg). They then followed the fate of the two groups and found an exciting result. More than half of the experimental nests were depredated, either at the egg or young chick stage, compared with only 10% of the control nests. Two observations suggest this was not simply due to predators. First, injured chicks were sometimes left in the nest (crows always remove and eat their victims). Second, in one case a radio-tracked female Cuckoo that had earlier parasitized the nest returned to peck at the eggs after the researchers had removed her egg. This suggests that the Cuckoos themselves were responsible for at least some, and perhaps all, of the predation differences between the two groups.[41] Remarkably, it also implies that despite egg mimicry the Cuckoos can distinguish their own eggs from the Magpie eggs, and so tell when their own egg is missing.

Why should the Great Spotted Cuckoo destroy host nests where rejection has occurred? One benefit is that this induces repeat laying by the hosts, and so makes

Experiments in Spain show that Great Spotted Cuckoos sometimes destroy the eggs or chicks of Magpies that dare to reject the Cuckoo's egg.

available more nests for parasitism. Beyond this, it may also teach hosts to obey. Perhaps next time they will be more likely to accept the Cuckoo's egg? Another experiment was done in 1996 and 1997 to test for this possibility.[42] This time the Magpies were given model Cuckoo eggs made from plaster of Paris and painted to look like those of the Great Spotted Cuckoo. A few days later, the nests were checked and this revealed that about half of the pairs had thrown the model egg out of their nest. These pairs were punished by the experimenters, who crushed all the eggs in their nests to simulate what a Mafia-cuckoo would do. The Magpies then built a replacement nest in their territory and the researchers parasitized them again with another model egg. Half of those that had rejected before now changed their behaviour and accepted the Cuckoo egg. This was not simply because the Magpie population at large showed more acceptance later in the season, so it seems to be a specific response to the punishment received in the first nest. Moreover, the change in Magpie behaviour was most marked in areas with lots of Cuckoos, which suggests that the hosts were assessing their probability of being punished again if they rejected a second time.[42]

These results provide striking support for the Mafia hypothesis. Magpies may be particularly susceptible to Cuckoo control because they are strictly territorial and build conspicuous nests. It would therefore be easy for the Cuckoo to parasitize or punish a pair over subsequent nests within a season or even over several seasons. Both Cuckoos and Magpies are likely to return to the same territory and so will meet again in future years. Like a kiss from the Godfather, pecks from a Great Spotted Cuckoo may be a sign that the hosts have an offer they cannot refuse.

At first sight, it might seem odd that the Mafia hypothesis fits this case so well. If the Great Spotted Cuckoo can control the Magpies through Mafia tactics, why has it evolved a mimetic egg, which would surely make checking for host rejection so much harder? And why are the Guadix Magpies now evolving increased rejection of Cuckoo eggs?[28] This implies that the Mafia tactics are not working very effectively. In fact, on average the Magpies do seem to do better to reject. Despite the greater predation on nests where the Soler team simulated rejection, these Magpies still tended to raise more of their own chicks to fledging than did those whose young were left to compete with young Cuckoos.[43] Thus, by removing a Cuckoo egg, the researchers gave the Magpies a helping hand. This may explain why rejection is slowly increasing in the Guadix Magpie population, despite the Cuckoo's attempts at Mafia-like control.

Perhaps Mafia behaviour persists in the cuckoos because hosts vary in their responses. Just as the human Mafia might find it easier to control some victims rather than others, so Mafia cuckoos might be better able to control particular host individuals, say those that are less able to defend their nests, or those with fewer reproductive opportunities elsewhere. So we may find some individual hosts in a population that do not submit to cuckoo control, and reject cuckoo eggs, while others are forced to accept to make the best of their poor circumstances.

CHAPTER 9

Cuckoos versus hosts: who wins?

Hosts suffer dearly if they are parasitized by a cuckoo. Either all their own eggs or chicks get thrown out of the nest, or at least some of their brood get crushed to death, or starve, in competition with the large and greedy cuckoo chick. It is not surprising that many hosts have evolved defences. However, this is not like evolving defences against the physical environment, for example the cold or the rain, where dense and waterproof feathers may bring a final solution to the problem. Cuckoos are living enemies and they fight back. The result is an evolutionary arms race.

The evidence in the previous chapters has shown that cuckoos and hosts have exerted a powerful selection pressure on each other. Hosts have clearly evolved egg rejection in response to cuckoos, because species untainted by cuckoos (the unsuitable hosts) accept. And cuckoos have evolved egg mimicry in response to host rejection, because variation in the degree of egg mimicry among European gentes of Common Cuckoos reflects variation in discrimination by their respective hosts.

This arms race is exactly like that between a predator and its prey; as a predator evolves improved tactics for finding and killing its prey, the prey evolve improved defences, so selecting for further improvements in the predators. It is important to realize exactly how selection is working here. In one sense, the predator or cuckoo is certainly engaging in a contest with its prey or host. The predator or cuckoo wants to succeed, while their victims want to avoid being eaten or parasitized. But the evolutionary contest takes place within each party, as individual predators or cuckoos compete with each other to pass genes on to future predator and cuckoo generations, and as individual prey compete with each other to pass copies of their genes to future prey generations. A story will help to make this point clear. Two tourists were walking in a game park in Africa, when they came upon a pride of lions. One of them immediately began to take off her backpack. 'Don't be crazy', said her companion. 'You'll never outrun a lion.' 'I don't have to', came the chilling reply, 'I just have to run faster than you.'

ADAPTATIONS AND COUNTER-ADAPTATIONS

Here is a summary of the various adaptations and counter-adaptations of the two parties.

HOST	CUCKOO
1. Learn own eggs and reject those that differ from this learnt set.	Mimic host eggs. Strong-shelled egg to make ejection harder.
2. Distinctive signatures (spots, scribbles) on own eggs. Decrease variation within own clutch. Increase variation between clutches of individuals.	Mimic host signatures. Punish hosts that reject (non-evicting cuckoos only).
3. Reject any egg that appears before own clutch begins.	Delay laying until host eggs in the nest.
4. Reject large eggs.	Lay small egg.
5. Attack cuckoo and increase egg rejection if see cuckoo at the nest.	Rapid laying when host likely to be absent. Male may lure hosts away from nest.
6. Reduce probability of parasitism: nest architecture (e.g. entrance tube) or colonial nesting.	Improved stealth or surprise. Strong-shelled egg that can be dropped into nest.
7. If parasite chick raised with host chicks, learn to recognize chicks as a defence.	Mimic host chicks in appearance and begging calls.
8. Favour large hungry chicks, to maximize own success in unparasitized nests.	Cuckoo chick becomes largest in nest because it hatches first (internal incubation gives its development a head-start) and has rapid growth. Eject or outcompete host chicks. Beg more vigorously than host chicks.

These intricate adaptations by either side are testament to a long history of co-evolution. Indeed, molecular evidence suggests that the cuckoo family is an ancient one, which appeared in the Cretaceous Period, some one hundred million years ago. Song-bird families evolved later, with the main radiation from one hundred million to thirty million years ago. We do not know exactly when the first parasitic cuckoos appeared but it is likely that many host families have been subjected to cuckoo parasitism for much of their evolutionary history.

The question we now have to tackle is: what is the outcome of this arms race? Does it continue for ever, with both hosts and cuckoos evolving ever more refined tactics to keep up with improvements in their opponents? Charles Darwin himself recognized this possibility:[1] 'Wonderful and admirable as most instincts are, yet they cannot be considered as absolutely perfect: there is a constant struggle going on throughout nature between the instinct of the one to escape its enemy and of the other to secure its prey.'

This kind of never-ending arms race has been coined 'Red Queen Evolution', after the Red Queen in Lewis Carroll's *Through the Looking Glass*.[2] In this story, the Red Queen grabs Alice by the hand and they run together, faster and faster. To Alice's surprise, they never seem to move but remain in the same spot. 'In our country,' she says, 'you'd generally get to somewhere else if you ran very fast for a long time.' The Queen replies, 'A slow sort of country! Here, it takes all the running you can do to keep in the same place.'

The same idea might apply to the evolutionary battle between cuckoos and hosts. Over time, each party evolves better trickery or better defences with the result that their relative success remains the same. Richard Dawkins and John Krebs liken this to a human arms race in which the balance of power remains equal even though both sides continuously escalate their weapons and defences. The implication is that although today's cuckoo is no better at exploiting its hosts than one forty million years ago, if we could somehow pit a modern cuckoo against the defences of a host in ancient times then the cuckoo would easily win, just as a modern jet would annihilate a Spitfire.[1] Such one-sided contests are not simply things to dream of; they occur in nature every time a predator invades an isolated prey population with no co-evolved defences. The result is extinction of the Dodo and the Great Auk, and many other island birds, as soon as they encounter Man, cats and rats.

Continuous improvements in the adaptations of the two sides is not the only potential outcome of a cuckoo-host arms race. The other possibility is that one side can no longer afford to invest in costly offences or defences. Either the cuckoo could win, in the sense that the host is doomed to accept cuckoo eggs or chicks for ever more. Or the host could win, by evolving such good defences that the cuckoo is forced to turn to new victims.

A Co-Evolutionary Sequence

Let's consider the battle at the egg stage. The cuckoo's egg can either have no mimicry of the host eggs or it can be mimetic. The hosts can either accept or reject. The evidence from the previous chapters suggests the following evolutionary sequence:[3]

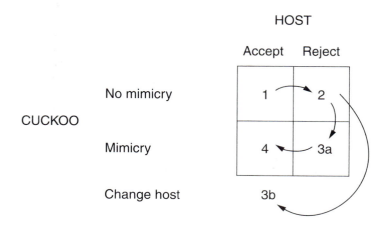

Stage 1

Initially, before it becomes a victim of the cuckoo, the host shows no rejection of eggs unlike its own. The evidence for this is that species unsuitable as hosts, and so untainted by an arms race with cuckoos, show little or no rejection (chapter 4). Either they never learn what their own eggs look like or, if they do, they nevertheless decide to accept odd-looking eggs in their nests. The starting point of the arms race is therefore no host rejection and no cuckoo egg mimicry (the top left-hand box).

Stage 2

In response to parasitism, hosts then evolve rejection of non-mimetic eggs, so we move to the top right-hand box. This involves learning their own eggs and then rejecting eggs that look different. The evidence for this stage is that most species that are suitable as hosts show at least some, often strong, rejection of odd-looking eggs. In theory, the time taken for hosts to evolve rejection will depend on the frequency of parasitism. With parasitism rates of 20% or more, rejection will spread rapidly through the host population by natural selection, so that after a few hundred generations most of the hosts will be 'rejectors'. However, if parasitism is just 2–5%, a typical average for the main hosts of the Common Cuckoo in Britain, then rejection could take many hundred, perhaps several thousand, generations to evolve. The reason is that most hosts never encounter cuckoos, so 'rejectors' have only a small selective advantage compared with 'acceptors'.

Stage 3

Once hosts begin to reject eggs unlike their own, the cuckoo has two possible courses of action. First, it could turn to a new host, one that does not reject. Second, it could persist with the same host, in which case natural selection will start to favour those cuckoos that lay mimetic eggs, ones more likely to escape host detection. So we now move to the bottom right-hand box in the diagram above.

Of course, our diagram is too simple; hosts will not suddenly evolve from a state of 'accept all foreign eggs' to 'reject them all'. Their rejection is expected to improve gradually, perhaps as they get better at learning their own eggs, or as they evolve better egg signatures which permit discrimination with fewer recognition errors. Similarly, cuckoos won't suddenly go from 'no mimicry' to 'mimicry'; their match of the host eggs will improve gradually as hosts improve their rejection. The evidence that perfection of cuckoo egg mimicry goes hand in hand with the intensity of host discrimination comes from comparing the various gentes of the Common Cuckoo in Europe (chapter 4; **Plate 2c**). Where hosts show no rejection, the Cuckoo has no mimicry (Dunnock-Cuckoos). Where hosts show moderate rejection of eggs unlike their own, the Cuckoo exhibits moderate mimicry (Robin-Cuckoos). Where hosts show strong rejection, mimicry is best of all (Reed Warbler-Cuckoos and Great Reed Warbler-Cuckoos).

In theory, there will be three stages in this co-evolution of host rejection and cuckoo egg mimicry. At first, most hosts will be 'acceptors', because the rejection habit will increase slowly in the host population. Likewise, the improvement in egg mimicry among cuckoos, from generation to generation, will also be very slow. Mimetic cuckoo eggs will gain an advantage only on the rare occasions that they encounter rejecting hosts. As host rejection increases, however, the evolution of cuckoo egg mimicry speeds up. We now enter a stage where it increases much more rapidly than the increase in the rejection habit in the host population. The reason for this is as follows. Imagine that 50% of the hosts are rejecting eggs unlike their own. Cuckoos that lay mimetic eggs will enjoy a huge advantage over those that lay non-mimetic eggs, so egg mimicry increases rapidly in the cuckoo population from generation to generation. But at this point, still only 5% or so of the hosts are encountering cuckoos. Thus at 95% of nests, acceptor hosts do just as well as the rejectors, so the rejection habit continues to increase more slowly in the host population. Richard Dawkins has called this the 'rare enemy effect'.[4] It provides a general reason for expecting the cuckoo to be one step ahead in the arms race. The reason is that whereas every cuckoo encounters a host, not every host encounters a cuckoo. This means that there will be stronger selection pressure for improvements in the cuckoo than for improvements in the host.

In the final stage of the co-evolution of host rejection and cuckoo egg mimicry, there is an unexpected and subtle twist. In theory, as mimetic eggs become more and more common, the increase in host rejection slows down and may even come to a halt.[5] This arises because rejector hosts that encounter mimetic eggs will not detect that they have been parasitized, so they will do no better than acceptors. Therefore as more and more of the cuckoo eggs become mimetic, rejector hosts begin to lose their advantage compared with acceptors. The result, at least according to theoretical models, is that the cuckoos will eventually all lay mimetic eggs but only a proportion of the host population will reject non-mimetic eggs.

Stage 4

Finally, once the cuckoo has evolved mimetic eggs, it may pay the hosts to accept them, provided there are sufficient costs of rejection and parasitism rates are not too high. The result is a stable end to the arms race in the bottom left-hand box of our diagram.[6] The Reed Warblers on Wicken Fen, and many other hosts, seem to be at this stage. The mimicry is sufficiently good that most cuckoo eggs are accepted, unless the hosts have additional information to alert them to parasitism, for example from the sight of a cuckoo at their nest (chapter 5).

If a host becomes freed from parasitism, either because its cuckoo gens has become extinct or has changed to exploit other victims, then it may revert to being an acceptor of eggs unlike its own. The speed with which it evolves back to its ancestral acceptor state will depend on the costs of rejection behaviour. If rejection is very costly, for example the host throws out many of its own eggs from its unparasitized nests, then reversion to acceptance may be fast. As a result there will always be a pool of acceptor species available for subsequent re-cycling through the co-evolutionary sequence.[7] On the other hand, if rejection had little cost then old hosts might remain as strong rejectors for a long time, perhaps never losing their 'ghost of adaptation past', just like our own retention of an appendix or wisdom teeth.

If old hosts retain rejection behaviour, then it will be harder for cuckoos to exploit them the second time round. In this case, the option of changing to a new host every time the current host evolves rejection will become unviable. Once all suitable hosts have evolved rejection of eggs unlike their own, then the only possibility for the cuckoo is to evolve better mimicry of one host's eggs. The result will be several gentes of specialist cuckoos or cuckoo speciation (see below).

Stable Resolutions or a Continuing Arms Race?

Current cuckoo-host systems seem to lie at all four stages of this proposed evolutionary sequence. Some examples are summarized below:

		HOST	
		Accept	Reject
CUCKOO	No mimicry	Common Cuckoo : Dunnock (Ch. 4) Jacobin Cuckoo : Bulbul (Ch. 8) Red-chested Cuckoo : Cape Robin	Common Cuckoo : Azure-winged Magpie (Ch. 3)
	Mimicry	Common Cuckoo : Reed Warbler (Ch. 4) Diederik Cuckoo : weaverbirds (Ch. 7)	Great Spotted Cuckoo : Magpie (Ch. 8)

How do we explain this variation? One possibility is that the bottom left-hand box is not the only stable conclusion. Perhaps the arms race can come to a halt in the other boxes too, depending on the costs and benefits involved for particular cuckoos and hosts.[3,8] This is the 'evolutionary equilibrium' theory. For example, the top left-hand box could be an equilibrium. Perhaps rejection is peculiarly costly for the Dunnock, so that at the current low level of parasitism in Britain, just 2% of nests parasitized, it is better for them to accept foreign eggs.

At first sight this seems unlikely. There is nothing obviously odd about Dunnocks which would preclude rejection. They have just as large bills as other rejector hosts and so should be able to eject a cuckoo egg. They do not nest in unusually dark places where detection of a foreign egg would be difficult; Robins' nests are equally dark and they reject. Finally, other hosts with blue eggs (Redstarts) have evolved rejection. Furthermore, Dunnocks suffer similar rates of parasitism in Britain to Meadow Pipits (3%) and a much higher rate than Pied Wagtails (0.5%), both strong rejectors.

However Fugo Takasu, from Nara Women's University in Japan, points out that these data on current parasitism rates may not be a fair comparison.[6] It is possible that the rejection behaviour of the pipits and wagtails evolved under higher parasitism levels in the past. Perhaps, as they evolved rejection, this drove down the population sizes of their Cuckoo gentes, resulting in the low present parasitism rates. The Dunnock parasitism rate, by contrast, may have always been at the low current level and this may be below the threshold at which rejection would pay, because of its costs (chapter 5). According to this view, acceptance by Dunnocks could be a stable situation. If we came back in a few thousand generations, they would still accept non-mimetic Cuckoo eggs.

Bulbul hosts of the Jacobin Cuckoo in southern Africa also accept a non-mimetic cuckoo egg. This, too, could be a stable end to the arms race if, as we suggested in chapter 8, the Cuckoo's white egg is a 'super-normal' stimulus, or if the Jacobin Cuckoo adopts Mafia tactics and forces the hosts to accept.

Evolution could also reach an equilibrium in either of the two right-hand boxes. In Japan, the eggs of the Common Cuckoo gens that parasitizes Azure-winged Magpies look nothing like the host eggs.[9] The Cuckoo's eggs are smaller and they have brown scribbles rather than greenish spots. Although it may be possible to improve the colour mimicry, it may be impossible to evolve a much larger egg within one gens, so if the hosts discriminate against smaller eggs the Cuckoo may simply have to tolerate a high rejection rate.

In Spain, the egg mimicry by Great Spotted Cuckoos for their Magpie hosts is better in both colour and size, but still there is plenty of host rejection. Perhaps the Cuckoo has to get by with the small proportion of the host population that it can terrorize through Mafia-like punishment? Alternatively, Manuel Soler and his colleagues suggest that there may be cyclic changes in parasitism rates and host rejection, as cuckoos move between host populations.[10] In this case, any 'equilibrium' will be a dynamic one, with each host population evolving stronger rejection as parasitism increases and then reduced defences as parasitism declines.

The alternative to the evolutionary equilibrium theory is that cuckoos and their hosts are still evolving. The variation in rejection and mimicry that we now see could be snap shots of the different stages of our proposed co-evolutionary cycle.[3] According to this view, hosts in the top left-hand box, like Dunnocks, are at the start of the arms race. They are relatively new victims of cuckoos and simply have not had time to evolve defences. In other words, they show 'evolutionary lag'. If we come back in a few thousand generations, they will have evolved rejection and their cuckoos will have evolved mimetic eggs.

Swynnerton (1918) was the first to propose that cuckoo-host interactions provide an opportunity to 'watch natural selection at work'. Both he and Stuart Baker (1923) suggested that the Dunnock is a recent host while the Redstart is a much older host, which has had time to evolve rejection and so select for a mimetic blue egg in its gens of Common Cuckoo. David Lack (1968) also favoured the idea of evolution still in action and wrote, 'the regular hosts of *Cuculus canorus* are perhaps continually changing, partly through changes in habitat, and partly through local extinction of a particular gens because the host species has temporarily evolved such good discrimination that a high proportion of cuckoos' eggs are rejected.'

Could Dunnocks be recent hosts of the Common Cuckoo in Britain? At first, it seems that references from old literature would argue against this view. As we saw in chapter 4, Gilbert White (1789) mentioned the Dunnock as a Cuckoo host. We can go back further, to Shakespeare's *King Lear*, written in about 1605. In Act I, Scene IV, the Fool warns Lear that his daughters will prove to be his ruin if he continues to dote on them, just as 'the Hedge Sparrow [= Dunnock] fed the Cuckoo so long that it had it head bit off by it young'. Shakespeare intended this metaphorically, but there is one curious account where this actually happened! The Cuckoo chick normally swallows with its bill closed only when the delivery of the meal from the foster parent is complete, so it avoids injuring the host, which bows deep into its gape. One exception to this usually smooth operation is described by Hens:[11] the Cuckoo nestling clamped its mouth shut on a hapless Dunnock, which suffered fatal injuries!

There is an even more ancient reference to Dunnocks and Cuckoos in Chaucer's poem *The Parlement of Foules* (1382), where the Merlin chastises the Cuckoo (line 612): 'Thow mordrer of the heysugge on the braunche that broghte thee forth!' Heysugge is Old English for Hedge Sparrow and probably refers to the bird we now call the Dunnock.

Even so, though the Dunnock has been a host for at least 600 years, it could still be a recent host on an evolutionary time scale. With just 2% parasitism, most Dunnocks never encounter Cuckoos, so their lack of discrimination will bring only a small selective disadvantage compared with hypothetical 'rejector' Dunnocks. Calculations suggest that discrimination would take several thousand generations to spread through the Dunnock population.[5] Most of Britain was covered in woodland until a few thousand years ago and the Dunnock is not common in this habitat. For example, in the primeval temperate forest of the Bialowieza National Park in eastern Poland, there are on average only five pairs per square kilometre, and in the New Forest, southern England, just 0.6 pairs per square kilometre. This is probably too low a density to make them profitable as hosts for the Cuckoo. On present-day farmland in Britain, by contrast, Dunnock density is 28 pairs per km². It is possible, therefore, that the Dunnock did not become a common victim of the Cuckoo until extensive forest clearance occurred 6500 to 2500 years ago, within the time which calculations suggest it would take rejection to evolve.

Both Stuart Baker (1942) and David Lack (1963) claimed that Dunnock-Cuckoo eggs in some collections had a blue-grey tint to the background and that selection was, therefore, already taking place. However Michael Brooke and I are not convinced by this and our results with the model eggs show no hint of Dunnock rejection.[12]

The idea that Dunnocks may be recent hosts seems plausible, but how could we test it critically? One possibility is to leave instructions for our descendants to repeat the model egg experiments a thousand years hence. But there is another method that enables us to look back in time. This involves a detailed analysis of the genetic differences between the Cuckoo gentes. Recall from chapter 3 that some of a bird's DNA gets passed on down the female line only, namely the DNA of their W chromosomes and their mitochondrial DNA. Over time, we would expect each gens to have 'clocked up', by mutations, increasing differences in this female-specific DNA because of its isolation from the other gentes. The degree of difference between two gentes could be used to measure the time for which they have been isolated. The greater the difference, the longer their separation must have been. So if the Dunnock gens of Cuckoo really is a newly formed gens, it should be less genetically distinct in its female-specific DNA than the other gentes, simply because it will have had less time to accumulate differences arising by mutation.

This prediction is now being tested. For the present, it is an unsolved mystery whether the Dunnock's acceptance of a non-mimetic Cuckoo egg reflects an equilibrium or evolutionary lag. The same alternatives apply to the Cape Robin in southern Africa, which is the main host of the Red-chested Cuckoo, with an average of 5% nests parasitized over the region as a whole, but with local rates of up to 22%.[13] Cape Robins lay variable eggs, ranging from cream or pink to greenish-blue in ground colour, usually speckled with brown. By sharp contrast, the Cuckoo's egg is uniform chocolate- or olive-brown. Michael Cherry, from the University of Stellenbosch, has shown that the Cuckoo's egg does in fact look a little like the host eggs in the ultra-violet part of the spectrum, invisible to humans, but even so the overall mimicry is very poor. Experiments with model eggs show that, like Dunnocks, Cape Robins will accept non-mimetic eggs.[14]

In this case there is a hint about the origin of the Cape Robin gens of Cuckoo, because the dark-brown Cuckoo egg is an excellent match for three other robins who are occasional hosts, the Heuglin's, Natal and Chorister Robins. Perhaps the Cape Robin gens is recently derived from Cuckoos that once specialized on these other hosts? This would explain very neatly why the Cuckoo's mimicry is so good for rare hosts and so poor for the favourite host. To explain this with the equilibrium theory we would have to imagine that rejection costs are very much higher for the Cape Robin than for the other robins.

How New Cuckoo Gentes Arise

It is easy to see how a new cuckoo gens might form. Although individual female cuckoos have favourite hosts, they occasionally parasitize another species if nests of the main host are in short supply. Edgar Chance's Meadow Pipit-Cuckoos sometimes laid in Skylark, Yellowhammer or Linnet nests if they failed to find a suitable pipit. From their study of host clutches in museum collections, Arne Moksnes and Eivin Røskaft estimated that in 5–10% of cases a Common Cuckoo egg was laid in the 'wrong' host's nest.[15] Hiroshi Nakamura's detailed radio-tracking in Japan revealed a similar level of 'mistakes', with 8% of eggs laid in the nests of alternative hosts.[16]

Some of these eggs will be doomed. For example, Linnets feed their young on a seed diet and never successfully raise a Cuckoo chick to fledging. Nevertheless, they are still often parasitized, probably by desperate Dunnock-Cuckoos who can't find a Dunnock nest at the right stage for parasitism. Other cuckoo eggs, no doubt, will be rejected because they are a poor match of the host eggs. Occasionally, however, some of the mistakes will produce a surviving offspring. If it is a female and imprints on the new host species, then this will be its chosen victim when it becomes an adult cuckoo and a new gens will be born.

Many of these new gentes will be short-lived. They may last for just one or two generations because the adult cuckoos die before they have produced sufficient female offspring to keep their line going. But sometimes the choice of the new host will spread. At first, cuckoos specializing on the new host may do even better than their relatives that stick to the old host. There will be less competition from other cuckoos for the new host's nests and the new host may also be less likely to reject cuckoo eggs, especially if it has not been exploited before. As the new gens increases in numbers and the host begins to reject, the stage is then set for the evolution of a different cuckoo egg type, one that matches the new host. Note that the behavioural specialization comes first, through imprinting, followed by the evolution of egg mimicry later on.

Richard Dawkins has pointed out that there may be multiple origins of cuckoo specializations on particular hosts.[17] For example, there may be several gentes of Reed Warbler-Cuckoos in Europe, which have built up their egg mimicry independently. There could be accurate egg mimics, descended from female Cuckoos that moved to Reed Warblers a long time ago, and less accurate mimics, descended from females that colonized Reed Warblers more recently. Furthermore, these various lines could have come from several previous gentes. Some may have been derived from Robin-Cuckoos that used a Reed Warbler as an alternative host, others may have come from Sedge Warbler-Cuckoos, and so on. This diversity of origins and ages of the female lines may explain why cuckoo eggs laid in the nests of each host species vary so much in their degree of egg mimicry. It may also complicate the analysis of differences between gentes in mitochondrial DNA.

Cuckoos are more likely to turn to alternative hosts, and so set new gentes in motion, when competition for the favourite host is more intense and when the habitat is more fragmented, so nests of the favourite host are harder to find. In vast marshes, for example, Great Reed Warbler-Cuckoos may be better able to specialize on their main host than where small reed beds are isolated in a landscape modified by Man. In fact, habitat fragmentation could either slow down or prevent the evolution of host egg mimicry altogether, simply because the gentes are not sufficiently isolated.[18]

In the Czech Republic, Ingar Øien, Arne Moksnes and Eivin Røskaft have radio-tracked female Common Cuckoos which parasitize four warbler hosts, all in the genus *Acrocephalus*, namely Great Reed Warbler, Reed Warbler, Marsh Warbler and Sedge Warbler. Although the four host species breed in slightly different habitats, these were mixed together in a patchwork, so all four species occurred in the same small area. The radio-tracking showed that each female Cuckoo favoured one of these hosts, so imprinting is likely to occur, but there were no differences in egg type between the four gentes. Perhaps habitat fragmentation and the high frequency of mistakes prevents precise egg mimicry from evolving.[19]

A NEW CUCKOO GENS IN JAPAN

The most convincing evidence that cuckoos change their use of hosts over time comes from Hiroshi Nakamura's studies of the Common Cuckoo in central Honshu, Japan.[20] Historical records suggest that 60 years ago the three most common gentes were those that specialized on Bull-headed Shrikes, Great Reed Warblers and Siberian Meadow Buntings. Nowadays, these first two hosts continue to be Cuckoo favourites, with 10–20% of their nests parasitized in many areas. However, although the Bunting is still abundant in the region, it has become a rare host, with less than 1% parasitism. Nakamura's experiments with model eggs show that it is the most discriminating of the three hosts, so although the Cuckoo egg is often a good match, copying the little brown scribbles on the host eggs, it is possible that this gens is being driven to extinction by host rejection.

In its place, a new gens is evolving, one that parasitizes the Azure-winged Magpie.

These Magpies have spread dramatically in recent years, particularly into areas of higher elevation, and have come more and more into contact with Cuckoos. The first record of parasitism in Japan was in 1956, followed by other single records in 1965 and 1971. Since then, the Magpie has rapidly become one of the main Cuckoo hosts in central Honshu. The increase in parasitism has been documented particularly well at Nobeyama Heights by S. Imanishi. Azure-winged Magpies first colonized this area in 1967. From 1981 to 1983, 30% of nests were parasitized (about 30 nests monitored each year). By 1988, when 49 nests were studied, parasitism had reached 80%, with many nests containing more than one Cuckoo egg. Similar rapid increases have been recorded elsewhere, with 30–60% of Magpie nests now parasitized in several areas.[21]

This remarkable spread of a new Cuckoo gens does not all originate from one female Cuckoo, because right from the start there was a lot of variation in the Cuckoo eggs in Magpie nests. Nakamura believes that many female Cuckoos simultaneously began to use Azure-winged Magpies as secondary hosts, as the Magpies spread into their range.[20] The Cuckoo eggs in Magpie nests are particularly variable and reflect multiple origins, some coming from Great Reed Warbler-Cuckoos and some from Bull-headed Shrike-Cuckoos. There are even some of the scribble-marked eggs typical of Siberian Meadow Bunting-Cuckoos. The rapid rise in Magpie parasitism might reflect its increased use as a secondary host by all three old gentes, as well as the spread of their female descendants which have presumably imprinted on the new host and use it as their favourite. Nakamura's radio-tracking has revealed that some female Cuckoos now specialize on the Azure-winged Magpie (chapter 3). As a result, the new host suffers much higher parasitism rates than the old hosts. In some areas, almost every Magpie nest is parasitized.

It seems unlikely that this situation can persist. Already Nakamura has found that some local Magpie populations have declined due to the heavy parasitism, and one has been wiped out altogether. But in other areas, the Magpies are fighting back. At Nobeyama Heights the new hosts lacked defences in the early years of parasitism but now they are beginning to reject Cuckoo eggs, either by ejection or by deserting the clutch, and they are also more likely to defend their nests against adult Cuckoos. One Magpie population at Azumino, which has been parasitized for 20 years, rejects Cuckoo eggs at 42% of the nests, while the Magpies near Nagano city, about 50 km away, which have been parasitized for 15 years, reject at 35% of nests.[20] This must be exerting strong selection for egg mimicry by the Cuckoo. It will be fascinating to see how quickly the new gens begins to match the host eggs.

This increase in host rejection has been so fast that we might wonder whether it really reflects evolution, in the sense of genetic change, or whether Azure-winged Magpies were once hosts in the distant past and have retained some legacy of their old battle with the Cuckoo. Perhaps the increased frequency with which they now see Cuckoos at their nests has 'turned on' the defences that they evolved long ago.[20] Although there are no old records of parasitism in Japan, the Azure-winged Magpie is parasitized in China by another *Cuculus* cuckoo, the Indian Cuckoo, so it's perhaps unlikely that the Japanese host populations are completely naïve. Similar rapid changes in host defences occur in Britain, both between years and even within a season, and are likely to reflect individual flexibility in host behaviour (chapter 5). Of course, the changes that are taking place in the Japanese Magpies could reflect both genetic change and flexible behaviour. Individuals may already be equipped to show some defences and these could now be being refined by natural selection.

A NATURAL EXPERIMENT IN THE WEST INDIES

How could we test the idea that a cuckoo host would lose its defences if it was no longer parasitized? The perfect experiment might involve taking some individuals of a favourite host and releasing them on an island where there are no brood parasites. We would need an island to be sure that the hosts did not disperse, so we could easily follow their descendants over time. We could then test their responses to eggs unlike their own, to see whether rejection rates declined over successive generations. After a while, perhaps we could introduce a brood parasite to see whether the host then re-gained its defences, as might now be happening with the Japanese magpies.

Amazingly, this exact experiment has already been done, though it started in shameful circumstances. During the eighteenth century, the Atlantic slave trade reached its peak with ships making regular trips from West Africa to the West Indies, ferrying cargos of slaves to work in the sugar plantations. Some West African Spottedbacked Weaverbirds (= Village Weaverbirds) must have been on board too, probably taken as cage-bird pets. On the island of Hispaniola, the second largest in the West Indian island chain after Cuba, some of the weaverbirds escaped. They spread rapidly through the island and have now become an agricultural pest. As in their ancestral African home, they breed in colonies, with up to 150 nests per tree.

In Africa, Spottedbacked Weaverbirds are a favourite host of the Diederik Cuckoo and they are strong rejectors of eggs unlike their own (chapter 7). However, until recently, Hispaniola was free from brood parasites, so the island Weaverbirds had no parasitism from another species for about two hundred years. Did their rejection frequency decline during this time? In the period 1974–1982, Alexander Cruz and James Wiley, from the University of Colorado, studied their responses to foreign eggs. As with the African population, eggs were very variable between individual females, differing in background colour and spotting pattern (**Plate 3b**), so it was easy to find non-mimetic eggs for the experiments from other nests within the colony. The results showed that non-mimetic eggs were rejected at only 14% of nests, well below the rate of 50–93% found by Victoria in experiments with captive birds recently bred from the African stock (chapter 5). Cruz and Wiley concluded that rejection had indeed declined, but the island birds still retained some discrimination from their ancestors' arms race with the cuckoo.[22] A complication is that Spottedbacked Weaverbirds suffer brood parasitism from their own species too (chapter 14). It is not known whether the Hispaniolan weavers have similar rates of con-specific parasitism to those in Africa. Some rejection may be maintained as a defence to this other source of foreign eggs.

The second part of this experiment occurred naturally. During the last hundred years, the Shiny Cowbird has spread north from South America through most of the islands in the West Indies (page 184). It was first seen in Hispaniola in 1972 and by the 1980s it was well established. Shiny Cowbirds parasitize a wide range of host species (chapter 12) and so the Spottedbacked Weaverbirds soon became parasitized once more. In 1974–1977, Cruz and Wiley reported parasitism rates of just 1%, but by 1982 this had risen to 16%. Shiny Cowbird eggs are similar in size to those of the Weaverbirds, but they are white with red-brown speckles, and clearly different from the Weaverbirds' eggs, which are light to dark blue in background colour, either plain or with spots. Unlike the Diederik Cuckoo, the Cowbird chick does not evict the host young, but it usually outcompetes them so that the Weaverbirds raise only half as many of their own young as in unparasitized nests. Therefore, under selection from this new brood parasite, we would expect the Weaverbirds to increase their defences again.

Diederik Cuckoo

Spottedbacked Weaver

Shiny Cowbird

The egg rejection behaviour of Spottedbacked Weavers (left) declined when they were introduced to Hispaniola in the eighteenth century, and became isolated from the Diederik Cuckoo (top right), their parasite back in Africa. When Shiny Cowbirds (bottom right) invaded Hispaniola in 1972, these weavers became parasitized once more and their egg rejection increased.

In 1998, Magali Robert and Gabriele Sorci, from the Université Pierre et Marie Curie in Paris, visited Hispaniola to test the Weaverbirds' responses again. This time they found much higher rejection rates of non-mimetic eggs, namely at 68–89% of nests, depending on the exact type of egg used in the experiment.[23] These rejection rates are now back at the levels shown by the African ancestral population, so within just 26 years of the Shiny Cowbird's arrival the Weaverbirds have regained their former defences.

Once again, we are faced with the question of how this rapid re-armament occurred. Is it because natural selection has caused genetic change in the Weaverbird population, favouring 'rejectors' over 'acceptors'? Or have most hosts retained their ability to reject all along, and this is now switched on again by the frequent sight of parasites at the nest? As with most hosts, parasitism on Hispaniola is likely to vary between Weaverbird colonies. It would be interesting to see if defence levels vary with parasitism rate. Given the ease with which these Weaverbirds can be bred in captivity, it might also be possible to study the heritability from parent to offspring of rejection responses. This would help determine whether the rapid changes in the wild are likely to involve a genetic component.

OLD HOSTS IN EUROPE?

Let's draw up a list of what makes a species a good host for a cuckoo. It must have the following main features:

- *An accessible nest.* This means either an open cup, or a hole big enough for the laying female to enter. Dropping her egg through a tiny hole with rigid sides (e.g. a tree hole) is no good because the fully grown cuckoo chick will not be able to get out. Inserting an egg through the small entrance of a domed nest might work, provided the chick can burst the lid off the nest as it grows, which happens with some Common Cuckoo chicks reared in Wren nests.
- *A suitable size for efficient incubation.* The smallest regular hosts of the Common Cuckoo are *Phylloscopus* warblers, such as the Chiffchaff, whose eggs are 35% the volume of the Cuckoo's egg. The smallest hosts of Australian cuckoos have egg volumes 38% of that of their cuckoo.[24] These figures might reflect a lower limit to host size because too large a cuckoo egg may receive inadequate incubation from a very small host. So the Goldcrest would be excluded as a Common Cuckoo host, though its nest is so small that it would not be able to accommodate the enormous chick anyway. There may also be an upper limit to host size because too small a cuckoo egg may receive too little contact with the host's brood patch if it is hidden among much larger host eggs. Nevertheless, several cuckoos parasitize hosts larger than themselves. In Europe, the Great Spotted Cuckoo's egg is only 46% the volume of a Carrion Crow egg, yet it has just as high hatching success as in Magpie nests, where the cuckoo egg is similar in size to the host egg.[25] In Australia too, the Pallid Cuckoo's egg is only 46% of the volume of its largest host, the Red Wattlebird.[24] This figure could reflect an upper limit to host size for each parasite.
- *A suitable chick diet.* This usually means invertebrates; there are no regular hosts of the Common Cuckoo, nor of any Australian cuckoos, that raise their young primarily on seeds. However, there are exceptions, such as the Diederik Cuckoo raised by Red Bishops (chapter 7).
- *Host chicks which the cuckoo can outcompete.* Cuckoo chicks will find it harder to eject the eggs of larger hosts, and from deeper nests. Nevertheless, Common Cuckoo chicks can eject the large eggs of Azure-winged Magpies, even though the Cuckoo

chick hatches from an egg that is only 60% the volume of the host eggs and the nest cup is 8 cm deep. The Common Cuckoo also occasionally parasitizes Blackbirds, where the Cuckoo's egg is only 47% the volume of the host eggs, yet the Cuckoo chick again is able to eject the host eggs from a nest cup 7 cm in depth. All hosts smaller than the Blackbird should, in principle, be suitable for this cuckoo species. If ejection is impossible, then the cuckoo chick can outcompete the host chicks, as Great Spotted Cuckoos do in crow nests. By hatching early and growing fast the cuckoo can survive well even when the host chicks are potentially over three times their weight.

- *An abundance of nests to parasitize.* Individual female cuckoos are specialists, so their favourite hosts must be reasonably common. They must also have a laying season that spans the period when cuckoos are able to breed. Among European species that might serve as Common Cuckoo hosts, this excludes perhaps only the Crossbill, which breeds at the end of the winter before there are any caterpillars available for the adult cuckoos. But the Crossbill is excluded as a host anyway, because of its seed diet. Many other potential hosts complete their first clutches before the Cuckoo arrives, but still have later clutches available for parasitism.

The current main hosts of the Common Cuckoo (chapter 3) fulfil these five criteria very well. In Britain, for example, the three favourite hosts are among the commonest species in their respective habitats: Reed Warblers in marshland, Meadow Pipits in moorland and Dunnocks in farmland and scrub. However, there are many other suitable species that the Cuckoo does not use. In marshland, Reed Buntings are often common. In the birch and conifer scrub on the edge of moorland, the most abundant birds are Willow Warblers and Chaffinches. In farmland and scrub, Blackbirds are usually more abundant than Dunnocks. Why are there not Cuckoo gentes exploiting these and other such potential hosts?

One possibility is that these were old favourites of the cuckoo in the past, but they evolved such strong rejection that their gentes became rare or extinct. Michael Brooke and I tested the rejection responses of these 'suitable but rarely used' host species in Britain,[12] and Arne Moksnes and Eivin Røskaft and their colleagues did so in Norway.[26] The experiments involved 'parasitizing' nests with model Cuckoo eggs that were unlike the host eggs. There are two problems with comparing the strength of rejection between different species. First, host populations vary their rejection in relation to parasitism frequency (chapter 5), so an average score of '% nests where model egg was rejected' will conceal interesting variation within each species. Second, different host species have different coloured eggs and we used a range of model eggs unlike the host eggs. This means that the term 'non-mimetic' is not quantified or standardized.

Nevertheless, despite these two caveats, there was good agreement between the '% rejection' scores of those species studied both in Britain and Norway.[27] The graph on the next page summarizes the results and presents, for each species, the average of the % rejection scores in the two countries. Among the suitable hosts, the current favourite species are starred. The lower graph refers to unsuitable host species, namely seed-eaters, hole-nesters and those that regurgitate food to their chicks (chapter 4).

The results show that many of these rarely used suitable hosts are just as strong

Suitable hosts (N=24)

			Reed Warbler*	Blackbird	
			Chaffinch	Pied Wagtail*	
Wren*			Icterine Warbler	Great Reed Warbler*	
Dunnock*			Spotted Flycatcher	Brambling*	
Fieldfare	Redstart*		Song Thrush	Willow Warbler	
Sedge Warbler*	Meadow Pipit*		Blackcap	Reed Bunting	
Robin*	Redwing	Bluethroat	Yellow Wagtail	Chiffchaff	
				Yellowhammer	
0	20	40	60	80	100

Unsuitable hosts (N=12)

Redpoll					
Bullfinch					
Linnet					
Blue Tit					
Great Tit					
Pied Flycatcher					
Swift					
House Sparrow					
Wheatear	Greenfinch				
Swallow	Starling				
0	20	40	60	80	100

% nests non-mimetic eggs rejected

rejectors, if not more so, than the current favourite hosts.[28] For example, in marshland Reed Buntings rejected a greater percentage of non-mimetic eggs than did the main host, the Reed Warbler. In woodland scrub, Willow Warblers and Chaffinches were stronger rejectors than the main host on adjacent moorland, the Meadow Pipit. In farmland, Blackbirds, Yellowhammers and Blackcaps were stronger rejectors than the two main hosts, Dunnocks and Robins.

How did these rarely used hosts evolve their strong rejection? Given that unsuitable species, those untainted by cuckoos, are acceptors (chapter 4), the inescapable conclusion is that they did so in response to cuckoos. It seems likely that in the past they suffered higher parasitism and the strong defences they evolved drove their Cuckoo gentes to extinction. What will happen in the future? One possibility is that the current favourite hosts will eventually evolve stronger rejection so that today's gentes, in turn, will decline in abundance. The Cuckoo may then re-cycle through the old hosts if they have meanwhile lost their strong defences. Alternatively, the present situation may represent an equilibrium.[8] Perhaps the current hosts have higher costs of rejection that preclude them from evolving better defences?

A HOST THAT HAS BEATEN THE CUCKOO

Karen Marchetti, from the University of California at San Diego, has discovered a host that has apparently beaten the cuckoo.[29] In the foothills of the Himalayas, north India, the Lesser Cuckoo parasitizes Tickell's Leaf Warbler but not Hume's Yellow-browed Leaf Warbler. These are two *Phylloscopus* warblers of similar size and appearance, both have domed nests made of grass and moss and both lay white eggs speckled with reddish-brown. Why should the Cuckoo parasitize one but not the other?

Although the Lesser Cuckoo's egg is similar in appearance to the eggs of these two warblers, it is nearly three times the volume of a warbler egg. Marchetti tested the response of both warblers to artificial cuckoo-sized eggs, made from plasticine and painted white. The Tickell's Leaf Warbler accepted them, but the Hume's Warbler rejected them all, pecking a hole in the plasticine and throwing the egg out of the nest. Hume's Warblers accepted con-specific eggs and plasticine eggs the same size as their own, so their rejection response seemed to be triggered by the large size of the model cuckoo egg.

In further experiments, Marchetti showed that rejection was not a response to absolute size, but rather to an egg that was much larger than the others in the clutch. For example, Hume's Warblers accepted a whole clutch of large artificial eggs, and continued to incubate if these were suddenly swapped for their own natural clutch. But if they were then given a single large artificial egg, they immediately rejected it. Similarly, if they were given a whole clutch of artificial eggs smaller than their own (each egg 30% smaller by volume), they accepted them. But if one of their own eggs was then added to the clutch, it was rejected.[29]

The Hume's Warbler seems to have evolved a perfect defence. It seems unlikely that the Lesser Cuckoo, 50 g in weight, will ever be able to match the egg size of a tiny 6 g warbler. Yet unless the cuckoo can evolve a smaller egg, it will never be able to use this species as a host. Perhaps the warbler uses size as a cue, rather than colour and appearance, because the domed nest is rather dark inside. However, there are costs to defences based on size, just as with those based on colour and spotting pattern (chapter 5). Marchetti found that Hume's Warblers sometimes rejected one of their own eggs rather than an artificial egg, especially when the artificial egg was more similar in size to their own. Furthermore, individuals that had more variation in size within their own clutch were more prone to make recognition errors. Even in nests where no experiments were performed, the warblers rejected one of their own eggs in 5% of the cases.

Why does the Tickell's Leaf Warbler lack defences? Marchetti's measurements show that it has more variability in egg size within a clutch than does the Hume's Warbler.[29] This means that it would be more likely to make recognition errors, so acceptance may be the best option provided parasitism rates are not too high. Perhaps, in time, this host will evolve lower egg size variation which will permit discrimination based on size to evolve. The other possibility is that variation in egg size is such an advantage to Tickell's Leaf Warbler, that things will remain pretty much as they are now. We can only speculate on what that advantage may be. One idea is that more variable egg sizes within a clutch leads to greater variation in chick size. A size hierarchy in the brood may be advantageous for parents if food becomes short, because the smallest chicks will die more quickly, and so reduce the brood to a number the parents can raise. With no clear hierarchy, the parents may end up with a whole brood of weedy chicks, none of which survive. If Tickell's Leaf Warbler faces more unpredictable food supplies than the Hume's Warbler, it may pay to keep its variable-sized eggs and pay the price of occasional cuckoo parasitism as a consequence.

EGG REPLACEMENT BY COMPETING CUCKOOS

So far, we have imagined that the only selection pressure leading to cuckoo egg type is host rejection. But competition among cuckoos, in the complete absence of any host defences, could also lead to evolutionary change in cuckoo eggs, provided cuckoos are selective in their egg removal prior to laying (chapter 4). In the same way, competition among predators for limited prey can lead to changes in predator lineages even in the absence of any evolutionary response by prey.

The evidence that cuckoos are selective when they remove an egg is equivocal (chapter 4), and *Clamator* cuckoos do not remove an egg before they lay (chapter 8). Nevertheless, cuckoo egg replacement may be an important selection pressure in some cases. In particular, the Australian hosts studied by Michael and Lesley Brooker showed no rejection of odd eggs, yet their cuckoos lay mimetic or cryptic eggs, which are likely to be good defences against removal by other cuckoos. The Brookers have shown that it may be less costly for some Australian hosts to accept cuckoo eggs, because of their long breeding seasons (chapter 7). So it is possible that cuckoo egg replacement was the more powerful selection pressure here, driving the evolution of egg mimicry or egg crypsis before the hosts had time to evolve defences.[30] Once the cuckoos had begun to evolve mimetic or cryptic eggs, selection for host rejection would become even less strong because of greater recognition costs. Thus, the system may have ended up in the bottom left hand box of our co-evolutionary cycle (mimetic egg – host accept) without the hosts ever going through a stage of evolving defences against non-mimetic eggs. When the fairy-wrens and thornbills are now given odd eggs by experiment, they are presented with a situation that their ancestors never had sufficient time to deal with, so they accept.

The Brookers favour cuckoo egg replacement as the major selective force for cuckoo egg mimicry in all cuckoo-host systems.[31] Although parasitism levels in the past could certainly have been much higher, and involved stronger competition among cuckoos for host nests, I believe that host discrimination is likely to have been the more important selection pressure. Among *Clamator* cuckoos, at least, cuckoo egg replacement cannot have been important. And the fact that egg mimicry in the gentes of Common Cuckoos reflects discrimination by their respective hosts also points to host defences as the key. Furthermore, we now have good evidence for rejection of non-mimetic eggs by cuckoo hosts on three continents (Africa, Europe and Asia), while the evidence for selective egg removal by cuckoos is, at best, weak. Nevertheless, cuckoo egg replacement needs more study. Given the low frequency of second cuckoos at a nest, an experimental approach might be best, in which all the hosts in a population are given model eggs to test whether cuckoos remove odd or conspicuous eggs before laying their own.

COMPETITION AMONG CUCKOOS AND CUCKOO SPECIATION

Over most of its wide range through Europe and Asia, the Common Cuckoo is the only parasitic bird. Although individual females are host-specific, the species as a whole parasitizes many hosts, varying in size from tiny warblers to large shrikes and the Azure-winged Magpie. By contrast, where several cuckoo species coexist, each tends to parasitize just one or a few host species. Here are three examples.

In Australia, a survey by Michael and Lesley Brooker reveals that the nine most common cuckoo species each target different main hosts, as follows:[32]

- Channel-billed Cuckoo (610 g): crows and currawongs.
- Australian Koel (225 g): Magpie-lark, Figbird, friarbirds.
- Pallid Cuckoo (83 g): honeyeaters with open cup nests.
- Fan-tailed cuckoo (46 g): White-browed Scrubwren, Brown Thornbill, Inland Thornbill, Origma.
- Brush Cuckoo (36g)
    North Australian subspecies: honeyeaters with enclosed nests.
    South Australian subspecies: fantails and robins.
- Black-eared Cuckoo (29 g): Speckled Warbler, Redthroat.
- Horsfield's Bronze-Cuckoo (23 g): fairy-wrens (thornbills).
- Shining Bronze-Cuckoo (23 g): Yellow-rumped Thornbill, Brown Thornbill.
- Little Bronze-Cuckoo (17 g): Gerygones.

In southern Africa, M.K. Rowan has shown that each of the nine cuckoos whose hosts are well known again favour different host species.[13]

- Levaillant's Cuckoo (124 g): babblers.
- Great Spotted Cuckoo (124 g): crows, starlings.
- Thick-billed Cuckoo (115 g): helmet-shrikes.
- African Cuckoo (110 g): drongos.
- Black Cuckoo (85 g): bush-shrikes.
- Red-chested Cuckoo (75 g): robins, thrushes.
- Jacobin Cuckoo (72 g): Fiscal Shrike, bulbuls.
- Diederik Cuckoo (32 g): weaverbirds, bishops, sparrows.
- Klaas's Cuckoo (26 g): sunbirds, warblers, flycatchers, batises.

Of the 73 species recorded as cuckoo hosts in southern Africa, Rowan noted that 68 are exploited regularly by just one cuckoo species, while the other five are used by two cuckoos.

Finally, in Japan, Hiroyoshi Higuchi has shown that the four species of cuckoo on the island of Honshu also favour different main hosts:[33]

- Common Cuckoo (115 g): Great Reed Warbler, Bull-headed Shrike, Siberian Meadow Bunting, Azure-winged Magpie.
- Oriental Cuckoo (90 g): Crowned Willow Warbler.

Levaillant's Cuckoo

Arrow-marked
Babbler

Red-chested Cuckoo

Cape Robin

Klaas's Cuckoo

Greater Double-collared
Sunbird

♂

♀

- Hodgson's Hawk Cuckoo (83 g): Siberian Blue Robin, Blue and White Flycatcher, Siberian Bluechat, Narcissus Flycatcher.
- Lesser Cuckoo (52 g): Bush Warbler, Wren.

Why should different cuckoo species favour different hosts? Herbert Friedmann (1928) was the first to suggest that this was to avoid competition. David Lack (1968) spelt out exactly how this would work; 'If a cuckoo species is sufficiently common to exploit effectively the available hosts in its area, then one would expect the principle of competitive exclusion to hold, for the chance is negligible that two species would be equally well adapted to the same host species. Hence they will normally have different hosts.'

Imagine, for example, two cuckoo species, one large and one small. Initially they may overlap in their use of hosts. But it is easy to see that the larger cuckoo will be better at exploiting larger hosts. Not only would its chick be better able to evict the host eggs, it might also win any battle with the smaller cuckoo's chick for possession of a nest. Alternatively, the larger cuckoo adults may simply chase the smaller cuckoo species away from the host nests. On the other hand, the smaller species is likely to be better at exploiting smaller hosts. It will find it easier to gain access to their nests, especially if there is a small entrance. It will also be better able to match the size of the host egg, if hosts discriminate against large eggs. In time, as a result of competition, the large cuckoo will come to specialize on the large host and the small one on the small host. They might diverge in size as each becomes better adapted to its particular victim. Thus in southern Africa, for example, the two commonest Bronze-Cuckoos differ in size; the smaller Klaas's Cuckoo goes for smaller hosts, sunbirds and warblers, while the larger Diederik Cuckoo goes for weaverbirds.

How can we tell whether such competition really goes on in nature? There are three lines of evidence. First, although cuckoos living in the same area have different main hosts, they often overlap in secondary hosts. In Japan, for example, four host species are used as secondary hosts by three cuckoos while seven other host species are used by two cuckoos. So there is potential competition between the four cuckoo species there even today.[34]

Second, when competition is removed because a cuckoo species is absent from an area, another cuckoo may take over its hosts. The Lesser Cuckoo does not occur in central Hokkaido, the second largest island of Japan, lying just north of Honshu. In its absence, the Bush Warbler there is exploited by a gens of the Oriental Cuckoo which has evolved a mimetic brown egg. The egg is not such a good match as that of the Lesser Cuckoo for Bush Warblers on Honshu. Perhaps the Oriental Cuckoo gens is a recent one, derived from the gens which lays a whitish egg for the main host, the Crowned Willow Warbler.[35] Another example like this comes from two

---

Different cuckoo species (left) parasitize different hosts (right). Three cuckoos from South Africa. Top: The large Levaillant's Cuckoo parasitizes the Arrow-marked Babbler. Middle: The medium-sized Red-chested Cuckoo parasitizes robins, including the Cape Robin. Bottom: The small Klaas's Cuckoo parasitizes sunbirds, including the Greater Double-collared Sunbird.

islands in the Gulf of Guinea off West Africa. The only breeding cuckoo here is the African Emerald Cuckoo. In the absence of Diederik Cuckoos, it parasitizes a weaverbird, in addition to its normal sunbird and warbler hosts.[36]

Third, there is the opposite phenomenon – a cuckoo drops a large host from its repertoire in the presence of a larger cuckoo species. Over most of Asia, the Asian Koel parasitizes crows, which are larger than itself. In Australia, the very similar Australian Koel parasitizes smaller hosts, and avoids crows altogether, perhaps because they are exploited by the enormous Channel-billed Cuckoo. This has had a knock-on effect on host choice by Pallid Cuckoos. In western Australia, they parasitize large species of honeyeaters (averaging 60 g). In eastern Australia, where these are parasitized by the larger Australian Koel, the Pallid Cuckoo has turned to smaller honeyeaters (averaging just 19 g).[32] Similarly, in south Africa Jacobin Cuckoos avoid babblers, their normal hosts throughout the rest of Africa and India, perhaps because the babblers here are parasitized by the larger Levaillant's Cuckoo.

It may seem surprising at first that cuckoos should compete for hosts, given the low average parasitism rates, often 5% or less. However, as we have discovered in previous chapters, only a limited proportion of nests is available for parasitism, namely those nearer bushes or trees and those at a suitable stage for laying. Edgar Chance's experiments (chapter 3) show clearly that availability of host nests limits a female cuckoo's reproductive success; when he made more host nests available, the cuckoo laid more eggs. On a larger scale, there is also evidence that cuckoo abundance is linked to host availability. In South Africa, comparing *Chrysococcyx* cuckoos, the Diederik Cuckoo is more abundant than Klaas's Cuckoo, and the Diederik's hosts, weaverbirds, are commoner than the Klaas's hosts, sunbirds. Among the *Cuculus* cuckoos, the Red-chested Cuckoo, which uses many hosts, is more abundant than the Black and African Cuckoos, which are host specific. The Thick-billed Cuckoo, which is restricted to helmet-shrikes, is also rare. Among the *Clamator* cuckoos, the Jacobin and Great Spotted Cuckoos, which use several hosts each, are more common than the Levaillant's Cuckoo, which is restricted to babblers. Widening our comparison, the generalist cowbirds of America are far more abundant than any of the cuckoos of the Old World, all of which are more specialized in host use.

All this suggests that the abundance of a brood parasite can be limited by host availability, so there is likely to be competition for hosts whenever several parasites coexist. This competition has played an important role in the evolution of host specificity by cuckoos.

FROM CUCKOO GENTES TO CUCKOO SPECIES

Competition among cuckoos is not the only force leading to host specialization. Although the Common Cuckoo faces no competition from other brood parasites over most of its range, it still exploits only a small proportion of the available hosts. We have seen that many of the unused host species are stronger rejectors than the favourite hosts. This suggests that cuckoo specialization can also evolve as an outcome of a cuckoo-host arms race. In the early stages, a female cuckoo would do best by laying indiscriminately in any host nest she finds. As more and more hosts evolve discrimination against eggs unlike their own, it would pay the cuckoo to specialize on those hosts for which her egg is a good match. Imprinting would be favoured as a way of making sure that a cuckoo chose the 'right host', leading to the evolution of specialist gentes with mimetic eggs.

Could escalating host defences cause these cuckoo gentes to evolve into different cuckoo species? At present, the only difference between the gentes of Common Cuckoos seems to be their egg colour. If this difference can be determined entirely by the female's genes, perhaps on the W chromosome (chapter 3), then male cuckoos will be free to mate with any female cuckoo they encounter. From a male's point of view, the more females he mates with the greater his reproductive success, so the tendency of males to mate with females from several gentes prevents speciation.

In fact, it is precisely the promiscuous nature of males that is likely to have led to the evolution of female control of egg colour. To see this, imagine the arms race has reached the stage where hosts have begun to reject, so it now pays female cuckoos to lay mimetic eggs. Imagine that egg colour is affected by both male and female, because it is coded by genes on the autosomes (chromosomes common to both sexes). This is what happens in domestic chickens and Spottedbacked Weaverbirds, the two species where egg colour inheritance has been best studied. Given that male cuckoos will be keen to mate with every female cuckoo they encounter, it is hard to see how egg mimicry can get started. For example, if random mating doubled the number of females a male could inseminate, compared with selective mating, it would pay a male to mate randomly until this reduced the effectiveness of his daughter's egg mimicry by 50% or more. Any female that could gain control of egg colour through genes on the W chromosome, unique to females, would clearly gain an advantage. Her daughters could inherit a mimetic egg despite random male mating.

Female-specific gentes may be a stable end point of the arms race between the Common Cuckoo and its hosts. However, what if hosts evolved even better defences, so that they demanded more than just a mimetic egg? They could require chicks that matched the gape markings of their own chicks, like hosts of parasitic finches (chapter 13). Female control of mimicry, using the W chromosome, would be no good, because then only daughters would be mimetic. Or perhaps the hosts demand an egg that matches their own for size, as in the warblers studied by Karen Marchetti. This may require the cuckoo to evolve a smaller body size. Again, this is a fundamental change in body design that needs the contribution of both male and female genes. The result would be host specialization by both males and females, leading to cuckoo speciation. This is exactly what has happened in the African parasitic finches, where both males and females imprint on the hosts that rear them, with the result that the parasites have evolved into separate species, each specializing on just one host (chapter 13).

Our speculations here have left the evidence far behind. We still don't know for certain that only female Common Cuckoos imprint, nor do we know how Cuckoo egg colour is inherited. Only in the Japanese study do we know for sure that male Cuckoos mate with females from several gentes. Perhaps in other areas where Cuckoo egg mimicry is better, the Cuckoo needs to use genes on the autosomes to gain a perfect match. In this case males would have to restrict their matings to females raised by the same host. The 'Cuckoo' could therefore comprise a complex mixture of female gentes and different species.

A Continuing Arms Race or an Equilibrium?

The variation that we now see in the strength of host defences and the perfection of cuckoo egg mimicry is likely to reflect a mixture of systems at equilibrium and those at intermediate stages of a continuing arms race. It is clear both from mathematical models,[6] and from measurements of the costs and benefits of host defences, that the arms race can come to a halt at a point where the hosts accept most cuckoo eggs despite the fact that they are not a perfect match of their own eggs.[8] But equally clear is the fact that there are large changes going on in nature, both in parasitism rates and in host defences. This makes it unlikely that all systems will be at equilibrium. We shall encounter more examples of dynamic changes in parasite-host interactions in the cowbirds and parasitic finches.

Still unresolved is the question of whether current changes in host defences reflect evolution, involving genetic change, or simply change brought about by flexible individual behaviour. Perhaps one day we shall have the luck to watch natural selection cause evolutionary change, as in Darwin's finches and the migrating Blackcaps (chapter 1). To document this we shall need to determine the heritability of host rejection behaviour and cuckoo egg patterns, as well as measuring the costs and benefits involved.

CHAPTER 10

The Brown-headed Cowbird and its conquest of North America

The Brown-headed Cowbird is the only brood parasite that is widespread in North America. In the early days of European settlement they were largely restricted to the great grassy plains of the mid-continent, where they followed the vast herds of Buffalo (= American Bison). Cowbirds feed by walking on the ground to search for seeds and insects. Buffalos not only created the short-grass areas that were ideal for foraging, they also made foraging easier by flushing insects, especially grasshoppers and beetles which are among the Cowbird's favourite prey items.[1]

It is estimated that some sixty million Buffalo once roamed the North American plains and they, with their attendant Cowbirds, must have been a wonderful sight. Charles Murray[2] describes his travels in the prairies in the 1830s, and refers to the Cowbirds as 'the tamest of the bird creation that I have seen in any country. They repeatedly perched upon the back of the Buffalo, and of our horses ... the young Indian boys practise their early archery by shooting them at the distance of two or three yards.' In the early 1900s, another traveller, E.T. Seton,[2] comments on the remarkable close association between the Cowbirds and the Buffalo:

> In all this pastoral scene, there is a flock of small blackbirds, cowbirds or buffalo-birds they are called. They haunt the Buffalo ... sometimes on it, sometimes on the nearest land, but always moving when it moved, and recognising it as headquarters ... Sometimes the cowbirds walk sedately behind their grazing monster; sometimes they flit over snapping at flies; often they sit in a line along the ridge-pole of his spine. The attachment to the Buffalo was so close that an Indian myth tells of their nesting in the wool between the horns of the big bull – rather a fearsome homesite, one would think, during a combat of the bull with some huge rival.

The last five hundred years has witnessed a dramatic change to this scene. The European invasion of North America has driven both native Americans and Buffalo to near extinction as successive waves of hunters, herdsmen and farmers have swept west across the continent. These new settlers have changed the landscape through deforestation and the introduction of livestock and agriculture. As a result, the Cowbird has spread and increased in numbers. This has set in motion a vast and fascinating experiment in co-evolution. Fragmentation of the forests has exposed new species to parasitism, hosts which have apparently not had time to evolve defences. Many song birds now suffer such high rates of parasitism that there are claims that the Cowbird might drive them to extinction. Europeans returning from a day's bird watching will announce with delight that they have seen, or even just heard, a Cuckoo. Few North Americans would impress friends with a sighting of a Cowbird – they would be more likely to claim approval from the numbers they have shot! Within a couple of hundred years, the delightful buffalo-bird of the prairies has become the most unpopular bird in the country.

However, as we shall see, the Cowbird is not the arch villain responsible for the declines in song-bird populations. Habitat destruction by Man is the main cause, and the Cowbird has often been a convenient scapegoat. We shall begin by describing the Cowbird's dramatic spread. Then we'll discuss its parasitic behaviour, which provides a remarkable contrast to cuckoo-host interactions in the Old World. In the next chapter, we'll consider host defences against Cowbirds and the causes of today's conservation problems.

Brown-headed Cowbirds used to associate with the vast herds of Buffalo (American Bison) that roamed the great grassy plains of North America.

THE COWBIRD'S DRAMATIC SPREAD

The remarkable spread east from the Great Plains has been documented by Harold Mayfield.[3] It began in the mid to late 1700s as European settlers cut down the eastern forests for settlements, livestock and agriculture. Prior to this, there were probably few places east of the Mississippi River which provided extensive short grass areas suitable for Cowbirds, except perhaps a few clearings in the forests, so the Cowbird must have been scarcer there three hundred years ago. It did not appear in the tenth edition of Linnaeus's *Systema Naturae* (1758), though two other American blackbirds, the Red-winged Blackbird and Common Grackle, were included along with other conspicuous birds of the first settled areas in the East.

As herdsmen took their cattle, sheep and pigs westwards, they created corridors of short grassland through which Cowbirds could disperse from the Great Plains to the new agricultural land in the east. The increasing forest clearance had two effects. First, it provided Cowbirds with more open country in which they could feed. In the farmland pastures they began to associate with cattle, which took over the Buffalo's role in maintaining short swards and disturbing insects. Agricultural land also provided good foraging and the waste grain increased the Cowbird's winter food supply. Second, fragmentation of the forests exposed more forest song birds to 'edge' habitats where they came into contact with Cowbirds and so became parasitized.

The result was a dramatic spread in Cowbird range and an increase in abundance. By 1790 they became common at scattered sites throughout eastern North America, when the population of settlers was almost four million and some areas had been under cultivation for six generations. By the late 1800s Cowbirds were widespread in eastern North America, primarily in cultivated areas. Although the main destruction of the eastern forests came to an end in the nineteenth century, the Cowbird continued to extend its range elsewhere, as the number of cattle increased and as more short-grass areas became available. High reproductive success with naïve hosts is also likely to have increased population numbers, forcing Cowbirds to seek new areas. In Ontario, the Cowbird spread its breeding range northwards more than 300 km during the twentieth century. To the northeast, it colonized Nova Scotia in the 1930s and Newfoundland in the 1950s. In the southeast, it reached Georgia and Florida in the late 1950s and had spread as a breeder through Alabama by 1960.

We have more detailed information on the Brown-headed Cowbird's increase in the far west because it occurred more recently. It has been documented by Stephen Rothstein from the University of California, Santa Barbara.[4] Cowbirds must have long been present in some parts of southern and western North America because there has been sufficient time for two subspecies to evolve here which show minor differences in size and colour from the eastern subspecies *Molothrus ater ater*.[5] The larger 'Nevada Cowbird' *M. a. artemisiae* was present to the north, though it may not have colonized areas west of the Rocky Mountains until the last few hundred years. It has certainly increased in numbers since the late 1800s in the Great Basin and the Sierra Nevada, probably due to the spread of agriculture and cattle.

The smaller 'Dwarf Cowbird' *M. a. obscurus* occurred to the south, along the Colorado River and east through Arizona, probably to Texas. However, it began to

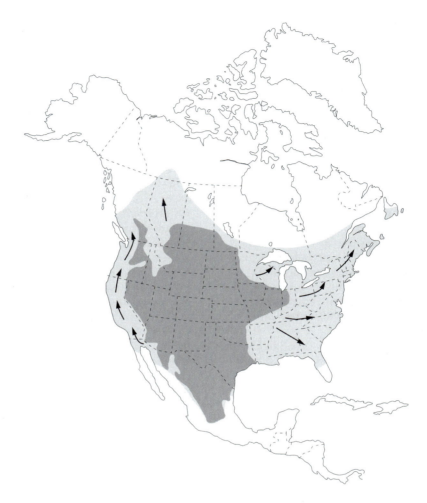

Figure 10.1 Today's breeding range of Brown-headed Cowbirds (light tint),[1] and their likely distribution immediately prior to European settlement (heavy tint).[3] Arrows indicate the expansion in the east[3] and the far west.[4] Cowbirds may have originally been present in some areas of the east, but in lower numbers than today.

move west into southern California around 1900. Since then it has spread 1600 km north along the Pacific coast and reached British Columbia by 1955. This recent invasion of the far west has been aided by increased agriculture and forest clearing, which has made more feeding habitat available for Cowbirds. An early field guide to the birds of California, written in 1904, commented: 'Californians are to be congratulated that as yet the Cowbird is only an irregular winter visitant to the south-eastern corner of their state.'[4] Now, less than a hundred years later, it has become one of the commonest birds here.

Although the Brown-headed Cowbird probably increased in abundance throughout North America during the first half of the twentieth century, breeding bird surveys suggest that overall numbers have remained stable, or have even declined a little, since the mid-1960s.[6] Nevertheless, it is now one of the most widespread of all North American birds and is recorded as a breeder in a greater proportion of censuses than any other species.[4]

HOSTS AND PARASITISM RATES

Much of our knowledge of the parasitic habits of Brown-headed Cowbirds stems from the pioneering work of Herbert Friedmann, who studied them for nearly 70 years. His book published in 1929 is still a wonderful source of information. By 1985, Friedmann and his co-workers had recorded parasitism of over 220 host species, of which 144 had successfully reared Cowbird young. The most frequent hosts are those that feed their nestlings on a diet of invertebrates, which the young Cowbird needs for normal growth. Victims range in size from 6 g gnatcatchers to 100 g meadowlarks. Some common hosts are of similar size to the Cowbird (40–50 g), but most are smaller. They include the majority of the North American song birds: flycatchers, Wood Thrush, Veery, gnatcatchers, vireos, wood warblers, meadowlarks, tanagers, blackbirds, orioles, Northern Cardinal, grosbeaks, buntings, Dickcissel, towhees and sparrows.[1]

Not only does the Brown-headed Cowbird parasitize far more host species than does any cuckoo, the parasitism rates are also extraordinarily high compared with cuckoos simply because the Cowbird is so numerous. In the heart of the historic range in central North America, still the area with greatest Cowbird abundance, many host species suffer parasitism at 20–80% of their nests.[7] For example, Spencer Sealy[8] from the University of Manitoba recorded 21% parasitism of 1885 Yellow Warbler nests studied in Delta Marsh from 1974 to 1987 and Phillip Elliott[9] from Kansas State University found 70% parasitism for three ground-nesting species studied in the Kansas prairies from 1974 to 1975, namely the Dickcissel, Grasshopper Sparrow and Eastern Meadowlark. Other examples for host populations in areas of high Cowbird abundance are 24% parasitism for the Eastern Phoebe, 76% for the Red-winged Blackbird, 52% for the Chipping Sparrow, 63% for the Song Sparrow and 69% for the Red-eyed Vireo.[7] Parasitism rates generally decline away from the central parts of North America. For example, in the eastern States typical rates for many hosts are 0 to 20%. In the west too, parasitism is often lower but there is substantial local variation. In Washington state, average parasitism of Red-winged Blackbirds is just 8%.

Parasitism rates are also high in the fragmented forest landscape of the Midwest, where the patchwork of habitats provides Cowbirds with an ideal mixture of places to feed (farmland, suburbia) and breed (grassland, scrub, forest). Scott Robinson from the Illinois Natural History Survey, together with colleagues, coordinated a study from 1989 to 1993, which involved more than one hundred field workers.[10] They monitored some five thousand nests in nine study plots throughout Illinois, Indiana, Minnesota, Missouri and Wisconsin. These plots varied from 90% agricultural land to 90% forested. The nine most common hosts were Wood

Thrush, Red-eyed Vireo, Ovenbird, Worm-eating Warbler, Kentucky Warbler, Scarlet Tanager, Northern Cardinal, Indigo Bunting and Acadian Flycatcher. All showed highest parasitism rates (55% or more) in the plots with the least % forest. For example, where forest patches were less than 200 ha and no more than small islands in a sea of farmland, 80–100% of Wood Thrush nests were parasitized, usually with several Cowbird eggs (**Plate 5c**). In some areas Wood Thrushes had twice as many Cowbird eggs in their nests as their own eggs! By contrast, in the most heavily forested landscapes parasitism was much lower, from 0 to 20%.

Why does parasitism increase with forest fragmentation? One of the first studies was in an area of extensive forest in Wisconsin, and it found that parasitism rates were much higher on the edges than in the middle of the forest.[11] Because smaller blocks of forest have a higher ratio of edge to interior, this may lead to increased parasitism as forests become more fragmented. However, it is now known that 'edge effects' vary between host species and they are not found in all landscapes. Even when they do occur, the reasons for increased parasitism may be complex.[12] Cowbirds may find it easier to observe hosts in edge habitats, or they may prefer edges because host densities are sometimes greater there. In addition, Cowbird numbers are likely to be higher where forests are fragmented because the intervening agricultural land provides more food. For example, a recent study in Illinois found that Kentucky Warblers suffered 60% parasitism in forest patches next to a Cowbird feeding site on agricultural land, but parasitism declined to 3% just 2 km away.[13]

Breeding Ranges and Social Systems

In the southern States, many Brown-headed Cowbirds are year-round residents but northern populations migrate south for the winter, down as far as Mexico. Winter roosts often number tens of thousands or even millions. They arrive on their breeding grounds in late March to early May, often in flocks in association with Red-winged Blackbirds and Common Grackles. Egg laying usually begins from April to May and ends by late July, at which time the Cowbirds begin to form flocks again and migrate south from northern areas. Just as with some hosts of the Common Cuckoo (chapter 3), early nesting species in some areas may be more likely to escape parasitism of their first clutches, which are laid before most Cowbirds arrive. For example, in Washington Brewer's Blackbird clutches begun before 9 May suffered just 7% parasitism compared with 50% for those that began later.[12]

Because Brown-headed Cowbirds do not care for their offspring, they are free to feed in areas well away from where they breed. Like Common Cuckoos (chapter 3), they often commute between nest-searching sites and distant feeding sites. Radio-tracking shows that the Cowbirds typically spend the mornings either alone or in pairs in host-rich habitats, such as forests, scrubland or grassland. Females lay before dawn and spend the rest of the morning searching for nests they can parasitize on subsequent days. In the afternoons they then visit prime feeding sites up to 7 km away where they often feed in flocks.[14] These include farmland and fields with livestock, where there is grain and insects, and also suburbs which provide short-grass areas plus food scraps from humans. In the Sierra Nevada of California, commuting to feed at just one horse corral could enable Cowbirds to parasitize hosts over an area of 154 km² that contained no other suitable feeding sites.[14] In more fragmented habitats Cowbirds can feed much closer to their breeding sites, just 1 km or less, and they may make more frequent journeys between the two each day.[15]

Studies of individually marked birds on the breeding areas show that the size and exclusiveness of a female's home range is likely to vary with both host density and Cowbird density. In the Sierra Nevada female morning ranges averaged 68 ha, far larger than the 1–3 ha typical of a normal 40 g bird that tends its own young.[14] These enormous ranges would clearly be impossible to defend and, not surprisingly, there was a great deal of overlap between females. All the copulations occurred in the morning on these breeding ranges, none at the communal feeding sites later in the day. Nevertheless, females were often seen alone in the morning and it might be supposed that the large distances over which they roamed would make it unlikely that they maintained permanent pair bonds. However most females chose to mate with just one male even though they were courted by several others, so monogamy appeared to be the main mating system.[16] Some pair bonds did not last the whole season – a female consorted first with one male and then he was replaced by another male.

In other studies females had much smaller breeding ranges. In a study in New York state, females defended exclusive breeding territories of 10–33 ha and males followed their females closely, chasing off rival males to maintain a monogamous pair bond.[17] The breeding system was therefore one in which a female defended a territory against other females while males engaged in mate defence. In studies in Ontario, females had 8–10 ha ranges but these overlapped substantially, perhaps because of greater Cowbird density. Again observations suggested that monogamy prevailed, with males following females to guard them, though a few males managed to guard two or even three females at a time.[18] Finally, in a study in the Kansas prairies there was a very high density of Cowbirds at the breeding site because the feeding areas, pastures with cattle, were where the hosts had their nests (ground-nesting Dickcissels, Eastern Meadowlarks and Grasshopper Sparrows). Here there were no long-term pair bonds, perhaps because the high density intensified competition for nests and mates, and both sexes mated with several partners.[19]

A recent study at Delta Marsh, Manitoba, by Gerald Alderson, Lisle Gibbs and Spencer Sealy, is the first to link observations on social behaviour of colour-ringed Brown-headed Cowbirds to actual parentage of offspring.[20] Analysis of DNA markers, from blood samples taken from the adults and nestlings, revealed that the egg laying areas of individual females rarely overlapped. All the eggs laid by a particular female were almost always fertilized by a single male. Likewise, most of the eggs fertilized by a single male were laid by one female. Therefore, monogamy was the predominant genetic mating system in this population.

In summary, Brown-headed Cowbirds behave remarkably like Common Cuckoos (chapter 3). Both species may commute long distances between feeding areas and breeding areas. In both females compete for host nests while males compete to mate with females. Finally, both show variation in ranging and mating systems depending on dispersion of host nests and the intensity of competition with conspecifics.

EGG LAYING

Like cuckoos, the Brown-headed Cowbird monitors host nests and selects her victim in advance of the laying visit. Females search alone for host nests in three ways.[21] Sometimes they sit quietly in shrubs or trees and watch for nest building. This is a good method in forests or edge habitats and probably explains why the nests of some host species are more likely to be parasitized if they are nearer suitable Cowbird look-out posts,[22] just as is found for Cuckoo hosts (chapter 4). In areas away from perches Cowbirds walk on the ground, watching out for breeding activities in other birds. Finally in dense vegetation they make short and noisy flights, landing on the leaves and flapping their wings to flush hosts from their nests.[21]

Most nests are parasitized during the host laying period. Nevertheless, Cowbirds often seem to get their timing wrong. In a remarkable study of Prairie Warblers,[23] one of the most detailed of any North American bird, Val Nolan Jr. of Indiana University found that of 121 Brown-headed Cowbird eggs, 30 were laid during nest building, 76 during warbler laying and 15 during incubation. Eggs laid during the host building stage often fail because they get buried in the nest lining, and those laid in late incubation fail to hatch. Why then should Cowbirds lay such a large proportion of their eggs at inappropriate times? It is tempting to suggest that Cowbird behaviour has not been so well refined by natural selection as that of the cuckoos. However, the greater numbers of Cowbirds means that there is more intense competition for host nests, so the Cowbird may simply be unable to afford to be too choosy. It would be interesting to discover whether a female lays more of her eggs at the best time (during host laying) when she has sole command of a greater number of host nests.

Like Common Cuckoos (chapter 3), female Brown-headed Cowbirds depredate host nests discovered at the late incubation or nestling stage to force the hosts to lay again, and so increase the number of suitable nests at their disposal. Some studies have caught the Cowbird red-handed (red-beaked would be a better description) as she pecked or threw the host chicks out of the nest, or pecked all the eggs. In a study of Song Sparrows on Mandarte Island, British Columbia, Peter Arcese, James Smith and Margret Hatch obtained circumstantial evidence that Cowbirds were the major nest predator.[24] Predation increased when Cowbirds were laying on the island and decreased when they left or were removed by experiment. Furthermore, parasitized nests suffered lower predation which is exactly what you would predict if Cowbirds remembered the sites they had already used and left these free from interference. Michael Brooke and I found the same result for Reed Warbler nests on Wicken Fen; those parasitized by Common Cuckoos were less likely to be depredated, implying that Cuckoos were up to the same trick.[25]

Recent studies have revealed that cowbirds have brain specializations that are likely to help them find host nests and to remember where they have laid. The area of the brain used to process spatial information is called the hippocampus. This is unusually large in those bird species that require special feats of memory, like food storers (which have to remember where they have hidden their food) or migrants (which have to find their way home). Compared with the non-parasitic Bay-winged Cowbird, parasitic cowbirds have an enlarged hippocampus.[26] Furthermore, the hippocampus is larger in female Brown-headed Cowbirds than in the males, just what you would expect from the fact that females do all the monitoring of host nests.[27] The same is true for Shiny Cowbirds, where females also search for host nests alone. However, in Screaming Cowbirds, where males and females search for nests together, there are no sex differences in hippocampus size.[26] It would be interesting to discover whether cuckoos have these brain specializations too.

Female Brown-headed Cowbirds lay at dawn, before the hosts lay their egg for the day. Here the Cowbird has disturbed a female Prairie Warbler, which had spent the night on her nest prior to laying the final egg of her clutch (drawing based on description by Val Nolan Jr[23]).

Whereas Common Cuckoos try to avoid attracting host attention by laying in the late afternoon (chapter 3), Brown-headed Cowbirds do so by a raid at dawn.[28] Most nests are parasitized during the hour before sunrise, well before the hosts arrive to lay their own eggs. Just like parasitic cuckoos, the Brown-headed Cowbird also lays very quickly, spending an average of 41 seconds on the host nest (range 4 to 119 seconds).[29] Diane Neudorf and Spencer Sealy observed laying on seven occasions during dawn watches of host nests from hides in Delta Marsh, Manitoba.[30] On all four occasions that they observed parasitism of Red-winged Blackbirds, the hosts were absent. In one case at a Northern Oriole nest, the host arrived just as the Cowbird was leaving and chased her. In two cases the host female was roosting on the nest because incubation had begun. In one, a Clay-coloured Sparrow chased the Cowbird off but she then returned within seconds and laid despite being attacked by both the female sparrow and her mate. In the second case the female Cowbird squeezed onto the nest while the host, a Northern Oriole, was still sitting. The Oriole pecked at the intruder and screamed continuously for the two minutes the Cowbird was on the nest, but the Cowbird still managed to lay. Clearly the Cowbird's strategy involves a mixture of stealth and brute force.

Female Brown-headed Cowbirds often remove a host egg from the nests they parasitize, but they don't always do so and, unlike Common Cuckoos, egg removal usually occurs during a separate visit before laying, perhaps the morning before.[8,31] Sometimes a host egg is removed after the laying visit. If this was by the laying female then she would risk removing her own egg, unless she could distinguish it from the host eggs. Perhaps these later removals are often the work of other females? As with cuckoo hosts, experiments show that egg removal does not affect acceptance of the Cowbird's egg.[8] Nor does this affect its incubation period or hatching success in the nests of small hosts (sparrows or warblers) or medium-sized hosts (Red-winged Blackbirds). However, with larger hosts egg removal may both decrease incubation time and increase the chance that the Cowbird egg hatches.[32] Some evidence suggests that Cowbirds are more likely to remove an egg when they parasitize larger hosts. For example, an egg is almost always removed when Red-winged Blackbirds are parasitized[33] but only in about a third of the cases that Yellow Warblers are parasitized.[8]

Therefore, as with Common Cuckoos (chapter 4), egg removal does not help to fool the hosts but rather increases the hatching success of the Cowbird's egg and, perhaps, provides the female with a free meal. However, Cowbirds eat only 60% of the eggs they remove – the rest are dropped to the ground. Again like cuckoo hosts, there is a limit to the number of eggs the Cowbird can remove because hosts desert if their clutch is reduced. Clay-coloured Sparrows were more likely to desert their clutch if Cowbirds removed two or more host eggs than if they removed just one or none at all.[34]

Brown-headed Cowbirds are prolific egg layers. They lay daily in sequences of one to seven eggs, with pauses of a few days between each sequence. A female has the potential to lay about 40 eggs during an eight-week breeding season.[35] Free from all parental duties, she could be up to five times more productive than a typical passerine that has to care for its own young, whose seasonal output may involve two clutches, each of about four eggs. One captive female Brown-headed Cowbird laid 77 eggs in one season, including 67 in a single sequence.[36] No wonder this parasite

Plate 1a Common Cuckoo laying in a Reed Warbler nest (Cambridgeshire, England). She first removes a host egg. Holding it in her bill, she then lays directly into the nest and leaves. All this takes just 10 seconds. (photo: © Ian Wyllie – OSF).

Plate 1b The Cuckoo egg (right) is a good match of the Reed Warbler eggs, but a little larger. (photo: © N. B. Davies).

Plate 1c The Cuckoo chick hatches first. Just a few hours old, and still naked and blind, it ejects the host eggs, one by one. (photo: © Ian Wyllie – OSF).

Plate 2a (*left*) A Reed Warbler feeding a nestling Common Cuckoo. (photo: © Mike Birkhead – OSF).

Plate 2b (*below*) A Reed Warbler feeding a fledgling Common Cuckoo. (photo: © Ian Wyllie – OSF).

Plate 2c (*left*) Left column: Eggs of some Common Cuckoo hosts in Europe. From top to bottom: Robin, Pied Wagtail, Dunnock, Reed Warbler, Meadow Pipit, Great Reed Warbler. Central column: An egg from each of these Common Cuckoo gentes, opposite its respective host egg. Right column: Model eggs painted to represent various Cuckoo gentes. (photo: © Michael Brooke; from Brooke & Davies 1988).

Plate 2d (*above*) A "Meadow Pipit-Cuckoo" model egg in a White Wagtail nest in Iceland. Icelandic Wagtails, isolated from Cuckoos, accept these models, but parasitised populations in Britain reject them. (photo: © N.B. Davies).

Plate 3a A male Diederik Cuckoo in Kruger National Park, South Africa. (photo: © Ian Wyllie – OSF).

Plate 3b (*right*) Variation in the eggs laid by different female Spottedbacked Weavers, a host of the Diederik Cuckoo. Each egg is from a different clutch from a colony in South Africa. (photo: © Anna Lindholm).

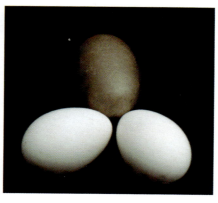

Plate 3c (*left*) Two Australian Bronze-Cuckoos. Left: The Horsfield's Bronze-Cuckoo egg (top) mimics the eggs of its host, the Splendid Fairy-wren. Right: The Shining Bronze-Cuckoo egg (top) is difficult to see in the dark nest of its host, the Yellow-rumped Thornbill, which lays white eggs. (photo: © Lesley and Michael Brooker).

Plate 4a Great Spotted Cuckoo (photo: © Fischer Berndt BIOS).

Plate 4b Magpie nest in Spain with three Great Spotted Cuckoo eggs (left) and three Magpie eggs (right). The top-most host egg has been damaged by the Cuckoo during laying. (photo: © Manuel Soler).

Plate 4c A Great Spotted Cuckoo chick (centre) with two Magpie chicks. The white papillae in the Cuckoo's mouth stimulate the host parents to feed it. (photo: © Manuel Soler).

Plate 5a A male Brown-headed Cowbird (photo: © R. & A. Simpson – Vireo).

Plate 5b A Western Meadowlark nest in Manitoba with two host eggs (bottom) and eight Brown-headed Cowbird eggs. The nest eventually fledged only five cowbird young. (photo: © Stephen K. Davis).

Plate 5c A Wood Thrush nest with three host eggs and two Brown-headed Cowbird eggs. (photo: © T. Fink and R. Day – Vireo).

Plate 6a (*above*) Male Shiny Cowbird in Argentina. (photo: © Bruce Lyon).

Plate 6b (*above*) Rufous-collared Sparrow, a common host of Shiny Cowbirds in South America. (photo: © Bruce Lyon).

Plate 6c (*left*) Rufous-collared Sparrow nest in Argentina with one host egg (centre) and five Shiny Cowbird eggs, two of the spotted morph and three of the plain white morph. (photo: © Bruce Lyon).

Plate 6d (*right*) Feathered Screaming Cowbird chicks (right) are excellent mimics of the Baywinged Cowbird host chicks (left) with which they are raised. The paint marks were added to remind the experimenter which was which! (photo: © Gabriela Lichtenstein).

Plate 7a Egg of a Greater Honeyguide (centre) in a clutch of Striped Kingfisher eggs, Kenya. (photo: © Heinz-Ulrich Reyer).

Plate 7b Boran honey-gatherer from Kenya, whistling with a hollow palm nut to attract a Greater Honeyguide. The bird will lead him to a bees' nest. (photo: © Hussein A. Isack).

Plate 7c Egg of a Village Indigobird (centre, bottom row) in the nest of its host, the Red-billed Firefinch, Zambia. (photo: © Robert B. Payne).

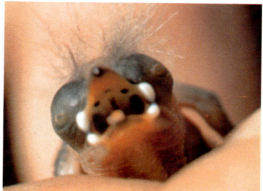

Plate 7d The mouth spots of the Village Indigobird nestling (bottom) mimic those of the Red-billed Firefinch host chicks (top), with which it is raised. (photos: © Robert B. Payne).

Plate 8a (*left*) Wood Duck host female in Missouri about to leave her nest, with a parasitic female on top of the box, waiting for an opportunity to lay. (photo: © Brad Semel).

Plate 8b (*below*) Nest box chaos. An abandoned Wood Duck clutch with more than thirty eggs – the result of parasitism by several females. (photo: © Paul W. Sherman).

Plate 8c (*left*) A Moorhen clutch (Cambridgshire, England) with four host eggs and three parasite eggs (smaller spots: two on far left, one far right). (photo: © Susan McRae).

Plate 8d (*right*) A Giraffe-eye view of an Ostrich nest in Kenya. The major female has pushed some eggs laid by minor (parasitic) females to the periphery. (photo: © Brian Bertram).

has been called 'a passerine chicken'. Together with Shiny Cowbirds (chapter 12), Brown-headed Cowbirds may lay more eggs than any other wild bird. Nevertheless, as we found with Common Cuckoos (chapter 3), the number of eggs laid in a season may often be well below the maximum potential, because of limits set by availability of suitable host nests and competition with other parasites.

ARE INDIVIDUAL FEMALES GENERALISTS?

The Brown-headed Cowbird's egg has a white or greyish-white background with brown or grey spots, usually denser at the larger end (**Plate 5b**). In sharp contrast to many parasitic cuckoos, there are no obvious differences in the Cowbird eggs laid in the nests of different host species.

Three lines of evidence suggest that many female Cowbirds are not as selective as cuckoos in their choice of hosts. First, the eggs from different females vary slightly in spotting density and size and these differences can sometimes be used to recognize individuals. In 1922 Herbert Friedmann followed three females, each over a period of four or five days. One laid five eggs in the nests of three host species, one laid five eggs in two species' nests and the third laid four eggs for three different species.[2] Other studies have managed to track individual Cowbirds for longer periods and again often show that they are generalists.[37] For example, one female was followed for 41 days in Michigan during which she laid 19 eggs, 11 in Song Sparrow nests, six in Yellow Warbler nests and two in Traill's Flycatcher nests. However, some females seem to specialize. There are records during one season of 18 eggs from one Cowbird, all in Yellow Warbler nests,[37] and 25 eggs from another, of which 23 were laid in Field Sparrow nests and two in towhee nests.[38]

Robert Fleischer from the University of Kansas used a different technique. He collected all the Cowbird eggs from host nests in a small pasture and found that he could identify the eggs from individual females by differences in the proteins of their egg yolks. All six female Cowbirds that laid two or more eggs parasitized the nests of two or three different hosts. Overall, Fleischer found that the choice of hosts simply reflected the proportion of nests of the different host species breeding in the pasture.[39]

Finally, on Delta Marsh, Manitoba, the use of DNA markers to identify chicks belonging to individual female Cowbirds, revealed that of 13 females which laid two or more eggs, seven parasitized two or three hosts while six parasitized just one host.[20] With small samples from individual females it is hard to tell whether parasitism of one host species arises by chance, or whether it reflects true specialization by some females. The most fecund female in this study laid 13 eggs, all in the nests of Red-winged Blackbirds. However, her egg-laying range was in a marsh where this was by far the commonest species available. It would be interesting to know whether she was a specialist on this host and so chose to lay in the marsh, or whether she was in fact a generalist and her habitat restricted her choice to this one species.

The generalist laying habits of many females, together with the lack of differences between Cowbird eggs laid in different host nests, suggests that Brown-headed Cowbirds are not divided into distinct 'host races', like some of the parasitic cuckoos. In support of this, genetic analysis revealed no differences between Cowbird chicks raised in the nests of the two most commonly used hosts in Delta Marsh, namely Red-winged Blackbirds and Yellow Warblers.[40] Generalist laying by many female Cowbirds would prevent the formation of cuckoo-like gentes (chapter 3).

The conclusion from all three kinds of study is that individual female Cowbirds often parasitize several species. Further work is needed to show whether some females are true specialists or whether they parasitize one host simply because it is the most abundant species nesting in their range. Nevertheless, even generalist females may not lay completely at random. In aviary experiments, Andrew King of Cornell University gave captive Cowbirds a choice of artificial nests and found that they preferred to parasitize nests with eggs smaller than their own.[41] In the wild too, small hosts are often preferred. Host choice may also be constrained by host aggression. For example, in Delta Marsh Yellow Warblers are three times as abundant as Least Flycatchers yet they are parasitized six times as frequently. The Least Flycatcher is more aggressive and may be better able to chase the Cowbird away from its nest.[42]

NUMBER OF COWBIRD EGGS PER NEST

A female Cowbird usually lays just one egg per host nest. However, she will parasitize a nest twice, or even three times, if hosts are in short supply. Robert Fleischer's analysis of yolk proteins showed that, on his study site, nests with more than one Cowbird egg had usually been parasitized by several females.[39] By contrast, in the Delta Marsh study most nests with two or more Cowbird eggs had been parasitized again by the same female.[20]

When female Cowbirds defend territories, they can avoid parasitizing nests that have been victimized by other Cowbirds. However, when their ranges overlap, several Cowbirds may compete for the same host nests. In these cases there is no evidence that they avoid laying in nests that have already been parasitized by other females. The number of Cowbird eggs per host nest often follows a random distribution, so that by chance alone some host nests avoid parasitism altogether while others are unlucky and may receive up to 12 Cowbird eggs.[43] Because Cowbirds are so numerous, multiple parasitism is far more frequent with Cowbird hosts than cuckoo hosts (**Plate 5b**). On average, about 40% of all parasitized nests have more than one Cowbird egg.[44]

THE COWBIRD CHICK

Like cuckoos, Brown-headed Cowbird chicks usually hatch before the host young provided their egg was laid during host laying. Most host eggs have incubation periods of 12–14 days compared with just 11–12 days for the Cowbird egg. Female Cowbirds lay daily, so they cannot adopt the cuckoo's trick of internal incubation to give their egg a head start in development (chapter 4). Nor do they lay unusually small eggs, another cuckoo trick for reducing incubation time. Nevertheless, the

Cowbird egg hatches early for two reasons. First, the embryo develops unusually fast so that the Cowbird chick hatches after 0.7 days less incubation compared with non-parasitic birds with eggs of the same size.[45] Second, in small host nests the presence of a Cowbird egg prolongs the incubation of the host eggs by about a day, probably because the larger parasitic egg reduces the host eggs' contact with the female's brood patch.[46]

The Cowbird chick usually has the benefit of hatching first, so that it can grow before the host eggs hatch, and most hosts are smaller than the Cowbird so it already has a clear size advantage in competition with the host chicks. In addition Cowbird chicks beg more vigorously than the host young, as expected from the fact that they have no genetic interest in the survival of their nest mates nor in the host parents' future reproduction (chapter 6). Herbert Friedmann[2] noted how the Cowbird chick continued to beg despite his own interference or alarms from the hosts: 'It is a matter of common observation to approach nests of various birds and find that the young occupants crouch down and remain quiet. Not so with the nestling Cowbird ... the young parasite will beg for food, confidently expecting the world to minister to its wants ...'

In the nests of small hosts, like warblers, it is not uncommon for all the host chicks to starve to death in competition with the larger Cowbird. However, with larger hosts, like Red-winged Blackbirds, the host chicks can hold their own and they grow and fledge just as well as if they were competing with another chick of their own species.

Recent studies at the nest using video cameras have shown exactly how the Cowbird chick wins the battle for food with small host young. Gabriela Lichtenstein from Cambridge University joined Spencer Sealy in Manitoba to study Cowbird begging behaviour in Yellow Warbler nests.[47] Adults of this host are 10 g in mass, compared with 40 g for an adult Brown-headed Cowbird. In each nest the researchers placed one Warbler chick and one Cowbird chick of the same age. The Cowbird chicks were about twice the mass of the host chicks. In most visits the host parents fed just one of the chicks and in 60% of the occasions the Cowbird got the food. This was simply because it was quicker to beg and reached up higher towards the food. When the two chicks reached up together to the same height they had an equal chance of being fed. Thus the Cowbird did not present any special features that were particularly attractive to the hosts – it won the competition for food simply because it could outreach the Warbler chick.

Experiments by David Eastzer from the University of North Carolina, and his colleagues, also suggest that the Cowbird chick does not provide any special 'super-normal' stimuli for parental care.[48] They placed various chicks in the nests of Barn Swallows (not a usual Cowbird host) and found that chicks of other species, such as Gray Catbirds, Eastern Phoebes and Red-winged Blackbirds, did just as well as Cowbird chicks in growth and survival to fledging. Donald Dearborn from the University of Missouri found further evidence that any advantage the Cowbird chick enjoyed was mainly due to its size.[49] In the nests of Indigo Buntings (adults 14–15 g) the Cowbirds got twice as much food as a host chick but in nests of Northern Cardinals (45 g – about the same size as the Cowbird) they fared no better than host chicks.

In one of the Indigo Bunting nests, Dearborn's video film revealed some

Brown-headed Cowbird chicks are raised alongside the host young. However, in the nests of small hosts, like this Yellow Warbler, the larger parasite chick easily outcompetes the host young for food, and often most or all of the host chicks starve to death (drawing from video film by Gabriela Lichtenstein and Spencer Sealy).

extraordinary events, never recorded before for any cowbird.[50] The nest originally contained three Bunting chicks and one Cowbird chick. On the fourth day after hatching the smallest Bunting chick was found on the ground under the nest, still alive. Dearborn put it back but the next day it was missing. The following day another Bunting chick disappeared and the sequence was captured on film. As a result of the shuffling in the nest as the chicks reached for food, one of the Buntings had been pushed towards the nest rim and was balanced on the Cowbird's back.

After the parent left, it tried to wriggle down into the centre of the nest. Three minutes later, in Dearborn's words: 'the Cowbird then slowly stood up, backing towards the nest rim as it straightened up. The pushing/standing action appeared to be quite deliberate, and lasted for roughly 10 seconds. Once the bunting was off the Cowbird, and completely out of the nest, the Cowbird slowly lowered itself, taking approximately 4 seconds to return to a resting position in the bottom of the nest cup, with its head down. Meanwhile, the ejected Bunting clung to the outside of the nest with one foot for approximately 6 seconds before falling 2 metres to the ground.'

Presumably this cuckoo-like ejection behaviour is rare, otherwise surely it would have been noted before. But it may be responsible for at least some of the host losses in parasitized nests in addition to the trampling and starvation suffered by the host chicks as they compete for food with the larger Cowbird.

The Brown-headed Cowbird chick leaves the host nest at 9–13 days of age and is then fed for a further 16–28 days before it becomes independent. The begging calls of the fledgling are unusually loud and persistent and, like parasitic cuckoos, the Cowbird occasionally attracts feeding by other birds in addition to its foster parents. The young Cowbirds follow their hosts and so perch at different heights depending on the species that feeds them; with flycatchers they perch higher up than with ground-feeders such as sparrows and wrens.[51]

WHY NO IDENTITY CRISIS?

One of the most engaging images from studies of animal behaviour is that of Konrad Lorenz swimming with his family of Greylag Geese. When Lorenz reared them from the egg stage, the newly hatched goslings regarded him as their parent and trailed after him wherever he went, seeking his company rather than that of other geese. This had remarkable long-term consequences. The males that imprinted on Lorenz later preferred to court humans rather than their own species.

Similar effects have been found in song birds. For example, if the eggs of Zebra Finches are fostered out to pairs of Bengalese Finches for rearing, the young often prefer to pair with Bengalese Finches when they reach adulthood, rather than with their own species. Experiments have shown that the young learn visual characteristics of the adults that raise them, and then use these as cues for mate choice later on. Vocal cues may be learnt too. Some results suggest that a male's mate choice may be more affected by imprinting than that of a female.[52]

For the first four or five weeks of its life, the young Brown-headed Cowbird has little social contact with its own species. Instead, it receives all its food, warmth and protection from the host species. How, then, does it avoid the problem of mis-imprinting? In other words, how does the Cowbird know that it's a Cowbird? This problem applies to all the brood parasites, of course, but it has been best studied in Brown-headed Cowbirds, particularly with regard to the development of their vocalizations.

Many species of birds have complex songs. These are usually acquired by learning, so that if young birds are kept in isolation they end up singing only simple versions of the song. However, in nature birds will not copy just any song they hear.

They have a genetic 'template', which predisposes them to learn their own species song. They often learn their songs either as juveniles, or during their first breeding season, by listening to territorial neighbours.[53]

Unlike parasitic cuckoos, which have simple songs that are likely to develop without the need for learning, the songs of the Brown-headed Cowbird are extremely complex. It was initially thought that these must be genetically programmed, because of the young Cowbird's early isolation from its own species. However, soon after reaching independence the Cowbird associates with other Cowbirds, often in large flocks. Somehow, it must avoid mis-imprinting on the hosts and, instead, have a genetic predisposition to seek out Cowbird-specific cues, perhaps visual or vocal signals that enable it to find its own kind. Or perhaps it could imprint on its own features? Whatever the mechanism, this association with its own species then opens up the possibility of learning, just as in other song birds. Experiments have shown that Cowbirds do in fact develop their songs in similar ways to other species, by an interaction between genetic predisposition and learning. The importance of learning varies between the three main vocalizations.[54]

Female 'chatter calls'

Female Brown-headed Cowbirds produce a loud chatter, a rapid series of notes given both in flight and when perched. Males occasionally produce a short version of this call. Female chatters are sometimes given in response to male song and may then attract the male. They are also given when other females or males approach too closely, as part of an aggressive display. The chatter calls show only slight variation throughout North America, and they may develop without learning, though this has not been investigated.

Male 'perched song'

Perched males give an elaborate series of whistles and other notes, often accompanied by a display in which the male fluffs up his body feathers, spreads his wings and tilts his body downwards. The song begins with a series of very low-pitched notes, which sound like bubbling water, and these are then followed by an extraordinary jump in pitch to a louder whistle. The perched song may be directed as a threat to other males or as courtship to females. Unlike most song birds, males develop a reasonably good perched song even if they are raised in isolation.[55] Furthermore, female Cowbirds raised in the laboratory in complete isolation from other Cowbirds still recognize male Cowbird perched song. In response to playbacks, they adopt copulatory postures when they hear Cowbird song, but not when they hear the song of other species (e.g. Red-winged Blackbirds). Both normal song from wild Cowbirds, and the song produced by isolated males, are stimulating to females.[55] Therefore, neither male nor female Cowbirds require experience with other Cowbirds in order to recognize each other.

However, in the wild learning plays an important role in modifying both the details of the male song and how females respond. Males modify their innate song by learning, so males within a local area tend to sing similar songs and there are differences between the subspecies of Cowbird. Experiments by Meredith West and

Andrew King, both now at Indiana University, have revealed that males may not simply copy details of their perched song by listening to other males in their local area. In addition, females play an active role, by encouraging males to sing certain songs rather than others.[56] The way females influence male song is fascinating. Juvenile males of the eastern subspecies (*M. a. ater*), which have never heard Cowbird song, develop perched song typical of their own subspecies if they are housed with wild-caught females of their own subspecies. However, if they are housed with wild-caught females of the southern subspecies (*M. a. obscurus*), they develop songs containing elements of this other subspecies song. How can this happen, given that females themselves do not sing?

West and King discovered that females became particularly excited when they heard elements from their own subspecies song. They gave a brief display called 'wing-stroking', in which the wings are moved rapidly to and fro out from the body. Males are more likely to repeat songs that stimulate the females in this way. So the wing strokes of the female act like a conductor's baton, training the males to produce sounds that the female prefers.

Male 'flight whistles'

This second type of male song is mainly used in long distance communication. It is most commonly given in flight, but males also give flight whistles when they are close to a female, just before copulation. Most males give just one type of flight whistle, but there are distinct local dialects.[54] The clearest boundaries between neighbouring dialects are where there are gaps in Cowbird distribution, caused by unsuitable habitat. The flight whistles usually consist of from two to four pure tone, whistle-like syllables, but they vary in pitch and duration and may be accompanied by various buzzes or trills. The differences between local populations are so marked that even observers who are familiar with Cowbird flight whistles may fail to recognize those from other dialects as belonging to this species. Dialect differences occur even in areas of California where Cowbirds have colonized since the 1930s, so they can develop rapidly.

Experiments show that these flight whistles are learned from other males in the area where a young male settles to breed. So a male dispersing to a new dialect area will learn to sing that new kind of song, either during his first year of life or later on during his first breeding season. Females, too, presumably get to know the local flight whistle dialect when they settle to breed. In captivity, playback experiments show that they are more likely to solicit copulations if they hear the local song rather than that from neighbouring or more distant populations. This means that a male will be more successful in pairing if he gives a good rendition of the local dialect.[57]

Why do females prefer males who sing the local dialect? Males don't help females by defending a territory where a female could enjoy exclusive use of resources, such as food or host nests. Nor do they assist in the search for host nests. All they do is provide a female with sperm to fertilize her eggs. So female choice and mate fidelity is most likely to reflect a quest for a male of good genetic quality.[58] Stephen Rothstein and Robert Fleischer suggest that a male's song may help the female to make a good choice.[59] Because the song is complex, and there are distinct differences between populations, it takes time for a male to perfect the local dialect.

Once he has mastered it, he provides the female with a reliable signal of his long-term residence in the area. So song is a sure sign of a male's age and experience, both of which are likely to indicate his genetic quality as a partner. The dialect differences may be arbitrary, and arise in geographical isolation in the same way as human dialects or regional accents. But in Cowbirds they are then reinforced by female preference for experienced mates.

These studies show that Brown-headed Cowbird behaviour is strongly influenced by learning, just as in other species. The Cowbird's trick is to delay learning until it has become independent and has followed a genetic predisposition to seek company with its own kind. This means that its mate preference is not disrupted by its early life with foster parents, so it avoids the problems encountered by Lorenz's geese and the cross-fostered Zebra Finches.

CHAPTER 11

Old and new hosts of the Brown-headed Cowbird and conservation problems

When Friedmann wrote his classic book *The Cowbirds* in 1929, it was known that some hosts rejected Brown-headed Cowbird eggs. In one report a Cowbird was seen to lay in the nest of an American Robin.[1] Having chased the Cowbird off, one of the Robins returned, 'looked in the nest, gave two syllables of its distress call and then drove its bill through the Cowbird egg and, with a jerk of its head, threw the egg out.' Friedmann placed foreign eggs of various species into the nests of American Robins and Grey Catbirds and found that they rejected eggs unlike their own. He suggested that their rejection response explained why they were so rarely recorded with Cowbird eggs. However, the fact that so many hosts suffered high parasitism rates, even those whose eggs were different in colour from the Cowbird egg, suggested to him that 'the great majority of species seem not to mind the strange eggs in the least'.

ACCEPTER AND REJECTER HOSTS

This is a fascinating puzzle and it is extraordinary that no-one investigated it further until Stephen Rothstein began his pioneering experiments with model eggs in 1966. Rothstein is a cowbird fanatic – even the number plate of his car bears the bird's name. It is his work in particular that has inspired much of the current interest in co-evolution of brood parasites and their hosts. Rothstein's experiments involved removing one host egg and replacing it with an artificial egg made of plaster, painted to look like the egg of a Brown-headed Cowbird. Experiments with real Cowbird eggs gave the same results so the use of plaster eggs did not affect host responses. Eggs were scored as 'rejected' if they disappeared from the nest, or had peck marks, or if the clutch was deserted. They were scored as 'accepted' if the hosts continued to incubate them for at least five days.

The results showed that most species could be categorized as either 'accepters' or 'rejecters' because all, or almost all, individuals within a species gave exactly the same response.[2] Nine species were rejecters: American Robin, Grey Catbird, Eastern Kingbird, Blue Jay, Northern Oriole, Cedar Waxwing, Brown Thrasher, Crissal Thrasher and Sage Thrasher. Most of the rejections (80%) were by ejection, often within minutes of the experimental parasitism. For example, Grey Catbirds ejected Cowbird eggs at 50 out of 53 nests, Eastern Kingbirds did so at all 33 nests and American Robins did so at 45 out of 46 nests. Only the Cedar Waxwing regularly rejected the Cowbird egg by desertion.

In further experiments, Rothstein showed that rejecter species did not simply follow the rule 'eject an odd egg' because they ejected Cowbird eggs if they formed the majority of the clutch or even if the whole clutch consisted of Cowbird eggs.[3] Instead, rejecters learnt the characteristics of their own eggs the first time they bred and then rejected eggs that differed from their learnt set (chapter 5). All these rejecter species have eggs that differ in appearance from the Cowbird's eggs. For example, Catbird and Robin eggs are blue, completely unlike the smaller, white spotted egg of the Cowbird. This means that the hosts can easily discriminate against all the Cowbird eggs by imprinting on the very first egg they lay and then rejecting eggs that differ in background colour, size or spotting.[4] Rapid learning from their first ever egg enables them to avoid the mis-imprinting costs we discussed in chapter 5, which is a problem for hosts who face the task of recognizing mimetic parasite eggs.

Although some species were rejecters, the majority accepted all Rothstein's experimental eggs. Some of the accepters were unsuitable as hosts, like the Mourning Dove, which feeds its chicks by regurgitation on crop milk, an unsuitable diet for Cowbirds. They are rarely parasitized and their lack of rejection is no surprise. Like unsuitable hosts of the Common Cuckoo (chapter 4), there will have been no pressure in nature for them to evolve rejection. However, also included among the accepters were some of the most common Cowbird hosts, for example Red-winged Blackbird, Wood Thrush, Eastern Phoebe, Song Sparrow, Chipping Sparrow, Northern Cardinal and Red-eyed Vireo. The high parasitism rates suffered by many other common hosts suggests that they too are accepters. Indeed, Rothstein estimates that accepter species outnumber the rejecters by a ratio of at least four to one.[5]

Unlike the rejecter species, the accepters apparently never learn what their own eggs look like. For example, Red-winged Blackbirds, Chipping Sparrows and Eastern Phoebes will accept clutches that contain a majority of Cowbird eggs or even a whole clutch of Cowbird eggs.[3] Herbert Friedmann's conclusion is correct: the majority of Cowbird hosts lack defences against the Cowbird egg.

Do Accepters Have Alternative Defences?

If an accepter species has alternative ways of defending its nest from parasitism then acceptance of Cowbird eggs may not matter. For example, although Rothstein's experiments show that the Common Grackle is an accepter, it is rarely parasitized in nature.[6] Perhaps its large size or colonial nesting dissuades the Cowbird?

Some accepter species defend their nests against Cowbirds and, like hosts of the Common Cuckoo (chapter 4), they show specific reactions to Cowbirds which reflect its threat as a parasite. For example, female Yellow Warblers are more aggressive to female than to male Cowbirds[7] and they respond with a special alarm call and rush to their nest and sit tight, in an attempt to block the Cowbird's access,

Experiments reveal that some hosts reject Brown-headed Cowbird eggs, but most hosts accept them. Top: Some rejecter hosts that grasp the parasite egg in their bill and eject it – American Robin, Grey Catbird, Eastern Kingbird, Brown Thrasher. Centre: Some rejecter hosts that puncture the parasite egg and then eject it – Northern Oriole, Warbling Vireo. Bottom: Some accepter hosts – Red-winged Blackbird, Wood Thrush, Eastern Phoebe, Chipping Sparrow.

a response not given to other enemies.[8] Red-winged Blackbirds are especially aggressive to presentations of a stuffed Cowbird during laying and early incubation, when parasitism is more likely, but they are aggressive to a stuffed Common Grackle throughout the egg and chick stage, which reflects the fact that this species is a nest predator at both stages.[9] Many host species are also more aggressive to model Cowbirds in populations that are more heavily parasitized.[10]

However, the high parasitism rates suffered by most accepter hosts suggest that any alternative defences are not adequate to keep Cowbirds at bay.

DO COWBIRDS AVOID REJECTER HOSTS?

Cowbird eggs are rarely found in the nests of rejecter hosts. Is this simply because they are rejected before we have the chance to record them, or do Cowbirds avoid these hosts altogether?

Some rejecter species are certainly parasitized. David Scott, from the University of Western Ontario, recorded 1% parasitism for Gray Catbird nests that were checked casually during the egg stage, but when he visited nests daily during the early morning, when Cowbirds lay, he found 44% parasitism.[11] Other studies have recorded 70% parasitism for Northern Orioles[12] and 8% for Cedar Waxwings.[13] The Cedar Waxwing is not only a rejecter of Cowbird eggs, but any Cowbird that survives to the chick stage usually starves to death anyway because it cannot grow on a diet of fruit.

The only clear evidence that Cowbirds avoid a rejecter species is from a study of Eastern Kingbirds in Delta Marsh, Manitoba.[14] Although experiments showed that they ejected 99% of real Cowbird eggs, about 40% of the eggs remained in the nest for 24 hours or more. Nevertheless, daily inspections recorded natural parasitism at just one out of 402 nests. Kingbirds are very aggressive but they do not guard their nests before sunrise, so Cowbirds should be able to gain access. Perhaps Cowbirds avoid this host.

Why do Cowbirds still parasitize some rejecters even though all these eggs will be doomed to destruction? Stephen Rothstein suggests that rejecter hosts are such a diverse group that it would be impossible for natural selection to provide Cowbirds with an innate program to avoid them all.[13] Given that most hosts are accepters, the simplest solution may be to design the Cowbird as a generalist despite the occasional losses from the rejecter species.

WHY DO MOST HOST SPECIES ACCEPT?

Most cuckoo hosts reject eggs unlike their own and this has led to the evolution of egg mimicry by the cuckoo (chapter 9). Here in North America we have the extraordinary contrast of a parasite with no refined host egg mimicry, which affects a much larger proportion of host nests, yet whose eggs are accepted by the majority of its hosts. How can we explain this? Once again we encounter the two hypotheses we discussed for accepter hosts of cuckoo eggs, namely equilibrium and evolutionary lag.

Equilibrium: acceptance is better than rejection

When hosts reject they face two costs. First, they may make recognition errors and reject their own eggs rather than the parasite's eggs. Second, there are ejection costs because they may crack their own eggs while trying to remove the parasite egg (chapter 5). Could either of these costs be so great that some Cowbird hosts do better to accept?

Three accepter hosts have eggs very like Cowbird eggs. These are the Song Sparrow, the Northern Cardinal and the Rufous-sided Towhee. Rothstein suggested that for these three species recognizing the Cowbird egg might be such a problem that acceptance could be better than rejection.[3] However, most accepter hosts have eggs that differ from Cowbird eggs just as much as those of the rejecter species. For example, Indigo Buntings and Eastern Phoebes have plain white eggs and those of the Wood Thrush and Chipping Sparrow are blue (**Plate 5c**). The first two lack the spotting of Cowbird eggs and the second two differ in background colour, two features which rejecter species use to discriminate against foreign eggs. Rothstein concluded that recognition costs could not provide a complete explanation for the rejecter-accepter dichotomy among Cowbird hosts.

What about ejection costs? If a host of the Common Cuckoo knows for certain that it has been parasitized, then it should always reject. The young Cuckoo will eject the host's eggs or chicks, so acceptance leads to zero reproductive success for hosts, unless the Cuckoo egg fails to hatch. Large hosts simply pick the Cuckoo egg up in their bill and throw it out of the nest. Small hosts have bills that are too small to grasp the Cuckoo egg, so they either puncture it to get a better hold or try to roll it out. If they fail to eject the egg, then they desert. Desertion is a more costly way to reject, of course, because the hosts lose their current clutch, but it is better than being lumbered with a Cuckoo chick. By deserting, the hosts can either start a new clutch or save themselves for next season. Therefore, although small hosts of the Common Cuckoo are more likely to have to resort to desertion, they still reject just as often as larger hosts.[15]

For hosts of the Brown-headed Cowbird, however, the situation could be different because they can raise some of their own young in parasitized nests. Ejection would be the best response provided it could be done without too much damage to the host eggs, because it releases the hosts from the burden of raising a Cowbird chick. However, if smaller hosts found ejection difficult, or impossible, then acceptance might sometimes be the best option.[3] This would be true provided the hosts could raise more of their own young in a parasitized nest than they could from attempting to eject the Cowbird egg or by deserting and starting again. Desertion could bring poorer rewards than acceptance if other nest sites were hard to find, or if food supplies were declining, or if there was not time for another brood that season.

Rejecter hosts are, indeed, larger on average than the accepters.[2] The largest rejecter species (Blue Jay, Catbird, Robin, Kingbird, thrashers) easily grasp the Cowbird egg in their bills and can eject it without any damage to their own eggs. However, the two smallest rejecter species in Rothstein's list, the Northern Oriole and the Cedar Waxwing, are 'puncture-ejecters', perhaps because they find it difficult to pick up the whole Cowbird egg. Northern Orioles occasionally crack one of their own eggs when puncturing the Cowbird egg, a loss of 0.26 host eggs per ejection. Experiments in which Cowbird chicks were added to Oriole nests showed that the presence of a Cowbird chick in an average-sized brood of four Orioles reduced the number of Orioles fledged by 0.4 young. So the Oriole's rejection behaviour still makes good economic sense; it is better to lose 0.26 eggs while ejecting the Cowbird egg than to lose 0.4 young in competition with a Cowbird chick.[12]

Cedar Waxwings apparently find it even harder to eject the Cowbird egg because they crack their own eggs more often when rejecting, and about half of their rejections are by desertion. Experiments show that they are more likely to reject Cowbird eggs placed in their nests during laying or early incubation than later on. This change in response is adaptive because later-laid Cowbird eggs are unlikely to hatch.[13]

Sievert Rohwer and Carol Spaw, from the University of Washington, suggest that for hosts much smaller than orioles and waxwings rejection often becomes so costly that it is better to accept.[16] Small hosts are unable to remove the Cowbird egg by grasp ejection because their bills are too small. They may also not have the strength to puncture the egg because, like eggs of parasitic cuckoos (chapter 4), Cowbird eggs have unusually thick shells.[17,18] Even if they did eventually manage to remove the Cowbird egg, they may end up damaging most or all of their own clutch. Small hosts may therefore be confronted with just two viable alternatives, 'accept or desert', and they may choose acceptance as the lesser of these two evils. Rohwer and Spaw propose that by evolving a thick-shelled egg, the Cowbird has forced small hosts to accept, so it has won the arms race without the need for egg mimicry.

The most convincing evidence that acceptance can sometimes be best is provided by the variable responses of some small hosts to natural parasitism. Both Yellow Warblers[7,19] (10 g) and Blue-grey Gnatcatchers[20] (7 g) are more likely to desert their nests if they are parasitized early on in laying rather than later on during incubation. A correctly timed parasitism produces a Cowbird chick that outcompetes their own young, so they usually have no reproductive success. However, later-laid Cowbird eggs either fail to hatch or hatch too late to cause total destruction of the host brood. So 'reject early-accept later' may be a sensible response. Both these hosts are much smaller than the smallest puncture-ejecter species, so perhaps they are too small to puncture the Cowbird egg and can reject only by desertion.

Lisa Petit from the University of Arkansas studied Prothonotary Warblers, one of the few hole-nesters to be parasitized.[21] Although the Warblers accepted the Cowbird egg in 81% of cases, parasitized nests were more likely to be deserted if Petit had put up more alternative nest sites in the territory in the form of nest boxes. This host seems to suffer less than most warblers, rearing on average three of its own young from parasitized nests, compared with four if not parasitized. Therefore acceptance may be best unless it is easy to find another site for rapid re-nesting.

Amotz and Avishag Zahavi have even suggested that provided hosts raise some of their own young they should encourage Cowbirds to parasitize them! Their argument, which pushes the 'acceptance is best' idea to its extreme limit, is as follows.[22] A pair of hosts might fledge some of their own young from a parasitized nest, but if the Cowbird fails to parasitize them and finds their nest later on, she will destroy their clutch to force them to re-lay. If a female Cowbird is very efficient at finding all the host nests in her territory, it may be better for the hosts to expose their nests early to minimize the parasite's damage. It is better to accept the smaller cost of parasitism than to be found out later and have to pay a heavier price.

Song Sparrows on Mandarte Island show a puzzling behaviour which might be interpreted to support the Zahavis' idea. James Smith and his colleagues from the University of British Columbia found that female Sparrows older than two years of age mobbed the Cowbird much more than did yearling females breeding for the first time.[23] Mobbing is most intense near the nest and may actually help the Cowbird to locate it, because older Sparrows were parasitized twice as much as the yearlings. Why don't yearlings advertise their nests by mobbing? The Zahavis suggest that this is because they are less able to raise both their own young and the Cowbird chick. For yearlings, it may be best to lie low and hope the Cowbird will miss them.

However, there are two other plausible explanations for these results. First, the mobbing itself may not be the cause of the increased parasitism. Older female Sparrows are better parents and Cowbirds might prefer them anyway. Second, the mobbing may not be specifically designed for Cowbirds but rather as a defence against a variety of intruders. Perhaps, on average, it is an effective protection of the nest?

Two hosts of the Brown-headed Cowbird vary their rejection behaviour depending on the frequency of parasitism, just as we found for some cuckoo hosts (chapters 4 and 5). James Briskie, from Queen's University Ontario, and his colleagues tested the responses of American Robins and Yellow Warblers to experimental parasitism with real Cowbird eggs that they had collected from other host nests.[24] In southern Manitoba, where Cowbirds are common and have been present since well before European settlement, the Robins ejected 100% of the eggs and the Warblers deserted, or buried, 11% of them. At a site in northern Manitoba, 600 km away, where Cowbirds do not breed, the Robins rejected at 66% of their nests and the Warblers showed no rejection at all. The Warblers were also less aggressive to a stuffed Cowbird. As with the studies of cuckoo hosts, it is not known whether these differences in response reflect genetic differences within host populations or whether individual hosts are equipped with flexible behaviour. Either way, they still show that hosts are more likely to accept when the costs of parasitism are lower. This also provides some indirect evidence that acceptance may sometimes be best because rejection is costly.

* * *

The 'acceptance is best' hypothesis provides a neat explanation for why some hosts accept, but it cannot be the only solution to this puzzle. A recent study by Spencer Sealy in Manitoba has revealed that Warbling Vireos, just 15 g in mass, reject all Cowbird eggs that are placed experimentally in their nests, and they do so by puncture ejection. Furthermore their ejection costs, just 0.29 Vireo eggs lost per Cowbird egg ejected, are no higher than those of the Northern Oriole, which is over twice as large.[25] This suggests that puncture ejection may be feasible for many of the accepter species after all.

Other studies also cast doubt on the 'acceptance is best' hypothesis as a universal explanation for acceptance. First, Rothstein has shown that four accepter species (Red-winged Blackbird, Common Grackle, Eastern Phoebe, Chipping Sparrow) accept undersized model Cowbird eggs, smaller than their own, which they should easily be able to pick up and eject.[3] Furthermore, Red-winged Blackbirds will reject inanimate objects (dowel sticks) the same size and colour as Cowbird eggs, and they do so with no breakage of their own eggs.[26] This also suggests that their acceptance of real Cowbird eggs is not forced upon them because they are impossible to eject.

Second, accepters will incubate whole clutches of Cowbird eggs, which is clearly maladaptive – rejecters make the sensible decision in this case and reject them all. This suggests that accepters simply don't recognize the Cowbird's egg as foreign.[3,27]

Finally, we have to consider exactly what a host's reproductive success would be if it decided to accept. The nestlings of medium to large-sized hosts (Song Sparrow, Red-winged Blackbird) can usually stand up to the competition from a Cowbird chick, so the main or only cost of parasitism is the eggs lost when the female Cowbird removes or cracks them during laying. This loss is irrecoverable, and will occur in most re-nesting attempts by the hosts if parasitism levels are high. The best response is to eject the Cowbird egg, provided this can be done without damaging too many host eggs. Otherwise acceptance brings at least reasonable host success.

For small hosts, however, and for hosts with long incubation periods, acceptance usually leads to zero host success because the larger, greedier Cowbird chick monopolizes the food and all the host chicks starve. This includes the smaller flycatchers, vireos, warblers and sparrows and also the Eastern Phoebe.[3,28] These hosts fare no better when parasitized than hosts of the Common Cuckoo. Furthermore, they suffer such high rates of Cowbird parasitism that if there were any individuals that could reject the Cowbird egg then they would have such a strong selective advantage that their habit would spread very rapidly through the host population.

Stephen Rothstein calculated how rapidly rejection would evolve.[29] Consider, for example, the Eastern Phoebe. Its average clutch is 4.7 eggs, of which 94% produce fledglings provided the nest is successful. If the nest is parasitized, the female Cowbird removes one egg and replaces it with her own. This lost egg is not recoverable, of course, but a 'rejecter' Phoebe could still save production from 3.7 of its eggs if it ejected the Cowbird egg without damaging any of its own. If 94% produced fledglings, it would have 3.5 young. Compare this with the dismal production from a parasitized nest, where the Cowbird chick monopolizes the food and, on average, only 0.3 young Phoebes fledge. Under the present average parasitism rate of 19% (assessed from nest records), the huge advantage enjoyed by any rejecter Phoebes would mean that their habit would increase rapidly from generation to generation. In fact, calculations show that the proportion of rejecter individuals in the Phoebe population would increase from just 5% to 95% in about one hundred generations. For most small birds, which breed every year and have an expectation of further life of one to two years, this is equivalent to one or two hundred years. Calculations for some other common accepter hosts produce similar results.

Evolution might proceed more slowly than suggested by Rothstein's calculations. First, rejection costs would reduce the relative success of rejecters (chapter 5). Second, parasitism rates in the past may have been much lower, before the Cowbird's dramatic increase. Nevertheless, many accepters have probably suffered 20–50% parasitism for at least one hundred years. Many lose practically all of their young if there is a Cowbird in the nest. Many have eggs that look very different from the Cowbird's egg. For many, even the most costly method of rejection, namely desertion, would bring a selective advantage. Why, then, do they still accept Cowbird eggs?

Evolutionary lag: rejection would be best, but it has not yet evolved

Accepter hosts could be lagging behind in their defences either because they lack the genetic variations which would permit rejection to evolve,[29] or because there hasn't been sufficient time for evolution to change them to rejecters.[15] We can test for evolutionary lag by comparing 'old hosts' of the Cowbird with 'new hosts'. Old hosts are species that must have had long exposure to parasitism because they breed in grassland, grassland edge or riparian habitats in the centre of North America, right in the historic range of the Cowbird. New hosts are forest species, which are likely to have been less affected by Cowbirds until European colonization in the last 200–300 years fragmented the landscape and allowed Cowbirds to penetrate the forests (chapter 10).

This division of hosts into 'old and new' does not provide a satisfactory explanation for the dichotomy in host responses to Cowbird eggs placed into their nests by experiment.[2] Certainly some of the accepter species are likely to be new hosts (eastern wood warblers, Wood Thrush, Red-eyed Vireo) and, furthermore, all nine of Rothstein's rejecter species can be classified as old hosts. But the majority of the accepter species are old hosts too. They breed in grassland or scrubby edge habitat and have ranges that include the Great Plains of central North America.

Nevertheless, an early analysis by Harold Mayfield in 1965 hinted that old hosts might be less tolerant of natural parasitism, because Cowbird eggs in their nests were less likely to give rise to Cowbird fledglings.[30] His sample size was small and some of the differences in success could have been caused by predation. However, Mayfield's suggestion has been confirmed by a recent, more extensive, study by Aki Hosoi and Stephen Rothstein.[31] They found that old hosts are much more likely to desert their nests if they are parasitized naturally by Cowbirds. Their results are shown on the next page. I have included three species among the old hosts which could be classified as 'intermediate' because their habitat includes both forest and grassland edge (Eastern Phoebe, Blue-grey Gnatcatcher, Chesnut-sided Warbler).

These results were even more striking when Hosoi and Rothstein analysed them in more detail. They defined 'highly sensitive' species as those that often lost all, or nearly all, of their own young when their nest was parasitized. These were mostly small hosts (less than 13 g), but the Solitary Vireo (17 g) and Eastern Phoebe (20 g) are also highly sensitive because they have long incubation periods, which means that the Cowbird chick gets such a head-start in its growth that the host chicks are easily outcompeted. 'Less sensitive' hosts tended to be larger species (16 g or more), whose young could compete well with the Cowbird chick, and they suffered heavy losses only if their nest was multiply-parasitized. Within each of these categories, the old hosts had much higher desertion rates than the new hosts. This means that even if we control for host sensitivity, length of exposure to Cowbirds still explains variation in desertion. Especially intriguing is the finding that within the old hosts the sensitive species have higher desertion than the less sensitive species, exactly what you would expect if hosts varied their responses sensibly in relation to the costs of raising a Cowbird. However, among the new hosts there was no tendency for the highly sensitive hosts to be more likely to desert. For example, some eastern wood warbler species readily accept Cowbird eggs despite the fact that their own

NEW HOSTS

0	10	20	30	40	50	60	70	80
Kirtland's Warbler								
Wood Thrush								
Louisiana Waterthrush								
White-throated Sparrow	Dark-eyed Junco							
Swamp Sparrow	Prothonotary Warbler	Ovenbird	Magnolia Warbler					
Solitary Vireo	Acadian Flycatcher	Mourning Warbler	Red-eyed Vireo		Veery			

OLD HOSTS

0	10	20	30	40	50	60	70	80
			Northern Cardinal					
			Chipping Sparrow	Blue-grey Gnatcatcher				
		Eastern Phoebe	Clay-coloured Sparrow	Chestnut-sided Warbler		Yellow Warbler		
		Grasshopper Sparrow	Lark Bunting	Eastern Meadowlark	Indigo Bunting	Field Sparrow		
Song Sparrow	Dickcissel	Common Yellowthroat	Yellow-breasted Chat	Prairie Warbler	Willow Flycatcher	Brewer's Sparrow	Golden-cheeked Warbler	

% naturally parasitized nests deserted

reproductive output is all but eliminated in parasitized nests. This suggests that new hosts simply haven't had time to evolve sensible responses.

Finally, Hosoi and Rothstein compared closely related host species, within the same genus or subfamily, and again found that old hosts rejected more than new hosts. As with hosts of the Common Cuckoo (chapter 4) there was therefore no hint that taxonomic constraints affected responses to parasitism. Rather, hosts tend to evolve defences when it is economic for them to do so, and provided there has been sufficient time for sensible responses to evolve. There are still some exceptions unexplained by the separation into old and new hosts. Why, for example, does the Dickcissel so rarely reject despite the fact that it is an old host and the Cowbird egg is unlike its own? Nevertheless, this analysis provides striking support for the idea that evolutionary lag is part of the explanation for the lack of host defences.

However, the results now leave us with an unresolved puzzle. If many old hosts have evolved nest desertion as a defence against the Brown-headed Cowbird, why have not more of them evolved egg ejection? This is a widespread defence among cuckoo hosts and is surely the more effective method because it saves having to start a new nest.

One possibility is that even the old hosts may not all have had sufficient time to evolve the best rejection responses. Stephen Rothstein points out that rejection by desertion may evolve more quickly because it is already in the behavioural repertoire of all small birds, as part of a general response to any intruder or disturbance at the nest.[3] Indeed, some of the desertion of parasitized nests may be a response to disturbance rather than a specific reaction to Cowbirds. Experiments by Dorothy Hill and Spencer Sealy[32] have shown that Clay-coloured Sparrows desert 60% of parasitized nests in Delta Marsh, but they never desert when Cowbird eggs are placed in their nests by experiment, nor do they do so when presented with a stuffed Cowbird at the nest. Instead, desertion is stimulated by the reduction in their clutch which accompanies natural parasitism when the female Cowbird removes some of their eggs. These hosts rarely fledge any of their own young from a parasitized nest, so desertion is clearly adaptive, but even so it is not a direct response to either the Cowbird or its egg.

In contrast to desertion, egg rejection involves the evolution of completely new behaviour patterns in hosts, including learning about their own eggs and decisions about when to eject. These may well take considerable time to evolve. Perhaps they will eventually replace desertion as the major host defence? In the next chapter we shall return to the difficult question of whether cowbird-host interactions might eventually become more highly co-evolved, like those of cuckoos and their hosts in the Old World.

A complication for any comparison of so-called 'old' and 'new' hosts is that the North American landscape experienced huge changes well before those recently wrought by Man, so host-parasite interactions must have fluctuated in the distant past too, as habitat changes led to changes in bird distribution. For example, at the end of the last Ice Age, some 10,000 years ago, grassland was more extensive and Cowbirds may well have been more widespread than in the period immediately prior to the European invasion. Perhaps some of today's 'new' hosts had ancestors who were heavily parasitized because they too lived in small forest patches in a sea of grassland. Their parasitism rates may have then declined as the forests began to spread across the continent and the Cowbird's range contracted.

A key question is whether we would expect today's descendants to have retained any legacy of their ancestors' ancient battles with parasites, as some cuckoo hosts seem to have done (chapter 9). The strong difference in the response of 'old' and 'new' Cowbird hosts suggests either that few of the 'new' hosts were exposed to heavy parasitism in the distant past, or if they were, it was so long ago that they have since lost their defences.

EFFECTS ON HOST POPULATIONS

The picture that emerges from our discussion of host defences is one in which most hosts are at the mercy of Brown-headed Cowbirds. Some may decide to accept the Cowbird egg because this is the best thing to do, given that attempts to reject it are costly. Others accept simply because the Cowbird is a new threat in their lives and selection has not had time to equip them with defences. Either way, the result is that millions of North American birds spend their summer raising Cowbird chicks rather than their own young. In his 1989 book, John Terborgh from Princeton University lamented the loss of song birds that used to live in the North American woods during his boyhood days and he asked, 'Where have all the birds gone?'[33] Could Cowbird parasitism provide part of the answer?

The economics seem simple. For a species to survive, sufficient young must be raised to replace the adults that die. If a host loses all or most of its young in a parasitized nest, then there will be a critical frequency of Cowbird parasitism above which it raises too few young to maintain its numbers, so it will eventually become extinct. The Brown-headed Cowbird's generalist habits make it a particularly insidious threat, because even when a host species declines in numbers it may continue to suffer high parasitism rates as Cowbird numbers are maintained by other hosts.[34] Contrast this with a specialist parasite, like a cuckoo, where, as a host declines in numbers, the parasite will decline too. The cuckoo's host may then gain a temporary respite and be able to increase its population again.

To calculate the critical parasitism frequency at which Cowbirds could drive their hosts to extinction, we need to measure three parameters; adult female mortality, seasonal production of young and survival of those young to breeding age.[35] None of these measurements is straightforward.

Adult female mortality

In many species adults return to the same area to breed each year, so if individuals disappear they have probably died. However, in some species females may disperse to new areas even within a season and mortality is hard to estimate. So far, only one study has examined the possible long-term costs to a host of raising a Cowbird. Robert and Laura Payne from the University of Michigan found that Indigo Buntings that had been parasitized survived just as well, and had just as great reproductive success the next season, as unparasitized birds.[36] This suggests that, as for cuckoo hosts, raising a Cowbird is not unusually arduous compared with the task of raising a host brood. It means that the main costs of parasitism come from the reproductive losses from parasitized nests.

Seasonal production of young

It is easy to measure the number of host young that fledge from parasitized and unparasitized nests. However, what we need to know is a host pair's seasonal productivity. This takes account of whether the pair can re-nest, and their probability of success if they do so.[37] For hosts that fail to raise any of their own young from a parasitized nest, parasitism can have a large effect on seasonal productivity because there may not be time to breed again after raising a Cowbird. On the other hand, there may be parts of the season when the hosts can escape parasitism, perhaps because Cowbirds breed later than the hosts.

Survival of young to breeding age

This is hard to measure. If a young fledgling disappears, is this because it has died or dispersed from our study area? This is an important distinction because in some areas host populations may fail to replace themselves but their numbers may be maintained by other populations which produce a surplus of young each year. Thus some less parasitized populations may provide a 'source' of young to replenish other, heavily parasitized, populations which act as 'sinks'.[38]

*   *   *

One of the few studies that is sufficiently detailed to calculate seasonal production of young and the effect of Cowbirds on a local population is Val Nolan Jr.'s wonderful study of the Prairie Warbler.[39] His population suffered 24% parasitism. From successful unparasitized nests, the Warblers produced 3.4 fledglings compared with just 0.9 from a parasitized nest. However, 80% of all nests failed owing to predation and females could have up to four attempts per season. Nolan calculated that at current levels of parasitism, a population of 100 females produces 69 young that will survive to breed the next season. Of these, about half will be females. This productivity almost exactly balances the annual female mortality of 35%. Therefore the population is just barely replacing itself, mainly because predation is already taking a terrible toll. Any increase in parasitism could cause this Warbler population to become extinct, unless it is maintained by dispersal from other areas.

For small song birds that lose most or all of their young from a parasitized nest, high parasitism by Cowbirds must certainly mean that many local populations are 'sinks'. This must apply to many heavily parasitized species in the fragmented forest blocks of the mid-west. For example, the Wood Thrush populations in Illinois that suffer 80–100% Cowbird parasitism are essentially just raising Cowbirds. The flute-like song of the Wood Thrush will continue in these woods only as long as there are more productive populations nearby to replenish their numbers.[40] This highlights the importance of reserves to maintain areas of extensive forest which can act as song-bird reservoirs.

Could Cowbirds threaten populations of larger hosts, whose nestlings are better able to compete with Cowbird chicks? In general, these species will be less vulnerable and will produce a surplus of young to replace the dying adults provided parasitism rates are not excessive. For example, the long-term study by James Smith and Peter Arcese of Song Sparrows on Mandarte Island shows an annual average of 25% nests parasitized. Nevertheless, a female can still raise an average of three young to independence each year, which far exceeds the numbers needed to replace the dying adults. The seasonal loss in productivity due to parasitism is just

0.3 Sparrow young per breeding female. Furthermore, when Sparrow numbers decline on the island there are too few pairs to make it worthwhile for Cowbirds to spend the whole summer there and so parasitism rates decline. Overall, Cowbirds have had a negligible effect on the population and the numbers of Sparrows now breeding on the island is about the same as in the 1960s, before the Cowbirds arrived.[41]

COWBIRDS – VILLAINS OR SCAPEGOATS?

Although Brown-headed Cowbirds must have contributed to local population declines of some North American song birds, it is often difficult to distinguish their effect from that of habitat change. At one extreme we could imagine the following chain of causation, with the Cowbird as the arch villain:

Change in landscape → Increase in Cowbirds → Decline in song birds

At the other extreme, we could imagine habitat change as the main factor, having independent effects on both Cowbirds and song bird hosts. Here the Cowbird is entirely blameless and is a scapegoat for the havoc we ourselves have caused:

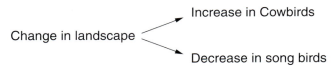

This last scenario is likely to apply at least to some song bird populations, which have declined even though they are not parasitized by Cowbirds.[42] For parasitized species, the true picture in nature is likely to be an intermediate, as follows:

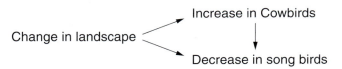

For example, in the study by Scott Robinson and colleagues in Illinois, nest predation also increased as forests became more fragmented and was a major factor limiting host productivity.[40]

There are further complications. First, other factors may lead to dynamic change in populations, such as survival in winter quarters. Second, at any one time some local populations may be increasing while others are decreasing, so it is unwise to make general conclusions about the health of a species from just one or two studies. In fact, in some areas the changes in the landscape have led to a decline in song birds which, in turn, might have led to a Cowbird decline.[43] Nevertheless, it is clear that Cowbird parasitism can threaten a species when it is reduced, by habitat loss, to a few small populations, all of which are heavily parasitized. Four cases have been well studied in recent years.[43–45]

Kirtland's Warbler

It was Harold Mayfield's study of this species, published in 1961, which first raised the alarm and suggested that Brown-headed Cowbirds could drive a host to extinction.[46] Kirtland's Warblers are restricted in distribution to a small part of Michigan, where they breed in young jack pine forests, 6–24 years after fires. This habitat was never very extensive and even prior to European settlement in the area, Mayfield estimates that there were only about five thousand birds.

Settlement by farmers in the late 1800s was bad news for the Kirtland's Warbler. First, suppression of natural fires caused the pine forests to mature beyond the stage that provided suitable breeding habitat. Second, the arrival of livestock and agriculture attracted Cowbirds. Counts of the Warblers in 1951 and 1961 revealed just 432 and 502 singing males and by 1971 the population had crashed to 201 singing males.

High parasitism rates suggested that Cowbirds might be part of the problem. In the period 1944–1957, 55% of the Warbler nests were parasitized, rising to 69% in 1966–1971. This gave considerable cause for concern as the Warblers have no defences against the Cowbird and always accept its egg. The young Cowbird usually has a two-day head start in growth, so the newly hatched Warbler, just 1.5 g, faces

Kirtland's Warbler. Female in foreground, with male singing behind.

competition from a 10 g nest companion. Not surprisingly, most Warbler chicks get trampled or starve to death and production from parasitized nests is just 0.3 Warbler young, compared with 1.3 from unparasitized nests (including failed nests). On top of this, the breeding season is short, with time for just one brood per year.

Since 1972, Cowbird traps have been put out across an area of 19,200 km², near the breeding sites used by the Warblers. Wild Cowbirds are attracted to a large cage containing live decoys and grain. They enter through slits or funnels in the cage and then, once inside, can't find their way out. By 1994, over 90,000 Cowbirds had been removed from the Warbler's nesting area and the control proved to be very effective. In the first decade of the removal program parasitism plummeted to 3.4% and the Warbler's reproductive success increased three-fold. Nevertheless, despite this dramatic increase in productivity, the breeding numbers remained stable at around the same two hundred pairs that there had been immediately prior to Cowbird removal. Only when new habitat was created, after a wildfire went out of control in 1981, did the population increase. The great irony is that, despite all human efforts, the most important conservation success for Kirtland's Warblers in recent years arose as an accident.[45]

There is still debate about whether Cowbird control saved the Kirtland's Warbler from the brink of extinction. Some estimates of juvenile and adult mortality indicate that without Cowbird removal, the Warbler population would not have been self sustaining. On the other hand, it is strange that numbers did not increase even in the early years of the removal program. This suggests that the population was limited by habitat rather than by juvenile recruitment.[45] Nevertheless, ecologists rarely have the luxury of waiting until all the evidence is in, and Cowbird removal was certainly the sensible approach.

There is a fascinating new twist to the Kirtland's Warbler story. One recent study[47] suggests that the periods of decline in the breeding population this century, coincided with the destruction of the Warbler's main habitat in winter quarters, namely pine forest in the Bahama archipelago. Furthermore, the breeding population increase since 1990 has coincided with the regrowth of these forests following logging. This implicates winter habitat as a key factor limiting population numbers. However, another study[48] claims that the birds are not dependent on pines during the winter, but rather use a diversity of habitats with a good shrub layer, which are widespread and not limiting for the current small population. Further work is needed to resolve this issue. Whatever the outcome, it is clear that Cowbird control on the breeding grounds is not enough. The long-term security of the Kirtland's Warbler depends on safeguarding their habitat.

Black-capped Vireo

Unlike the Kirtland's Warbler, the distribution of this host is within the historical range of the Brown-headed Cowbird, namely scrub habitat in south central North America. However, it has suffered habitat loss because suppression of fires has allowed the Vireo's preferred early successional habitat to mature. Many populations are now in small isolated scrub patches.

In the old days, when they followed the Buffalo herds, Cowbirds were likely to have been more localized in their distribution and so parasitism was probably highly variable between Vireo populations. Today, with the introduction of sedentary cattle in the southern Great Plains, Cowbirds are almost everywhere and so the Vireos suffer increased parasitism. Several local populations have 70–100% of their nests parasitized and some have been driven to extinction. In Oklahoma, Vireo populations unprotected by Cowbird control produced just 0.4 young per pair per year, well below what is needed to maintain their numbers without immigration. With removal of Cowbirds, the production increased to over two young per pair per year. Continued control of Cowbirds, combined with habitat management, will be necessary to safeguard many of the Vireo populations.[45]

Least Bell's Vireo

This subspecies used to be common in the riparian woodland of the Central Valley and coastal southern California. Its decline began in the 1930s and coincided with the Cowbird's invasion of the state. By the early 1970s it had disappeared from the Central Valley and by 1987 there were just 440 territorial males left, all in pockets of woodland in the south.

The Cowbirds must have had an impact because the Vireos were heavily parasitized (50% or more of the nests in most studies) and parasitized nests usually produced only Cowbird young. However, habitat loss was the main cause of the decline – the Central Valley has lost 95% of its riparian vegetation this century as a result of drainage and the spread of agriculture. In the presence of more extensive habitat, the Vireos could probably survive the onslaught from Cowbirds. For example, another subspecies, *Vireo bellii arizonae*, which bred along the lower Colorado River, was heavily parasitized as early as 1900, but it did not begin to decline until the 1950s, when much of the habitat was destroyed.[49]

Unlike the Kirtland's Warbler, the Least Bell's Vireo showed a rapid increase in its breeding population immediately Cowbird control began in 1983, so Cowbird removal alone was sufficient to allow local vireo populations to recover.[50] The goal of long-term management plans is to restore lost habitat.

Southwestern Willow Flycatcher

This is another endangered riparian species that has suffered an enormous decline in the southwest, especially in California and Arizona, probably mainly owing to severe habitat loss, followed by increased Cowbird parasitism. In the mid-1980s, the Californian population was less than 150 pairs and parasitism rates were around 50%. Cowbird control might be needed to maintain the remaining lowland populations, though so far Cowbird removals have not led to an increase in flycatcher numbers.[51] Unlike Least Bell's Vireo, this species also occurs at higher elevations, in woodland patches of moist meadows and streams. Here, parasitism levels are much less and habitat loss seems to be the major threat.[49]

In the central part of its range, Willow Flycatchers breed in more extensive tracts of riparian habitat, within the historic range of the Cowbird, and have presumably survived parasitism for thousands of years. As with the Least Bell's Vireo, therefore, this species seems to come under severe threat from the Cowbird only when habitat destruction exposes more breeding pairs to edges and fragmented plots where Cowbirds have easy access to their nests.[49]

Although the details differ for each of these four endangered species, they all carry the same broad message for conservation. Cowbird parasitism may well hasten the decline of some fragmented local host populations, but we must accept responsibility as the major villains, through our destruction of the landscape. The long-term security for all these species demands restoration of suitable habitat.

A DANGEROUS INVASION?

Brown-headed Cowbirds migrate in flocks. Given their recent expansion into eastern Canada, it is not too far-fetched to imagine that one day they might cross the Atlantic and colonize Eurasia. So far, there have been just two records in Europe.[52] An adult female was found dead in Norway in 1987, and a male was seen feeding with a flock of Starlings on the island of Islay, western Scotland, in 1988. These records provoked advice from a North American ornithologist, who urged that, 'any further Cowbirds which turn up in Europe be instantly shot, without debate or delay ... if the species were to become established in the Old World, it would be an ecological disaster. The effect of Cowbird parasitism on a totally naïve population of hosts would be utterly devastating.'[53]

Would it? Most potential hosts of the Cowbird in Europe have already been equipped with defences by their evolutionary battle with the Common Cuckoo. They reject eggs unlike their own, so the Cowbird might not have the easy time it has enjoyed with new hosts in North America. In fact, colonization would be the perfect natural experiment to test between the two hypotheses for the prevalence of host acceptance in North America. If 'evolutionary lag' is important, European hosts should reject much more than their ecological equivalents in North America. If 'acceptance is best', they should show similar responses.

It seems likely that the first Cowbirds in Europe would meet some rejection from most of their hosts, as shown by the experiments with model eggs (chapter 9). The worry is that even moderate reproductive success might lead to a rapid increase in Cowbirds because food would be abundant. They would survive well on agricultural land and in suburbia, unlike Common Cuckoos, which have to commute between Europe and Africa in search of hairy caterpillars. As a result, European hosts may soon face 50% parasitism from Cowbirds on top of the 5% parasitism from Cuckoos. This could have an interesting 'knock-on' effect: perhaps the increased pressure from a generalist parasite would force hosts to be more discriminating and so select for better mimicry by their specialist Cuckoos?

Although European hosts may already be able to increase their defences rapidly as parasitism rises (chapter 5), heavy Cowbird parasitism could still have severe effects on the production of young by small hosts that are unable to eject the Cowbird egg, and so have to choose between acceptance and desertion. History has taught us that introductions by Man, or natural invasions, often have disastrous effects on the indigenous wildlife, especially when their populations have already been reduced and fragmented by habitat destruction. Prudence would be best, and my sympathies lie with our American correspondent. For Europe, Cuckoos are enough – we don't need cowbirds too!

CHAPTER 12

'Shot-gun' Shiny and specialist Screaming Cowbirds, with cowbirds and cuckoos compared

The Brown-headed Cowbird is just one of five parasitic cowbird species. The other four are from Central and South America. They vary in their parasitic habits from the generalist Shiny Cowbird, which exploits nearly as many host species as the Brown-headed Cowbird, to the Screaming Cowbird, which is largely a specialist on the one non-parasitic species of cowbird, the Bay-winged Cowbird.[1] This variation is summarized below.

Why do different cowbird species exploit different numbers of hosts? Could this represent an evolutionary progression towards cuckoo-like specialization?

Species	Distribution	Number of host species	Main hosts
Brown-headed Cowbird	Widespread through North America	226	Passerines
Shiny Cowbird	South America Trinidad and Tobago; recent expansion throughout West Indies and into southern U.S.A.	214	Passerines
Bronzed Cowbird	Central Arizona, S.W. New Mexico, S. Texas, through Mexico and central America to Panama.	82	Passerines
Giant Cowbird	Mexico, through South America to N. Argentina	7	Icterids (oropendolas and caciques)
Screaming Cowbird	Bolivia, Paraguay, Uruguay, S. Brazil, Argentina	1	Bay-winged Cowbird

SHINY COWBIRDS: 'SHOT-GUN' LAYING

Shiny Cowbirds (**Plate 6a**) were originally confined to South America, Trinidad and Tobago. However, in the early 1900s they began to spread north through the West Indies archipelago. This invasion was mainly due to increased suitable habitat provided by deforestation and the spread of agriculture and livestock, the same causes of the Brown-headed Cowbird's expansion throughout North America. Shiny Cowbirds reached Florida in 1987 and appear to have become established in the southern part of this state.

In South America, Shiny Cowbirds are common in open country, especially where there are scattered trees and shrubs. Historically, their distribution was centred on the 'pampas', but they must have spread and increased in numbers since European colonization because they are especially abundant in cultivated land. At present, they are widespread and abundant throughout much of the continent except for the Amazon rainforest, but they have been quick to move into deforested areas.

Figure 12.1 The range of the Shiny Cowbird in south and central America.[20]

The Shiny Cowbird's parasitic behaviour was first studied in detail during the 1870s by William Henry Hudson, whose father had emigrated to Argentina from Britain. Hudson was born there and came to love the wild countryside. He lamented its loss to agriculture and the destruction of wildlife brought by hunting, fearing that all his generation would leave to posterity would be 'monographs of extinct species, and the few crumbling bones and faded feathers ... in some museums. Such dreary mementoes will only serve to remind them of their loss, and if they remember us at all, it will only be to hate our memory and our age'.[2] Hudson returned to Britain in later life to become a pioneer in conservation and a staunch supporter of the RSPB.

Hudson attributed the Shiny Cowbird's success to the fact that, freed from parental duties, it could lay more eggs than other birds. He noted that it parasitized many host species, that its egg required less incubation than the host eggs, that this 'head start' enabled the Cowbird chick to outcompete the host chicks and that the parasite chick was unusually vigorous in its begging behaviour. He also described how female, and sometimes male, Shiny Cowbirds pecked holes in host eggs, and he suggested that the unusually strong shell of the Cowbird's egg helped it to withstand destruction by other Cowbirds. Hudson embraced Darwin's theory of natural selection, published just over a decade earlier, and admired these parasitic adaptations, but he puzzled over the extraordinary wastage of Cowbird eggs. Often so many eggs were laid in one host nest, either by the same or several females, that the hosts deserted. Cowbirds would even lay in abandoned host nests or old nests that Hudson himself put out in trees and bushes. One deserted nest of the Rufous Hornero had 37 Cowbird eggs! 'If there is so much that is defective and irregular in [its] reproduction,' Hudson asked, 'how can the species maintain its existence, and even increase to such an amazing extent?'[3]

This wastage of eggs is surely a consequence of intense competition for host nests, rather than defective behaviour on the part of the Cowbird. In areas of high Shiny Cowbird abundance, often 50–100% of the host nests are parasitized, many of them with several Cowbird eggs. For example, a common host throughout much of the Cowbird's range is the Rufous-collared Sparrow (**Plate 6b**). In northwest Argentina, James King found an average of 66% nests parasitized over the whole breeding season, and 100% parasitism during the peak of laying.[4] With such competition for nests, the best parasitic strategy would be 'shot-gun' laying, where females simply laid in any nests they could find. If there was a premium on laying early, to ensure that the Cowbird chick hatched in good time, then it would pay to parasitize nests as soon as they were complete, despite the wasted eggs in abandoned nests. Provided eggs are cheap to produce, this would be better than careful monitoring of every host nest to ensure the timing was perfect for each one, especially as there is a good chance that other female Cowbirds will parasitize the same nest. Like Brown-headed Cowbirds, female Shiny Cowbirds are prolific egg-layers. It has been estimated that one female may be able to lay up to one hundred eggs per breeding season.[5]

Such 'scramble competition' for limited resources is well known in other circumstances. It occurs in many frogs and toads, for example, where males face intense competition for mates during a brief spawning period. They grab at any passing object in the hope that it might be a female. Some end up grasping goldfish or even lumps of bread and hang on with grim determination. These ludicrous mistakes are simply the penalty to be paid when there is pressure to be first – any 'slow but sure' individuals will always be outcompeted.

Two recent studies have provided particularly good data on 'shot-gun' laying by Shiny Cowbirds. In the Cauca Valley, Colombia, Gustavo Kattan[5] recorded parasitism of House Wrens at 59% of natural nests and 94% of nests in artificial nest boxes. Most parasitized nests had three or more Cowbird eggs (maximum 12) and up to six different females, recognized by characteristic egg markings, parasitized the same nest. In one case, six Cowbird eggs were laid in a Wren nest all on one day! The Wrens abandoned clutches with three or more Cowbird eggs. Nevertheless, female Cowbirds were just as likely to parasitize nests with many eggs, and over 30% of their eggs were laid in abandoned nests. This is a remarkable contrast to the careful laying by Common Cuckoos, which often have sole command of a group of host nests and choose their timing so it coincides with host laying (chapter 3).

In Buenos Aires Province, Argentina, Bruce Lyon[6] recorded 48% parasitism of Chestnut-capped Blackbird nests. Again, eggs were laid at random so that some nests, by chance, escaped parasitism while others had up to five Cowbird eggs. There was clearly no exclusive territory defence by females. For example, in one colony of just 12 host nests, eight different Cowbirds laid eggs. Lyon's analysis of parasitism of 11 host species showed that the frequency of multiple parasitism increased as the overall percentage of nests parasitized increased, and it did so exactly as you would expect from random laying by females.

Presumably the intense competition for hosts also explains why Shiny Cowbirds often lay in the nests of species that are not very suitable. In the pampas of Argentina, Michael Gochfeld[7] found 96% parasitism of the nests of Red-breasted Meadowlarks, yet no fledgling Cowbirds were seen, probably because they were outcompeted by the larger host young. Similarly, in Buenos Aires Province, Gabriela Lichtenstein[8] recorded 49% parasitism for Rufous-bellied Thrushes, yet the Cowbird chicks usually starved to death in competition with the much larger host young.

Although most studies show that Shiny Cowbirds waste many of their eggs, they can sometimes be more selective in their laying behaviour. Juan Carlos Reboreda and colleagues from the University of Buenos Aires found that 70–80% of parasitic eggs laid in the nests of two icterid blackbird hosts (the Yellow-winged Blackbird[9] and the Brown-and-yellow Marshbird[10]) were timed perfectly, namely during the host laying period. Perhaps Shiny Cowbirds are better at getting their timing right when they can more easily monitor host nests, or can afford to be more choosy when there is less competition for hosts.

PUNCTURING HOST EGGS TO TEST THEIR DEVELOPMENT

Like Brown-headed Cowbirds, Shiny Cowbirds often puncture host eggs. These damaged eggs are then removed by the hosts. There could be several advantages of egg-puncturing, including improved incubation of the parasite's egg, reduced competition for the parasite's chick, and forcing the hosts to re-lay if the nest is too advanced for parasitism.

Viviana Massoni and Juan Carlos Reboreda have recently discovered another function.[11] They studied Yellow-winged Blackbirds in Buenos Aires Province, and found that the Shiny Cowbirds punctured one or two host eggs before they laid their own egg, either later that same day or the day after. Curiously, the Cowbirds also punctured eggs at nests they did not later parasitize. This wasn't to force hosts to desert because, again, only one or two eggs were punctured. Massoni and Reboreda suggest that the main function of the pecking was to assess the development of the host clutch. In support of their idea, the Cowbirds were less likely to lay following pecking if the host eggs were at a more advanced stage of development, where parasitism would be pointless because the Cowbird egg would not receive sufficient incubation to hatch. Puncturing host eggs might provide the best guide to the correct timing of parasitism in cases where cowbirds are unable to use other cues, such as nest building or the onset of host laying.

Cuckoos usually don't remove a host egg until the laying visit itself, so they cannot use 'egg tasting' as a regular cue to time their laying. However, female Common Cuckoos occasionally remove a host egg a day or two before they lay (chapter 4), so they might sometimes use this to assess whether the nest is suitable for parasitism.

THE SHINY COWBIRD'S VARIABLE EGGS

One of the most remarkable features of Shiny Cowbirds, and one of the few contrasts with Brown-headed Cowbirds, is the extraordinary variation in their eggs (**Plate 6c**). Some are pure white. Others are spotted, but the spots vary in colour from grey to reddish or brownish and while some eggs are sparsely speckled, others have heavy blotches, and there is all manner of variation between these extremes. Furthermore, the spots may be on backgrounds which vary too, from white, pale blue, pale green or buff. Hudson remarked that he had never seen a species with so much variation.[3] It is assumed that this variation is under genetic control, and that individual females lay eggs of a constant type, but this is not known for sure. Spotted eggs are found throughout the species' range, while the white morph is restricted to eastern Argentina, Uruguay and southeast Brazil.[12]

Why are the Shiny Cowbird's eggs so variable? The most obvious possibility is that hosts might reject eggs unlike their own so, like cuckoos, Shiny Cowbirds have evolved different host races. No-one has yet followed individual females to see how selective they are in their choice of hosts, but the variability in Cowbird eggs found within the nests of any one host species suggests that any host race formation cannot be as advanced as in cuckoos. Could Shiny Cowbirds, nevertheless, be at an early stage of this evolutionary transition from a generalist parasite to one with specialist gentes (chapter 9)?

Hudson[3] suggested that one host, at least, might selectively reject plain white shiny Cowbird eggs. He found a nest of the Brown-and-yellow Marshbird with two host eggs (which are spotted) and three spotted Shiny Cowbird eggs. However, on the ground beneath there were five more Cowbird eggs, all of the pure white morph. Recent experiments by Myriam Mermoz and Juan Carlos Reboreda[13] have confirmed that this host does indeed reject white eggs but accepts spotted eggs. Two other hosts with spotted eggs are more likely to eject the white type than spotted types, namely the Chalk-browed Mockingbird[14] and the Yellow-hooded Blackbird.[15] No host has yet been found to accept only white eggs.[16] Furthermore, 16 out of 24 host species, tested by experiment, accepted both plain and spotted eggs.[16,17] This suggests that, except for the three that reject the white morph, hosts do not provide a strong selection pressure for particular egg patterns. Even for the three host species that are selective rejectors, there is no evidence that they are more likely to be parasitized by Shiny Cowbirds with matching eggs. Mermoz and Reboreda[10] found that white eggs were just as likely to be laid in the nests of Brown-and-yellow Marshbirds, even though they would all get rejected, as in the nests of Yellow-winged Blackbirds, a host that accepts all egg types. Clearly, there is no evidence that the variability in Shiny Cowbird eggs reflects the start of host race formation in this parasite.

As we discovered in chapter 4, host defences are not the only selection pressure that may affect parasite eggs. Another possibility is predation. Perhaps different egg types do best in different host nests because predators would be more likely to notice clutches with eggs that are different from the host eggs. Paul Mason and Stephen Rothstein[18] tested this by placing single model eggs into the nests of Rufous-collared Sparrows, a ground nester which lays spotted eggs and which accepts odd eggs in its nest (**Plate 6c**). There was no difference in survivorship of clutches with 'cryptic' spotted model eggs versus those with 'conspicuous' white eggs and so, just as we found for cuckoos (chapter 4), no support for the predation hypothesis.

A third possibility is that the variability in Shiny Cowbird eggs reflects the outcome of discrimination by the Cowbirds themselves. Recall that some cuckoos remove an egg before they lay and this may lead to the evolution of either eggs like those of the host, or dark eggs that are hard to see against the nest lining, to decrease the chance that other cuckoos will be able to pick out a cuckoo egg for removal (chapter 7). Cowbirds also destroy eggs, though they usually do this on a separate, earlier visit to the host nest (it is not certain that the same female is always responsible for both the laying and the egg pecking). Given the fact that Cowbird eggs are likely to hatch first, and so produce chicks that are especially strong competitors, it would pay a female to select other Cowbird eggs for destruction. This could be a powerful selective pressure because of the high frequency of multiple parasitism – often most of the host nests have already been parasitized by other female Cowbirds. The Cowbird's best defence may be to mimic the host eggs, but if individual females are generalists then they might have to lay an egg which is an average match for several hosts. If the most common hosts vary in abundance between local areas, then the best egg type may vary from place to place and explain the variation in the parasite eggs.

So far there is no evidence for this idea. In his study in Colombia, Gustavo Kattan[5] found that Shiny Cowbirds did not target previously laid Cowbird eggs for removal. Indeed only 6% of them were pecked. Similarly, in Mermoz and Reboreda's study[10] host eggs were much more likely to be broken than Cowbird eggs, even in nests with multiple parasitism by several females. This suggests that Cowbird eggs are fairly well protected by their thick shells.

In conclusion, the problem of why Shiny Cowbird eggs are so variable is still a mystery. In particular, the persistence of the white type is a puzzle. Is it declining in frequency because of selective rejection by three common hosts? Or is something else maintaining it in certain parts of the parasite's range?

HOST DISCRIMINATION FOR EGG SIZE

Paul Mason and Stephen Rothstein have discovered a case of host discrimination which is apparently leading to evolutionary change in Shiny Cowbird eggs, a selection not for egg coloration but rather for size.[19] Rufous Horneros build an extraordinary oven-like domed nest out of mud, which becomes hard-baked in the sun. It is dark inside, and the hosts do not discriminate foreign eggs by visual cues. Nevertheless, they do so by size. Observations in Uruguay showed that they rejected Shiny Cowbird eggs whose width was less than 88% of their own eggs.

In Uruguay, Shiny Cowbird eggs have unusually large widths. Here, the Hornero has probably been parasitized for a long time and although it is only one of many hosts there, it is likely to have had an influence on the design of Cowbird eggs because its nests are relatively safe from predation and fledge many Cowbird chicks. On the south side of the Río de La Plata estuary, in the grasslands of Buenos Aires Province of Argentina, Horneros have probably become common only since European settlers planted trees and erected buildings and fences on which they could build their nests. Here, where Hornero parasitism has probably occurred for less than three hundred years, there has been no evolutionary change towards wider cowbird eggs.[19]

SHINY COWBIRD INVASION OF THE WEST INDIES – EVOLUTION IN ACTION?

Why do most hosts of the Shiny Cowbird accept the parasite's eggs? The recent invasion of the West Indies seems to provide an ideal opportunity to test between the two hypotheses we discussed in the last chapter for acceptance by Brown-headed Cowbird hosts. If acceptance is best, then hosts in South America should accept just as much as those in the West Indies. If rejection is best, but takes time to evolve in host populations, then the West Indian hosts should show more acceptance.

Shiny Cowbird colonization of the West Indies has been followed over the past 20 years by William Post from Charleston Museum, James Wiley from the U.S. Fish and Wildlife Service and Alexander Cruz and his colleagues from the University of Colorado.[20] The colonization is thought to have originated from Trinidad and Tobago. Here, host choice has remained stable over the past 50–60 years, with the three most heavily parasitized species in 1920–1940 remaining the favoured hosts today, namely House Wren, Red-breasted Blackbird and Yellow-hooded Blackbird.[21] The Shiny Cowbird's progress north, from island to island, is shown on the map overleaf, and charted by the following arrival dates: 1901 Grenada, 1916 Barbados, 1931 St. Lucia, 1948 Martinique, 1955 Puerto Rico, 1972 Hispaniola, 1982 Cuba. Host preferences on the new islands have remained similar to those in Trinidad, with icterids being among the most common hosts.

Host choice has been best studied on Puerto Rico.[22] As on the South American mainland, the Cowbirds avoid hosts (e.g. pigeons, nectar and fruit eaters) with an unsuitable diet for their parasitic chicks, and target those that fed their young on insects or a mixture of insects and seeds. Favourite hosts include the Yellow Warbler,

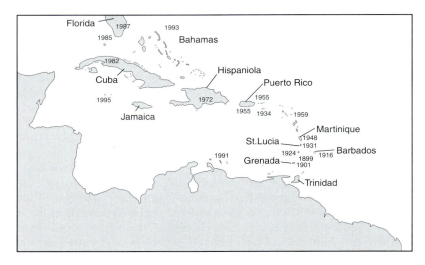

Figure 12.2 The recent range expansion of Shiny Cowbirds, northwards through the West Indies to southern Florida. Dates indicate when the Cowbird first reached the various islands.[20]

Black-whiskered Vireo, Puerto Rican Flycatcher, Yellow-shouldered Blackbird, Troupial and Black-cowled Oriole. These suffer parasitism at 75–100% of their nests. Other hosts, with 2–17% parasitism are the Gray Kingbird, Red-legged Thrush, Northern Mockingbird, Greater Antillean Grackle and Bronze Mannikin.

These parasitism rates are similar to those suffered by hosts in the Shiny Cowbird's ancestral home, so selection for the evolution of host defences is probably just as strong among these new host populations. How do their defences compare with those of hosts in South America? Experiments with model Cowbird eggs revealed that only three out of 11 host species tested on Puerto Rico showed strong rejection[23] (eggs rejected at 60% or more of nests). These were the Gray Kingbird, Northern Mockingbird and Greater Antillean Grackle. The first two species are parasitized by cowbirds on mainland America, so are not really naïve hosts. They have probably retained their rejection defences from ancestral populations, which were parasitized. In support of this view, Gray Kingbirds showed just as strong rejection in the Bahamas, when they were tested within three years of the parasite's first colonization in 1993.[40] The grackle is endemic to the West Indies, so may have evolved rejection within 30 years or so, unless it has retained some ability to reject from an ancestral species that had experienced parasitism.

This proportion of 'rejecter' host species in Puerto Rico is similar to that found by Paul Mason[16] in experiments in Buenos Aires Province, Argentina (where three out of 13 hosts were strong rejecters). At first sight then, these results seem to support the 'acceptance is best' hypothesis for accepter hosts – if rejection is best, then surely more of the hosts in the parasite's ancient home would have evolved rejection by now? However, this conclusion would be premature. As we saw in the last chapter, many old hosts of the Brown-headed Cowbird have evolved desertion as a rejection response to natural parasitism, perhaps in response to the sight of a female Cowbird at their nest. What we really need is a comparison of desertion rates in the West Indies and on mainland South America.

One hint that West Indian hosts may have lower desertion defences comes from the fact that on Puerto Rico desertion rates did not differ between parasitized and unparasitized nests for any host species, except the Yellow Warbler.[22] This host is heavily parasitized by Brown-headed Cowbirds in North America (chapter 10) and so may already be primed to desert because of defences its ancestors evolved long ago against this other parasite. Perhaps the other hosts on Puerto Rico have not had sufficient time to evolve desertion as a defence?

Another defence that may take time to evolve is aggression against female Cowbirds. On Trinidad, and in northern South America, a common host is the Yellow-hooded Blackbird. Although 40% of its nests are parasitized on Trinidad, parasitism has little effect on the Blackbird's productivity because its chicks are larger than the Cowbird chick and can fledge successfully from parasitized nests. The male Blackbirds are very aggressive towards female Cowbirds that approach their nests and apparently recognize them as a particular threat. This defence reduces the chances of parasitism and also is effective in preventing Cowbirds from puncturing their eggs.[15]

A closely related blackbird endemic to Puerto Rico, the Yellow-shouldered Blackbird, lacks this defence altogether.[24] As a result, it suffers much heavier parasitism, 90–100%, and although its chicks could compete just as well with the Cowbird chick, few of its chicks survive because of multiple parasitism and destruction of its eggs by female Cowbirds. These destroyed eggs are not recoverable by defences against Cowbird eggs, such as ejection or desertion. The best defence is clearly the one adopted by the old blackbird host on Trinidad, namely nest defence against female Cowbirds. It is possible that Yellow-shouldered Blackbirds may not evolve this defence in time and now need human help to survive. Their population on Puerto Rico has declined precipitously since Cowbirds arrived and production may be below the levels needed to maintain their numbers. Cowbirds are now being removed from some areas by trapping. This has reduced parasitism levels to 30–45% and has improved Blackbird productivity.[25] It remains to be seen whether this will lead to an increased population size. Other factors to blame are loss of habitat and predation by introduced rats.

BRONZED AND GIANT COWBIRDS

Bronzed Cowbirds occur from the U.S.–Mexico border through Central America to northern Colombia. They have spread during the last hundred years into Arizona, New Mexico, California, Texas and Louisiana, but their spread has been slow. They are less of a generalist than Brown-headed and Shiny Cowbirds, with some tendency to favour orioles and other large hosts.[26]

Giant Cowbirds favour larger hosts still, and specialize on oropendolas and caciques. These hosts nest in colonies, sometimes with a hundred or more nests high in the tree tops and often at the ends of the branches. Colonial nesting may help reduce parasitism in two ways. First, aggressive defence by a colony can drive the Cowbirds away. Second, it may help hosts to synchronize their laying which could 'flood the market' and reduce the chance that any one nest is parasitized. Giant Cowbirds may increase their access to host nests by visiting colonies later in the morning, when the hosts are more likely to be away feeding,[27] and by arriving in groups, with the males distracting the hosts while the females slip onto the nests unnoticed.[28]

In Panama, Neal Smith from the Smithsonian Tropical Research Institute suggested that in some host colonies the oropendolas and caciques actually benefited from parasitism because the young Giant Cowbirds preened the host chicks, removing the larvae of harmful botflies.[29] He argued that in these colonies the hosts encouraged parasitism by allowing the Cowbirds to enter their nests. However, it seems unlikely that a young cowbird chick would have the skills to remove botflies from its fellow nestmates. Gabriela Lichtenstein's videos of another species, the Bay-winged Cowbird, show clearly that it is the host adults which remove the botflies from the chicks.[30] This is a difficult task, requiring deft and precise pecking to extract the larvae from under the skin. Furthermore, other studies suggest that it is unlikely that hosts would gain from parasitism and have found strong aggression against Giant Cowbirds.[27,28]

SCREAMING COWBIRDS AND THEIR BAY-WINGED COWBIRD HOSTS

We now turn to a cowbird with very different parasitic habits. The Screaming Cowbird is an extreme specialist, almost entirely reliant on the Bay-winged Cowbird as its host.[1] W.H. Hudson[3] was the first to discover that it was a parasite (chapter 2), a clever piece of detective work because the eggs of the two species are similar and, most remarkably, their chicks (which are raised together) are practically impossible to tell apart at both the nestling and fledgling stage (**Plate 6d**). Herbert Friedmann[12] suggested that Screaming Cowbirds have evolved from Bay-winged stock and their common ancestry explained this close resemblance. However, the adults look very different – Bay-winged Cowbirds are brownish with a rufous patch on the wings, while Screamings are glossy black – and recent molecular studies reveal that they are not each other's closest relatives.[31] Therefore, the extraordinary resemblance at the nestling and fledgling stage is likely to reflect evolved mimicry rather than close ancestry.

Why is the Screaming Cowbird unique among cowbirds in showing such host specialization and chick mimicry? Its interactions with Bay-winged hosts have been studied in Buenos Aires Province, Argentina, by Rosendo Fraga[32] from the Asociacion Ornitologica del Plata and by Gabriela Lichtenstein[30] from Cambridge University, and the following account is based on their work.

Bay-winged Cowbirds are common in open woodlands, grasslands, agricultural land and suburbia in central and southern South America. They usually breed in the old abandoned nests of other species, particularly the domed, stick nests of the Leñatero (= Fire-wood Gatherer or Woodhewer) or domed, oven-like mud nests of the Rufous Hornero. Occasionally they take over active nests, by chasing off the owners, or build their own open-cup nests. This habit of occupying old nests

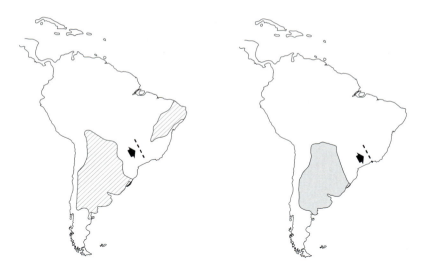

Figure 12.3 Distribution of Bay-winged Cowbirds (left) and their parasite, the Screaming Cowbird (right). Arrows indicate range expansions into southeastern Brazil.[32]

probably explains why Bay-winged Cowbirds breed much later than most other species.

Although Screaming Cowbirds are not as abundant (in Fraga's study area, Bay-wings outnumbered them by about four to one), they occur over most of the Bay-wing's range and are now following their host as it extends into the deforested areas of Brazil. In the non-breeding season the two species often occur together in feeding flocks. Once the Bay-wings begin to occupy their nests, the Screamings pay them frequent visits and an hour's watch of an active nest almost always brings several inspections by these parasites. Parasitism rates are often high. In Fraga's study 88% of the Bay-winged nests at one site were parasitized, and 100% at another site, with an average of three Screaming Cowbird eggs per nest. Lichtenstein recorded 100% parasitism at her site, with an average nest containing three Bay-winged Cowbird eggs and seven Screaming Cowbird eggs. The eggs of the Screaming Cowbird are spotted, like those of the Bay-winged, but the eggs of both species vary considerably in background colour and markings. This helps to distinguish host and parasite eggs in a particular nest, but in a large mixed collection from many nests they would be difficult to tell apart.[33]

With such intense competition for Bay-winged nests, Screaming Cowbirds are driven to lay in any nest they can find and many of their eggs are wasted. Fraga found that only 50% of their eggs were laid at the correct time, during the host-laying period. Of the others, 15% were laid too early, before the hosts had begun their clutch, and all these were ejected by the Bay-wings. The other 35% were laid too late, after incubation had begun, so they usually failed to hatch. Once the Bay-wings have started their clutch they accept all foreign eggs, even pure white eggs completely unlike their own.

Screaming Cowbirds often puncture host eggs (40% in Fraga's study) or previously laid parasite eggs. However, sometimes parasitism by several females leads to so many eggs in the nest (up to 28 have been recorded) that the Bay-wings either abandon it or eject the entire clutch and start again. The result of all this chaos is that while the Screamings appear to have the upper hand at the egg stage (55% of the eggs in Fraga's study were Screaming eggs), by the time the chicks fledge the Bay-wings have restored some advantage (only 24% of the fledglings were Screaming Cowbirds).

THREE COWBIRD SPECIES IN ONE NEST

To add to the mayhem, about 20% of the Bay-winged nests are also parasitized by Shiny Cowbirds! The lower rate of parasitism by this second parasite is partly due to the fact that, by the time the Bay-wings begin to breed, most of the Shinys have finished laying. A second reason is that Bay-winged Cowbirds are fierce defenders of their nests. Screaming Cowbirds can gain access because they visit the nests in pairs, sometimes several pairs together, so while the owners do battle with some of the intruders, the females can slip into the nests to lay.[34] Shiny Cowbird females, on the other hand, visit host nests alone and are more easily driven off.

So, if you peer into a Bay-winged Cowbird nest, it could contain the chicks of three different species! This is every bit as confusing for naturalists as for the birds themselves, so before we continue it may help if we remind ourselves who is who.

> *Bay-winged Cowbirds: the hosts.*
> *Screaming Cowbirds: a specialist parasite of the Bay-winged Cowbird.*
> *Shiny Cowbirds: a generalist parasite which includes the Bay-winged*
> *Cowbird among its many hosts.*

Rosendo Fraga was the first to discover how you can sort out which chick belongs to which species.[35] Shiny Cowbird chicks can be distinguished with experience because they have yellowish skin and a yellow bill. The chicks of the other two species have pinkish skin and pink bills, but newly hatched Bay-wings look a little more orange and have a darker tip to the upper mandible. However, by two to four days of age these differences have disappeared, so if you want to distinguish the two species you have to be quick. At the feathered fledgling stage the Shiny Cowbird chicks really stand out; they are uniform brownish and their calls are high-pitched whistles. By contrast, the Bay-winged and Screaming chicks have identical brownish-grey plumage and rufous wings (**Plate 6d**), and their calls are the same too, a series of fast nasal rattles.

Is such exquisite chick mimicry important to fool the Bay-winged foster parents? At the early nestling stage, the answer is firmly 'no'. Both non-mimetic Shiny Cowbird chicks and mimetic Screaming Cowbird chicks are treated just like host chicks. Gabriela Lichtenstein's video filming at nests[30] shows that the hosts feed them, and also clean them of botfly larvae, just as assiduously as their own young. However, there are hints that the Shiny Cowbirds may get rejected once they grow feathers and begin to look unlike the rest of the brood. Fraga[32] found very low fledging success for Shiny Cowbirds and those that did fledge seemed to get ignored by the host parents. Gabriela Lichtenstein also never saw Shiny Cowbird fledglings being fed by Bay-wings,[36] even though many of her Bay-wing nests had Shiny chicks. A small number of cross-fostering experiments by Fraga[32] suggested that Shiny Cowbirds were rejected around fledging time. It would be fascinating to investigate this further. If it is confirmed, then it explains why the Screaming Cowbird has evolved such good chick mimicry.

Why should the Bay-wings delay rejection until the chicks are feathered? Gabriela Lichtenstein suggests that this avoids discrimination errors that would be likely earlier on, when the young nestlings are all rather alike, in a dark nest, and changing in appearance from day to day as they grow.[30] Later on, the Shiny Cowbird chick can be easily picked out because it lacks the rufous wing patches. Even at the early fledgling stage, rejection will be worthwhile because it saves the hosts three weeks wasted further care and fledglings demand even more food than nestlings. It would be interesting to discover whether rejection of foreign-looking chicks by Bay-winged Cowbirds involves an innate program to feed only fledglings with rufous wings, or whether they have to learn what their own young should look like (chapter 6).

Only at independence do the Screaming Cowbirds reveal their true identity, by moulting into their characteristic black plumage. It was this apparent miraculous transformation of some of the 'Bay-winged' Cowbirds into another species that led to Hudson's marvellous discovery[3] of the Screaming Cowbird's parasitic lifestyle.

SELFISH SCREAMING CHICKS

Parasite chicks that are raised alongside the host young are often far more exuberant in their begging than the host chicks. In chapter 8, we discussed two explanations. It might reflect the fact that the parasite is unrelated to the host, so its greed is not constrained by kinship with its nestmates or with the host's future broods. Alternatively, the parasite might need an especially 'charming' begging display to compensate for the fact that it looks different from the host young, and would otherwise be rejected. Of course, the parasite might have exaggerated begging for both of these reasons.

The Screaming Cowbird nestling is a more or less perfect mimic of the Bay-wing host nestlings, in both size and appearance, so it has no need to charm its hosts to combat rejection. Therefore this provides a good opportunity to test whether lack of kinship alone can lead to more intensive begging by a parasite chick. Gabriela Lichtenstein compared the begging displays of the two species in the laboratory, under standard conditions of hunger.[30] She fed the chicks to satiation, and then recorded their begging displays at various times thereafter. Both Screaming and Bay-wing chicks begged more as they became hungrier, but the Screamings begged more intensively and they held their begging postures for longer. These begging displays were the same whether the chicks were tested alone, or with a parasite and a host chick together in the same nest. Therefore the Screaming chick's more exaggerated begging was not triggered by the presence of a nestmate alongside – rather, it has an inbuilt program to be more demanding.

Lichtenstein then offered the chicks food and recorded how much they ate before they stopped begging. For the same degree of food deprivation, host and parasite chicks ate exactly the same amount. Therefore, the Screaming Cowbird's more exuberant begging was not simply because it was more hungry than a host chick. This neat study shows that exaggerated parasite begging can evolve because of lack of kinship alone.[30]

In the experiments the nestlings were offered as much food as they wanted, but in the wild food is often in short supply and parents struggle to raise the whole brood. Lichtenstein's video recordings at Bay-winged Cowbird nests revealed that the Screaming chicks' more selfish begging performance was very effective – it tricked the host parents into giving them an unfair share of the food, so that they grew faster and were more likely to survive than the host young.[30]

GENERALISTS AND SPECIALISTS

In chapter 9, we concluded that early on in evolution cuckoos are likely to be generalists in their parasitic habits, exploiting many host species. Then, as more and more hosts evolve defences, they will be forced to specialize. Increasing host defences, combined with competition among cuckoos, has driven the evolution of cuckoo specialization and speciation. Are cowbirds at an earlier stage of this evolutionary progression? If so, could their variation in parasitic habits reflect the transition from generalist to specialist host use?

During the last twenty years or so, our understanding of evolution has been revolutionized by new techniques. It is now possible to compare similarity at the molecular level, namely in sequences of the chemical compounds (bases) that make up the DNA, the genetic code that passes down the generations. The DNA molecule is made up of a long string of bases of four kinds, which can be represented by the letters A, C, G and T (the first letters of their chemical names). When DNA is copied, a mistake is sometimes made: for example, a G replaces an A or a C is substituted for a T. Recall from chapter 3 that cells contain DNA in two places. In the nucleus, errors are usually quickly spotted and corrected by special repair molecules. But in the mitochondria the correction mechanism works less well so mistakes accrue at a more rapid rate. This means that mitochondrial DNA is especially good for revealing relationships between species. The longer that two species have been separated, the greater the difference in their mitochondrial DNA simply because there will have been more time for differences to 'clock up' by accumulated copying errors. It's even possible to estimate the time that two species last shared a common ancestor from the degree of difference in their DNA sequences, by calibrating the molecular clock from known dates of divergence in the fossil record. Although endless sequences of the four letter code might appear to be the dullest message ever written, they contain not only the genetic information to build bodies but also clues to the ancestry of each species. It is as if each species carried around an enormous parish register, with details of its own history.

Scott Lanyon, from the Field Museum of Natural History, Chicago, was the first to study cowbirds by molecule watching rather than by bird watching.[31] He was able to work out the relationships between the five parasitic cowbirds and other icterid blackbirds by comparing DNA sequences of one gene in the mitochondria, the cytochrome-b gene. His results suggested the following evolutionary tree. The branches represent evolutionary transitions from a distant common ancestor on the far left hand side of the diagram. The shorter the branches between two species, the more closely they are related.

Brown-headed Cowbird (226 hosts)
Shiny Cowbird (214 hosts)
Bronzed Cowbird (82 hosts)
Giant Cowbird (7 hosts)
Screaming Cowbird (1 host)
other icterid blackbirds, including
Bay-winged Cowbird

The first exciting result is the close relationship between the five parasitic cowbirds. The tree suggests that the parasitic habit evolved just once in the cowbirds and all five species inherited this lifestyle from a common ancestor. Unfortunately, the molecular results did not resolve the precise position of the Bay-winged Cowbird in this tree, but it has certainly not shared a recent common ancestor with the parasitic cowbirds.

Lanyon also made a second conclusion. Because the most specialist cowbirds (Screaming and Giant) are more ancient species, and the most generalist cowbirds (Brown-headed and Shiny) are the more recently evolved, he suggested that the tree indicates that specialists evolve into generalists. This is the exact opposite of what we argued from our cuckoo results in chapter 9. However, it is difficult to make conclusions about the evolution of host specialization from the cowbird tree because 'number of hosts' is unlikely to be a fixed characteristic of a species. It could equally well be argued that because the younger species are generalists, then this is the likely starting habit. Older species have occupied their ranges for longer and so have had more time to evolve specialist habits suited to their host avifauna. There is also still debate about the cowbird phylogeny itself.[37]

COWBIRDS AND CUCKOOS COMPARED

Compared with the Old World parasitic cuckoos, the parasitic cowbirds are a relatively young lineage. They include just five species, all rather similar in appearance. The molecular clock evidence suggests that the Screaming Cowbird separated from the lineage leading to the other parasitic cowbirds about 2.8 to 3.8 million years ago, while the Brown-headed Cowbird and Shiny Cowbird have existed as independent species for only one million years or so.[38] By contrast, the cuckoos belong to an ancient group which evolved 65–144 million years ago, and they have evolved into many more parasitic species with a much greater range in appearance. This comparison suggests that the cuckoos have had much more time to evolve their specialist habits.

When Stephen Rothstein published the results of his experiments in 1975, showing that the majority of North American hosts accepted cowbird eggs, he concluded that 'the host-parasite system of the Brown-headed Cowbird is not a highly evolved interaction'. Certainly, a comparison with the cuckoo-host systems of the Old World supports this view. Experiments show that for both European and African hosts, only about a quarter of host species are 'accepters' of eggs unlike their own[39] (defining an 'accepter' species as one where rejection of eggs placed into their nests by experiment occurs at less than 25% of nests). The cuckoos are specialist parasites, many have mimetic eggs evolved to deceive their particular host species, and parasitism rates tend to be low on average, often 5% or less. By contrast, the majority of hosts in the New World are 'accepters'; in North America about 80% of host species accept eggs unlike their own and in South America the proportion is about 60%.[17] The most common parasites, the Brown-headed and Shiny Cowbirds, are generalists, with no special egg mimicry, and parasitism rates are often heavy, 50–100% of host nests.

As we pointed out in chapter 11, the cowbird-cuckoo comparison is complicated by the fact that, for some cowbird hosts, acceptance may be better than rejection. However, there are strong reasons for believing that many cowbird-host systems are undergoing dynamic change. First, the range expansions of both Brown-headed and Shiny Cowbirds have certainly brought them into recent contact with new hosts. Second, old hosts have stronger defences than new hosts (chapter 11), which suggests that for many 'accepter' hosts lack of defences reflects evolutionary lag, and that in time they will evolve stronger rejection. There is the exciting prospect of being able to study this in the east and far-west of North America, where Brown-headed Cowbirds are recent invaders, and in the West Indies, recently colonized by Shiny Cowbirds. Perhaps, as more and more hosts evolve defences, these cowbirds will be forced to evolve mimetic eggs and so will split into separate host races. Certainly they have the potential to do this. There is considerable variation in their eggs and some female Brown-headed Cowbirds, at least, may already specialize on particular host species.

The recent range expansions of cowbirds may also enable us to see what happens when two cowbird species come into competition. In central America, the two cowbird species, Bronzed and Giant, tend to go for different hosts. In South America, too, Shiny Cowbirds and Screaming Cowbirds largely avoid competition by breeding at different times. Bronzed Cowbirds come into competition with the smaller Brown-headed Cowbird in Mexico, and there is currently much overlap in host use, though the Bronzed Cowbird tends to go for larger hosts.[41] In time, will these two parasites diverge further in their host choice so as to avoid competition? Perhaps they will evolve further divergence in body size, as each becomes better adapted to its own suite of hosts. These kinds of host shifts have frequently occurred in cuckoos and have led to host specialization and cuckoo speciation (chapter 9). Similarly, if Shiny Cowbirds invade the U.S.A., their competition with Brown-headed Cowbirds may lead to increasing specialization, perhaps with the two cowbirds diverging to exploit different hosts.

It is neither easy, nor wise, to predict the future with great certainty, especially in nature, where interactions are so complex. But the cowbird-host systems of the New World surely offer a wonderful opportunity for molecule watchers and bird watchers to combine forces to document evolution in action, both as hosts evolve stronger defences and as cowbird species come into competition. I would dearly love to be around in a few thousand years' time to see what has happened!

CHAPTER 13
The parasitic finches of Africa: mimicry of host chicks and host songs

In Africa, it is the big things that first catch the eye – the vast savannahs, ancient baobabs, herds of elephants crashing through the bush, giraffes browsing in the tree tops. But the greatest biological treasures are often to be found on a smaller scale. At first sight, a flock of drab-coloured finches at a dry season water hole seems to present little of interest, but come the rains and the onset of breeding, these small birds will be transformed. The males moult into extravagant plumage and pour out extraordinary songs, while the females engage in parasitic behaviour which rivals even that of the cuckoos in its intricate trickery.

There are 20 species of parasitic finches and they all live in Africa. Nineteen of them are classified in a single genus, *Vidua*. The females and non-breeding males are sparrow-like in plumage but breeding males are partly or entirely glossy-black and some have long tails, often with remarkable shapes. All the *Vidua* finches parasitize grassfinches (Estrildidae) and most of them specialize on just one host species, so they are the most specialized of all the brood parasites. Genetic studies have revealed that the estrildids are, in fact, the *Viduas'* closest living relatives and that the *Vidua* finches evolved away from the estrildid stock some thirty million years ago.[1] As we shall discover, although these parasites are an ancient group, they are still showing evolutionary change today as they colonize new host species.

The other parasitic finch, the Cuckoo Finch, looks different from the rest and is more like a weaverbird, with a stubby bill and yellowish, streaky plumage. Unlike the others, it parasitizes warblers and it is not a specialist but exploits several host species. It was originally classified as a weaver, and is sometimes called the Parasitic Weaver, but genetic studies show that the *Vidua* finches are its closest relatives. This implies that brood parasitism evolved just once in the African parasitic finches.[1]

In this chapter we shall first discuss the *Vidua* finches. Why are they so specialized in their use of hosts? How do they ensure that they stick to the same host species from generation to generation?

THE *VIDUA* FINCHES AND THEIR HOSTS

The 19 species and their hosts are listed in Appendix 1. Like their estrildid hosts, the *Vidua* finches are birds of open woodland and grassland and they occur throughout sub-Saharan Africa. They feed on the small seeds of grasses and weeds, which they collect from the ground, with occasional supplements of termites during the rainy season. The *Vidua* finches can be divided into three groups.[2]

The paradise whydahs

There are five species, each specializing on a different species, or subspecies, of *Pytilia* finches as hosts. The tails of the breeding males are spectacularly ornate. When I first flicked through a field guide to African birds, these were among the species I was most eager to see. The central pair of long tail feathers is twisted and rounded to form a 'keel' shape and either side there is another pair of even longer broad feathers which taper to a point, adding an extra 15–23 cm to a body length of 15 cm in the non-breeding plumage (see page 203). The five species all look rather alike, but they differ in geographical distribution and males differ in their songs. The only two species with extensive range overlap are the eponymous Paradise Whydah and the Broad-tailed Whydah and their breeding males are readily distinguished by the latter's shorter and broader tail.

The waxbill whydahs

There are four species, all using waxbills as hosts (*Granatina* and *Estrilda* species). Two species are host specific (Shaft-tailed and Straw-tailed Whydahs). The Resplendent or Steel-Blue Whydah parasitizes two very similar waxbill species. The Pin-tailed Whydah, which has by far the widest distribution of the four, mainly parasitizes the Common Waxbill but uses five other host species in parts of its range. Breeding males of this group also have two pairs of elongated central tail feathers, but they are much slimmer than in the paradise whydahs. In the Shaft-tailed Whydah they have spatulate tips (see page 23) while in the other three species they are more or less uniformly thin along their length.

The indigobirds

These are a taxonomist's nightmare! Females and non-breeding males are streaky-brown and all look very similar. Breeding males are blackish, with short tails, but they differ in their metallic gloss (which may be green, blue or purple) and in the colour of their wings (brown to black), bills and feet (white, grey, red). Originally, some taxonomists thought that they all belonged to one species, with the different male forms simply being variants. However, careful studies since the 1960s have shown that there are distinct species and currently 10 are recognized, though there may be more.

The discovery of the different species is largely due to the remarkable field studies of Robert Payne, from the University of Michigan. On his first field trip to

Africa he lived in an old truck and spent two years travelling 55,000 miles on rough roads all over the continent, using five kilometres of audiotape to record indigobird songs. He has made many subsequent trips during the last 30 years, and has shown that the confusing taxonomy reflects a beautiful case of evolution in action with new species still forming now. His work is a fine example of the rule; if nature appears complicated, don't ignore the complications – they're likely to hide a wonderful story.

Payne discovered that, just like the whydahs, each indigobird species sang a different song, that males which sang the same songs looked alike, and that there were also subtle differences in the appearance of the females that mated with these different types of males.[3] Furthermore, nine of the indigobird species are specialist parasites on just one host species. Most of the hosts are various species of firefinches (*Lagonosticta*), but they also include twinspots and others. The one indigobird that parasitizes several hosts (the 'Cameroon' Indigobird) may well turn out to consist of several distinct species.[2]

EGG LAYING AND PARASITISM RATES

Like all the estrildid finches, the *Vidua* finches lay plain white eggs, so there is always a perfect match between parasite and host egg (**Plate 7c**). However, this reflects common ancestry rather than evolved mimicry as in cuckoos.[4] Thus when the *Vidua* finches began to evolve their parasitic habits and diverged from their ancestral estrildid stock, they suddenly presented their hosts with perfectly mimetic eggs. Unlike cuckoo hosts, the estrildid hosts never experienced a transitional stage with non-mimetic eggs and so there has been no selection for them to evolve discrimination against odd-looking eggs in their nest. This probably explains why estrildids accept eggs unlike their own.[5]

Although *Vidua* eggs are white, like the host eggs, they are easy to recognize because of their larger size. This is not because the parasites have evolved larger eggs; their egg size is exactly what you would expect for an estrildid finch of their body size. Parasite eggs are larger simply because the *Vidua* are larger in body size than their hosts.[4] For example, the indigobirds are 13–16 g, compared with 7–11 g for their firefinch hosts, and the paradise whydahs are 19–22 g, compared with 14–15 g for their *Pytilia* hosts. It may be advantageous for the parasite to be larger so its chicks gain a competitive advantage in the brood.

Vidua finches lay at daily intervals in 'sets' of about three eggs, with rests in between, and in a three-month breeding season they may lay 22–26 eggs.[4] This is many more eggs than in normal parental estrildids, where the average clutch of open-woodland and grassland species is about four eggs. Even with the maximum of four clutches in a season, they cannot match the parasite's productivity. As with parasitic cuckoos and cowbirds, the freedom from parental duties enables parasitic finches to increase their fecundity.

Estrildid finches breed later than most birds, usually delaying their egg laying until one or two months after the peak rainfall, when there will be an abundance of fresh green grass seeds and termites with which to feed their young.[6] They build dome-shaped nests from grass, with a side entrance, and these are hidden among the leaves of a bush or tree. Males do most of the work in collecting nest material, but females may help with nest construction. The female *Vidua* finches follow the hosts to observe their mating and nest-building activities. Robert Payne had captive firefinches and indigobirds flying freely around his house in America and the female indigobirds would follow the firefinches to watch them build their nests behind his bookcases, in roof crevices and, in one case, in an old Christmas tree.[3] Male indigobirds showed no interest in these activities so, like Common Cuckoos, the female parasitic finches search for host nests alone.

It is likely that the female *Vidua* coincides her egg laying with that of the host by responding to the same cues that the host female herself uses to trigger her laying, namely the sight of the male collecting nest material and the sound of his song.[3] The importance of host nest building as a cue for the parasite is suggested by the fact that when firefinches re-use an old nest, the female indigobird is more likely to get her timing wrong and lay too late, well after the host clutch is complete.[7] Even with freshly built nests, the parasite may find timing difficult because although host laying may commence a few days after the nest is complete, sometimes it is delayed for two weeks. It would be interesting to know whether this variability is a tactic designed to confuse the parasite. Despite being larger, the parasite egg hatches after less incubation than the host egg, just as in parasitic cuckoos.[4] For example, Village Indigobird eggs need just 10–12 days' incubation compared with 13–14 days for the Red-billed Firefinch host eggs. This means that even if the parasite lays her egg three days after the host clutch is complete, her chick will still hatch out in good time to compete successfully with the host brood.

Whereas hosts of cuckoos and cowbirds are often aggressive towards the laying female parasite, estrildid hosts are remarkably tolerant of *Vidua* females. During his studies of estrildid finches in the Transvaal, South Africa, David Skead of the Barberspan Ornithological Research Station, observed a nest of a Violet-eared Waxbill being parasitized by two female Shaft-tailed Whydahs during one morning.[6] The nest contained four eggs and at the start of Skead's watch the male waxbill was incubating. At 0846, the female waxbill settled in a tree nearby and was very agitated. Two minutes later, a female whydah arrived and entered the nest. The female waxbill followed her in, but then left immediately. The parasite spent 45 seconds inside the nest and then left, whereupon the host female entered the nest again briefly. The host male was in the nest all this time. At 0928 the male and female changed over, so the female was now incubating. At 0956 another female whydah arrived and appeared to peck at the female waxbill through the nest entrance. It then got right inside the nest and left 30 seconds later, with the host female following her. When Skead checked the nest, he found two parasite eggs alongside the four host eggs.

Other observations also suggest that *Vidua* finches are able to enter host nests freely. Skead watched a male Melba Finch guarding his nest while the female incubated and the male paid no attention to two female Paradise Whydahs, who inspected his nest together, but chased off two other Melba Finches who passed nearby. Similarly, firefinches seem to tolerate laying visits by female indigobirds.[7] In many cases, the firefinch is incubating when the female indigobird arrives and the parasite must either lay on top of the host, or at the edge of the nest, by squeezing in alongside. Presumably the parasite egg then rolls into the bottom of the nest. Is this extraordinary tolerance of the parasite simply because the hosts are afraid of the large intruder, or do the parasites have a special trick to dissuade attack?

By far the most extensive study of parasitism rates and effects on hosts is that by Marie-Yvonne Morel, from the University of Rennes, who did a 10-year study of Village Indigobirds parasitizing Red-billed Firefinches in Senegal.[7] The Firefinches nested in the bush but they also entered local villages to feed on grain and weed seeds from human cultivation and built nests in the thatched roofs of traditional houses. Morel found that 36% of the Firefinch nests were parasitized. Of these, about half had just one parasite egg while the others had several, usually two or three, but up to six. Multiple parasitism was sometimes the result of several Indigobirds laying in the same host nest (two eggs appeared on the same day), but some females certainly laid more than one egg per nest because their eggs appeared on successive days and were recognizable by their distinctive size and shape. Morel concluded that Village Indigobirds did not remove host eggs, because parasitized nests contained just as many host eggs. However, Robert Payne's aviary studies have shown that several *Vidua* species (including indigobirds, Paradise Whydahs and Pin-tailed Whydahs) remove eggs from host nests and eat them, and he has also found egg shells in the crops of laying female Village Indigobirds that he collected in the wild. So it seems likely that host eggs are sometimes removed. In her field study, Morel never recorded any cases of hosts rejecting the parasite egg.

Other studies that have recorded parasitism rates in local host populations are as follows:

- In Zambia, 42% of Red-billed Firefinch nests parasitized by Village Indigobirds (62% parasitized nests had one Indigobird egg, 38% had two).[4]
- In Tanzania, 87% of Melba Finch nests parasitized by Paradise Whydahs in one year, and 94% in another, and 73% Purple Grenadier nests parasitized by Straw-tailed Whydahs.[8]
- In Transvaal, South Africa, 33% Violet-eared Waxbills parasitized by Shaft-tailed Whydahs and 28% Melba Finch nests parasitized by Paradise Whydahs.[6]

The parasite chicks are raised alongside the host young and, unlike most cuckoo and cowbird chicks, seem to have little depressive effect on host success. Morel[7] found that unparasitized Red-billed Firefinch nests fledged on average 2.8 young per successful nest compared with 2.1 Firefinch young plus 1.3 Indigobird young from successful parasitized nests, a reduction in host success of just 25%. However, if there was a longer delay to the next clutch after raising a larger brood, parasitism could have a large effect on a pair's seasonal productivity. It would be interesting to study this further.

Why do the *Vidua* young have relatively little effect on the number of host chicks produced per nest? One possibility is that they constrain their aggression and greed because they often share the nest with siblings (chapter 8). Alternatively, perhaps the host parents can easily increase their provisioning rates to cope with an enlarged brood because they are exploiting an abundant food supply, namely a flush of new seeds and insects brought about by the rains. If this is true, why don't the hosts lay a larger clutch themselves? Perhaps their seasonal production is highest if they pace themselves with several smaller broods, and this then enables the parasites to exploit their spare capacity in each attempt.

The estrildid finch 'boom and bust' lifestyle, in response to a seasonal flush of food might also provide the clue to why they are so tolerant of parasitism. Morel ringed more than seven thousand firefinches during her 10-year study. She found that they had an unusually high rate of reproduction. Pairs often had four broods in a season, and young birds themselves began to breed at four months of age if food was plentiful. These high rates of reproduction brought their toll, because most breeding birds lived for one year or less. Estrildids seem to be designed to exploit the good times while they last and put all their effort into one breeding season, whatever the cost. If it is difficult to defend the nest against *Vidua* parasites (because they are larger), and to discriminate parasitic eggs and chicks (because they are mimetic), then the best host strategy may be to ignore parasitism altogether and to go for as much nest building and chick feeding as possible while seeds and insects are available. Any 'slow but sure' individuals, that spent time defending their nests, and rejecting or deserting in response to parasitism, would simply miss the boat.

WONDERFUL MOUTHS AND MIMICRY

If you have never peered into the mouth of a gaping estrildid nestling, then you are in for a shock! Most nestling birds have bright gapes, often yellow or red, but in estrildids they are such a riot of colours and patterns that nature the artist seems to have gone quite mad. The palate (roof of the mouth) may be whitish, red, yellow or blue. It also has black and violet spots in various numbers and patterns. In addition, there are grotesque swellings on the edge of the gape of ivory white, cornflower blue, yellow, red or violet. These may be simple thickenings or in the form of little pearl-shaped warts. Some are highly reflective, so the mouth appears to be surrounded by shining lights.[9]

Most species of estrildids have a unique mouth pattern, and each *Vidua* parasite mimics precisely the mouth colours and patterns of its particular host species (**Plate 7d**).[9] For example, the gapes of Melba Finch nestlings and those of its parasite, the Paradise Whydah, both have a single black spot on a pinkish palate, with two blue spots either side, and four white swellings around the gape margins. By contrast, the gapes of the Purple Grenadier and its parasite, the Straw-tailed Whydah, have three black spots on a yellowish palate, with blue swellings on the gape margins.

The nestlings also adopt strange postures when they beg. Most nestling birds stretch their necks and try to reach higher than their nestmates towards the parent's bill. The domed nest of estrildids may make this impossible so, instead, the chicks keep their head low and twist their neck to one side so that the open mouth is directed upwards to present the parents with a large target. The chicks then sway their heads from side to side, perhaps to attract the parent's attention, and in some species the tongue is waggled too. These astonishing postures of the host chicks are also copied exactly by the *Vidua* chicks and the host parents treat them just like their own young; the parent inserts its bill into the open gape and pumps in a mass of regurgitated seeds.[10] These identical begging postures might reflect common ancestry of the *Vidua* parasites and their estrildid hosts, rather than evolved mimicry.

This wonderful mouth mimicry was discovered in 1929 by Neunzig,[11] and confirmed by studies in the 1960s by Jürgen Nicolai, from the Max Planck Institute for Behavioural Physiology in Seewiesen, Germany. Nicolai suggested that host specialization and precise mouth mimicry has evolved because hosts reject chicks unlike their own.[9,10] According to Arnon Lotem's theory (chapter 6), nestling mimicry is exactly what you would expect in parasites that are raised alongside the host young, because it pays the hosts to imprint on the appearance of the young in their nest, and to then reject chicks that look different.

The history of this idea has followed the same curious path as that of egg mimicry by cuckoos – host discrimination seems so likely to be the mechanism that it is hardly worth testing! However, as we have discovered in the cuckoo chapters, experimental tests of host defences at the egg stage have revealed many surprises, not least the possibility that egg mimicry can evolve without any host discrimination whatsoever (chapter 7), so it is important to test critically even what seems to be obvious.

So far, the evidence for chick discrimination by estrildid parents is surprisingly slim. The first experiments were with Zebra Finches, an Australian estrildid which has no brood parasites. Normal Zebra Finch nestlings have distinctive dark spots on their palate, but there is a white morph, bred in aviaries, which lacks these spots. In one study, both normal adults and white morph adults preferred to feed nestlings with spotted mouths, when given mixed broods.[12] However, other studies have found that when food is abundant, unmarked nestlings grow just as well as those with spotted mouths. Only when food is restricted do the spotted-mouth chicks do better.[13,14]

Recently, Robert Payne and his co-workers have provided the first evidence that an African host species might discriminate against odd-looking young.[15] In cross-fostering experiments in aviaries, they found that Red-billed Firefinches were more likely to rear successfully either their own species' young, or young Village Indigobirds, which have matching mouth patterns, than the young of other estrildid species with mis-matching mouths. Nevertheless, young with mis-matching mouths were often accepted and fed, both by these firefinches and other estrildids. This suggests that a parasite would not need perfect mimicry right from the start, but could succeed by colonizing a new host, with selection then perfecting the mouth mimicry gradually over successive generations[15] (see later).

Why are the mouth markings of estrildid nestlings so elaborate? In chapter 4, we discussed the possibility that complex spotting on host and cuckoo eggs might be the outcome of a signature-forgery arms race. The same idea might be suggested for estrildid–*Vidua* nestling gape spots. However, this does not seem to be the explanation because Australian estrildids, which have no brood parasites, have just as complicated mouth patterns as those of the African species.[2,16] The complexity is also unlikely to have evolved to beat parasitism by other estrildid species; this would be selected against anyway because any parasitic offspring would mis-imprint on the host species and would misdirect their sexual preferences later on. Somehow, the complex mouths must be important in the normal family life of these finches.

The most likely explanation is that the mouth spots and colours are signals to the parents,[2] and their variety reflects their different functions. The reflective swellings around the edge of the gape must produce a better target in the dark, domed nest and the black spots on the palate may then help the parents to aim for the centre of the mouth. The colours, on the other hand, might help to signal the chick's condition. Like some other seed-eating finches, perhaps there is a flush of colour to the mouth which signals a chick's level of hunger (chapter 7). The various colour spots may well be signals of health.[2] Robert Payne has noted that chicks infested with parasites have faded mouths, and that the colours quickly fade altogether within minutes of death. Why, then, do different estrildid species have different mouth colours and patterns? Some differences may reflect adaptations to different environments (dark versus lighter nests, for example), while others may simply be the kinds of arbitrary differences that evolve once a species has been isolated for a long time.

These speculations need to be tested by experiment, but they still leave us with the puzzle of why estrildid mouth patterns are more complex than in other birds. One possibility is that this is linked to the fact that estrildid chicks hatch very asynchronously, over several days. In some species it pays the parents to have staggered hatching because if food becomes scarce, the smallest chicks can then be quickly runted off, and all parental effort can be directed towards saving the lives of the largest chicks. If food is plentiful, then the parents will be able to feed the smallest chicks too. However, in the estrildids, which usually have an abundant supply of food during breeding, staggered hatching may have another advantage; it might reduce the peak energy requirements of the whole brood because the nestlings will not all have their maximum energy demands at the same time. Signals of health and need may be particularly likely to evolve when there are chicks of different sizes and ages in the nest because parents should choose carefully which to feed, to make sure that the larger chicks do not monopolize an unfair share. Perhaps the mouth colours and markings help parents distinguish the small and needy from the large and greedy?

Once this kind of signalling system is in place, the signals could then become exaggerated by evolution. Just as males of many bird species have evolved elaborate sexual ornaments, such as wattles, crests and tails, to increase the chance that they attract a female, perhaps estrildid nestlings have evolved more elaborate mouths as ornaments to increase their attractiveness to parents. To the human eye, the mouth appears to be an outrageous advertisement; perhaps it is precisely this – a riot of colour and patterns aimed to brainwash the parent into providing more food.

Ornamented chicks have been described for just one other species. Young American Coots have bright orange plumes on the throat and back, and brilliant red spiky feathers around the face, which contrast with their black down.[17] Intriguingly, these chicks face exactly the same problem as the young estrildids. They hatch over a prolonged period, five days or more, and observations show that parents often pick out the youngest chicks to feed, even when their older and larger siblings are demanding food. Experiments, in which the orange plumes were trimmed, showed that the ornaments were particularly important for attracting feedings in these small, late-hatched chicks. Young Coots have a bare patch of skin on the top of the head which varies in colour, and may signal hunger in the same manner as the red flush in a finch nestling's gape. The ornamental feathers are similar in colour and may be advertisements to attract the attention of parents, which are tuned to respond to red and orange as a signal of chick condition.[17]

The theory that mouths are health signals which have been exaggerated in evolution, may explain why estrildids are parasitized only by their closest relatives. In ancient times, before estrildids were ever parasitized, they would already be paying close attention to their nestlings' mouths, so any parasite that tried to invade would have to have mouth signals of health, right from the start. *Vidua* finches, derived from the estrildid stock, would indeed be pre-adapted to exploit the system, so then evolution could proceed and perfect the mimicry. This contrasts with the evolution of egg discrimination and egg mimicry in cuckoos where, at the start of the arms race, the hosts pay no attention to their eggs, so a parasite with no mimicry whatsoever can invade and gradually perfect its mimicry as the hosts begin to evolve discrimination (chapter 9). In this case, no 'head start' in adaptation is needed, because the host is initially completely unresponsive to egg patterns.

HOW DO *VIDUA* FINCHES SELECT THE RIGHT HOST?

The *Vidua* finches now have an intriguing problem. How do they ensure that they choose the right host species, namely the one for which their nestling mouth pattern is a perfect match? In cuckoos, we argued that females alone could be host specific, because the key adaptation for tricking the host is a mimetic egg, and egg patterns might be controlled by the female genotype alone (chapter 9). In the *Vidua* finches, however, the mimicry of host nestling mouth patterns and begging postures could not be coded for by genes unique to females (on the W chromosome), otherwise only daughters would be mimetic. The mimicry must arise from genes on the autosomes (chromosomes common to both males and females). This requires host specialization by both sexes. Therefore, not only must a female *Vidua* parasitize the same host species that raised her as a nestling, but she must also somehow make sure that she mates with a male *Vidua* also raised by that same host species.

The way that Nature has solved this problem is beautiful in its simplicity. It was first suggested by Jürgen Nicolai in 1961, who made the exciting discovery that his male captive Village Indigobirds mimicked the song of their Red-billed Firefinch hosts.[18] He then went on to show that most of the other *Vidua* finches also sang songs just like those of their particular host species, so male Paradise Whydahs sang like Melba Finches, male Straw-tailed Whydahs sang like Purple Grenadiers, and so on. Therefore, when male *Viduas* sing they advertise the identity of the host that reared them. This immediately suggested to Nicolai how host specificity could come about.[19] Female *Vidua* finches might imprint on the song of their foster parent species, and then use this as a 'mental image' to guide both their choice of mate and their choice of host for egg laying. If they mated with a *Vidua* male that sang the song of their foster parent species, this would ensure that they mated with a male raised by the same host, and if they then chose to lay in a nest where the resident male sang that same song, this would ensure that they parasitized the same host species that reared both them and their mate. The result would be that the parasites produce offspring with mouth patterns that mimic their host.

Nicolai's evidence to test his theory was rather anecdotal, but certainly supportive. In his aviaries, he arranged for some male Straw-tailed Whydahs to be reared by Bengalese Finches, with no contact with their natural hosts, nor with other adults of their own species. These males developed songs like Bengalese Finches, showing that the parasites did indeed learn songs from their hosts.[19]

Nicolai's field observations also suggested strongly that song was the key for attracting females.[8] In Tanzania, he watched male Paradise Whydahs defending territories with spectacular aerial displays and loud calls. The males would fly up to a height of 20–100 m and then make straight sweeps across their territories in slow flight, with their long tails held in line with the body and the keel feathers slightly raised. These displays must serve as a 'keep out' signal to other males and may also attract females from a distance. The male then dives down towards the tree tops, sits on a favourite perch and pours out his songs which mimic those of the Melba Finch host. Females visit males at these singing perches and it is here that all the mating occurs. The importance of the song for mating was shown by a natural experiment. One of the male Paradise Whydahs studied by Nicolai had typical breeding plumage, with the long tail, and he displayed normally and defended his territory successfully against other males. However, when he perched and tried to sing, although his mouth and throat moved, no sound came out. This silent male failed to attract any females to his song perches.[8]

The male Paradise Whydah in a display flight over his territory, with the keel feathers raised and his long tail streaming behind.

Experiments by Robert Payne provided the first critical evidence that the mimetic song of the Paradise Whydah is the key for attracting females. He caught wild females and broadcast various songs to them from little loudspeakers in an aviary. The females approached the songs of male Paradise Whydahs that mimicked Melba Finch song, and they also approached Melba Finch song itself, but they did not respond nearly so much to the songs of another species of *Pytilia* finch.[20]

More recent studies show that males of other whydah species also defend territories and display from favourite perches, where they sing their mimicry songs and are visited by females for mating.[21,22] Some males appear to be much more successful than others, perhaps because they have a territory which contains scarce resources which females want, such as food or water for drinking.[22] There appears to be intense competition for territories, especially the more successful sites, because males without territories are constantly patrolling for vacancies and males with poor sites try to take over better sites. If males are removed by experiment, their places are quickly taken by others.[21] The most successful males may mate with a dozen or more females in a season, while each female mates with just one or a few males.

LONG TAILS

Although female whydahs demand host-mimicry songs from a male before they will mate with him, the male whydah's plumage is an important attractive feature too. In aviary experiments at the University of the Witwatersrand, South Africa, Phoebe Barnard gave some male Shaft-tailed Whydahs even longer tails, by glueing on an extra length snipped from other males.[23] In choice experiments, females preferred to solicit to the longer-tailed males and, intriguingly, these males boosted their song output, perhaps because the increased attention they received made them realize that they were more attractive and so would gain from extra advertisement.

Phoebe Barnard suggests that female whydahs may go for longer tails because this is a sure sign of a fertile male in peak breeding condition. This preference has driven the evolution of more exaggerated tails, so now the poor males have to fly around all breeding season with tails that are even longer than their bodies. This must be expensive in terms of energy and, perhaps, increased risks of predation, which may explain why some males don't come into full breeding plumage until the middle of the breeding season.[24] Perhaps these individuals cannot afford to carry their ornaments for a full season? An indication of the way that the tails hinder flight is shown by comparing the hovering displays that the whydah males perform in front of females that arrive at their singing perches. Male Shaft-tailed and Pin-tailed Whydahs, which have narrow tails, can hover for a minute or more while male paradise whydahs, with broader and much heavier tails, can keep this up for only a few seconds.[24] The costs to males of growing and bearing these crazy tails must have set the limit to how much they can be exaggerated in evolution by female choice.

As an aside, we might wonder why other brood parasites have not also evolved these kinds of extravagant ornaments. They are typical of species where males play no part in parental care and so put all their effort into attracting mates, species such as the birds of paradise and pheasants. During the breeding season, male cuckoos and cowbirds likewise have nothing to do all day except eat and attract mates. Why, then, haven't they evolved ornaments to enhance their attractiveness?

One possibility is that, by chance, females have latched on to other male features as a sign of fertility or quality, such as amount of calling, so these have been exaggerated instead. The rather arbitrary nature of female choice for male signals is suggested by the variety of plumes and colours of different species of birds of paradise, for example, and the fact that male indigobirds have not evolved long tails. The other possibility is that in some of the other brood parasites males cannot afford to develop ornaments, perhaps because they have to follow females around to guard them from other males (some cowbirds) or to help them gain access to host nests (some cuckoos). This, in turn, would reduce the number of females a male could mate with and so there would be less pressure to be attractive. Thus, while male whydahs have apparently been designed to be 'beautiful', perhaps male cowbirds and cuckoos are designed as 'mate guarders' instead. It would be interesting to know whether these different male tactics are ultimately linked to differences in the abundance and dispersion of host nests, which will influence the local distribution of the female parasites and hence the way that the male parasite has to compete for mates.

SONG LEARNING AND IMPRINTING IN INDIGOBIRDS

The observations we have described so far suggest that a male *Vidua* might learn his songs from the host species that raises him and then he uses these songs to attract females. However, we still have not tested Nicolai's suggestion that females develop their mate preference by imprinting on their host species' song, nor the idea that this same song then directs their choice of which host to parasitize. Evidence for this comes from studies by Robert Payne and his co-workers on indigobirds. In fact, Payne's studies provide the only really critical tests of each stage of Nicolai's theory and are a model of how to combine field observations with incisive laboratory experiments.

Unlike the whydahs, a male indigobird does not have an elaborate tail, but his glossy-black breeding plumage enhances his visibility and he advertises his readiness to mate by perching on the top of a favourite tree. Here he sits, usually on exactly the same twig, for more than half the day, singing his songs under the blaze of the African sun. Most males have one favourite singing tree and they keep this throughout the breeding season and from year to year. Replacement males may sing from exactly the same spot so traditional sites are maintained across the generations.[3]

Indigobird mating behaviour is best known for the Village Indigobird, where Payne has studied colour-ringed individuals in Lochinvar National Park, Zambia.[25] Traditional male singing trees are spaced several hundred metres apart and males defend them vigorously against any other male *Vidua*, including males of other indigobird species and whydahs. Females visit these singing sites alone, and this is where all the matings occur. A female may visit several males, often in quick succession, so she seems to sample the males in her neighbourhood before she decides which to copulate with. Once she has chosen, she tends to mate repeatedly with the same male throughout the season. Some males are much more successful than others. For example, among local populations of 10–20 males, the most successful male may attract more than half the females to his site and so mate with a dozen or so females during a season. The most successful males were those with the most stamina, that spent the most time at their call sites and that sang the most. Unlike some of the whydah studies, Payne found no obvious resources at the singing sites which attracted the females, so the mating system can best be described as a 'dispersed lek'. The term 'lek' is applied to aggregations of males at display sites which females visit solely for the purpose of mating.

As a female approaches his singing site, the male usually flies over to greet her and then, as she lands at his site, he performs a hover display in front of her, dancing up and down in mid-air as if he were suspended on a string. If the female is ready to mate, she usually solicits straight away and he then mounts. At the peak of the breeding season, Payne recorded the most successful males mating with four females in one day. Males are rather undiscriminating and will court not only all indigobirds (both their own and other species) but any other bird that lands at their call site, including sparrows, shrikes, sunbirds and doves. On two occasions, Payne saw a male Village Indigobird copulate with a female Paradise Whydah that happened to land nearby and was taken by surprise while she was looking the other way![25] The undiscriminating nature of the males explains why a territorial male needs to keep all other *Vidua* males at bay, not just males of his own species.[26] Sometimes there are four indigobird species and three whydah species all living in one area – there would be chaos if the females did not exert careful choice of their mates.

Each male indigobird mimics the songs and calls of one particular firefinch species. These songs are such good mimics, that it is often impossible to tell whether they come from a firefinch or an indigobird unless you can see the bird itself. By comparing the details of the indigobird songs and those of the hosts, Payne found that the parasite does not simply learn songs from his foster father, but also from other male firefinches of the same species, and from adult indigobirds that sing these kinds of songs.[27] This shows that learning continues for several weeks after the young indigobird reaches independence.

Aviary experiments by Robert Payne, Laura Payne and Jean Woods, with captive breeding stock at the University of Michigan,[28] have confirmed that there is no genetic predisposition to learn the normal host species songs. If Village Indigobirds are raised by Red-billed Firefinches, then they learn Red-billed Firefinch song, but if they are raised by Bengalese Finches, they will learn Bengalese song just as readily, and they stick to this even if they hear their normal host's song soon after independence. So a young male indigobird learns his song first by focusing on his foster parents, and then on other birds with similar songs, whether they be other males of his foster species or indigobirds that mimic these song types. By incorporating a whole range of songs in his repertoire, a male increases his attractiveness because he's more likely to include the songs imprinted on by a range of females raised by the same host.[27]

The songs learnt from other indigobirds include not only the musical whistles and trills that comprise the mimicry songs of the foster species, but also harsh chatter notes. These 'non-mimicry' songs are used especially when other males

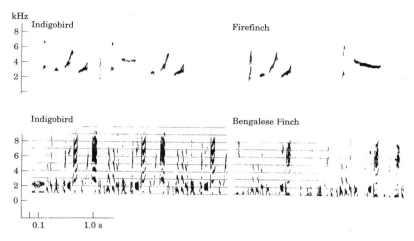

Figure 13.1 Aviary experiments show that male Village Indigobirds learn their songs from their foster parents, and from other individuals that sing similar songs. Top: This male indigobird (left) was raised by the normal host, a Red-billed Firefinch, and mimics the whistled notes of firefinch song (right). Bottom: This male (left) was raised by Bengalese Finches, an Asian species it would never encounter in the wild, and mimics their twittering song.[28]

approach and seem to be aggressive, whereas the 'mimicry' songs are most often directed at females.[27]

The final piece of the puzzle is to show that a female imprints on the song of the host that raises her. Recent aviary experiments have revealed that this is indeed what happens.[29] The songs that a female finds attractive are those that she experienced during her period of foster care. If she was raised by firefinches, then she will mate only with an indigobird that sings that firefinch species' song. If she was raised by the 'wrong' host, for example a Bengalese Finch, then she will be attracted only to a male indigobird that sings Bengalese song, and so a male that must have been raised by that same host species.

Does a female's imprinted song also guide her choice of which host species to parasitize? Robert Payne found anecdotal evidence that this was likely to be true from the behaviour of the captive firefinches and indigobirds that had the freedom of his house. A female Village Indigobird, raised by Red-billed Firefinches, became very excited when a pair of Red-billed Firefinches began to build a nest behind a bookcase, and she often inspected it. By contrast, a female Jameson's Firefinch Indigobird, raised by Jameson's Firefinches, took no interest at all.[3] Experiments have now confirmed that imprinting influences female host choice.[29] When given a choice in an aviary containing a mixture of breeding species, female Village Indigobirds raised by Red-billed Firefinches choose this same species to parasitize, whereas females raised by Bengalese finches prefer to parasitize Bengalese Finches.

These elegant studies by Payne and his co-workers are a brilliant confirmation of Nicolai's suggestion nearly 40 years ago, that learning of host songs provides the key to both host choice and mate choice in the parasitic finches, and this enables each *Vidua* species to stick to one host species. The two key questions that still need to be answered are: Would matings between different *Vidua* species produce hybrid offspring with mismatching mouths? And, would these then be more likely to suffer discrimination by the hosts? These would both be predicted if the main advantage to a female from mating with a male raised by the same host, was to maintain the mouth mimicry pattern in her chicks.

Finally, it would be interesting to know how the female *Vidua* directs her mating to a male *Vidua* rather than to a male of the host species. Presumably, she must have an innate ability to recognize a male *Vidua* as a mate, perhaps based on his appearance or display, with her imprinted song guiding her to a male reared by the correct host species. Then, her egg-laying choice is directed by that same song, but now in a different context, namely a complete nest where egg laying has just begun.

COLONIZING NEW HOSTS AND THE MAKING OF NEW *VIDUA* SPECIES

Jürgen Nicolai assumed that the estrildid hosts would always reject parasite young unless their mouths were a perfect match of their own young. Therefore, he suggested that the host and parasite species must evolve together in pairs,[9,10] a process known as 'co-speciation'. Imagine, for example, an estrildid species 'A' which is parasitized by a *Vidua* species 'a'. If some of these estrildids became isolated from the rest, for example by a mountain or a desert, they might begin to evolve into a new species 'B', with adaptations suited to their local conditions. As they evolved away from the parental stock, they might evolve new nestling mouth patterns too. According to Nicolai, the only way that a *Vidua* could exploit this new species would be if *Vidua* species 'a' evolved alongside, into a new species 'b', so that the perfect mouth mimicry could be maintained at every stage of evolution. It is easy to envisage how this might happen; the new host and parasite populations could become isolated together and so they would evolve together. According to this theory, parasite species 'b' should be exactly the same age as its host, species 'B'.

However, recent molecular studies have shown conclusively that co-speciation does not occur in estrildids and their *Vidua* parasites. Nedra Klein and Robert Payne analysed mitochondrial DNA to produce evolutionary trees for the hosts and the parasites and there is no suggestion that the two have evolved together into new species.[30] First of all, the *Vidua* finches are clearly a much younger evolutionary group because they differ much less from one another in their mitochondrial DNA than do the estrildid host species. The indigobirds, in particular, are all very similar, which is exactly what you would predict from their appearance – they look almost identical. This suggests that the *Vidua* parasites evolved well after their hosts split into new species.

A detailed look at the evolutionary trees also shows no evidence for co-speciation.[30] The most closely related *Vidua* often parasitize distantly related host species. For example, there are distinct populations of the Cameroon Indigobird, which cannot be separated by the genetic techniques used by Klein and Payne, that go for very different host species and mimic the songs of their respective hosts.

These must be very recently evolved parasite populations, yet they have clearly been able to parasitize a variety of hosts, with different mouth patterns.

As another example, there are two species of paradise whydah that exploit different subspecies of Melba Finch, one in West Africa and one in South and East Africa. If co-speciation had occurred, then these two paradise whydahs should be closely related – but they are not. The West African whydah's closest relative is another West African whydah that parasitizes Aurora Finches, while the South and East African whydah's closest relative parasitizes the Orange-winged Pytilia. The two paradise whydahs that go for Melba Finches must have each colonized this host independently, from an ancestor that parasitized another species altogether.

These results suggest that a new *Vidua* species can form simply through colonization of a new host species.[30] The experiments on nestling discrimination show that chicks with odd mouth patterns are not always rejected, so this would allow the parasite to gain some initial success. The nestling mouth mimicry could then be improved gradually by selection in exactly the same way that egg mimicry improves in cuckoos.

Field observations also support the idea of parasite colonization after the host has already speciated. About 1% of wild indigobirds sing songs of the 'wrong' host.[31] Presumably their mothers laid eggs in the wrong host nest. Occasional mistakes like this may not be sufficient to give birth to a new species, because single birds with strange songs and song preferences may fail to find a mate. However, sometimes several females may simultaneously choose to lay in a new species nest because there are too many females competing for too few nests of the regular host. This may arise if the regular host declines in abundance. In the next generation, therefore, there may be several females imprinted on the new host and several males singing the new host's song. A new mating group of parasites will be formed, held together by the new tune. This new culture will then set the stage for natural selection to do its work over the generations and match the parasite mouth to that of the new host.

Thus the colonization of new host species follows exactly the same path as in cuckoos (chapter 9), except that 'mistakes' in cuckoos may lead only to new female races (because only females are faithful to the host species that raises them) whereas in the *Vidua* finches they lead to the formation of new species.

Robert and Laura Payne have recently described what is likely to be the formation of a new species of indigobird in West Africa.[32] Most indigobirds parasitize species of firefinches, but there are distinct populations of the 'Cameroon Indigobird' where the males mimic the songs of the Brown Twinspot. Indigobird nestlings raised by these twinspots do not mimic the host's gape pattern. Instead, they have mouths just like those of the Black-bellied Firefinch, another common host used by the 'Cameroon Indigobird' in the same region. Adults which parasitize these two host species are identical in appearance – the only way to distinguish the males is by their songs, and the females by their song preferences. It seems certain that these twinspot-specialists are a new indigobird species in the making, derived recently from the indigobirds that parasitize the firefinch, and there has not yet been time for selection to produce a matching mouth for the new host. Other populations of the 'Cameroon Indigobird' sing songs that mimic another twinspot species and these, too, are likely to represent new isolated breeding groups derived from the firefinch specialists.[33]

In our brief allotted span of 'three score years and ten', we may sometimes get the impression that evolutionary change is occurring only in small creatures, like the parasites that attack our own bodies and our food crops. However, evolution is in action everywhere. The illusion of the fixity of larger creatures, such as birds, comes about simply because they have longer generation times and are slower to change. However, the brood parasites remind us that birds, too, live in a changing world. Ecological changes bring not only changes in their numbers and distribution, which we can easily monitor, but also evolutionary changes, as they adapt to new suites of selection pressures.

THE CUCKOO FINCH

Although this finch is closely related to the *Vidua* finches, it differs markedly in the base sequences of its mitochondrial DNA. This 'molecular clock' (see chapter 12) suggests that the Cuckoo Finch diverged from the ancestor that gave rise to the *Vidua* finches some 15 to 30 million years ago.[1]

Its parasitic habits are very different from those of the *Vidua* finches.[34] The Cuckoo Finch is not host specific but parasitizes various *Prinia* and *Cisticola* warblers, which build domed nests, with a side entrance, in grass or other low vegetation. Its egg is bluish-white, sometimes with red speckles, and mimics the eggs of these hosts. Egg laying has not been observed, but the appearance of a parasite egg usually coincides with the disappearance of one or more host eggs, so the female Cuckoo Finch seems to remove host eggs when she lays. The parasite chick is usually raised alone in the nest, probably because it outcompetes the host chicks, which then starve to death and are removed by their parents. However, there are occasional records of two Cuckoo Finches being raised successfully in the same nest. Finally, the parasite chick is strikingly different from the host chicks, with dark skin (the hosts are pink) and a purple gape without spots (the host gapes are yellow). Because it is raised alone, the parasite chick apparently does not have to mimic the host young to fool the host parents into accepting it (chapter 6).

So the Cuckoo Finch is well named. It is much more like a cuckoo than its parasitic cousins, the *Vidua* finches. It provides a good example of how nature can produce similar adaptations from different ancestral stocks when faced with the same problem, in this case persuading warblers to raise chicks of another species.

CHAPTER 14

Cheating on your own kind

As a schoolboy, I was often woken early on spring mornings by the Starlings that nested under the eaves just outside my bedroom window. Sometimes, one of their pale blue eggs would appear on our lawn and I supposed that these were laid by birds without nests, or perhaps by a poor nesting female that had failed to get back to her nest in time.

Now to Texas, where researchers studying Black-bellied Whistling ducks counted 17 eggs in one nest box and then, two days later, there were 50.[1] No bird can lay more than one egg per day, so during these two days at least 17 females came to lay the 33 new eggs that appeared in this nest. Perhaps, with nest boxes in short supply, many females were competing for this site and ownership was confused?

However, a closer look reveals that neither of these is likely to be the result of mistakes. Studies of Starlings in which eggs are marked in nests as they are laid, shows that the eggs that appear on the ground nearby are all marked ones.[2] They have probably all been removed by parasitic females, which sometimes adopt cuckoo-like tactics and remove a host egg before replacing it with one of their own. Studies of waterfowl have revealed that many females lay eggs parasitically, not through confusion over nest sites, but as a sneaky way of increasing their reproductive success.

Cheating on your own kind turns out to be a regular part of the lives of many species. In the first review,[3] published in 1980, Yoram Yom-Tov from Tel Aviv University defined it as 'the laying of eggs in a conspecific nest without taking part in the processes of incubation and/or caring for the hatchlings'. He reported the behaviour in 53 species and noted this early record in the Bible (Jeremiah 17: 11).[3]

> Like a partridge which incubates in its nest
> Eggs which it has not laid,
> So is the man who amasses wealth unjustly;
> Before his days are half done he must leave it
> And prove but a fool at last.

A decade later, the next review[4] recorded conspecific brood parasitism in 141 species, and the latest count (1998) is 185 species.[5] No doubt this total will increase as more studies follow individual behaviour in detail or use molecular markers to identify maternity. For example, the first study of wild Zebra Finches in Australia to use DNA fingerprinting to analyse parentage found that 36% of broods contained a chick which did not belong to the nesting female and must have come from an egg laid by a parasitic female, with 11% of all chicks the result of parasitic layings.[6] This was the first record of conspecific brood parasitism for this species, but since then observers have had a closer look and found, by more regular checking of nests, cases where two eggs appeared on one day, and they have even caught females in the act of laying in another female's nest.

WHY CHEAT?

These discoveries should come as no surprise. Caring for eggs and chicks is a costly business. For a small bird, like the Starling, it takes several weeks to find and defend a suitable nest hole and then a week to build the nest. This is followed by 12 days' incubation, three weeks' care of the nestlings and two further weeks of fledgling care. In theory, these time and energy costs open the way for the evolution of parasitic behaviour by three alternative routes.[7]

Some females could choose parasitism as an equally profitable alternative to nesting

Imagine that all the females in a population are honest nesters, which lay their eggs at home and care for their own young. Now imagine a female that breaks the rules and becomes a parasite. She avoids the trouble of defending a nest site, building and parental care, so she can devote all her effort to laying eggs. With a huge pool of honest parents to exploit, she is likely to enjoy greater success because she can lay many more eggs than the other females. Assuming her offspring inherit her parasitic tendency, the parasitic habit will become relatively more and more common from generation to generation.

   As the parasitic habit begins to pollute the population, the average reproductive success of the honest nesting females will decrease, because they are spending more and more effort raising parasitic chicks rather than their own. However, the success of the parasitic females will decline too because competition for the dwindling supply of host females will become intense. Perhaps the hosts will begin to evolve defences, which will make parasitism harder still. Eventually a point will be reached where the average success of the parasites equals that of the nesters, and now the situation will stabilize, with a mixture of the two kinds of females living together in the population. If the frequency of parasites increased beyond this point, then parasitism would now become less profitable than nesting. For example, a parasitic female would often turn up at a nest only to discover that it is already so full of eggs that it's not worth laying (late hatching chicks in larger broods are unlikely to survive). Nesting females, however, would occasionally escape parasitism and so their average success would be better. The balance of advantage has now swung the other way and the relative frequency of nesters would increase again. Thus the equilibrium is maintained at equal success for the two types of female.[7]

These two female behaviours, parasite and nester, could reflect different genetic types, in which case the sequence I have just described would occur as evolutionary change, with the 'choices' made by natural selection. The result would be a genetic polymorphism in the population – a stable mixture of two types of female, each genetically programmed to play just one strategy. Alternatively, all the females could be equipped to play either role because they have flexible behaviour. They should then make adaptive choices depending on what everyone else is doing. For example, if a female assessed that more than a given proportion of the population was nesting, she might choose to be a parasite that year. In this case, natural selection would design individuals to adjust their choices so that the frequencies of females playing the two options was such that their average success was the same. This might seem far fetched, but birds often make these kinds of adaptive choices in other contexts. For example, if you offer a flock of Starlings or ducks a choice between two feeding sites, one with lots of food and one with a little, the first arrivals will settle at the best site. But eventually, because of competition, food intake per individual will decline to the point where it pays the next arrivals to settle at the poor site. Individuals may then move back and forth, maintaining a distribution which results in the same average success at both sites. We do exactly the same when choosing between queues in supermarkets, where the best line to join depends on what everyone else is doing.

The key prediction from this theory for parasitism is that the average success of parasitic females and nesting females should be the same. Testing this prediction is tricky, because by 'success' we mean lifetime reproductive success. The advantage gained by the parasites initially would be an increased number of eggs laid per year, but once the population has settled down to equilibrium, parasites may no longer enjoy this advantage. In fact they may produce fewer viable offspring per year, because of the problems in finding suitable host nests and in timing their parasitism correctly. Nevertheless, this disadvantage could be offset by their increased lifespan due to reduced parental effort each season.

Some females could be forced to become parasites to 'make the best of a bad job', because they fail to nest normally

According to this theory, nesting is the best way to reproduce but sometimes females have to settle for parasitism as a second best option. They might do this because nest sites are limited, or because they do not have sufficient energy reserves to cope with the demands of a normal nesting cycle, or because their clutch is destroyed by predators or bad weather during laying. In all these cases, females might try to salvage at least some success through parasitic laying. Although they won't do as well as nesting females, even one or two eggs would be better than nothing.

Some females might enhance their success by parasitism in addition to nesting

Even if a female had a nest of her own, she might still gain by laying some eggs in other females' nests. These could be eggs additional to her normal clutch, which might boost her reproductive success without the need for any extra parental effort. Or perhaps she could distribute some of her normal clutch in other nests to reduce her parental burden and increase the chance that she survives to breed again the next year.

Testing between these theories is a challenging task. With cuckoos, cowbirds and parasitic finches it is easy to distinguish the adult parasites and hosts and, with practice, the parasitic eggs can also be recognized even when they are mimetic. With conspecifics, however, hosts and parasites are identical and their eggs are much harder to tell apart so ingenious detective work is often needed to discover which females are parasitic and to follow their success. So far, there have been detailed studies of only a few species. We shall consider them in turn because differences in their natural history illuminate both the advantages and problems of life as a cheat on your own kind.

STARLINGS: PARASITIC LAYING BY FEMALES WHO FAIL TO FIND A NEST

The first report of Starling parasitism was in 1974, when Yoram Yom-Tov and colleagues studied a nest-box colony near Aberdeen, Scotland.[8] Normally, a female lays one egg each day, in the early morning, until the clutch is complete, whereupon her ovary regresses and she cannot lay more eggs unless she prepares for a new clutch. There were three signs of parasitic laying. Sometimes two eggs appeared in a nest on the same morning, sometimes new eggs were added to a clutch several days after a clutch of normal size had been completed, and occasionally there were abnormally large clutches.

Similar odd events during laying have been recorded in subsequent studies of nest-box colonies in Britain,[9] Belgium[10] and North America.[11] They suggest that 5–46% of the Starling's first clutches are parasitized per colony, usually with just one parasitic egg per clutch but occasionally up to five. These frequencies, based on routine checks of nests, must be underestimates because parasitic layings will be missed when parasites remove a host egg (see below) or lay immediately before or after the host's own clutch sequence. Another method used in some of the Starling studies is to compare blood proteins of chicks with those of their putative parents. This suggests that up to a quarter of the nests of early broods contained a chick which did not belong to the nest's attendant female.[11] But this method will also be an underestimate because some parasites may share protein types with the resident female. A third, but drastic, method is to kill females soon after they begin incubation and to inspect their ovaries. After an egg is released from the ovary it leaves a little chamber-like scar. By counting these, it is possible to determine the number of eggs the female has laid. One study found that 36% of females had more eggs in their nest than they could have laid themselves, indicating that parasitic females must have added eggs to their clutch.[12]

Which are the parasitic females? Some studies noted that parasitism rates increased as unoccupied nest boxes became scarcer, which suggests that the parasites might be females that fail to find a nest site. The first direct evidence for this comes from a clever recent study by Maria Sandell and Michael Diemer from the University of Lund, who watched a colony in southern Sweden.[13] First, they established that limitation of nest sites excluded some females from breeding. These 'floater' females roamed among the boxes looking for vacancies and were quick to replace any nesting females that disappeared. By putting up some extra boxes, containing an artificial nest and plastic eggs, Sandell and Diemer were able to trap the floaters – when they entered the box, the birds released a shutter which closed off the entrance hole. All these females had fully developed incubation patches, which is a sign that they were ready to lay and some of them carried fully developed eggs, which could be felt gently through the belly wall. Some even laid an egg in the nest box. On average, these females were younger or smaller than the nesting females.

To make sure that these floaters did not have nests elsewhere, 12 were fitted with small radiotransmitters, attached to the tail feathers. They were then followed for a week or two. None of them had nests at the time of capture and instead spent all their time visiting other females' nests, probably to check for vacancies or to seek opportunities for parasitic laying. However, some of them eventually settled in the colony to breed, either by joining a male whose female had died or by occupying a vacant nest box to become a polygynous female with a male that was already paired. These observations show that the parasitic females were those unable to compete successfully for a nest site or mate early in the season, that laid some eggs parasitically while awaiting the chance to become nesters.

While the majority of parasitic eggs are laid by females without nests, a few come from females whose nests are depredated during laying and which then try to salvage the remainder of their clutch by laying in other females' nests. In a study in southern Britain, Chris Feare followed seven females which laid eggs of an unusual and distinctive colour or shape. After they had begun to lay in their own nests, he removed their eggs to simulate predation. During the next few days, the eggs of five of these females appeared in the nests of other females nearby.[14] In a similar study in New Jersey, North America, some females were injected with tetracycline, which causes their eggs to fluoresce under ultraviolet light. Again, when these females were made to desert during laying some of their subsequent eggs turned up in other females' nests.[15]

Parasitic Starlings adopt two cuckoo-like tactics. First, they sometimes remove a host egg.[16] At least some, and perhaps all, of these removals occur during the laying visit because parasites have been seen to enter nest boxes to lay and then to fly off with a host egg in their bill. From the disappearance of marked host eggs, it is estimated that egg removal occurs at about a quarter or a third of parasitized nests. This is certainly advantageous to the parasite because it reduces competition from the host chicks.

Second, the parasites lay later in the day than the host females to increase the chance that they gain access to the nest.[17] Nesting females lay in the early morning and then go off to feed, followed closely by their males who have to guard their paternity. Parasitic females lay later, often around mid-day. If they are caught on the nest, there is sometimes a terrible fight, which can lead to serious injury or even death. The two females grip one another with their feet, screaming, and stabbing with their bills.

While the hosts are constrained in their defence by their need to feed and mate guard during laying, they certainly keep a close eye on the nest contents because any eggs that appear before the host female begins her clutch are immediately ejected.[18] Experiments with model Starling eggs, by Rianne Pinxten and colleagues from the University of Antwerp, have revealed that females will remove foreign eggs right up to the time they lay their first egg whereas males cease removing eggs about three days before their female begins to lay, perhaps because they are less certain whether the egg is a parasitic egg or one laid by their mate.[19] Once the host begins her clutch, however, parasitic eggs are all accepted, presumably because they are difficult to distinguish from the rest of the clutch.

Now this causes a problem for the hosts. Starlings are apparently 'determinate' layers, which means that the female decides on a clutch size before she begins to lay. Given that she cannot know beforehand whether she will be a victim, parasitized females lay just as many eggs as those not parasitized. If the parasitic female removes one of their eggs then hosts raise a normal brood size, and they simply rear one fewer of their own young. But often the parasite adds her egg to the host clutch. In these cases, the hosts might raise even fewer of their own young because there is not enough food to go round the enlarged brood. Harry Power and colleagues from Rutgers University have suggested that Starlings might minimize these costs by pre-empting the arrival of a parasitic egg and laying one fewer egg themselves.[20] This would ensure that their own productivity is not compromised by an extra egg. According to their calculations, it would pay all the Starlings in their population to reduce their clutch by one egg provided more than 26% of nests are parasitized during host laying. They found that 33% of nests were parasitized during this stage (i.e. were likely to produce chicks which would compete with the host chicks) and suggest that this might explain why their Starlings lay, on average, a clutch of five eggs even though a clutch of six would produce more surviving young per brood.

There are other reasons why Starlings might lay small clutches (e.g. they are saving themselves for future broods) but the idea that they leave space for parasitic eggs is fascinating. The key prediction from this hypothesis is that lucky females, which escape parasitism, would have produced more offspring during their lifetime if they had laid one extra egg per clutch. Another prediction is that species subject to heavy conspecific brood parasitism should be more likely to lay clutches smaller than that which maximizes the number of surviving young per brood.

* * *

Other studies of hole-nesting passerine birds have also found that parasitic laying occurs when females cannot obtain a nest site (e.g. Eastern Bluebirds)[21] or when females are disrupted while laying a clutch (e.g. White-fronted Bee-eaters).[22] In both cases, parasites are making the best of a bad job and fare less well than honest nesters. Why are there no professional parasites, who do just as well as nesting females?

Several factors limit the success of cheating.[23] First, there's the problem of getting to the host nest. Although some species are colonial, so nests are easy to find, hosts are often at their nests for most of the laying period. For example, female White-fronted Bee-eaters remain in their nest chambers (holes in banks), where they are brought food by their mates. If a parasitic female enters the burrow, she is attacked.

In one case, an intruding female was grabbed by the bill and grappled with the host female for two and a half hours! Finally, she broke free and flew to a tree nearby where, clearly exhausted, she laid an egg from her perch and it smashed on the ground below.[22] In other species, like Blue Tits and Great Tits, pairs are spaced out, which makes it hard for parasites to visit many nests, and residents are also very territorial during laying so intruders cannot gain easy access to nests. This probably explains why Bart Kempenaers and colleagues found no evidence for any brood parasitism in more than 150 nests monitored near Antwerp, Belgium. There were floater females present, and experiments revealed that foreign eggs would have been accepted, but DNA profiles showed that all the chicks (1394 of them!) belonged to the resident females.[24]

Second, in some species the nesting females lay synchronously, which puts a severe limit on the period of potential parasitism. In Starling populations, for example, most females start their first clutches within 7–10 days of each other. A parasite would have to find a suitable host nest just about every day to beat the productivity of a nesting female. Many studies report that about half the parasitic eggs are mistimed, either too early (those laid before the host eggs are ejected) or too late (those laid during incubation are unlikely to hatch). This further suggests that professional parasites are likely to do worse than nesters.

SNOW GEESE: WHITE GOSLINGS FOR BLUE PARENTS

In the Canadian Arctic, David Lank, Fred Cooke, Robert Rockwell and their co-workers from Queen's University, Ontario, have made a long-term study of the colony of Lesser Snow Geese breeding at La Perouse Bay in Northern Manitoba. The research team collects data on the reproductive success of more than two thousand pairs each season. The geese arrive on their breeding grounds in May or early June, having wintered in the Gulf Coast. They stop off during their spring migration in the northern prairies to form body reserves for nesting and egg production.

Snow Geese occur in two colour morphs. Colour is determined by a pair of alleles, one inherited from the mother and one from the father. Adults with all blue plumage have genotype BB, while those with white plumage are bb. Adults with one of each type of gene, Bb, are mainly blue, but have white feathers on the belly. The goslings come in two colour types; dark goslings are either BB or Bb, while white goslings are bb.

The first hint that some females were cheats came from odd-coloured goslings in some families.[25] About 4% of the offspring of blue pairs (BB male with a BB female) were white. These were clearly unrelated to both male and female adults and must have resulted from parasitic layings. Sometimes there were blue goslings (BB or Bb) in the nests of parents who were both white (bb). These could be the result of parasite laying too, but they could also be the progeny of unfaithful white females that had a sneaky copulation with a blue male. Combining these data with observations on unusual laying sequences in nests, the researchers estimated that 12–31% of the nests each year were parasitized and that 2–10% of all the goslings hatched from parasitic eggs.

Nesting females never laid parasitic eggs, even if their clutch was depredated during laying. Instead, all the parasites were females that failed to start a nest. Some failed because they couldn't find a safe, dry nest site. This was a particular problem in years of heavy snow or with high water levels. Others failed because they did not have sufficient food reserves to breed normally. This was most likely in drought years, when food was scarce on the migration staging grounds in the prairies. Under both these conditions, females tried to salvage at least some success by parasitism.[26] However, they never did as well as the nesting females because host nests were well defended and the colony laid synchronously so the period of opportunity for parasitism was short.[27]

During laying, the nest is sometimes left unattended. Provided the parasite can find the nest, she may be able to lay an egg in peace. But the nesting female is often sitting and her male is on guard nearby. Under these circumstances a lone parasite has little chance of getting to the nest because the resident male will either chase her off or try to copulate with her. However, the parasite's male often follows her, to guard his paternity, and this then helps her to gain access to the nest. While the resident male is kept busy displaying to her mate, the parasite female goes straight to the sitting female and tries to push her aside so that she can lay directly into the nest. The resident female usually sits tight and if she cannot be dislodged the parasite sits alongside and lays either on the edge of the nest cup or outside it, perhaps up to a metre away. It can take her up to 30 minutes to lay. All the while she is attacked by the sitting female (and sometimes by the resident male too) and she shields her head in an attempt to ward off their blows.

After laying, the parasite runs off and then something extraordinary happens.[25] If the parasite has laid outside the nest, the resident female leans out, tucks the egg under her chin, and tries to roll it gently in to join the rest of her clutch. If the egg is nearby, she usually succeeds. But the manoeuvre is tricky if the egg is far off or has to be rolled uphill and if the first few attempts fail she soon gives up. Why is the host female so keen to accept the parasite's egg after she has gone to so much trouble trying to prevent the parasite from laying?

One possibility is that retrieval is advantageous because sometimes the host's own eggs are accidentally displaced. The parasite would then simply be taking advantage of a host response which, on average, is beneficial for the host's own reproductive success. However, there is likely to be another important factor.[28] When the nest is unattended it is vulnerable to predation by skuas and gulls, so the female covers her eggs with down to conceal them. The presence of a large, conspicuous white egg nearby clearly attracts these predators. In cases where the host female failed to roll an egg back into her nest, her clutch was more likely to get eaten. Typically, the egg outside the nest would disappear first and then those inside the nest would disappear soon after, indicating that the predator first found the lone egg and then returned for the rest of the clutch. Provided acceptance of a parasite egg is not too costly, it will be better for the host female to roll it in to her nest and cover it up. In fact, the addition of a single parasite egg had no measurable effect on host reproductive success. Only if the nest had several parasitic eggs did the hosts suffer, because with a very large clutch their hatching success decreased.

Two other studies of geese have produced a similar story. In both Barnacle Geese, nesting on small islands in the Baltic Sea,[29] and Bar-headed Geese, in a captive

Lesser Snow Goose rolling the egg laid by a parasite female into her nest. In the background, her mate is chasing the parasite female off.

colony in Germany,[30] the parasitic females were again those with no nest of their own, and they had much lower success than the nesting females. Parasitic Barnacle Geese often laid in the evening, when the host females were more likely to be off the nest for a brief feed before nightfall, but sometimes they sat alongside the sitting host, which then rolled the parasitic egg in to the nest.[31] In both species, hosts attacked the parasites and their vigorous defence limited parasite success.

SWALLOWS: NESTING FEMALES LAY EXTRA EGGS NEXT DOOR

So far, all our examples of parasitism fit the second of the hypotheses at the start of the chapter, namely females trying to salvage at least a little success when they fail to enjoy the better productivity from nesting. Now we encounter evidence for the third hypothesis, parasitic laying by nesting females to boost their success above the average.

Cliff Swallows breed throughout North America in colonies, typically of several hundred pairs but sometimes more than three and a half thousand. They build gourd-shaped nests from pellets of mud and these are placed in tightly packed clusters under the sheltered eaves of buildings or bridges, or on cliff faces. Charles Brown and Mary Bomberger Brown, from the University of Tulsa, have made a remarkable study of colonies in Nebraska. They have ringed thousands of adults and nestlings to follow their survival and reproductive success. They check nests daily, using a dental mirror and flashlight, and mark eggs as they are laid. Finally, so that the behaviour of individuals at the colony can be followed, some of the swallows have their white forehead patches painted with distinctive colours.

The Browns found that up to a quarter of the nests were parasitized, usually with just one parasite egg per nest.[32] All the parasites were nesting females, which placed a few extra eggs in neighbouring nests, just a metre or two away, while at the same time raising a normal-sized clutch in their own nest. Several lines of evidence suggested that these parasitic females were high quality individuals.[33] First, the offspring they raised in their own nests survived better than average and second, parasitic females themselves were more likely to survive to the next year than non-parasitic females that raised similar sized broods.

It is difficult to follow behaviour at a colony when there are hundreds of pairs flying to and fro, but individuals were often seen to visit neighbouring nests. Sometimes they simply made a quick inspection, but sometimes they grabbed an egg and tossed it out! These raids may have been a prelude to parasitic visits because the arrival of a parasite egg was sometimes accompanied by the disappearance of a host egg. However, in only one of 27 observations of parasitic laying did the parasite remove an egg during the laying visit itself.[34] Inspection visits may have enabled the parasites to assess the suitability of their neighbours' nests because parasites targeted neighbours with high quality nests, namely those least likely to collapse during bad weather and those with the lowest infestations of blood-sucking bugs and fleas.[35] While the parasite is intent on avoiding the costs of parental care for her extra eggs, she is nevertheless keen to make sure that they get a good foster home.

Parasites adopted two tactics. First, they made furtive visits to lay in unattended nests.[34] These laying visits usually occurred two to three days before the parasite began her own clutch, and she chose neighbouring nests where laying had just begun or was about to begin in a day or two. It paid the parasites not to be too early because experiments showed that foreign eggs appearing more than four days before the hosts began their clutch were all rejected, whereas those appearing just a couple of days beforehand were accepted. These parasitic laying visits occurred later in the day (0800–1600 hrs) than normal egg laying (before 0800), presumably to reduce the chances of meeting the host female. They were also extraordinarily quick, usually just 15 to 120 seconds. In one case, a parasite sneaked in to lay while the owner was nearby, but busy fighting another intruder. So every time a female leaves her nest during the laying period, even for a moment, she runs the risk of a parasitic laying.

The discovery of the second tactic came as a real surprise.[36] Sometimes the Browns noted the arrival of a parasitic egg several days after the hosts had begun incubation, yet it hatched the same time as the host eggs. At first, they thought that parasitic eggs might have accelerated development. But then they began to notice

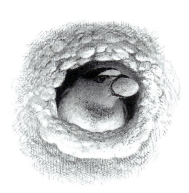

Eggs on the move. Left: A female Cliff Swallow removes a partly incubated egg from her own nest to put in the nest of a near neighbour. Right: A parasitic female Starling has just laid her egg and is flying off with one of the host female's eggs.

that marked eggs sometimes moved to neighbouring nests! These transfers occurred any time after laying right up to one or two days before they were due to hatch. Eventually, the Browns caught the perpetrators with their beaks full. All five transfers they observed were by incubating females, who carefully picked up an egg from their own nest and placed it in a nest next door while the owner was away. From the movements of marked eggs, and the appearance of eggs that arrived well after clutch completion yet still hatched in synchrony with the others, it was estimated that 6% of nests have one or more parasite eggs transferred to their nests by the bill.

One of Edgar Chance's proudest triumphs was to show that Common Cuckoos lay directly into host nests and do not, as was widely believed at the time, insert their own egg by carrying it in their bill (chapter 3). Chance ridiculed the 'beakers' and offered to wager 'a considerable sum of money' to anyone who could show that a cuckoo ever laid other than directly into a host nest. He would have been surprised, and delighted too (I'm sure), by the discovery that swallows both play at cuckoos and use their beaks for cheating.

Cliff Swallows clearly gain an advantage from parasitism. It enables them to lay extra eggs without commitment to increased parental effort and without jeopardizing the lives of their brood at home through increased competition. The Browns suggest that another advantage is gained by scattering eggs in several nests rather than having all your eggs in 'one basket'.[34] Scatter-laying decreases the chance of total failure, for example through parasite infestation or nest collapse. However, theoretical calculations suggest that risk spreading is unlikely to have a major effect.[37] Birds should simply choose the option that gives them the best average success, not the one which minimizes the chance of complete failure. Nevertheless, if a female discovered half way through laying or incubation that her nest was likely to fail, she might certainly gain by transferring eggs to neighbouring nests. There is some evidence that the swallows might indeed resort to parasitism if their chance of failure is high; parasitism rates are highest in colonies with the greatest proportion of failed nests, due to blood-sucking parasites or nest collapse.[34]

European swallows also cheat. In Barn Swallows, the parasites are again nesting females that lay eggs in their neighbours' nests, especially when these nests are less well defended.[38] In Bank Swallows (= Sand Martins), DNA fingerprinting at a colony in Scotland revealed that 13% of nests contained a parasitic egg. Intriguingly, some of these had been fertilized by the resident male.[39] Perhaps some females allow males extra-pair copulations in exchange for permission to lay eggs in their nests?

WEAVERBIRDS: COMBATING PARASITISM BY EGG SIGNATURES

Transfer of partly incubated eggs into other nests also occurs in Northern Masked Weavers. Wendy Jackson, from the University of Washington, Seattle, studied a population breeding at Lake Baringo, Kenya.[40] In one case an egg she had marked moved to another nest. In two cases unmarked eggs appeared well after the host had completed her clutch yet they hatched eight and four days later. The normal incubation period is two weeks, so these eggs must have been incubated elsewhere before they arrived. Unusual laying sequences suggested that other parasitic eggs were laid directly in host nests. There was no evidence that parasites ever removed a host egg.

The parasites were probably nesting females who were trying to increase their success beyond the brood size they could rear themselves. Most clutches were of three eggs. When Jackson added a fourth egg, the fourth hatching chick starved to death. Given that it is not worth rearing a fourth egg in your own nest, the best thing to do is to place it in another nest where it has the chance of being one of the first to hatch.[40]

Like some of the other species of weavers (chapter 7), Northern Masked Weavers have remarkably variable eggs. Each female lays a constant type, but there is enormous variation between females in background colour (dark brown to blue-green) and spotting (no spots through to heavily spotted). Jackson suggests that egg variation has evolved as a defence against conspecific brood parasitism; with a distinctive signature, it is much easier to recognize a foreign egg. Her experiments showed that hosts did not count eggs and reject a fourth one, but they rejected other females' eggs that differed from their own type.[41]

Jackson quantified egg variation and found that the presence of an odd egg could give a reliable measure of parasitism, though it is likely to be an underestimate because hosts may have rejected some foreign eggs before they could be recorded.[42] For her population of Northern Masked Weavers, up to 35% of the nests were parasitized by conspecifics. The frequent appearance of odd eggs in the nests of other weaver species suggests that conspecific parasitism is rife in this family. Colonial nesters are likely to be most prone to parasitism by nesting neighbours, so it is especially interesting that the most colonial species are the ones with the most variable eggs.[43] This suggests strongly that conspecific parasitism has selected for egg signatures in this group.

As we discussed in chapter 4, egg signatures might also evolve as a defence against cuckoo parasitism. It is tempting to suggest that conspecifics are a greater selective force for the weavers because conspecific parasitism (up to a third of the nests) is far more frequent than cuckoo parasitism (on average, about 5%). However, cuckoo parasitism is more damaging (the hosts lose all their eggs) and may have been more frequent in the past, so it is difficult to separate the effects of the two.

WHY ARE EGG SIGNATURES NOT MORE COMMON?

There are very few species that reject conspecific eggs from among their own clutch. Apart from four weaver species (Spottedbacked,[44] Northern Masked,[41] Masked[45] and Yellow[46]), the only other passerines shown by experiment to do this are the Chaffinch, Brambling[47] and Reed Bunting.[48] Among non-passerines, discrimination against conspecific eggs has been found in American Coots[49] and Sora Rails.[50] These species all have very variable eggs and females can probably easily pick out a foreign egg. The majority of species reject conspecific eggs appearing in their nests before they have begun their clutch ('any egg that arrives before I begin to lay can't be mine!'). However, once laying has begun they always accept. Acceptance is likely to be best simply because in most species the eggs of all the females look pretty much the same. Rejection of odd eggs would incur severe costs from recognition errors (chapter 5). Even among species with variable eggs, there are likely to be recognition costs associated with rejection, so rejection may vary between populations depending on the frequency of parasitism.

Why don't more species protect themselves against conspecific brood parasitism by evolving variable eggs? This is an unsolved puzzle, which might have several answers. First, perhaps in most species variation is constrained by other factors, particularly the need to have camouflaged eggs as a protection against predators. Second, many species may protect themselves against parasitism in other ways (e.g. nest defence) and so have no need for a second line of defence. Third, there may be a positive disadvantage in having eggs that are different from everyone else's. While it may protect you against parasitism, it also precludes you from parasitizing others. Perhaps the usual outcome of the cheating game in evolution is for everyone to have similar eggs. Finally, it may be advantageous to have some variation in your own clutch, which outweighs the disadvantage of accepting an occasional foreign egg. Often the last egg of a female's clutch is distinctly paler than the rest. The female could have simply run out of colour! But it is more likely that it pays her to mark the last egg. Yoram Yom-Tov has suggested that she may do this to signal to conspecific parasites that her clutch is now complete, to dissuade them from parasitism.[3] The signal would be of benefit to the parasite (a late laid egg is unlikely to hatch) and to the host (additional eggs may decrease hatching success of her own clutch). Robert Magrath, from the Australian National University, has suggested another explanation.[51] The female herself may want to identify her last egg. Once it has hatched, any remaining eggs must be infertile so are not worth continued incubation. It would be fun to test these various ideas.

American Coots

All the cheats we have encountered so far nest in colonies, where it is easy to find nests to parasitize. But parasites can also crack the defences of territorial species, where nests are widely spaced. Two of the best studies have been of species in the rail family, which nest in marshes and on lake margins.

Bruce Lyon, now at the University of California, Santa Cruz, studied American Coots breeding on lakes in central British Columbia. He identified parasitic eggs by a combination of daily nest checks, which revealed some unusual laying sequences (two or more eggs laid per day, or eggs added well after clutch completion), and by variation in egg features (shape, colour, spotting), which enabled him to assign eggs to particular individuals. Over 40% of nests were parasitized, with hosts receiving 1–17 eggs from 1 to 5 parasitic females.[52]

Lyon followed the success of host and parasite eggs by marking them with indelible felt pen numbers as soon as they were laid, and then by marking the chicks with coloured nape tags and rings soon after hatching. Coot chicks hatch asynchronously over five days or more, so with just one chick hatching at any given time it is usually easy to tell which chick belongs to which egg. Sometimes, however, several chicks were due to hatch on the same day (because the parasites synchronized their laying with host eggs). When this happened, Lyon ensured he assigned chicks to the correct eggs by a neat trick. The day before the chick was due to hatch, he cut a little window in the egg shell, gently pulled out a foot and clipped the end of one of the claws. He then popped the foot back inside and sealed the shell piece in place. By clipping different claws for each chick he could later work out which one came from each egg. Within a day of hatching the chicks can swim and they follow their parents, which feed them for several weeks.

These observations revealed that there were two kinds of parasitic females.[52] About a quarter of the parasitic eggs were laid by 'floater' females with no territories or nests of their own. Were these parasites by choice, gaining success equal to the nesting females? Or were they forced to become floaters as a second best option? The evidence supported the second alternative. Floater females laid fewer eggs than the nesters (on average five rather than nine per season) and they produced even fewer fledged young (0.2 rather than 2.8) because some of their layings were badly timed or rejected. About a third of all parasitic eggs were either ejected or buried under the nest material by the hosts. Whenever a Northern Harrier killed a territorial female, a floater was quick to fill the vacancy. This suggests that some females were forced to become floaters because the habitat was saturated by territorial pairs.

The rest of the parasitic eggs (three-quarters of them) were laid by nesting females. In fact a quarter of all the nesting females laid eggs parasitically. These were usually laid just before the female began a clutch in her own nest and were often part of one continuous sequence.[53] For example, one female laid 10 parasitic eggs on successive days and then over the next nine days she laid a clutch of nine eggs in her own nest. The arrangement of 'parasitic eggs first, own clutch next' makes good sense. Once a female begins her own clutch, parasitic layings would conflict with demands at home.

Most hosts were immediate neighbours or lived next door but one.[53] Females that laid a few parasitic eggs tended to lay them all in one host nest while those that laid five or more usually parasitized several nests. The record was held by one female that laid 20 parasitic eggs in six different host nests. Parasites would have done best by laying just one egg per host nest because hosts were more likely to desert if their clutch became too large, and chick survival declined in larger broods. However, with a limited number of neighbours parasites were often forced to use some nests more than once.

Just as with the swallows and weavers, parasitic laying augmented the success of nesting females. Their own clutch is limited by their capacity for parental care. Laying more than nine eggs in their own nest would lead to a net reduction in the number of healthy fledglings because they couldn't cope with the extra food demands of a larger brood.[54] By laying extra eggs next door, they can increase their success by tricking others into doing the work. Parasitic eggs are not as successful as eggs laid at home, because of host rejection and mismatched timing. But the average of three to four eggs that some nesting females managed to foist onto neighbours increased their seasonal output of fledglings by 8%.[52]

MOORHENS

On the other side of the Atlantic, Moorhens are up to similar tricks. A colour-ringed population with about 80 breeding territories at Peakirk Waterfowl Gardens, on the edge of the fens in eastern England, has been studied by David Gibbons and Susan McRae from Cambridge University. McRae used DNA fingerprinting to identify parasitic eggs from a sample of clutches and then assessed the validity of various field methods.[55] The presence of an 'odd egg' alone was a poor guide to parasitism. Although there was considerable variation between females in the size and appearance of their eggs, many last-laid eggs in a clutch were more different from the rest than a parasitic egg. Nevertheless, parasitic eggs could be reliably identified by a combination of criteria, including egg appearance and laying sequences in host nests and other nests nearby (**Plate 8c**).

Each year, 10–20% of nests were parasitized, with hosts receiving from one to six parasitic eggs per clutch. Parasitic eggs came from three sources.[56]

- 56% came from nesting females, which parasitized a close neighbour before laying a normal-sized clutch in their own nest.[57] About a quarter of all nesting females augmented their success by parasitism. On average they produced 3.3 independent young per season, 3 raised at home and 0.3 by neighbours, compared with 3 young produced by females that were honest nesters only.
- 19% came from females whose nests were depredated during laying on their own territories, which then tried to salvage the remainder of the clutch by laying eggs parasitically next door. This source of parasitism increased in a year of heavy nest predation by rats.[58]
- 25% came from a small number of females excluded from breeding because the habitat was saturated with territories. These females laid fewer eggs than nesting females and did very poorly because they often mis-timed their parasitism. Their

low success may partly reflect the fact that they were low quality individuals, but it also suggests that any attempts to make a living as a professional parasite would be unrewarding for Moorhens. A cuckoo can survey a dozen or more host territories in a day and often monitors host activities from a concealed perch. A Moorhen is clumsy and conspicuous in flight and would have to walk from territory to territory. It would find it much harder to watch hosts and to gain access to sufficient nests at the correct laying stage to beat the payoffs from nesting.

Parasites did not remove any host eggs – they simply added their egg to the host clutch. Parasite eggs appearing in an empty nest were quickly ejected or pecked and eaten by the hosts, but once the hosts began their clutch they never ejected parasite eggs. However, hosts sometimes deserted if their clutches were enlarged by foreign eggs at the one or two egg stage, though not after they had laid three or more eggs.[59] Why did they do this? Imagine you are a Moorhen. You notice an extra egg or two in your clutch, but you are not sure which eggs are your own. What should you do? One option is to carry on laying in the nest. The benefit is that you will then keep all your own eggs. The cost is that you will also have some parasitic eggs, and maybe the parasite will return to lay some more. As with the coots, Moorhen chicks are fed by the adults for three weeks or so after hatching and there is a limit to the number of young that a pair can feed. So raising parasitic chicks is likely to reduce your own success. The second option is to desert and lay the rest of the clutch in another nest. The benefit is that you'll avoid the parasitic eggs. The cost is that you'll leave the first part of your own clutch behind too. And, of course, you might get parasitized again in your new nest.

McRae calculated what the hosts would gain, in terms of the number of their own chicks raised to independence, if they followed either option. The observed behaviour was exactly what you would expect if the hosts were designed to maximize their own success.[59] If a female had laid just one or two eggs then desertion was best. Once she had laid more eggs it was best to carry on. Desertion would sacrifice too many of her own eggs in return for too small a clutch in the new nest. This example makes an important general point. To understand animal behaviour you have to immerse yourself in the animal's own world and understand its constraints. Moorhens do not have the benefit of DNA fingerprinting to identify parasitic eggs and odd eggs are an unreliable cue. But even the limited knowledge that 'there are more eggs here than I've laid myself' can be used to good advantage.

Moorhens lay their eggs in the evening, usually just after darkness falls. At this time the male takes over the incubation duties, perhaps because he is larger and better able to defend the nest against nocturnal predators. Parasitic eggs are laid at the same time too, so this raises the possibility that the host male might copulate with the intruding female and fertilize either the parasitic eggs, or some of the eggs that she lays later on in her own nest. Susan McRae's DNA fingerprinting results showed that this never happened. All the parasitic eggs were fertilized by the parasite's mate and he also was the father of all the eggs that parasites laid back home in their own nests.[60] This means that parasitic eggs will be just as costly for the host males as for the host females, so both members of the pair should try to keep parasites at bay.

Susan McRae was keen to find out how the parasites laid their eggs, so she set up video cameras with image intensifiers that could film during dusk and in the moonlight. Often a parasite would return to the same host nest on successive nights, so the cameras were set up the evening after a nest had been first parasitized in the hope that she would come back again. Nine parasitic layings were filmed as well as several layings by the host females. They made a fascinating contrast.[61]

During normal laying, the host female arrives at the nest, stops next to it and calls softly 'puck, puck' to her sitting mate. She has her head raised, is relaxed and often preens while she waits for him to leave. He then steps aside and stands nearby while she climbs slowly onto the nest. She sits there for about half an hour to lay. Then she leaves and the male resumes incubation once more.

Contrast this with parasitic laying. The parasite's mate stays at home, so she arrives alone. Her entry to the territory is probably easiest at night, when the male is on the nest, because during the day, when the female incubates, the male is vigorous in his defence against all intruders. The parasite female charges quickly towards the nest and in silence, with her head held low. She has no hesitation and must know the exact location of the nest from previous visits. In one of the nine cases, there were no hosts present and she laid in peace, though she was clearly nervous. In two cases, the host female was on the nest, laying her egg for the evening. She sat tight, while the parasite squeezed alongside, facing in the opposite direction and protecting her head from the resident female's pecks. In one of these cases the host female called and her mate arrived to join in the attack.

A parasite female Moorhen laying in a host nest at dusk. The parasite (foreground) squeezes alongside the sitting host male, and faces in the opposite direction while she lays, in an attempt to protect her head from his pecks (drawing based on video film by Susan McRae[61]).

In the other six parasite layings, the host male was on the nest when the parasite arrived. Again, she squeezed alongside him, head to tail, and sat there quietly while his blows rained down on her. Parasites never fought back and always remained motionless. The hosts may have limited their aggression because a violent struggle would have cracked their own eggs. Parasite females laid very quickly, in two to three minutes, and then ran off back to their own territories, often pursued by the host male. These remarkable film sequences show how parasites need a combination of stealth, speed and bravery to succeed.

PARASITIC DUCKS

In most of the examples we have discussed so far (in fact all but the geese) the adults have to feed their young and the number they can raise is limited by their capacity for parental care. Every parasite young raised is likely to be at the expense of one of their own young, so there will be strong selection for host defences. Some species, however, have young that can feed themselves straight after hatching, for example the waterfowl (ducks, geese and swans) and galliforms ('game birds'). Here parents have less work to do, mainly brooding young chicks, protecting them and leading them to suitable feeding areas. It is in these species with self-feeding young that conspecific parasitism seems to be most common. In a survey in 1989, nearly half of the 141 species then known to parasitize their own kind were waterfowl or galliforms.[4]

Why do we find this pattern? One suggestion is that when the young can feed themselves it is much less costly for their parents to have a few extra young in the brood, so selection for defences against parasitism is less strong.[4] For example, most north temperate ducks lay a clutch of about 10 eggs. They can hatch out a much larger clutch and it is commonly supposed that it would be just as easy to protect, say, 15 ducklings as 10.

If this is true, why don't female ducks lay more eggs in their own nests? Like coots and moorhens, some ducks lay parasitic eggs just before a normal-sized clutch in their own nests. This increases their success, but a parasitic egg often fares less well on average than an egg in the female's own nest (because of the now familiar problem of mis-timed layings). Surely if there is spare capacity for incubation and care it would be better to lay these extra eggs at home? This is an unsolved puzzle. The most likely answer is that there are costs of enlarged broods after all, even though they might not be as severe as for species which feed their offspring. At the laying stage, increasing clutch size can be costly for a duck because egg viability declines with time (so there is pressure to begin incubation as soon as possible) and because the more eggs you lay the longer the nest is exposed to predators.[62] For both these reasons it may be better to lay your extra eggs next door rather than at home. After hatching too, enlarged broods may be costly. Two experimental studies of clutch size in species with self-feeding young show that, as brood size increases beyond the normal size, either fewer young are raised[63] or the attendant female suffers through reduced condition.[64] Perhaps protection of a larger brood is sometimes both less effective and harder work?

Within the waterfowl, conspecific brood parasitism is most frequent in hole- and cavity-nesters; all 38 species suffer parasitism, with an astonishing average of 45%

nests parasitized per species. This is likely to reflect competition for limited nest sites (as we found for Starlings). In ground-nesters parasitism is rarer, but it is more common in colonial or island nesters, perhaps again because of nest-site limitation or increased opportunities to parasitize close neighbours.[5]

Let us look at three duck studies in detail. Each raises interesting new points about conspecific parasitism.

GOLDENEYES: NESTERS AND PARASITES IN BALANCE?

Barrow's Goldeneyes nest in tree cavities created by broken branches or large woodpeckers. Suitable sites are scarce and competition among breeding females has led to the evolution of a mixture of nesting and parasite behaviour. So far, this is the best candidate for the first of our hypotheses at the start of the chapter, namely a balanced frequency of the two behaviours in which each type of female enjoys the same success. The fascinating story has been unravelled by John Eadie, now at the University of California, Davis, and John Fryxell from the University of Guelph. They studied a population breeding in nest boxes and natural cavities on the margins of freshwater lakes in British Columbia.[65]

Females were marked individually with colour-coded nasal saddles and their activities were monitored by observation and with cameras set up above the nest boxes. Whenever a female entered or left the box, she triggered a photograph of herself. Parasitic eggs were identified from laying sequences and variation in eggs between females. Success of host and parasite eggs was followed by marking them individually as soon as they were laid. To ensure the fate of young from each egg was known, ducklings were marked while still in the egg. At the pipping stage, when they were in the process of hatching, a small window was cut in the shell. A foot was pulled out, given a numbered web-tag and then popped back inside.

Eadie and Fryxell found that 35% of the nests were parasitized and 17% of all eggs were laid parasitically. Within any one season, most females followed just one tactic and were either a nester or a parasite. However, individuals often switched tactics between years, so their behaviour was flexible. Let's compare the two types of behaviour.

- A nesting female lays on average eight eggs, all in her own nest, and then she incubates them for a month. Once they hatch, she accompanies the ducklings to the safety of a pond where she cares for them for a further two months. Male goldeneyes are typical ducks and do not help. As soon as the female has completed her clutch and he has ensured his paternity, his job is done and he leaves. You might wonder how the ducklings get to the water from a nest hole which may be 10 m up a tree. The answer is simple – they jump! They are so light and fluffy they have a soft landing, even if they bounce on the ground before waddling down to the pond.
- A parasite female lays on average nine or ten eggs, usually all in the nest of one host female. She then abandons all care to the host. Her lack of care is not because she tries to help but is driven off by the host female. If the host is removed before incubation begins, the parasite still abandons the nest once she

has completed her clutch and if she is tricked, by experiment, into laying in a decoy nest, with eggs but no host, she still does not incubate. Thus parasite females seem to be set on a different course of action right from the start of laying.

Goldeneyes did not reject parasitic eggs, so the result of parasitism by one female was simply that the host ended up with double the normal clutch. However, if two or more parasites laid in her nest, so she had more than 20 eggs, the host usually deserted. This set a limit to the frequency of successful parasitism in the population – if there were too many parasites they got in each other's way. Eadie and Fryxell calculated the predicted stable mixture of nesters and parasites at which each would enjoy equal success at producing fledglings.[65] The prediction was for around 20% of eggs to be laid parasitically, which is very close to the observation of 17%. This suggests that females may choose freely between nesting and parasitism, with the proportion adopting each option exactly as predicted from our theoretical argument under hypothesis 1.

Goldeneyes and Starlings both nest in holes and both compete for limited sites. Why, then, can parasitic goldeneyes do just as well as nesters while parasitic Starlings do much worse? The key difference may be that goldeneyes do not defend their nests as strongly during laying as hole-nesting species which have to feed their young (owls, woodpeckers, tits, starlings), because parasitism is less costly for ducks. Perhaps only when defence is lax, and parasites have easy access to nest sites, can parasites and nesters play their game of free choice, leading to equal success for each.

However, while this is likely to be at least part of the explanation, Eadie and Fryxell point out that there is more going on in the goldeneye world.[65] First, not all females have a free choice of what to do. Some young females are parasitic probably because they are unable to compete for a nest site. Second, a few nesting females lay in neighbouring nests as well as their own nest to augment their success. Third, the calculations ignore the savings that the parasite females make in avoiding three months of parental care. Perhaps this increases the chance that they survive to breed again? Finally, the situation is also more complicated because the stable mixture of parasites and nesters is likely to vary between years, depending on the density of breeders. When they compared different lakes and different years, Eadie and Fryxell found that parasitism levels increased as population density increased.

In theory, there may be interesting interactions between population numbers and the frequency of parasitism, as shown below.[5]

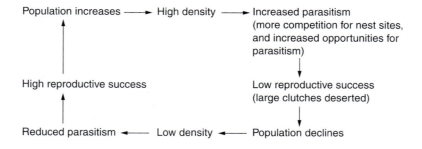

Depending on the details of these interactions, the sequence could produce stable populations, regular cycles in numbers, or even chaotic fluctuations which lead to extinction.[65, 66] This is not just arm-chair speculation. There are strong hints from our next example that this sequence may well happen in some duck populations and understanding it is essential for conservation efforts.

WOOD DUCKS: NEST-BOX CHAOS

Wood Ducks inhabit wooded swamps in North America and also nest in tree cavities, usually near water. Under natural conditions, parasitism is kept in check because nests are widely spaced and hard to find. About 30% of natural cavities are parasitized, usually with just one or two extra eggs per clutch.[5]

Wood Duck populations declined in the early 1900s owing to a combination of deforestation, loss of wetlands and hunting. Protection and conservation efforts have led to a population recovery in the last 50 years. One of the methods used to help them is to put up nest boxes. These are often arranged at high densities and placed on poles over open water, where they are very visible. Boxes may be clustered back to back in duplexes or even multi-box 'apartment blocks'.

The Wood Ducks readily take to these sites, but the result is chaos.[67] Nesting females sometimes kill one another in fights over boxes and parasite females have such an easy time finding nests that parasitism rates often reach 100%, with up to eight females laying per box. In one case, four females entered a box to lay within a period of 20 minutes! In the mayhem, eggs are cracked, clutches may end up with 30 or 40 eggs, and nesting females often desert (**Plates 8a, b**). As a result, duckling production plummets. The shy and solitary Wood Duck simply cannot cope when it is suddenly forced to breed in a crowded colony. Well meaning, but misguided, provision of high density nest sites could cause local populations to crash to extinction.[5]

This problem occurs whenever dense populations have free access to a limited resource. In a brilliant essay written in 1968, Garrett Hardin from the University of California, Santa Barbara, referred to it as 'the tragedy of the commons' and used it to illuminate the human condition.[68] Hardin imagined a pasture open to all. Each herdsman will try to keep as many cattle as possible on this common land. Should he increase his herd by one? He would receive all the proceeds from the sale of this extra animal while the costs from overgrazing will be shared by all the herdsmen. So the only rational course of action is to keep adding cattle to his herd. All the herdsmen think the same way. The number of cattle on the common increases as everyone rushes to pursue his own interests. The result is destruction of the common and ruin for all. The message is clear; for common read planet, for cattle read humans.

Humans can escape their tragedy by voluntary restriction on consumption and the freedom to breed. Wood Ducks have no such luxury. Natural selection is relentless in favouring individuals that produce the most surviving young. Under natural conditions, limited nest sites holds both population density and parasitism at low levels. But the tragedy of the nest boxes leads parasitic females to keep adding eggs to clutches until the rate of duckling production drops to zero.

Paul Sherman and Brad Semel, from Cornell University, have found that these problems can be avoided if nest boxes are put up in well hidden locations in woodland, and spaced out so that the Wood Ducks can enjoy the benefits of their normal secretive lifestyle.[69] The result is a reduction in parasitism and an increase in duckling production. Their work is a nice example of how an understanding of behaviour can aid conservation. Goldeneyes are less susceptible to unnatural chaos when nest boxes are put up for them because they are territorial. This sets a limit to the number of pairs that can breed on a lake.[5]

REDHEADS AND CANVASBACKS

In Hans Christian Andersen's story, the Ugly Duckling is the last to hatch. It is different from the rest of the brood, is taunted and runs away. But this odd bird is not a duck and grows up to become a beautiful swan. Despite the happy ending, there is a dark side to this tale. How did a swan's egg end up in a duck's nest? Did the mother make a mistake or did she deliberately abandon her offspring?

The events of this fairy tale may well have been based on real life because many waterfowl that parasitize conspecifics also occasionally parasitize other species too. This could arise by mistake, but in some cases it is so frequent and appears to be so deliberate that it is likely to reflect attempts by parasites to lay more eggs by widening their net of potential hosts.[70] The best evidence for this second view comes from studies of Redhead ducks in North America. Classic early studies in the 1950s, by Milton Weller of Iowa State College, showed that Redheads targeted a larger species, the Canvasback, as their main host.[71] In 1954, the doyen of duck biologists, Frank McKinney from the University of Minnesota, was the first to observe and photograph a female Redhead parasitizing a Canvasback nest. The Redhead squeezed alongside the sitting host female and had to withstand five minutes of intense pecking while she laid.[72]

The most detailed study of this interaction has been by Michael Sorenson, now at Boston University. He worked in the pothole wetlands in the prairies of Manitoba, just south of Minnedosa. The ducks arrived on the breeding grounds in mid-April and many were caught and marked individually with coloured nasal tags. Both species built their nests in emergent vegetation. Cameras were set up to take time-lapse photographs (one per minute) to reveal the comings and goings at each nest. The Canvasbacks were the first to nest and they were visited by two kinds of parasites.[73]

- 41% of Canvasback nests were parasitized by other Canvasbacks. Most of these were neighbouring females, which laid one or two parasitic eggs just before initiating a clutch in their own nest, while others were salvaging part of a clutch because of predation during laying.
- 65% of Canvasback nests were parasitized by Redheads. Female Redheads wandered over a wide area, so it was impossible to get a complete record for each one, but many (perhaps most) first laid a clutch of parasitic eggs, which they distributed among several Canvasback nests. Then, a week or more later, they built their own nest and laid a second clutch which they cared for themselves. Redheads did not begin their own nests until late May or June, by which time

most of the Canvasbacks had finished laying. Nevertheless, the Redheads, in turn, suffered some parasitism by Canvasbacks (6% nests) and by other Redheads (61% nests).

The Redhead's dual strategy of 'parasitic clutch first, own nest later' is a ploy that enables them to fit two clutches into a short season where there is only time to raise one clutch themselves. However, this luxury may not be possible every year.[74] In one year of drought, Sorenson found that the Redheads laid only one clutch. The young females just laid a parasitic clutch while the older females just had a nesting clutch, but much earlier than usual. This shows that in normal years the Redheads must delay their own nest in order to fit in the parasitic clutch. It also suggests that parasitic laying can be a low cost alternative to nesting when environmental conditions are unfavourable. However, parasitic laying is less productive too. On average, a parasitic egg had half the chance of hatching compared with an egg laid in a female's own nest, because a third of them were laid too late in the host's laying cycle and a quarter got displaced into the water during the laying struggle with the host female.[73]

Redhead eggs are ivory-coloured and glossy, while Canvasback eggs are larger and olive-green. Despite these differences, neither species rejects the other's eggs and conspecific eggs are accepted too. Females spent most of the day on their nests once the first few eggs had been laid, so in almost all cases they were sitting when the parasite arrived. All parasites behaved in the same way, whether they were of the same or a different species. The host sat tight while the parasite pushed and tunnelled beneath her so she could squeeze alongside to lay. Hosts pecked the intruders but their attacks were limited probably because a serious fight would have attracted predators (half of the nests were raided by raccoons) or displaced their own eggs.[73] The restrained resistance of the Canvasbacks is shown by the fact that Redhead females spent about the same time laying when the hosts were sitting as when they were absent, during short breaks from incubation.[75] The costs of escalation are shown vividly in the following account from another study:[75]

One Canvasback aggressively pecked and pushed against a parasitic Redhead for four minutes as it tried to climb on the nest. While the Redhead was clawing with its feet to displace the host, it kicked all nine host eggs backwards out of the nest. The Redhead eventually pushed the host off the nest, then spent seven minutes laying its egg while the Canvasback continued to vigorously peck the intruder. The Canvasback intermittently tried to incubate the Redhead egg but ... finally deserted ....

Sorenson found that, overall, 80% of his Canvasback nests were parasitized, either by Redheads, other Canvasbacks, or both, with an average of between 4 and 5 parasite eggs per parasitized nest. Hosts did not reduce their clutch size if they were parasitized and there was no evidence that their enlarged clutches or broods reduced their own success, so increased defences would probably have no selective advantage, given the costs they would entail.[73]

Up to half of the Redhead ducklings in a population are reared by Canvasback females. If these young Redheads imprinted on their hosts (either the brood female or their brood mates), then their courtship behaviour as adults might be misdirected to the wrong species. Michael Sorenson's cross-fostering experiments with captive Redheads and Canvasbacks suggest that mis-imprinting might indeed be a problem.[76] Single young males of either species were reared up to 60 days of age in broods composed entirely of the other species. This is the maximum period of care in the wild, by which time the young can fly. Then they were transferred to a large mixed-species flock. Some of these males later preferred to court females of their host species rather than of their own species. In fact, mis-imprinting seemed to be more of a problem for the Redheads, which suggests that this species may have no special mechanisms to avoid these costs, which you might have expected given their much higher frequency of parasitism of another species in nature.

Sorenson suggests that in the wild there may be two mitigating factors that could reduce these mis-imprinting problems.[76] First, several Redheads are often reared together, either because of multiple parasitism of a nest or because females desert their broods early and ducklings from different broods then join together. Perhaps the Redheads then imprint on one another? Second, Redheads and Canvasbacks have largely different wintering ranges in the south. This is where pair formation occurs, so perhaps there is little opportunity for courtship mix-ups, or perhaps any early mis-imprinting is overridden or reversed once each species associates with its own kind.

Nevertheless, the problem of mis-imprinting deserves more study. It might be an obstacle to the evolution of parasitism of another species.

CHICKS THAT RUN AWAY FROM HOME

So far, all our examples have involved adult parasites either laying directly into the host nest or transferring partly incubated eggs. But cheating can also occur at a later stage, when chicks try to join other families. This is brood parasitism too, except that here the choice of host is made by the chick rather than by its mother.[77] Chicks try to transfer to other families when they are receiving inadequate care from their own parents. Continuing our fairy tale theme, they behave like Hansel and Gretel and run away from home despite the risks that this entails.

The first evidence for this came from a study by Jeff Graves and Andrew Whiten from the University of St. Andrews, Scotland, who studied Herring Gulls breeding on the Isle of May.[78] The gulls are territorial and adults will attack and sometimes kill and eat any strange chick that trespasses on their land. Nevertheless, chicks frequently wandered onto neighbouring territories and about half of them succeeded in gaining adoption. Two observations suggested that these were not simply chicks that had got lost. First, the chicks that left home were those that had just one parent (the other had died or disappeared). They were malnourished and deliberately set off for other territories. Second, they adopted behaviour that increased the chance that they would be accepted, for example crouching down next to the neighbour's nest or chicks. In some cases, the adult picked them up and shook them, as if about to kill them, but they managed to wriggle free and then ran towards the nest where the adult seemed inhibited from continuing its attacks. This restraint in the vicinity of its own nest and chicks has probably evolved so that the adult gull avoids harming its own brood. After a couple of days on the new territory, the chick was treated like one of the fosterer's own young.

Other gull studies from around the world have found similar behaviour, with 5–35% of pairs adopting one or more foreign chicks.[77] The chicks that run away from home are those that are being badly cared for, either because a parent has died or because they are the smallest in the brood and are bullied by their siblings. They try to join other broods with younger chicks where they will have the advantage of being the largest. On average, only 20–30% of them succeed in getting adopted. The rest are killed by conspecific adults or starve to death. Nevertheless, calculations suggest that the starving chicks that choose to abandon their natal territory can double their survival chances by trying to seek foster care.[79]

In several gull species, parents do not begin to recognize their own young until they are a week old or more. Why don't they speed up their recognition so they can always discriminate against an impostor? It is costly to accept a foreign chick because the gull's own young get less food and are less likely to survive to fledging.[79] This puzzle becomes all the more intriguing when we discover that chicks can recognize their parents by voice at a much earlier age, soon after hatching. Why don't young gull chicks help their parents to recognize them by giving more distinctive calls? Michael Beecher, from the University of Washington at Seattle, suggests that selection would oppose any early advertisement of individual identity because it would preclude the chick from being able to parasitize care from other adults.[80] By hiding its identity it gains the best of both worlds. Its parents will feed it at home, using their territory as a cue for recognizing their own brood, and the option is still open to run off and parasitize neighbours if care from parents is inadequate. Only when the young follow their parents to feeding grounds away from the natal territory do they have to produce signatures to help with recognition because 'home' is no longer available as a cue.

In some herons, storks and birds of prey, nestlings may switch to other nests as soon as they can fly. They then parasitize care from foster parents for a few days or until independence. This has been well studied in White Storks breeding in colonies in southern Spain.[81] The young storks are fed by their parents, which regurgitate food onto the nest. From about 40 days of age, the young begin to take exercise flights and as they get older these flights become longer and more frequent. Parents will not feed them away from the nest, so the young have to keep returning for food. By 90 days of age, they leave home for good and become independent.

During the exercise flight stage, some young joined other broods instead of returning to their natal nest. These transfers were common; in about 40% of broods at least one chick left for another nest. The chicks most likely to switch broods were not the starving youngest, as in the gulls, but rather the greedy eldest chicks from the largest broods. Chicks got less food from their parents as they made the transition to independence and, furthermore, it became harder to return to the home nest because their growing siblings attacked them as they tried to land. So these older chicks sometimes tried to prolong their period of dependence by muscling in on other broods with fewer and younger chicks, where they would find it easier to compete for food. Resident adults and nestlings always attacked intruding chicks and often succeeded in driving them off. But if an intruder managed to land, it adopted a remarkable posture – it crouched with its neck extended and remained frozen for up to 30 minutes. Its immobility reduced attacks and after a while it was accepted. If the foreign chick succeeded in settling, the resident chicks got less food, but the costs were probably not severe because most adopted chicks stayed for only five or six days.[81]

In species that breed in dense colonies, and where chicks are mobile soon after hatching, there is a much greater chance that chicks will get mixed up at an early age, and parent-offspring recognition is more refined, and develops sooner, than in the gulls and storks.[80] In guillemots (= murres), where parents are packed on cliff ledges side by side, chicks learn their parents' calls while they are still inside the egg! And parents learn the calls of their chicks too within a few days.[82] Nevertheless, there is still scope for chicks to cheat. If food is scarce, both parents may have to go out to sea at the same time in search of fish. Unattended young may then approach neighbours and get brooded or fed by them. However, as soon as a parent returns the chick immediately recognizes the familiar voice and emerges to be fed. The temporary fosterers are usually failed breeders or females whose chicks have just fledged (only the male accompanies the chick out to sea). These birds are still hormonally primed for parental care and other chicks are easily able to exploit them.[83]

Similar temporary adoptions by failed breeders occur in the colonies of Emperor Penguins that breed on the sea ice of Antarctica.[84] Older chicks gather in large crèches while both parents go off foraging. They huddle together for protection against winds of up to 250 km per hour and temperatures down to −30°C. Chicks solicit food and warmth from any adults, but parents usually feed only their own young, which they recognize by its distinctive voice. However, failed breeders will often adopt young until their drive for care has subsided. Some failed breeders have such strong urges to continue care that they try to kidnap young chicks, which may get killed in a tug of war with the parents. Most adoptions last for just a day or two, after which the chicks are abandoned. Some are reclaimed by their parents, but others get lost in the crowd and die from cold and starvation, or they are killed by Giant Petrels.

WILLING HOSTS: ADOPTION AND KIDNAPPING

We are now familiar with the picture of hosts defending their nests to reduce the costs of raising parasitic young. But some hosts seem to welcome parasitism, either by allowing parasite females to lay in their nest or by willingly adopting or even stealing chicks from other females. These are not failed breeders, like the Emperor Penguins, tricked by their physiology into seeking a temporary outlet for their continuing drive to care. Rather they are breeding females with eggs and chicks of their own that seem intent on gaining a larger clutch or brood. Why should females behave in this extraordinary way? There is growing evidence that their motivation is entirely selfish. The hosts sometimes actually benefit from having extra eggs or chicks, even if they are foreign.

A good example comes from the study of Ostriches in Tsavo West National Park, Kenya, by Brian Bertram of King's College, Cambridge.[85] In the Bible, the Book of

Job refers to the Ostrich as a creature whom 'God hath deprived of wisdom' and the belief in this bird's stupidity persists today with the myth that it buries its head in the sand whenever danger approaches. However, Bertram has shown that the Ostrich's acceptance of parasitic eggs is far from stupid – it is a fascinating adaptation which increases the success of its own eggs.

Male Ostriches defend huge and exclusive territories, in which they make nest scrapes and display to females that wander past. The first female to lay, the major hen, forms a pair bond with the male and helps him to guard and incubate. She lays on average 11 eggs at two-day intervals. Over this three-week period, from one to five other females, called minor females, also come to lay in the nest, producing about 14 eggs between them. These females do not stay to help, so they are parasites. Some are major females from neighbouring territories who are laying extra eggs in addition to their own clutch. Others may have no nests of their own, though this is not known for sure (it's not easy to study a shy bird that can run off at 70 km per hour over territories up to 20 km²!).

What is so odd about this system is that the host pair shows no defence whatsoever. They step aside to allow the minor females to add their eggs to the clutch. It is possible that the male might fertilize some of the minor females' eggs, but why should the major female tolerate them? The result is a clutch of 25 eggs or more, which is more than can be incubated successfully.

Once the clutch is complete, it transpires that the major female is being more selfish than it might first appear. She rolls about half of the minor females' eggs out to the periphery of the nest scrape, where they cook in the African sun (**Plate 8d**). It is not known how she distinguishes the minor female eggs from her own. Bertram himself could recognize eggs from individual females by their distinctive pore patterns in the white shell, so perhaps the birds use this cue too. The result is that the host pair incubates a clutch of about 19 eggs, half of which belong to the major female and half to the minor females.

Why doesn't the major female roll out all of the parasitic eggs? Her ejection activities might be costly in terms of risking egg breakage or attracting predators. There are jackals and Egyptian Vultures at large searching for a nourishing meal, and each Ostrich egg has the food value of 25 chicken eggs. But there could be a positive advantage from retaining some parasite eggs in the clutch. It might reduce the chance that one of her own eggs is taken if a predator discovers the nest.

Bertram's calculations support this idea. Predators usually take just one egg at a time. If a major female had only her own eggs in the clutch, she would be bound to lose one every time a jackal arrived. With half the clutch consisting of foreign eggs, she reduces her chances of loss by 50%. Of course, this 'dilution advantage' would be nullified if doubling the clutch size doubled the number of predators attracted. But this doesn't happen – larger Ostrich clutches attract only a little more predation overall, so the acceptance of parasite eggs works to the major female's advantage. If major females can incubate 19 eggs, why do they lay only 11 themselves? Bertram shows that, with the two-day interval between eggs, the extra time to complete a larger clutch would be counter-productive because of increased time for predation.

The 'dilution effect' might work at the chick stage too and explain why some waterfowl apparently are willing to amalgamate their brood with other chicks.[86] Martin Gorman and Henry Milne, from the University of Aberdeen, studied

Common Eiders on the Sands of Forvie, on the northeast coast of Scotland.[87] They marked adults with wing-tags and the ducklings with spots of paint. Soon after hatching, the females took their broods on to the mudflats, where the ducklings fed on small snails and crustaceans. The broods joined up to form large crèches of up to five hundred ducklings, attended by up to 85 females. These crèches changed in size and composition from day to day and each female tended to stay for only a few days before abandoning her ducklings so she could go off to feed in other areas on mussels and crabs. Once a female left, she did not return. Thus the crèches were attended by a constant turnover of adults as new females arrived with their broods and other females departed.

The attendant females defended the crèches from attacks by crows and gulls. Another study in Canada has shown that ducklings are safer in larger crèches, because of the advantage of dilution, which might explain why females are keen to join up with other broods.[88] Their decision to stay or desert might then depend on whether they can feed at the same site (adults prefer larger prey) and on the number of other females present (guarding might improve with more females, but at a diminishing rate). It would be fascinating to study this further. Perhaps not all cases of brood amalgamation are adaptive – some may simply be mix-ups where chicks get lost.[89]

In geese, there may be another advantage of accepting foreign young. Larger families are able to displace smaller families from prime feeding sites, both soon after hatching and later on when the birds migrate in flocks to wintering grounds. This might explain why foreign goslings are accepted well after the time that parents can recognize their own young.[90] Perhaps it also pays some goslings to transfer between broods? In Barnacle Geese breeding on Spitzbergen, up to a quarter of the goslings were adopted by other families.[91] In Lesser Snow Geese at La Perouse Bay, up to a fifth of the broods each year adopted one or more young.[90]

Finally, there is the intriguing possibility that foreign chicks are sometimes so valuable that not only is it worth accepting them but it is even worth going out to kidnap them! Robert Heinsohn, from the Australian National University, Canberra, studied White-winged Choughs, which live in groups of up to 20 birds.[92] Usually one, but sometimes several, females lay in a nest and the whole group then helps to feed the young. The helpers include previous offspring of the breeders, which remain in their natal group. Teamwork is essential for success because food is hard to find and the young need to be fed for up to seven months after fledging to give them time to perfect their foraging skills.

When neighbouring groups meet, they line up along opposing tree branches and display to each other. During the battle, dependent fledglings sometimes transfer to the opposition! In two cases, Heinsohn observed individuals 'herding' fledged young from the other group towards their own team, while chasing their attendant adults off. They then preened the foreign young. This looks remarkably like kidnapping. In other cases the cause of the transfer was not known. Perhaps sometimes chicks made the decision to move? In most cases, the transferred young ended up in a larger group and they were then cared for exactly like the home young. Groups may benefit from the arrival of foreign fledglings, despite the costs of having to finish raising them to independence, because this increases their work force for raising future broods. The newcomers might also be a source of future mates.

The last two sections highlight the need to look at chick transfer as a four-way interaction between host parents, host chicks, parasite parents and parasite chicks. The various behaviour patterns we have observed, ranging from resistance through to kidnapping in the hosts, and from getting lost through to running away in parasite chicks, reflect the various balances of costs and benefits to the different parties in each case.

WHEN PARASITES STAY TO HELP

It is only a small step from parasitism to joint nesting. This occurs when the parasite stays to help the host female care for the eggs and chicks. Are these cases where the two parties have agreed to cooperate in perfect harmony? Not at all! There are just as severe conflicts as those we have encountered earlier in the chapter. The squabbles can be over whether the parasite stays or leaves, and over how reproduction is shared in the mixed clutch.

Sometimes, the host female would do best if she chased the parasite off and laid the whole clutch herself. This applies to the Pukekos (= Purple Gallinules) studied on the South Island of New Zealand, near Dunedin, by Ian Jamieson from the University of Otago.[93] Subordinate females, unable to find a territory of their own, become 'persistent parasites'. Breeding females always try to chase them off, but if the parasite is successful in adding eggs to the clutch she is eventually accepted on the territory and both females then cooperate to incubate the clutch and to feed the chicks. Neither female ejects the other's eggs, but they seem to engage in an egg-laying race. Both increase the number of eggs they lay in an attempt to gain a larger share of the clutch. The result is an unusually large clutch, with low hatching success, in which the dominant female has lower reproductive success than she would have enjoyed on her own. An added twist to this story is that the male gains from having a second female because the total number of surviving chicks increases when he has two females. So males might encourage second females to join them. It is only from the dominant female's perspective that the intruder is a parasite.

In other species, all the females in a group gain from joint nesting so the distinction between host and parasite becomes blurred. This occurs in Groove-billed Anis, a South American species of the cuckoo family, Cuculinae, which has been studied in Costa Rica by Sandra Vehrencamp from the University of California, San Diego.[94] Usually two or three monogamous pairs join together to share a communal territory. They all help to build a single nest, in which all the females lay, and then they all take turns at incubation and cooperate to feed the chicks. Sometimes these groups form by a son remaining on his natal territory and then gaining an incoming mate. However, the pairs are apparently often unrelated. For example, a roving pair might be accepted into the group and the female allowed to lay in the nest. In this case she might be regarded as 'welcome parasite'.

Although the anis apparently agree to share a communal clutch, there are conflicts during laying. Females behave exactly like many hosts of conspecific parasites – they eject eggs from the nest before they themselves begin to lay. Only when all the females have begun to lay does egg tossing cease. The main effect is to prevent early-laying females from racing ahead and gaining an unfair advantage in terms of more eggs or earlier-hatching chicks. In fact, this policing system means there is a disincentive to be first. The first female to lay ends up with fewer eggs incubated, even though she lays more eggs overall, because she suffers tossing until all the other females begin. The last female to start does best because none of her eggs are tossed out.

Walter Koenig and his colleagues from the University of California at Berkeley have discovered that the same kind of egg destruction occurs when close relatives share a nest.[95] In Acorn Woodpeckers, two or three females often lay in the same nest. They are usually sisters or a mother and her daughters. Once again, the females keep a close eye on each other to prevent anyone gaining an advantage from early laying. Females destroy any eggs that are laid before they begin their own clutch. The eggs are removed from the nest hole, balanced on a branch and then smashed open and eaten! Overall, a third of the eggs laid in communal nests are destroyed in this manner and the result is that each female has about an equal share of the final clutch (though, as with the anis, later females tend to do slightly better).

Why do anis and Acorn Woodpeckers breed in these communal groups? Cooperation in parental care or the defence of a high quality territory may reduce adult mortality and so increase an individual's lifetime success. In addition, it may pay parents to allow their offspring to remain at home so they have the chance to breed despite restricted vacancies elsewhere.

The advantage of allowing close kin to share your nest might limit host defences against parasitism.[96] For example, sometimes a young female Moorhen remains behind on her natal territory because she cannot find a breeding territory of her own. She then lays in the same nest as her mother. Her mother shows none of the aggression that she unleashes on neighbours that try to parasitize her nest. Both females cooperate to incubate the mixed clutch and to feed the chicks. The mother raises just as many of her own chicks as she would have done on her own, and she also gains extra grand-offspring by allowing her daughter the chance to breed. Perhaps this advantage of tolerating foreign eggs from close kin has constrained the evolution of better discrimination against parasitic eggs laid by unrelated females.[97]

CHAPTER 15

Origins

So far, we have explored two of Darwin's three ideas about the evolution of brood parasitism (chapter 1). We have shown that laying eggs in the nests of other birds can be advantageous because it reduces the costs of parental care. And we have encountered many marvellous adaptations that enable the parasite to exploit the 'mistaken instinct' of the host. What about the third of Darwin's suggestions, that the parasitic habit has evolved from a nesting ancestor? In *The Origin of Species*, Darwin pointed out how his theory of evolution by natural selection could be refuted: 'If it could be demonstrated that any complex organ existed, which could not possibly have been formed by numerous, successive, slight modifications, my theory would absolutely break down.' This criterion would apply equally to any complex behaviour pattern, such as the parasitic habits of the Common Cuckoo.

EVOLUTION STEP BY STEP

Has the Common Cuckoo's intricate trickery really evolved gradually from nesting behaviour? Some have found this idea hard to swallow. For example, Canon Raven[1] objected that 'a sequence of at least five distinct events, outside the run of normal behaviour and structure,' had to take place before the cuckoo could successfully leave its eggs in the nests of foster-species, 'yet each by itself is useless ... The odds against the random occurrence of such a series of coincidences are astronomical'.

However, the cuckoo would not have had to evolve its tricks all at once. At the start of the arms race hosts have few or no defences, so the cuckoo's trickery could evolve gradually (chapter 9). Furthermore, during our survey of parasitic behaviour around the world, we have met many examples where parasites have less intricate trickery than the Common Cuckoo, yet are still enjoying successful lives. Some are part-time parasites, some lay non-mimetic eggs, some have their young raised alongside the host young, and so on. This is not to imply that these are all on the way to becoming like Common Cuckoos in their habits, only that their behaviour reveals that intermediate stages can be fully functional. They may represent the steps through which ancestors of the present-day Common Cuckoo passed long ago.

A sceptic might object that surely it is too much to expect that normal family life could be the source of the newly hatched parasite chick's murderous intentions towards its nestmates. But recent observations have shattered the cosy view of animal families. Hungry chicks compete by trying to outreach their siblings when their parents return to the nest with food. If food is scarce, these contests may escalate to the point where older chicks peck their younger sibs to death or push them out of the nest.[2]

For example, in Kittiwakes it is not uncommon for the younger chicks to be pushed out of more than half the nests in a colony, where they crash to the rocks below.[3] Young egrets and boobies are also regularly pecked and evicted by their older siblings. Once out of the nest they are ignored by their parents and starve to death.[2] Young Cactus Wrens have been found impaled on cactus spines below their nest, still alive, probably again evicted by their stronger siblings.[4] There is even one report of a Barn Swallow behaving exactly like a cuckoo chick, balancing an egg on its back, between its wing stubs, and heaving it over the edge of the nest.[5]

What about the bill hooks with which young honeyguides and Striped Cuckoos lacerate the host chicks to death? Even these weapons have been found in one species with parental care. David Bryant and Paul Tatner, from the University of Stirling, studied Blue-throated Bee-eaters in Malaysia and discovered that the newly hatched chicks are equipped with a sharp, downward-pointing hook at the tip of their upper mandible.[6] If food is in short supply, the older chicks attack the younger ones, which often die from their wounds. The bill hook is ineffective against feathered nestmates and wears away after a week or so. It is unlikely to have evolved primarily for another function, such as grabbing food, because it disappears by the time of peak growth. Instead, it seems specifically designed as a weapon for attacking naked siblings.

In species where parents raise their own young, chicks normally restrain their aggression and selfishness provided there is enough food to go round. This makes good sense because nestmates will be siblings, which share genes in common. Any gene that programmed a chick to always murder its nestmates would lose out from the loss of copies of that gene in the bodies of its dead sibs. For the same reason, aggression is restrained in parasite species where the parasite chick is likely to share the host nest with a sib, because its mother lays several eggs per host nest (chapter 8). By contrast, where the female parasite lays just one egg per host nest (e.g. *Cuculus* and *Chrysococcyx* cuckoos, Striped Cuckoos and honeyguides), the parasite chick loses nothing if it always kills its nestmates. Natural selection has simply changed the sibling rivalry that occurs in nesting species from conditional killing to obligate killing.

David Lack was a champion of the power of natural selection. He reviewed the behaviour of avian brood parasites in 1968 and sympathized with those, like Canon Raven, who considered it impossible that such amazing adaptations could have evolved step by step. Nevertheless, Lack followed Darwin in concluding that this was only a difficulty of our imagination, not of logical reasoning. He concluded,[7] 'given that the marvellous adaptations of the brood parasites are a product of natural selection, it is perhaps as hard to concede that this same powerful force is likewise responsible for the dull conventional habits of the monogamous songbirds which raise their own young'. But Lack underestimated the conflicts that seethe away in a nuclear family. Natural selection has had a much easier job than he imagined. The raw material for parasite trickery is already there as part of normal, nesting family life.

TWO LIKELY ROUTES TO PARASITISM OF OTHER SPECIES

The hundred species of avian brood parasites belong to five families (chapter 2), which are likely to reflect six independent origins of the parasitic habit in birds (two in cuckoos). An examination of the nesting behaviour of their close relatives can perhaps give us clues to the origins of parasitism. However, as William Hamilton and Gordon Orians have pointed out, we have to be careful here.[8]

First, we should not, as did some earlier writers, think of parasitism as a 'degenerative' condition which arose through all members of a population developing 'faulty' nest building, laying sequences or incubation behaviour. For example, in 1870 W.H. Hudson strove to account for the unusually variable eggs of the Shiny Cowbird and wondered if 'an imperfection of the sexual organs, producing this diversity in the eggs, causes also that looseness in its breeding habits which makes this species so different from others'.[9] He was referring here to the bird's apparent wastage of eggs from laying in old nests, or in nests where hosts already had huge clutches and were likely to desert. But this is more likely to reflect the occasional maladaptive outcomes of a 'shotgun strategy' of laying, which itself is advantageous when eggs are cheap to produce and there is intense competition for host nests (chapter 12). Selection will not favour a change from nesting to parasitic behaviour if it involves a decrease in reproductive success through imperfections. Instead, we have to wonder how some precursors of parasitism might have improved reproductive success for individuals.

Second, if we do find precursors of parasitic behaviour in nesting relatives of the parasitic species, this does not imply that they are now evolving towards the parasitic way of life. Just like the parasites, the nesting species will have special adaptations. For example, the flimsy nest of *Coccyzus* cuckoos does not imply that they are on the road to losing nest-building behaviour. Instead, it is likely that a small nest reduces the chance that predators will find their eggs or chicks. Similarly, the Redhead Duck's dual strategy of 'nesting plus parasitism' (chapter 14) does not imply that it is now evolving to obligate parasitism. Its behaviour is likely to be adaptive under its current conditions and may represent a stable state in evolution.

Bearing these points in mind, we can suggest two likely routes to parasitism of other species, starting from a nesting ancestor.[8]

From the take-over of other species' nests

Many species either use old nests or take over occupied nests of other species for their own use by driving the owners off. It is then a small step to parasitic laying. All that has to happen is for the female to lay while the original owners are still there. If she is chased off, or leaves of her own accord, then her eggs might get incubated along with the owner's clutch. Selection could then refine the parasite's behaviour, favouring laying during the owner's laying period, rapid laying to escape detection, a reduction in tendencies to compete for the nest site, and so on. This is the likely route for the evolution of parasitism in cowbirds, parasitic finches and honeyguides.

The one nesting species among the cowbirds, the Bay-winged Cowbird, takes over the nests of other species (chapter 12). If the Bay-wing is the sister taxon of the parasitic cowbirds, as seems likely, then such 'nest parasitism' could be the preliminary step to brood parasitism in this group. W.H. Hudson occasionally saw Shiny Cowbirds attempting to build nests, which he suggested was a ghost of their past nesting habits, and he thought that their interest in the domed nests of woodcreepers also reflected their ancestral habit of taking over old nests for their own use. He then proposed how selection might favour parasitism;[10] 'Let us suppose that the [Shiny Cowbird] … once acquired the habit of breeding in domed nests, and that through this habit its original nest-making instinct was completely eradicated, it is not difficult to imagine how in its turn this instinct was also lost. A diminution in the number of birds that built domed nests, or an increase in the number of species and individuals that breed in such nests, would involve the [Shiny Cowbird] in a struggle for nests, in which it would probably be defeated.' Hudson's suggestion that competition for nests may favour parasitism anticipates, by over a century, the arguments we gave for the evolution of conspecific parasitism in chapter 14.

Nest parasites usually remove any eggs laid by the previous owners before they lay their own clutch. Herbert Friedmann regarded this as the precursor of the parasitic cowbirds' present-day habit of piercing or removing host eggs.[11] With the evolution of parasitism of already-tended nests, the destruction of all the host's eggs would be costly because it would cause the hosts to desert. Selection would therefore favour a reduction in its intensity. Friedmann interpreted egg piercing as a 'relic of past history'. This may certainly explain its origin, but by 'relic' we should not imply that it is an imperfection in the parasite's behaviour today. Egg piercing is still adaptive for parasitic cowbirds because it reduces competition from the host chicks, and enables the female cowbird to test whether the nest is at a suitable stage for parasitism (chapter 12).

The African parasitic finches are likely to share ancestry with the estrildid finches (chapter 13). Some estrildids take over the nests of other species,[12] and even in those that build their own nests the male plays the major role, with the female simply adding a lining. When females are accustomed to laying in nests they did not build themselves, it is easy to imagine a transition to parasitic laying in occupied nests.[13]

The honeyguides are most closely related to the woodpeckers, which are hole-nesters. These two groups in turn are most closely related to the barbets and toucans, which are again hole-nesters. These relationships (derived from similarities in DNA and anatomy) are shown in the diagram on the next page.

This implies that the honeyguides evolved from hole-nesting ancestors. Hole-nesters often face intense competition for nest sites. In the long term this may promote speciation, with large species winning the competition for large holes and small species evolving to exploit smaller holes. But breeding densities of many hole-nesters are still often limited by hole availability. Put up some nest

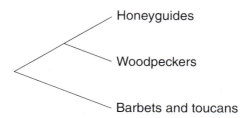

Honeyguides

Woodpeckers

Barbets and toucans

boxes and you can dramatically increase the numbers of tits or Pied Flycatchers nesting in a wood.

How should females behave when they cannot find a nest hole? One option is to simply wait for a vacancy. Another is to share a nest with a relative, either laying in the nest of their mother or sister, or helping them to raise offspring. Perhaps honeyguides took a third option and avoided competition altogether by cheating. If they were already used to laying in natural holes, it would be a small step to laying in occupied rather than unoccupied nests.

Honeyguides often parasitize hosts that are as large as, or larger than themselves. For example, Lesser Honeyguides (26 g) favour Black-collared Barbets (60 g; page 21), and Greater Honeyguides (55 g) often use nests of Hoopoes (60 g). Perhaps the honeyguides' ancestors were unable to compete with these larger species for occupancy of a nest site and so evolved into parasites instead. Their white eggs would already be a perfect match for hole-nesting hosts because of their past history of hole-nesting themselves. (Hole-nesters have evolved white eggs, presumably so they are visible in a dark nest). Being smaller than the host species, they would lay smaller eggs which would need less incubation and so would hatch out first. This would give their chicks a head start in development so they could compete successfully with the host young. Once the murderous bill hooks had evolved, the honeyguide chick could then command all the food. What better way to avoid competition from potentially larger nest mates than to kill them off while they are still small, naked and helpless?

From occasional parasitism by nest-building ancestors

A second likely route to interspecific parasitism is via the occasional parasitism we found in many nesting species, which lay eggs in other nests as well as their own, either to augment their success, or to salvage some success in unfortunate circumstances, or as an equally profitable strategy in balance with honest nesting (chapter 14). This route may have been taken by the one obligate parasitic duck, and perhaps by parasitic cuckoos too.

As we saw in the last chapter, many species of waterfowl sometimes lay in the nests of conspecifics. This could lead to parasitism of other species because of the advantage of increasing the number of potential hosts. In most ducks that parasitize only their own species, less than 20% of eggs laid are parasitic. But this increases to 60% in Redhead ducks, which parasitize Canvasbacks and other species too. Perhaps it is the ability to parasitize many host species that has enabled the

Black-headed Duck to become a successful obligate parasite and lay all its eggs parasitically.[14] It parasitizes at least 14 species in five orders, including Rosybill Pochards, coots, ibises and gulls. The Black-headed Duck's chicks become independent after a day or two and need no brooding or other care from their foster-parents. It is not known whether this extraordinarily rapid development of independence was an essential precursor for successful parasitism, or whether it evolved together with the parasitic habit.

The evolutionary relationships among the cuckoos are not well understood because information based on anatomy and gross similarities in DNA sometimes conflicts. Detailed comparisons of molecular sequences in DNA are needed to reveal the true family tree, as has been done for the cowbirds (chapter 12). Robert Payne has suggested the following as the most likely tree. He splits the cuckoo family Cuculidae into six subfamilies.[15] The numbers refer to the number of species. The parasitic groups are in bold.

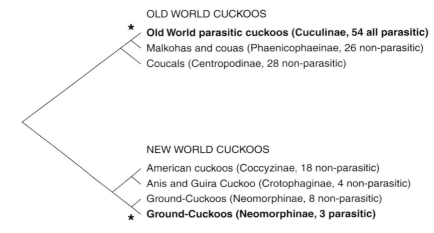

OLD WORLD CUCKOOS

* **Old World parasitic cuckoos (Cuculinae, 54 all parasitic)**
  Malkohas and couas (Phaenicophaeinae, 26 non-parasitic)
  Coucals (Centropodinae, 28 non-parasitic)

NEW WORLD CUCKOOS

  American cuckoos (Coccyzinae, 18 non-parasitic)
  Anis and Guira Cuckoo (Crotophaginae, 4 non-parasitic)
  Ground-Cuckoos (Neomorphinae, 8 non-parasitic)
* **Ground-Cuckoos (Neomorphinae, 3 parasitic)**

In this scheme, the branches indicate how the various subfamilies are likely to have evolved from a common ancestor on the far left. They suggest that there were two distinct origins of the parasitic habit in cuckoos (indicated by stars). One occurred among the Old World Cuculinae, all 54 species of which are parasitic. They are most closely related to the non-parasitic malkohas and couas. These two groups in turn are most closely related to the coucals, which are also non-parasitic. This implies that the Cuculinae derived their parasitic habits from a nesting ancestor, before they speciated and evolved into a separate lineage from the malkohas and couas. According to this classification, the New World cuckoos evolved their parasitic habits independently, within the ground-cuckoo lineage.

Some of the nesting cuckoos have odd breeding habits, suggesting that this family may be particularly prone to evolve parasitism. Among the New World cuckoos, the anis and Guira Cuckoo breed in groups where several females lay in the same nest.[16] There is conflict between them over how many eggs each should contribute to the communal clutch, which leads to egg tossing and occasional parasitic laying by females from outside the group (chapter 14).

Among the Old World cuckoos, male coucals perform most of the nest building, incubation and feeding of the young. This frees the females to build up reserves for a second clutch, or for a replacement clutch should the first one fail. In Black Coucals, which inhabit grassland with seasonally rich food supplies (grasshoppers and other insects), females may lay clutches for several males in quick succession.[17] This habit could be a precursor for parasitic laying. If a female had reserves to lay so many eggs that she ran out of nests built by males of her own species, she could exploit nests of other species too.

There is some evidence for this link between abundant food and parasitic laying in the American cuckoos, *Coccyzus*, which occasionally lay eggs parasitically, either in the nests of conspecifics or other species. This has been recorded in both Yellow-billed and Black-billed Cuckoos in North America[18] and in the Dwarf Cuckoo of South America.[19] In the two North American species, parasitic laying seems to be most frequent when there is an unusual abundance of caterpillars or cicadas. This glut of food enables the cuckoos to increase their clutch size and they attempt to augment their success by laying in other nests too. Among the 13 recorded hosts are American Robin, Northern Cardinal, Wood Thrush and Rufous-sided Towhee. If the ancestors of the parasitic cuckoos encountered regular flushes of food, perhaps this led to selection favouring those individuals that put less and less effort into nesting and more and more into parasitic laying.[18]

The Yellow-billed Cuckoo from North America is a nesting cuckoo that raises its own young, but occasionally it lays some eggs parasitically.

The *Coccyzus* cuckoos share two other traits with the parasitic cuckoos which might be regarded as useful precursors for successful parasitism.[18-21] First, they have short incubation periods of just 10–11 days, similar to that of the Common Cuckoo. This would enable their chick to hatch first in the nests of most host species, even those much smaller than themselves. Second, their chicks develop an active life style at a remarkably young age, leaving the nest when they are only a week or so old and clambering about the branches. Even four hours after hatching, the young Black-billed Cuckoo can cling with its feet to a twig and if suspended in mid-air it can pull its body up with its powerful leg muscles.[22] This surprising early demonstration of strength involves similar movements to those used by newly hatched parasitic cuckoos when they eject host eggs and chicks. In the nesting cuckoos, rapid development may be advantageous because it enables the young to reduce their chance of depredation by leaving the vulnerable nest at an early age, some two weeks before they can fly. This provides an alternative to sibling rivalry for the precursor of ejection behaviour.

However, this argument must be presented with some caution. Recent evidence from both anatomical studies and similarities in DNA has challenged the phylogeny above, suggesting instead that the New World *Coccyzus* cuckoos might have evolved from the Old World parasitic cuckoos.[23] If this is correct, then we have got our argument back to front. The *Coccyzus* cuckoos could have re-evolved nesting from a parasitic ancestor, so their habits would not be precursors of parasitism but rather an inheritance from their parasitic past, now put to good use in a nesting context. Whatever the direction of evolution, the main message is that it is not difficult to imagine how transitions might have occurred between nesting and parasitism in the cuckoo family.

Other possible precursors

Hamilton and Orians suggest that frequent depredation of nests during laying may lead to brood parasitism because females then try to salvage the remainder of their clutch by laying in other nests.[8] We have already seen that this can give rise to conspecific parasitism in Starlings, Moorhens and other species (chapter 14). However, not all species respond in this way,[24] and there is no evidence yet that it is a major source of interspecific parasitism.

It is also often pointed out that some of the brood parasites have odd feeding habits which could favour parasitism.[25] Cowbirds were presumably once nomadic, following the herds of Bison (chapter 10). If the herds frequently moved out of the commuting range of a nest site, then a female's foraging success would be compromised during breeding. Parasitic laying would enable her to avoid the constraints of having to return for a month or more to a fixed nest site.

It has been suggested that the honeyguide's unusual diet of wax, and the predilection of parasitic cuckoos for hairy, noxious caterpillars, have also favoured parasitism because these would be unsuitable for raising chicks. However, honeyguides also eat plenty of insects and because none of their close relatives eat wax, it is more likely that this odd diet evolved along with parasitism, as they escaped the constraints of parental care. Similarly, a diet of hairy caterpillars may not be a special predisposing factor for parasitism because many of the nesting cuckoos eat these too.

PARASITISM AND MODE OF DEVELOPMENT

Of the one hundred species of obligate parasitic birds, just one, the Black-headed Duck from South America, has precocial young, namely young which can run around soon after hatching. These young can often feed themselves too, so all the host has to do is brood and guard them. All the other parasites have altricial young; these are born naked and helpless and need much more care from the hosts, including brooding and feeding.

Why do 99% of the parasites have altricial young? This suggests strongly that it is much more profitable for birds with this mode of development to evolve into full-time cheats. Bruce Lyon and John Eadie have put forward an elegant argument to explain why this is so.[26] Parasitism is potentially of enormous benefit for species with altricial young because it enables them to avoid the high costs of parental care. And because their eggs are small (altricial young have few food reserves in their eggs), they can use their savings to boost their fecundity by several fold. Compared with related nesting species of the same size, brood parasites with altricial young lay many more eggs per season. Compare the following figures:

- An average of eight eggs, and often 15 or more, for Common Cuckoos (chapter 3), versus one or two clutches of three eggs for Yellow-billed Cuckoos.
- Forty eggs or more for Brown-headed Cowbirds, versus two clutches of four eggs for a typical nesting icterid (chapter 10).
- Twenty eggs or more for parasitic finches, versus two to four clutches of four eggs for a nesting estrildid (chapter 13).

A species with precocial young is unlikely to enjoy such a huge fecundity advantage if it changes from nesting to parasitism. First, the demands of parental care are less onerous, so there are fewer savings to be made. Second, these savings cannot be put to such good use because their eggs are much larger. Precocial young need large food reserves in the egg to enable them to hatch at their advanced stage of development. Many species with precocial young do augment their reproductive success by laying some parasitic eggs, usually in the nests of conspecifics (chapter 14). Some of them widen their net of hosts by including other species too. But the fact that only one of these species has abandoned nesting altogether, suggests that obligate parasitism is usually much less productive when your young are precocial.

Of course, there's another side to this argument. From the host's point of view, it is much more costly to receive parasitic eggs if the young are altricial and need lots of care. We used this to explain why these species defend themselves more against conspecific parasitism (chapter 14). Although conspecific eggs are usually accepted, because they are so hard to distinguish, nest defence often limits intruder access. Host defences are likely to provide a barrier to the easy evolution of parasitism by other species too. This might explain why, although parasitism is commoner in altricial species, it is nevertheless still rare.

Does Interspecific Parasitism Evolve Directly or Via Intraspecific Parasitism?

Nesting species might evolve to become parasites of other species via an intermediate stage of parasitism of their own kind,[27] or they might evolve directly to parasitism of other species.[28] Either transition is possible under both of the routes we have discussed above. For the honeyguides, parasitism of larger host species may have evolved directly from nesting as a way of avoiding struggles for limited nest sites with more powerful competitors. An experiment by Tore Slagsvold, from the University of Oslo, shows how parasitism of a smaller host species could also evolve directly from a nesting ancestor.[29]

Slagsvold switched single eggs between the nests of three species of tits, Great Tits (19 g), Blue Tits (11 g) and Coal Tits (10 g). These three have similar nest sites (holes in trees), similar eggs, and they all feed their chicks on caterpillars. The foreign chicks grew and survived best not in the nest of a conspecific but in the nest of a smaller species. This means, for example, that a female Great Tit would do 1.4 times better to parasitize the nest of a Blue Tit rather than a nest of another Great Tit. The reason is that the foreign young compete better for food when they are larger than the host chicks. And they do best of all when they hatch earlier, which gives them an improved size advantage owing to early growth.

These results suggest that interspecific parasitism might evolve directly from nesting species exploiting host species smaller than themselves, or species with longer incubation periods.[29] It would also be easier to overcome the nest defences of a smaller species than a conspecific, perhaps by muscling in while the hosts are present. However, there will be limits to how small a host can be, because very small hosts will have incubation periods which a larger parasite cannot match, and they may be unable to incubate large eggs or to rear unusually large chicks.

Comparisons with Parasitic Fish and Insects

Parasitic habits have been discovered in two other animal groups with parental care, namely fish and insects. There are often remarkable parallels with birds. And comparisons between the behaviour of related species gives strong hints as to how parasitism evolved from honest, nesting ancestors.

Facultative parasites in fish

Many species of fish are facultative parasites, occasionally farming out their eggs or young to other parents, either of their own or another species.[30] Some cichlids, which carry their small fry around in their mouths, escape parental duties by spitting their brood into a shoal of fry guarded by other individuals. Cyprinids (minnows and their relatives) often spawn above the nests of other species and their eggs drop down into the nests below. In both these cases, the hosts may sometimes benefit from accepting foreign eggs or fry, because a larger brood dilutes predation costs (as we found for eiders and ostriches). This advantage may explain the occasional kidnapping of foreign eggs or fry. For example, female Three-spined Sticklebacks prefer to lay in male nests with lots of eggs, which induces males to augment their clutch by stealing eggs from nests next door. Sometimes it is the offspring themselves which make the decision to join other broods (as in the gulls). In one damselfish, when older offspring are expelled from their parental territory, they join neighbouring shoals of smaller young to prolong their period of care (just like the storks).

A 'cuckoo' catfish

So far, only one species of obligate brood parasite has been described in fish. It was discovered in 1986 by Tetsu Sato, from the University of Kyoto, who was studying the fish of Lake Tanganyika in the east African rift valley.[31] The parasite is the catfish *Synodontis multipunctatus* and it uses cuckoo-like tactics to exploit its hosts, which are various species of mouthbrooders in the cichlid family. The laying sequence is remarkable.[32] The female cichlid lays one or two eggs and then she swims round to take them up in her mouth. Her partner is close by and he sheds sperm while she collects the eggs, so they are fertilized inside her mouth. This sequence is repeated until the female has laid a clutch of up to 50 eggs.

While the cichlid pair are spawning, a female catfish approaches, followed by up to three male catfish. At the exact moment that the host female releases her eggs, the female catfish releases her eggs too, and her attendant males release their sperm. So the host female takes up catfish eggs and sperm at the same time she collects her own eggs and her partner's sperm. Close synchrony is essential for the parasite's success because there is just a couple of seconds between the host female's egg release and the take up of eggs in her mouth. By comparison, the female cuckoo's timing problem seems a modest task.

The female catfish lays just a few eggs per host clutch, so a typical parasitized cichlid would have, say, 50 of her own eggs plus one to three catfish eggs.[31] The clutch develops in the safety of the female's mouth and all appears to be well. But the catfish hatch first, and as soon as they have absorbed their yolk sacs, they devour the host fry. So the poor cichlid ends up with a mouthful of mainly parasite young! Both the early hatching, and the destruction of the host's young are remarkably cuckoo-like, though in this case the host young are put to good use as food and not simply tipped out of the nest. Parasitism rates are also similar to those for cuckoo hosts; Sato found that 1–15% of host females had broods with catfish young.

Insects that cheat on their own kind

Intraspecific parasitism is widespread in insects, including burying beetles, lace bugs, and the stinging wasps, bees and ants. Lace bugs lay eggs on the undersides of leaves and then guard them until they hatch, and the young become mature and disperse. Parasitic females avoid these costs and can lay more eggs as a result.[33]

Wasps, bees and ants provide more elaborate parental care because they build a nest and also collect food for their young, so there is even more incentive for cheating. In many species of solitary wasps, the female digs a burrow and provisions it with one or more paralysed prey (e.g. caterpillars). She then lays and seals up the burrow. On hatching, the wasp larvae feed on these stores of food. Sometimes females behave parasitically. They may steal prey before the host female has begun to lay, or they may take over a nest and drive the owner away, or they may remove the host eggs and replace them with their own.[34]

In the social wasps, bees and ants, nests are much larger and are occupied for longer, sometimes for many years. A female (the queen) produces daughters that act as a worker caste. The queen then remains inside the nest to concentrate on laying, while the workers do all the other jobs, including enlarging the nest, defending it and stocking it with food. The nest and its workforce provide an attractive prize for parasitic queens. They try to muscle in on conspecific nests just before the first brood of workers hatch out (at later stages they find it more difficult to gain entry because the workers will attack them). The parasite then tries to kill the host queen. If she succeeds, she takes over the nest and when the workers hatch they regard the new queen as their mother and work away to help her raise her offspring. As these workers die, they are gradually replaced by the new queen's own workers. So this is an example of temporary social parasitism, where the parasite avoids the costs of the first stages of colony formation.

Just as we found for conspecific parasitism in birds, most of these female insects have flexible behaviour and can act as either a nester or a parasite.[34] Parasitism may be opportunistic (a female just happens to come across a nest), or it may depend on environmental conditions (parasitism increases when nest sites or food are scarce, or when a female's own nest has been destroyed), or it may depend on what other females in the population are doing (so there is a balanced frequency of nesters and parasites[35]). Again, this variation parallels what we found in birds (chapter 14).

'Cuckoo' beetles and bees

The food-laden nests of the social insects, with their bands of willing workers, have proved to be a great temptation for cheats. The result is the evolution of some obligate insect parasites whose trickery is even more remarkable than that of the cuckoos and parasitic finches. We live in a bird-like world of sight and sound and we marvel at matching eggs and gapes, or mimetic songs. But the social insects inhabit another world of taps, strokes and scents, so the parasite's trickery must involve cracking the tactile and chemical code of its hosts. To us, some parasitic insects appear to be totally unlike their hosts, yet the hosts welcome them as if they were one of their own kind. As the pioneer entomologist, William Morton Wheeler, wrote, 'Were we to behave in an analogous manner we should live in a truly Alice-in-Wonderland society,' and delight in welcoming porcupines, alligators and lobsters into our homes as if they were our own children.[36]

The use of chemical deception has been particularly well shown by the studies of Bert Hölldobler, from the University of Würzburg, who has discovered how the parasitic rove beetles *Atemeles* exploit *Formica* and *Myrmica* ants as hosts.[37] The female beetle gains entry to the ant nest, first by turning off the ant alarm system. She does this by secreting chemicals that suppress the worker ants' aggression. Then she produces another chemical cocktail that imitates the pheromones secreted by the ants' own young. This induces the worker ants to pick her up and carry her into the nest. Once inside, the beetle lays her eggs and she feeds there too, preying on the ant larvae and pupae and soliciting liquid food from the workers. When the beetle larvae hatch, they also secrete chemicals that are attractive to the worker ants, and beetle larvae beg for food just like an ant larva, rearing up towards the workers that pass by to sip droplets of food. Hölldobler tracked the flow of food through the colony using radioactive labels, and he found that the beetle larvae got more than their fair share. They behaved just like cuckoo chicks, begging more vigorously than the host young.

To imagine how extraordinary is this deception, think of a parasitic bird which arranges for the hosts to take her to their nest and then to feed both her and her growing offspring as if nothing were amiss. There are intermediate stages in other species of beetles, so it is easy to imagine how selection could have perfected this deception step by step. For example, highwayman beetles can induce ants to feed them but no more, whereas others can get ants to feed them and to carry them to their nests, but the beetle larvae are not fed by the ants.

There are also cuckoo bumblebees (*Psithyrus*). They produce no workers of their own, but instead the cuckoo bee queen barges into the nest of a *Bombus* bumblebee and uses the host workers to rear her brood of new cuckoo bee queens and males. *Psithyrus* bees have unusually tough integuments to help them withstand attacks when they first enter a colony, and they defend themselves with powerful jaws too. The workers may eventually accept them, perhaps because cuckoo bees have special appeasement substances or simply get coated in the colony's odour. Sometimes the cuckoo queen kills or drives off the host queen while sometimes the two share the nest.[38]

'Cuckoo' ants

Among the ants, it has been estimated that about 2% of the 12,000 species are interspecific parasites. Four types of parasites have been distinguished, which show various degrees of sophistication in their trickery.[39]

- *Guest ants.* These have small colonies which live inside the nests of a host species. They raise their own brood, but steal or beg food from the host workers.
- *Temporary parasites.* The parasite queen replaces the host queen and relies on the host species workers in the early stage of colony formation. But eventually her own workers replace the host's workforce. Parasite queens use some macabre tactics to invade colonies. Some perform a slow strangulation of the host queen, which may take several months (it may pay to keep her alive, but paralysed, so the host workers continue to receive her chemical signals and behave normally). Others secrete chemicals which induce the ultimate genetic madness in the host workers – they turn on their own queen and kill her. A cuckoo equivalent would be for the female cuckoo to induce the host parents to destroy their own offspring, so they could better care for the cuckoo chick.
- *Permanent parasitism with slave raiding.* The parasite queen invades the nest of a host species and kills or drives off the host queen and adult workers. She then relies on the newly hatching host workers to act as slaves to rear her own brood. However, the parasite's own brood does not contain the normal kind of workers. Instead, they are a specialized caste that go off and raid neighbouring host

species' nests to collect pupae, which will replenish the slave stock. When the pupae hatch, the young workers behave just as they would back home so, unwittingly, all their effort goes into raising the parasite's offspring. Darwin pointed out that this remarkable habit could have had a simple origin.[40] Ancestors could have raided nests for food (as some species now do) and occasionally pupae may have been kept beyond their 'use by date'. They would then hatch out and help. If this help were more beneficial than their use as food, it would pay to keep the pupae rather than to eat them. Food raids would then evolve into slave raids.

- *Permanent parasitism without slave raiding.* Here the parasite queen coexists with the host queen, so the host queen provides a continuous source of workers. These workerless social parasites, known as 'inquilines', are the ant-equivalent of a parasitic cuckoo. They contribute nothing to the rearing of their own offspring.

PARASITE SPECIES THAT EVOLVE FROM THE HOST STOCK

Most parasitic ants specialize on one host species. In marked contrast to the birds, parasites and hosts are often closely related. In fact, sometimes they are each other's closest relatives.[36] How can we account for this? One possibility is that parasites are more likely to succeed with related hosts. They will have similar larval food (so the hosts will provide the correct diet), and will share similar communication systems (so the host code is easier to crack). However, if a beetle can parasitize an ant this cannot be the whole story.

Another explanation is that the parasite species sometimes evolves directly from the host species. This may apply especially to the inquilines, which tend to be smaller than their hosts. They may have evolved from the 'miniature queens' found within some species.[41] These tiny queens are too small to compete for a nest site and have insufficient reserves to start up their own brood of workers. So they become cheats – they join a nest of their own species to exploit a normal queen's workforce. These conspecific cheats could evolve into another species which becomes a permanent parasite. For example, perhaps the sexual offspring (young queens and males) from the miniature queens develop faster (because they are smaller). They would then emerge earlier in the year and do their mating before the sexual offspring of the normal queens emerge. The two types of offspring would then be genetically isolated, allowing each to evolve their separate ways. This would enable the miniature queen stock to evolve into a separate species, with the improved trickery needed for life as a permanent parasite.[41]

This is an example where the variation in behaviour within a species can provide the origin for species diversity.[42] In birds, however, brood parasites have clearly not evolved from their host species. Most, including all the cuckoos, are distant relatives of their hosts. The nearest we get to the ant case is with Screaming Cowbirds parasitizing Bay-winged Cowbirds, but even these are not each other's closest relatives (chapter 12). The *Vidua* finches parasitize a related subfamily of finches, the estrildids, and the honeyguides also parasitize related families, woodpeckers and barbets. But in neither case have the parasites evolved directly from the host species. Instead, just like the cuckoos, they have colonized a host species and have then evolved specialized adaptations as a result of a host-parasite arms race (chapters 9 and 13).

Why hasn't conspecific parasitism in birds given rise to cuckoo-starling and cuckoo-goldeneye species? Perhaps variation within a bird species cannot be as extreme as that in ants, so there is less of a springboard for the start of a new species. Or perhaps conspecific parasites rarely do as well as nesters in birds because of limited opportunities for parasitism (host defences, synchronous laying) and the fact that there is less of a workforce to exploit (a host pair rather than a huge gang of workers).

WHY IS INTERSPECIFIC BROOD PARASITISM SO RARE?

The brood parasites include just 1% of bird species, 2% of ant species and a single fish. As the proverb says, there must always be more fools than knaves, or else the knaves will be deprived of their livelihood. But why are there so few species of professional parasites?

One possibility is that hosts are already primed to defend themselves because of parasitism by their own kind. Perhaps these defences limit the initial success of interspecific parasitism to such an extent that it rarely has the chance to get off the ground? However, most bird species accept eggs laid by conspecifics, probably because they are so similar to their own that rejection would entail severe recognition errors (chapter 14). So, prior to parasitism by another species, hosts would not have encountered non-mimetic eggs in their nest, and may not have any defences against them. In support of this, species untainted by cuckoos accept eggs unlike their own, even though they sometimes face regular parasitism with mimetic eggs from conspecifics (chapter 4). The success the Brown-headed Cowbird is now enjoying with new hosts in North America (chapter 10) also suggests that conspecific parasitism does not always prime hosts with effective defences against an interspecific parasite.

Here are three other explanations for why there are so few species of interspecific parasites.

- Parasitism is limited to five of the 160 families of birds, and mainly to two of the 11 sub-families of ants, where it is found in just a few genera.[36] This suggests that the habit is hard to evolve. Perhaps it needs special predisposing factors, which are present in just a few families.
- Honest nesting, with some occasional parasitism, may usually be a better way to reproduce. Permanent parasites have the problems of finding host nests, synchronizing their laying, making sure the hosts have a suitable diet, and avoiding costs of mis-imprinting. Once hosts begin to evolve defences, the parasites also have to overcome nest defence and egg and chick rejection. This long list may be sufficient to ensure that parasites are rarely selected in favour of nesters.
- Most parasite species are not abundant (the generalist cowbirds are an exception). Old World bird watchers are delighted to see a cuckoo. And the workerless ant parasites are usually so rare and local in their distribution that

Edward Wilson has written that 'they give the impression, quite possibly false, of having no more than a toehold on their host population and of existing close to the edge of extinction'.[36] Perhaps parasitic species are indeed short-lived in evolutionary time, and often doomed to early extinction owing to the evolution of host defences, or the chance factors that can eliminate small populations.

EPILOGUE

If cuckoos and their kind are destined for a precarious existence, then we should count ourselves fortunate that we have the privilege to study them. They inspire our wonder for Nature's ingenuity. They allow us to unravel the forces of natural selection by combining the pleasures of bird watching with simple field experiments. And the ludicrous sight of a little warbler feeding a monstrous cuckoo chick is a gentle reminder of how easily we, too, can be fooled by outrageous advertisements.

May there always be wild places for these miracles of evolution, where the interactions between hosts and parasites can be played, both for their own sake, and for the marvel of our future generations.

Notes on the Chapters

Chapter 1

[1] Peck (1970). [2] Hett (1936). [3] Riddle 9 in Hamer (1970), translated from the Old English by Dr. Audrey Meaney (pers. comm.). [4] Soyfer (1994). [5] In White (1789), Letter 30 to Daines Barrington. [6] Ridley (1993). [7] Grant (1986). [8] Berthold (1995). [9] Brehm (1869–73). [10] Darwin (1859). [11] Dawkins & Krebs (1979).

Chapter 2

[1] Sibley & Ahlquist (1990). [2] Payne (1997a). [3] Lack (1968). [4] Friedmann (1964). [5] Moreau & Moreau (1939). [6] Armstrong (1958). [7] Hudson (1874). [8] Ortega (1998). [9] Diamond (1985). [10] Isack & Reyer (1989). [11] Sorenson & Payne (1998). [12] Payne (1997b). [13] Vernon (1964). [14] Powell (1979). [15] Johnsgard (1997).

Chapter 3

[1] Payne (1997a). [2] Lack (1963). [3] Glue & Murray (1984). [4] Perrin de Brichambaut (1997). [5] Moksnes & Røskaft (1995). [6] Seel & Davis (1981). [7] Brooke & Davies (1987). [8] Lindholm (1999). [9] Jourdain (1925). [10] Brooke & Davies (1988). [11] Dunn (1985). [12] see also Löhrl (1979). [13] Bayliss (1988). [14] Chance (1940). [15] Wyllie (1981). [16] Newton (1893). [17] Collias (1993). [18] Punnett (1933); Jensen (1966). [19] Brooke & Davies (1991). [20] Teuschl et al. (1998). [21] Seel (1977). [22] Nakamura et al. (1998). [23] Nakamura & Miyazawa (1997). [24] Davies & Brooke (1988). [25] Molnar (1944). [26] Alvarez (1993); Øien et al. (1996). [27] Jeffreys et al. (1985). [28] Birkhead & Møller (1992). [29] Marchetti et al. (1998). [30] Gibbs et al. (1996). [31] Lisle Gibbs and Michael Sorenson; work in preparation.

Chapter 4

[1] Dawkins & Krebs (1979). [2] Davies & Brooke (1988). [3] Wyllie (1981). [4] see also Baker (1923, 1942). [5] see also Harrison (1968). [6] Davies (1992). [7] see also Mason & Rothstein (1987). [8] Davies (1999). [9] Seel (1973). [10] Molnar (1944). [11] Moksnes & Røskaft (1989); Moksnes *et al.* (1993). [12] Øien *et al.* (1996). [13] Alvarez (1993). [14] Craib (1994). [15] Duckworth (1991). [16] Payne (1974). [17] Noble & Davies (2000). [18] Brooker & Brooker (1991). [19] Picman & Pribil (1997). [20] Spaw & Rohwer (1987). [21] Lack (1968). [22] Dunn (1985). [23] Neufeldt (1966). [24] Perrins (1967). [25] first described for Jacobin Cuckoos by Liversidge (1961). [26] Arne Moksnes and Eivin Røskaft, pers. comm. [27] Brooke & Davies (1988). [28] see also Lotem *et al.* (1995). [29] Gärtner (1982); Nakamura *et al.* (1998). [30] Higuchi (1989, 1998). [31] Davies & Brooke (1989a). [32] von Haartman 1981; Järvinen (1984); Moksnes *et al.* (1995). [33] Moksnes *et al.* (1991). [34] Mason & Rothstein (1986); Marchetti (2000). [35] Davies & Brooke (1998). [36] Burton (1947). [37] Lerkelund *et al.* (1993).

Chapter 5

[1] Newton (1986). [2] Victoria (1972). [3] Lotem *et al.* (1992; 1995). [4] Rothstein (1974; 1975c). [5] Catchpole & Slater (1995). [6] Davies & Brooke (1989b). [7] Øien *et al.* (1995). [8] Soler & Møller (1996). [9] ten Cate & Bateson (1989). [10] Baerends & Drent (1982). [11] Alvarez (1999). [12] Davies & Brooke (1988). [13] Davies & Brooke (1989a). [14] Moksnes *et al.* (1991). [15] Molnar (1944). [16] Marchetti (1992). [17] Davies *et al.* (1996). [18] Lindholm (1999). [19] Pimm *et al.* (1988). [20] Lindholm & Thomas (1999). [21] Brooke *et al.* (1998). [22] Alvarez (1996). [23] Rodríguez-Gironés & Lotem (1999). [24] see also Stokke *et al.* (1999) for the same result within a species.

Chapter 6

[1] Jenner (1788). [2] Davies & Brooke (1988). [3] Dawkins & Krebs (1979). [4] Davies & Brooke (1989b). [5] Lotem (1993). [6] Lack (1968). [7] Fraga (1998). [8] Redondo (1993). [9] Brooke & Davies (1989). [10] Gill (1982); Brooker & Brooker (1989a); Grim & Honza (1997). [11] Davies *et al.* (1998). [12] Kilner (1997). [13] Noble *et al.* (1999). [14] Kilner & Davies (1998). [15] Kilner (1999). [16] Kilner *et al.* (1999). The chapter title comes from the commentary on this article by Mock (1999). [17] Kilner & Davies (1999). [18] Trivers (1974). [19] Dawkins (1976). [20] Briskie *et al.* (1994). [21] Godfray (1995). [22] Fry (1974). [23] Davies (1992). [24] Reed (1968). [25] McLean & Waas (1987). [26] McBride (1984). [27] Owen (1912).

Chapter 7

[1] Rowan (1983). [2] Payne (1997a). [3] Macdonald (1980). [4] Lawes & Kirkman (1996). [5] Lindholm (1997). [6] Victoria (1972). [7] Reed (1968). [8] Noble (1995). [9] Payne & Payne (1967). [10] Collias & Collias (1984). [11] Freeman (1988). [12] Rowley & Russell (1990).

[13] Brooker & Brooker (1989a). [14] Brooker & Brooker (1989b). [15] Brooker *et al.* (1988). [16] Payne *et al.* (1985). [17] Lesley & Michael Brooker, pers comm. [18] Payne & Payne (1998b). [19] Brooker & Brooker (1992). [20] Marchant (1972). [21] Brooker *et al.* (1990); Brooker & Brooker (1990). [22] Gill (1983). [23] Brooker & Brooker (1996; 1998). [24] Gill (1982). [25] McLean & Rhodes (1991). [26] Gill (1998).

Chapter 8

[1] Zahavi (1979); Zahavi & Zahavi (1997). [2] Rowan (1983). [3] Payne & Payne (1967). [4] Soler (1990). [5] Arias de Reyna *et al.* (1987). [6] Martínez *et al.* (1998b). [7] Cramp (1985). [8] Soler, J.J. *et al.* (1995). [9] Martínez *et al.* (1996). [10] Arias de Reyna (1998). [11] Manuel Soler, pers comm. [12] Martínez *et al.* (1998a). [13] Soler, M. *et al.* (1997). [14] Soler, M. *et al.* (1996). [15] Liversidge (1961); Steyn & Howells (1975). [16] Mundy & Cook (1977); Soler & Soler (1991). [17] Redondo (1993). [18] Soler, M. *et al.* (1995a). [19] Mundy (1973). [20] Redondo & Arias de Reyna (1988). [21] Redondo & Castro (1992). [22] Husby (1986). [23] Soler, M. *et al.* (1994a). [24] Alvarez *et al.* (1976). [25] Soler, M. *et al.* (1995b). [26] Beecher (1991). [27] Soler, M. & Møller (1990). [28] Soler, M. *et al.* (1994b). [29] Zuñiga & Redondo (1992). [30] Lamba (1963, 1966). [31] Dewar (1907). [32] Steyn (1973). [33] Gaston (1976). [34] Liversidge (1970). [35] Payne (1973c). [36] Bennett & Cuthill (1994). [37] Davies & Brooke (1988). [38] Hiroshi Nakamura, pers. comm. [39] Lotem *et al.* (1995). [40] Nevertheless, Pagel *et al.* (1998) have proposed that Common Cuckoo Mafia tactics could still evolve in some circumstances. [41] Soler, M. *et al.* (1995a). [42] Soler, J.J. *et al.* (1999). [43] Soler, M. *et al.* (1995c), page 773; 0.85 fledglings per experimental nest, compared to 0.54 per control, though the difference is not significant statistically.

Chapter 9

[1] Dawkins & Krebs (1979). [2] van Valen (1973). [3] Davies & Brooke (1989b). [4] Dawkins (1982). [5] Kelly (1987). [6] Takasu *et al.* (1993); Takasu (1998a,b). [7] Marchetti (1992). [8] Lotem & Nakamura (1998). [9] Nakamura *et al.* (1998). [10] Soler, M. *et al.* (1998). [11] Hens (1949). [12] Davies & Brooke (1989a). [13] Rowan (1983). [14] Cherry *et al.* (1998); Michael Cherry, pers. comm. [15] Moksnes & Røskaft (1995). [16] Nakamura & Miyazawa (1997); Marchetti *et al.* (1998). [17] Dawkins (1998). [18] Southern (1954); Harrison (1968). [19] Arne Moksnes & Eivin Røskaft, pers. comm. [20] Nakamura (1990); Nakamura *et al.* (1998). [21] see also Yamagishi & Fujioka (1986). [22] Cruz & Wiley (1989). [23] Robert & Sorci (1999). [24] Brooker & Brooker (1989b). [25] Soler (1990). [26] Moksnes *et al.* (1991). [27] Davies & Brooke (1998). [28] see also Moskát & Fuisz (1999). [29] Marchetti (2000). [30] Brooker *et al.* (1990). [31] Brooker & Brooker (1990; 1996). [32] Brooker & Brooker (1989b). [33] Higuchi (1998). [34] Lack (1963). [35] Higuchi & Sato (1984). [36] De Naurois (1979).

Chapter 10

[1] Lowther (1993); Ortega (1998). [2] In Friedmann (1929). [3] Mayfield (1965). [4] Rothstein (1994). [5] see also Ward & Smith (1998). [6] Smith *et al.* (1999). [7] Friedmann *et al.* (1977). [8] Sealy (1992). [9] Elliott (1978). [10] Robinson *et al.* (1995a). [11] Brittingham & Temple (1983). [12] Robinson *et al.* (1995b). [13] Morse & Robinson (1999). [14] Rothstein *et al.* (1984). [15] Thompson (1994). [16] Yokel (1986). [17] Dufty (1982). [18] Darley (1982); Teather & Robertson (1986). [19] Elliott (1980). [20] Alderson *et al.* (1999). [21] Norman & Robertson (1975). [22] Clotfelter (1998). [23] Nolan (1978). [24] Arcese *et al.* (1996). [25] Davies & Brooke (1988). [26] Reboreda *et al.* (1996). [27] Sherry *et al.* (1993). [28] Scott (1991). [29] Sealy *et al.* (1995). [30] Neudorf & Sealy (1994). [31] Scott *et al.* (1992). [32] Wood & Bollinger (1997). [33] Røskaft *et al.* (1990). [34] Hill & Sealy (1994). [35] Scott & Ankney (1983). [36] Jackson & Roby (1992). [37] McGeen & McGeen (1968). [38] Walkinshaw (1949). [39] Fleischer (1985). [40] Gibbs *et al.* (1997). [41] King, A.P. (1973). [42] Briskie *et al.* (1990). [43] Orians *et al.* (1989); Lea & Kattan (1998). [44] Friedmann (1963). [45] Briskie & Sealy (1990); Kattan (1995) suggests that the smaller yolk reserves in Cowbird eggs triggers earlier hatching compared with species with the same-sized eggs. [46] McMaster & Sealy (1998). [47] Lichtenstein & Sealy (1998). [48] Eastzer *et al.* (1980). [49] Dearborn (1998). [50] Dearborn (1996). [51] Woodward (1983). [52] Zann (1996). [53] Catchpole & Slater (1995). [54] Rothstein *et al.* (1999). [55] King & West (1977). [56] West & King (1985). [57] O'Loghlen & Rothstein (1995). [58] Yokel & Rothstein (1991). [59] Rothstein & Fleischer (1987).

Chapter 11

[1] Friedmann (1929). [2] Rothstein (1975a). [3] Rothstein (1982b). [4] Rothstein (1982a). [5] Rothstein (1992). [6] Peer & Bollinger (1997). [7] Burgham & Picman (1989). [8] Hobson & Sealy (1989). [9] Neudorf & Sealy (1992). [10] Robertson & Norman (1977). [11] Scott (1977). [12] Røskaft *et al.* (1993). [13] Rothstein (1976). [14] Sealy & Bazin (1995). [15] Davies & Brooke (1989b). [16] Rohwer & Spaw (1988). [17] Spaw & Rohwer (1987). [18] Picman (1989). [19] Clark & Robertson (1981). [20] Goguen & Mathews (1996). [21] Petit (1991). [22] Zahavi & Zahavi (1997). [23] Smith *et al.* (1984). [24] Briskie *et al.* (1992). [25] Sealy (1996). [26] Ortega *et al.* (1993). [27] Ward *et al.* (1996). [28] Rothstein (1986). [29] Rothstein (1975b). [30] Mayfield (1965). [31] Hosoi & Rothstein (2000). [32] Hill & Sealy (1994). [33] Terborgh (1989). [34] Takasu (1998a); Grzybowski & Pease (1999). [35] May & Robinson (1985). [36] Payne & Payne (1998a). [37] Pease & Grzybowski (1995). [38] Pulliam (1988). [39] Nolan (1978). [40] Robinson *et al.* (1995a); Trine (1998). [41] Smith & Arcese (1994). [42] Ortega (1998). [43] Smith *et al.* (1999). [44] Robinson *et al.* (1995b). [45] Rothstein & Cook (1999). [46] Mayfield (1961). [47] Haney *et al.* (1998). [48] Sykes & Clench (1998). [49] Rothstein (1994). [50] Griffith & Griffith (1999). [51] Whitfield (1999). [52] McKay (1994). [53] Brewer (1995).

Chapter 12

[1] Bay-winged Cowbirds occasionally parasitize two other hosts; Fraga (1996), Mermoz & Reboreda (1996). [2] Hudson (1892). [3] Hudson (1874). [4] King, J.R. (1973).

[5] Kattan (1997). [6] Lyon (1997). [7] Gochfeld (1979). [8] Lichtenstein (1998). [9] Massoni & Reboreda (1998). [10] Mermoz & Reboreda (1999). [11] Massoni & Reboreda (1999). [12] Friedmann (1929). [13] Mermoz & Reboreda (1994). [14] Fraga (1985). [15] Cruz *et al.* (1990). [16] Mason (1986a,b). [17] Rothstein (1992). [18] Mason & Rothstein (1987). [19] Mason & Rothstein (1986). [20] Ortega (1998). [21] Cruz *et al.* (1995). [22] Wiley (1985, 1988). [23] Post *et al.* (1990). [24] Post & Wiley (1977). [25] Wiley *et al.* (1991). [26] Lowther (1995). [27] Webster (1994). [28] Robinson (1988). [29] Smith (1968). [30] Lichtenstein (1997). [31] Lanyon (1992). [32] Fraga (1998). [33] Fraga (1983). [34] Mason (1987). [35] Fraga (1979). [36] Gabriela Lichtenstein, pers. comm. [37] Freeman & Zink (1995). [38] Rothstein *et al.* (MS). [39] Davies (1999). [40] Baltz & Burhans (1998). [41] Friedmann *et al.* (1977).

Chapter 13

[1] Sorenson & Payne (1998). [2] Payne (1997b). [3] Payne (1973a). [4] Payne (1977a). [5] Noble (1995). [6] Skead (1975). [7] Morel (1973). [8] Nicolai (1969). [9] Nicolai (1974). [10] Nicolai (1964). [11] Neunzig (1929). [12] Immelmann *et al.* (1977). [13] Skagen (1988). [14] Reed & Freeman (1991). [15] Payne *et al.* (2000a). [16] Immelmann (1965). [17] Lyon *et al.* (1994). [18] Nicolai (1961). [19] Nicolai (1973) and Payne (1973a, page 107). [20] Payne (1973b). [21] Shaw (1984). [22] Barnard (1989), Barnard & Markus (1989). [23] Barnard (1990). [24] Barnard (1995). [25] Payne & Payne (1977). [26] Payne & Groschupf (1984). [27] Payne (1983). [28] Payne *et al.* (1998). [29] Payne *et al.* (2000b). [30] Klein & Payne (1998). [31] Payne *et al.* (1992). [32] Payne & Payne (1994). [33] Payne & Payne (1995). [34] Vernon (1964).

Chapter 14

[1] Delnicki *et al.* (1976). [2] Feare (1984). [3] Yom-Tov (1980). [4] Rohwer & Freeman (1989). [5] Eadie *et al.* (1998). [6] Birkhead *et al.* (1990). [7] Andersson (1984); Eadie & Fryxell (1992). [8] Yom-Tov *et al.* (1974). [9] Evans (1988). [10] Pinxten *et al.* (1991a). [11] Romagnano *et al.* (1990). [12] Kennedy *et al.* (1989). [13] Sandell & Diemer (1999). [14] Feare (1991). [15] Stouffer & Power (1991). [16] Lombardo *et al.* (1989). [17] Feare *et al.* (1982). [18] Stouffer *et al.* (1987). [19] Pinxten *et al.* (1991b). [20] Power *et al.* (1989). [21] Gowaty & Bridges (1991). [22] Emlen & Wrege (1986). [23] Petrie & Møller (1991); Yamauchi (1993). [24] Kempenaers *et al.* (1995). [25] Lank *et al.* (1989b). [26] Lank *et al.* (1989a). [27] Lank *et al.* (1990). [28] Lank *et al.* (1991). [29] Larsson *et al.* (1995). [30] Weigmann & Lamprecht (1991). [31] Forslund & Larsson (1995). [32] Brown (1984). [33] Brown & Brown (1998). [34] Brown & Brown (1989). [35] Brown & Brown (1991). [36] Brown & Brown (1988). [37] Bulmer (1984). [38] Møller (1987). [39] Alves & Bryant (1998). [40] Jackson (1993). [41] Jackson (1998). [42] Jackson (1992). [43] Freeman (1988). [44] Victoria (1972). [45] Noble (1995). [46] Lindholm (1997). [47] Braa *et al.* (1992); Moksnes (1992). [48] Moksnes & Røskaft (1992). [49] Arnold (1987); Lyon (1993a). [50] Sorenson (1995). [51] Magrath, pers. comm. [52] Lyon (1993a). [53] Lyon (1993b). [54] Lyon (1998). [55] McRae (1997a). [56] McRae (1998). [57] Gibbons (1986). [58] McRae (1997b). [59] McRae (1995). [60] McRae & Burke (1996). [61] McRae (1996a). [62] Arnold *et al.* (1987). [63] Safriel (1975). [64] Lessells (1986). [65] Eadie & Fryxell (1992). [66] May *et al.* (1991); Nee & May

(1993). [67] Semel & Sherman (1986). [68] Hardin (1968). [69] Semel *et al.* (1988). [70] Lyon & Eadie (1991). [71] Weller (1959). [72] McKinney (1954). [73] Sorenson (1993, 1997, 1998). [74] Sorenson (1991). [75] Sayler (1996). [76] Michael Sorenson, pers. comm. [77] Pierotti & Murphy (1987). [78] Graves & Whiten (1980). [79] Brown (1998). [80] Beecher (1991). [81] Redondo *et al.* (1995). [82] Tschanz (1968); Lefevre *et al.* (1998). [83] Birkhead & Nettleship (1984). [84] Jouventin *et al.* (1995). [85] Bertram (1992). [86] Eadie *et al.* (1988). [87] Gorman & Milne (1972). [88] Munro & Bédard (1977). [89] Patterson *et al.* (1982). [90] Williams (1994). [91] Choudhury *et al.* (1993). [92] Heinsohn (1991). [93] Jamieson (1998). [94] Vehrencamp *et al.* (1986). [95] Koenig *et al.* (1995). [96] Andersson (1984). [97] McRae (1996b).

Chapter 15

[1] Raven (1953). [2] Mock & Parker (1997). [3] Braun & Hunt (1983). [4] Simons & Martin (1990). [5] Alvarez *et al.* (1976). [6] Bryant & Tatner (1990). [7] Lack (1968). [8] Hamilton & Orians (1965). [9] Hudson (1870). [10] Hudson (1874). [11] Friedmann (1929). [12] Payne (1998). [13] Friedmann (1960). [14] Sorenson (1998). [15] Payne (1997a). [16] Davis (1942). [17] Andersson (1995). [18] Nolan & Thompson (1975); Fleischer *et al.* (1985). [19] Ralph (1975). [20] Hamilton & Hamilton (1965). [21] Spencer (1943). [22] Herrick (1910). [23] Sibley & Ahlquist 1990; Hughes (1996). [24] Rothstein (1993). [25] Ortega (1998). [26] Lyon & Eadie (1991). [27] Yamauchi (1995). [28] Cichon (1996). [29] Slagsvold (1998). [30] Taborsky (1994). [31] Sato (1986). [32] Michael Taborsky, pers. comm. [33] Tallamy & Horton (1990). [34] Field (1992). [35] Brockmann *et al.* (1979). [36] Wilson (1971). [37] Hölldobler & Wilson (1994). [38] Fisher (1984). [39] Buschinger (1986). [40] Darwin (1859). [41] Bourke & Franks (1991). [42] West Eberhard (1986).

APPENDIX 1

The one hundred species of brood parasitic birds

Parasite	Breeding distribution	Main hosts
CUCULINAE (OLD WORLD CUCKOOS): 54 species[1]		
Jacobin (Pied) Cuckoo *Clamator jacobinus*	Sub-Saharan Africa. Indian subcontinent to Burma	South Africa – bulbuls and fiscal shrike Central and east Africa and Asia – babblers
Levaillant's Cuckoo *Clamator levaillantii*	Sub-Saharan Africa	babblers
Chestnut-winged Cuckoo *Clamator coromandus*	Northern India and Nepal east to China, Burma and Indochina	laughing thrushes
Great Spotted Cuckoo *Clamator glandarius*	Southern Europe east to Iran, and Africa	crows, magpies and starlings
Thick-billed Cuckoo *Pachycoccyx audeberti*	Sub-Saharan Africa and Madagascar	helmet shrikes
Sulawesi Hawk Cuckoo *Cuculus crassirostris*	Sulawesi	?
Large Hawk Cuckoo *Cuculus sparverioides*	Himalayas, China, S.E. Asia to Malay archipelago	spider hunters and laughing thrushes
Common Hawk Cuckoo *Cuculus varius*	Indian subcontinent, Burma	babblers and laughing thrushes
Moustached Hawk Cuckoo *Cuculus vagans*	Malay peninsula and archipelago	?

Hodgson's Hawk Cuckoo *Cuculus fugax*	S.E. Asia; from N. India, Nepal, China, E. Siberia, Japan; Burma south through Malaysia and Malay archipelago	flycatchers, shortwings and robins
Red-chested Cuckoo *Cuculus solitarius*	Sub-Saharan Africa	robins and chats
Black Cuckoo *Cuculus clamosus*	Sub-Saharan Africa	bush shrikes
Indian Cuckoo *Cuculus micropterus*	Southern Asia, from Indian subcontinent east through China and E. Siberia, south to Malay archipelago	drongos, shrikes, Azure-winged Magpie
Common Cuckoo *Cuculus canorus*	Throughout Palearctic, from western Europe through Russia, China to Japan, and south to northern Africa, Turkey, Pakistan, Himalayas and Burma	*Sylvia* and *Acrocephalus* warblers, wagtails, pipits, shrikes, chats, buntings, dunnock, wren
African Cuckoo *Cuculus gularis*	Sub-Saharan Africa	drongos
Oriental Cuckoo *Cuculus saturatus*	Eastern Eurasia, from Russia east through Siberia to Japan, and south through China to Malaya and archipelago	*Phylloscopus* and *Cettia* warblers
Lesser Cuckoo *Cuculus poliocephalus*	South-east Asia, from Pakistan, N. India, Burma, S. China to Japan	*Phylloscopus* and *Cettia* warblers
Madagascar Cuckoo *Cuculus rochii*	Madagascar	*Cisticola* and *Acrocephalus* warblers, paradise flycatcher *Terpsiphone*
Pallid Cuckoo *Cuculus pallidus*	Australia	honeyeaters
Dusky Long-tailed Cuckoo *Cercococcyx mechowi*	Sub-Saharan Africa	?
Olive Long-tailed Cuckoo *Cercococcyx olivinus*	Sub-Saharan Africa	?
Barred Long-tailed Cuckoo *Cercococcyx montanus*	Sub-Saharan Africa	?
Banded Bay Cuckoo *Cacomantis sonneratii*	Indian subcontinent, east to S. China, south to Malay archipelago	ioras and minivets

Grey-bellied Cuckoo *Cacomantis passerinus*	Pakistan and India	*Cisticola* and *Prinia* warblers and tailorbirds
Plaintive Cuckoo *Cacomantis merulinus*	Asia, from eastern India and southern China south to Malay archipelago	*Prinia* and *Cisticola* warblers and tailorbirds
Rusty-breasted Cuckoo *Cacomantis sepulcralis*	South-east Asia and Malay archipelago	shrikes, flycatchers and chats
Brush Cuckoo *Cacomantis variolosus*	Indonesia, New Guinea, Australia and S.W. Pacific islands	honeyeaters, flycatchers, robins, fairy-wrens
Chestnut-breasted Cuckoo *Cacomantis castaneiventris*	New Guinea and N.E. Australia	? scrubwrens *Sericornis*
Moluccan Cuckoo *Cacomantis heinrichi*	Moluccas	?
Fan-tailed Cuckoo *Cacomantis flabelliformis*	New Guinea, Australia and islands of S.W. Pacific	scrubwrens and thornbills
Long-billed Cuckoo *Rhamphomantis* *megarhynchus*	New Guinea	?
Little Bronze-Cuckoo *Chrysococcyx minutillus*	Malaysia and Malay archipelago to Australia	gerygones
Gould's Bronze-Cuckoo *Chrysococcyx russatus*	Malay archipelago through New Guinea to N. Australia	gerygones
Green-cheeked Bronze-Cuckoo *Chrysococcyx rufomerus*	Lesser Sunda islands	gerygones
Pied Bronze-Cuckoo *Chrysococcyx crassirostris*	E. Indonesia	gerygones
Shining Bronze-Cuckoo *Chrysococcyx lucidus*	Australia, New Zealand and islands of S.W. Pacific	thornbills (Australia) and gerygones (New Zealand)
Horsfield's Bronze-Cuckoo *Chrysococcyx basalis*	Australia	thornbills and fairy-wrens
Rufous-throated Bronze-Cuckoo *Chrysococcyx ruficollis*	New Guinea	?
White-eared Bronze-Cuckoo *Chrysococcyx meyeri*	New Guinea region	?

Asian Emerald Cuckoo *Chrysococcyx maculatus*	Himalayas, Tibet, S. China, Burma, Thailand	sunbirds and spiderhunters
Violet Cuckoo *Chrysococcyx* *xanthorhynchus*	N.E. India, Burma, to Indochina and Malay archipelago	sunbirds and spiderhunters
Black-eared Cuckoo *Chrysococcyx osculans*	Australia	*Sericornis* warblers
Yellow-throated Cuckoo *Chrysococcyx flavigularis*	Sub-Saharan Africa	?
Klaas's Cuckoo *Chrysococcyx klaas*	Sub-Saharan Africa	sunbirds, warblers, flycatchers and batises
African Emerald Cuckoo *Chrysococcyx cupreus*	Sub-Saharan Africa	? bulbuls, weavers, sunbirds, warblers
Diederik Cuckoo *Chrysococcyx caprius*	Sub-Saharan Africa	weavers, bishops and sparrows
White-crowned Koel *Caliechthrus leucolophus*	New Guinea	?
Drongo Cuckoo *Surniculus lugubris*	India and southern China, south through to Malay archipelago	babblers
Dwarf Koel *Microdynamis parva*	New Guinea	?
Asian Koel *Eudynamys scolopacea*	Indian subcontinent to south China and south through Malay archipelago to New Guinea	crows; some areas starlings and mynahs
Black-billed Koel *Eudynamys melanorhyncha*	Sulawesi	? mynahs
Australian Koel *Eudynamys cyanocephala*	Australia and ? New Guinea	honeyeaters, figbirds and magpie-larks
Long-tailed Koel *Eudynamys taitensis*	New Zealand	whitehead, yellowhead and brown creepers
Channel-billed Cuckoo *Scythrops novaehollandiae*	Sulawesi, eastern Indonesia and Australia	crows, butcherbirds and currawongs

NEOMORPHINAE (AMERICAN GROUND CUCKOOS): 3 species[1]

Striped Cuckoo *Tapera naevia*	Mexico south to Brazil and n. Argentina; Trinidad	spinetails
Pheasant Cuckoo *Dromococcyx phasianellus*	Mexico, south to Paraguay, Bolivia and Argentina	tyrant flycatchers and antshrikes
Pavonine Cuckoo *Dromococcyx pavoninus*	Tropical south America	tyrant flycatchers and antvireos

ICTERIDAE (PARASITIC COWBIRDS): 5 species[2]

Screaming Cowbird *Molothrus rufoaxillaris*	Bolivia, Paraguay, Uruguay, S. Brazil, Argentina	Bay-winged Cowbird is main host, also Chopi Blackbird and Brown-and- yellow Marshbird
Shiny Cowbird *Molothrus bonariensis*	South America, West Indies. Now colonising S.E. USA	numerous passerine hosts (over 200 species)
Bronzed Cowbird *Molothrus aeneus*	From southern Texas, New Mexico and Arizona south through Central America to northern Colombia	numerous passerine hosts (*c.* 70 species)
Brown-headed Cowbird *Molothrus ater*	Most of temperate North America	numerous passerine hosts (over 200 species)
Giant Cowbird *Scaphidura oryzivora*	From Mexico through South America to N. Argentina	oropendolas and caciques

INDICATORIDAE (HONEYGUIDES): 17 species[3]

Spotted Honeyguide *Indicator maculatus*	Sub-Saharan Africa	? barbets and woodpeckers
Scaly-throated Honeyguide *I. variegatus*	Sub-Saharan Africa	barbets, tinkerbirds and woodpeckers
Greater Honeyguide *I. indicator*	Sub-Saharan Africa	barbets, woodpeckers, bee-eaters, kingfishers, starlings, hoopoe and woodhoopoes
Lesser Honeyguide *I. minor*	Sub-Saharan Africa	barbets, bee-eaters, kingfishers, woodpeckers, starlings
Thick-billed Honeyguide *I. conirostris*	Sub-Saharan Africa	barbets
Willcock's Honeyguide *I. willcocksi*	Sub-Saharan Africa	?

Least Honeyguide *I. exilis*	Sub-Saharan Africa	? barbets
Dwarf Honeyguide *I. pumilo*	Sub-Saharan Africa	?
Pallid Honeyguide *I. meliphilus*	Sub-Saharan Africa	tinkerbirds
Yellow-rumped Honeyguide *I. xanthonotus*	Afghanistan, east through Nepal to Burma	?
Malaysian Honeyguide *I. archipelagus*	Malay peninsula, Sumatra, Borneo	?
Lyre-tailed Honeyguide *Melichneutes robustus*	Sub-Saharan Africa	? barbets
Yellow-footed Honeyguide *Melignomon eisentrauti*	Sub-Saharan Africa	?
Zenker's Honeyguide *Melignomon zenkeri*	Sub-Saharan Africa	?
Cassin's Honeyguide *Prodotiscus insignis*	Sub-Saharan Africa	flycatchers, *Apalis* warblers, white-eyes
Green-backed Honeyguide *P. zambesiae*	Sub-Saharan Africa	paradise flycatchers, white-eyes, sunbirds
Wahlberg's Honeyguide *P. regulus*	Sub-Saharan Africa	*Cisticola*, *Petronia* and *Cameroptera* warblers, sunbirds

ESTRILDIDAE (AFRICAN PARASITIC FINCHES): 20 species[4]

Cuckoo Finch *Anomalospiza imberbis*	Sub-Saharan Africa	*Prinia* and *Cisticola* warblers
Village Indigobird *Vidua chalybeata*	Widespread in Sub-Saharan Africa	Red-billed Firefinch *Lagonosticta senegala*
Jameson's Firefinch Indigobird *Vidua purpurascens*	East Africa south to South Africa	Jameson's Firefinch *Lagonosticta rhodopareia*
African Firefinch Indigobird *Vidua funerea*	Fairly widespread in Sub-Saharan Africa	African Firefinch *Lagonosticta rubricata* (Zimbabwe and Malawi)
Peters's Twinspot Indigobird *Vidua codringtoni*	East Africa	Peters's Twinspot *Hypargos niveoguttatus*

Bar-breasted Firefinch Indigobird *Vidua wilsoni*	Central Africa, from Senegal to Ethiopia	Bar-breasted Firefinch *Lagonosticta rufopicta*
Jos Plateau Indigobird *Vidua maryae*	Nigeria	African Firefinch *Lagonosticta rubricata*
Black-faced Firefinch Indigobird *Vidua larvaticola*	Guinea-Bissau to Sudan	Black-faced Firefinch *Lagonosticta larvata*
Cameroon Indigobird *Vidua camerunensis*	Cameroon, Sierra Leone	Black-bellied Firefinch *Lagonosticta rara* African Firefinch *L. rubricata*, Dybowski's Twinspot *Euschistospiza dybowskii* and Brown Twinspot *Clytospiza monteiri*
Goldbreast Indigobird *Vidua raricola*	Sierra Leone, Cameroon	Goldbreast, *Amandava subflava*
Quail-finch Indigobird *Vidua nigeriae*	Cameroon	Quail-finch, *Ortygospiza atricollis*
Paradise Whydah *Vidua paradisaea*	East Africa, south to southern Africa	Melba Finch, *Pytilia melba* (S. and E. Africa)
West African Paradise Whydah *Vidua orientalis*	Sub-Saharan sahel zone	West African Melba Finch, *Pytilia melba citerior*
Broad-tailed Paradise Whydah *Vidua obtusa*	Central Africa, south of Congo forest block	Orange-winged Pytilia *Pytilia afra*
Exclamatory Paradise Whydah *Vidua interjecta*	Central Africa, north of Congo forest block	Aurora Finch *Pytilia phoenicoptera*
Togo Paradise Whydah *Vidua togoensis*	Southern part of west Africa	Yellow-winged Pytilia *Pytilia hypogrammica*
Shaft-tailed Whydah *Vidua regia*	Southern Africa	Violet-eared Waxbill, *Granatina granatina*
Straw-tailed Whydah *Vidua fischeri*	East Africa	Purple Grenadier *Granatina ianthinogaster*

Pin-tailed Whydah *Vidua macroura*	widespread through Sub-Saharan Africa	Common Waxbill *Estrilda astrild* and some other *Estrilda* spp.
Resplendent (= Steel Blue) Whydah *Vidua hypocherina*	East Africa	Black-faced Grey Waxbill, *Estrilda erythronotos* and Black-faced Pink Waxbill, *E. charmosyna*

ANATIDAE (DUCKS): 1 species

Black headed duck *Heteronetta atricapilla*	South America: Central Chile and central to southern Argentina	other ducks, coots *Fulica* spp.

Footnote. Host families: bulbuls (Pycnonotidae), babblers and laughing thrushes (Timaliidae), shrikes and helmet shrikes (Laniidae), crows and magpies (Corvidae), starlings and mynahs (Sturnidae), sunbirds and spider hunters (Nectariniidae), flycatchers and batises (Muscicapidae), shortwings, robins, chats (Turdidae), drongos (Dicruridae), warblers and tailorbirds (Sylviidae), buntings (Emberizidae), pipits and wagtails (Motacillidae), honeyeaters (Meliphagidae), ioras (Irenidae), minivets (Campephagidae), fairy-wrens (Maluridae), scrubwrens, thornbills, *Sericornis*, whitehead, yellowhead, brown-creepers and gerygones (Acanthizidae), weavers, bishops and sparrows (Ploceidae), figbirds (Oriolidae), magpie-larks (Grallinidae), butcherbirds and currawongs (Cracticidae), spinetails (Furnariidae), tyrant flycatchers (Tyrannidae), antshrikes and antvireos (Formicariidae) oropendolas and caciques (Icteridae), barbets and tinkerbirds (Capitonidae), woodpeckers (Picidae), bee-eaters (Meropidae), kingfishers (Alcidinidae), white-eyes (Zosteropidae), coots (Rallidae).

References: [1] Payne (1997a). [2] Ortega (1998). [3] Fry *et al.* (1988). [4] Payne (1997b).

Scientific names of birds and other animals mentioned in the text

Acadian Flycatcher *Empidonax virescens*
Acorn Woodpecker *Melanerpes formicivorus*
African Cuckoo *Cuculus gularis*
African Emerald Cuckoo *Chrysococcyx cupreus*
akelat *Sheppardia* spp.
American Redstart *Setophaga ruticilla*
American Robin *Turdus migratorius*
American Coot *Fulica americana*
Arrowmarked Babbler *Turdoides jardineii*
Asian Koel *Eudynamys scolopacea*
Aurora Finch *Pytilia phoenicoptera*
Australian Koel *Eudynamys cyanocephala*
Azure-winged Magpie *Cyanopica cyana*
Bank Swallow (= Sand Martin) *Riparia riparia*
Bar-headed Goose *Anser indicus*
Barnacle Goose *Branta leucopsis*
Barn Swallow *Hirundo rustica*
Barred Long-tailed Cuckoo *Cercococcyx montanus*
Barred Warbler *Sylvia nisoria*
Barrow's Goldeneye *Bucephala islandica*
Bay-winged Cowbird *Molothrus badius*
Bell's Vireo *Vireo bellii*
Bengalese Finch *Lonchura striata*
Black-bellied Firefinch *Lagonosticta rara*
Black-bellied Whistling Duck *Dendrocygna autumnalis*
Black-billed Cuckoo *Coccyzus erythrophthalmus*

Blackbird *Turdus merula*
Blackcap *Sylvia atricapilla*
Black-capped Vireo *Vireo atricapilla*
Black-collared Barbet *Lybius torquatus*
Black Coucal *Centropus bengalensis*
Black-cowled Oriole *Icterus dominicensis*
Black Crow *Corvus capensis*
Black Cuckoo *Cuculus clamosus*
Black-eared Cuckoo *Chrysococcyx osculans*
Black-eyed Bulbul *Pycnonotus barbatus*
Black-headed Duck *Heteronetta atricapilla*
Black-whiskered Vireo *Vireo altiloquus*
Blue-and-white Flycatcher *Cyanoptila cyanomelana*
Blue-grey Gnatcatcher *Polioptila caerulea*
Blue Jay *Cyanocitta cristata*
Bluethroat *Luscinia svecica*
Blue-throated Bee-eater *Merops viridis*
Blue Tit *Parus caeruleus*
booby *Sula* spp.
Brambling *Fringilla montifringilla*
Brewer's Blackbird *Euphagus cyanocephalus*
Brewer's Sparrow *Spizella breweri*
broadbill *Smithornis* spp.
Broad-tailed Paradise Whydah *Vidua obtusa*
Bronze Mannikin *Lonchura cucullata*
Bronzed Cowbird *Molothrus aeneus*

Brown-and-yellow Marshbird
  Pseudoleistes virescens
Brown-headed Cowbird *Molothrus ater*
Brown Shrike *Lanius cristatus*
Brown Thornbill *Acanthiza pusilla*
Brown Thrasher *Toxostoma rufum*
Brown Twinspot *Clytospiza monteiri*
Brush Cuckoo *Cacomantis variolosus*
Buffalo (=American Bison) *Bison bison*
Bullfinch *Pyrrhula pyrrhula*
Bull-headed Shrike *Lanius bucephalus*
Bush Warbler *Cettia diphone*
caciques *Cacicus* spp.
Cactus Wren *Campylorhynchus
  brunneicapillus*
Cameroon Indigobird *Vidua
  camerunensis*
Canvasback Duck *Aythya valisineria*
Cape Bulbul *Pycnonotus capensis*
Cape Robin *Cossypha caffra*
Cape Sparrow *Passer melanurus*
Cape Weaver *Ploceus capensis*
Carrion Crow *Corvus corone*
Cedar Waxwing *Bombycilla cedrorum*
Chaffinch *Fringilla coelebs*
Chalk-browed Mockingbird *Mimus
  saturninus*
Channel-billed Cuckoo *Scythrops
  novaehollandiae*
Chestnut-capped Blackbird *Agelaius
  ruficapillus*
Chestnut-sided Warbler *Dendroica
  pensylvanica*
Chestnut-winged Cuckoo *Clamator
  coromandus*
Chiffchaff *Phylloscopus collybita*
Chipping Sparrow *Spizella passerina*
Chorister Robin *Cossypha dichroa*
Chough *Pyrrhocorax pyrrhocorax*
Clay-coloured Sparrow *Spizella pallida*
Cliff Swallow *Hirundo pyrrhonota*
Coal Tit *Parus ater*
Collared Dove *Streptopelia decaocto*
Common Babbler *Turdoides caudatus*
Common Cuckoo *Cuculus canorus*
Common Eider *Somateria mollissima*
Common Grackle *Quiscalus quiscula*

Common Waxbill *Estrilda astrild*
Common Yellowthroat *Geothlypis trichas*
Crissal Thrasher *Toxostoma dorsale*
Crossbill *Loxia curvirostra*
Crowned Willow Warbler *Phylloscopus
  coronatus*
Cuckoo Finch *Anomalospiza imberbis*
Dark-eyed Junco *Junco hyemalis*
Dickcissel *Spiza americana*
Diederik Cuckoo *Chrysococcyx caprius*
Dodo *Raphus cucullatus*
Drongo Cuckoo *Surniculus lugubris*
Dunlin *Calidris alpina*
Dunnock *Prunella modularis*
Dwarf Koel *Microdynamis parva*
Eastern Bluebird *Sialis sialis*
Eastern Kingbird *Tyrannus tyrannus*
Eastern Meadowlark *Sturnella magna*
Eastern Phoebe *Sayornis phoebe*
egret *Egretta* spp.
Emperor Penguin *Aptenodytes forsteri*
Fan-tailed Cuckoo *Cacomantis
  flabelliformis*
Fieldfare *Turdus pilaris*
Field Sparrow *Spizella pusilla*
Figbird *Sphecotheres viridis*
Fiscal Shrike *Lanius collaris*
Garden Warbler *Sylvia borin*
Giant Cowbird *Scaphidura oryzivora*
Giant Petrel *Macronectes giganteus*
Goldcrest *Regulus regulus*
Golden-cheeked Warbler *Dendroica
  chrysoparia*
Golden Plover *Pluvialis apricaria*
Grasshopper Sparrow *Ammodramus
  savannarum*
Gray Catbird *Dumetella carolinensis*
Gray Kingbird *Tyrannus dominicensis*
Great Auk *Alca impennis*
Great Grey Shrike *Lanius excubitor*
Great Northern Diver *Gavia immer*
Great Reed Warbler *Acrocephalus
  arundinaceus*
Great Spotted Cuckoo *Clamator glandarius*
Great Tit *Parus major*
Greater Antillean Grackle *Quiscalus
  niger*

Greater Honeyguide *Indicator indicator*
Greenfinch *Carduelis chloris*
Grey Warbler (= Grey Gerygone)
  Gerygone igata
Greylag Goose *Anser anser*
Groove-billed Ani *Crotophaga sulcirostris*
guillemot (= murre) *Uria* spp.
Guira Cuckoo *Guira guira*
Gyr Falcon *Falco rusticolus*
Hen Harrier *Circus cyaneus*
Herring Gull *Larus argentatus*
Heuglin's Robin *Cossypha heuglini*
Hodgson's Hawk Cuckoo *Cuculus fugax*
Honey Badger (= Ratel) *Mellivora
  capensis*
Hoopoe *Upupa epops*
Horsfield's Bronze-Cuckoo *Chrysococcyx
  basalis*
House Crow *Corvus splendens*
House Sparrow *Passer domesticus*
House Wren *Troglodytes aedon*
Hume's Warbler *Phylloscopus humei*
Icterine Warbler *Hippolais icterina*
Indian Cuckoo *Cuculus micropterus*
Indigo Bunting *Passerina cyanea*
Inland Thornbill *Acanthiza apicalis*
Jackdaw *Corvus monedula*
Jacobin (= Pied) Cuckoo *Clamator
  jacobinus*
Jameson's Firefinch *Lagonosticta
  rhodopareia*
Jameson's Firefinch Indigobird *Vidua
  purpurascens*
Japanese Quail *Coturnix coturnix*
Jay *Garrulus glandarius*
Jungle Babbler *Turdoides striatus*
Kentucky Warbler *Oporornis formosus*
Kirtland's Warbler *Dendroica kirtlandii*
Kittiwake *Rissa tridactyla*
Klaas's Cuckoo *Chrysococcyx klaas*
Large Grey Babbler *Turdoides malcolmi*
Large Hawk Cuckoo *Cuculus
  sparverioides*
Lark Bunting *Calamospiza melanocorys*
Lark Sparrow *Chondestes grammacus*
Least Bell's Vireo *Vireo bellii pusillus*
Least Flycatcher *Empidonax minimus*

Leñatero *Anumbius annumbi*
Lesser (= Little) Cuckoo *Cuculus
  poliocephalus*
Lesser Honeyguide *Indicator minor*
Lesser Masked Weaver *Ploceus
  intermedius*
Lesser Snow Goose *Chen caerulescens
  caerulescens*
Lesser Whitethroat *Sylvia curruca*
Levaillant's Cuckoo *Clamator levaillantii*
Linnet *Carduelis cannabina*
Little Bronze-Cuckoo *Chrysococcyx
  minutillus*
Long-billed Cuckoo *Rhamphomantis
  megarhynchus*
Long-tailed Koel *Eudynamys taitensis*
Louisiana Waterthrush *Seiurus motacilla*
Magnolia Warbler *Dendroica magnolia*
Magpie *Pica pica*
Magpie-lark *Grallina cyanoleuca*
Marsh Harrier *Circus aeruginosus*
Marsh Warbler *Acrocephalus palustris*
Masked Weaver *Ploceus velatus*
Meadow Pipit *Anthus pratensis*
Medium Ground Finch *Geospiza fortis*
Melba Finch *Pytilia melba*
Merlin *Falco columbarius*
Mistle Thrush *Turdus viscivorus*
Moorhen *Gallinula chloropus*
Mourning Dove *Zenaidura macroura*
Mourning Warbler *Oporornis
  philadelphia*
Narcissus Flycatcher *Ficedula narcissina*
Natal Robin *Cossypha natalensis*
Nightingale *Luscinia megarhynchos*
Nightjar *Caprimulgus europaeus*
Northern Cardinal *Cardinalis cardinalis*
Northern Masked Weaver *Ploceus
  taeniopterus*
Northern Mockingbird *Mimus
  polyglottos*
Northern Oriole *Icterus galbula*
Orange-winged Pytilia *Pytilia afra*
Origma *Origma solitaria*
oropendola *Psarocolius* spp.
Ostrich *Struthio camelus*
Ovenbird *Seiurus aurocapillus*

Pallid Cuckoo *Cuculus pallidus*
Paradise Whydah *Vidua paradisaea*
Pavonine Cuckoo *Dromococcyx pavoninus*
Pheasant Cuckoo *Dromococcyx phasianellus*
Pied Crow *Corvus albus*
Pied Flycatcher *Ficedula hypoleuca*
Pied Starling *Spreo bicolor*
Pied Wagtail *Motacilla alba yarrellii*
Pike *Esox lucius*
Pin-tailed Whydah *Vidua macroura*
Plaintive Cuckoo *Cacomantis merulinus*
Prairie Warbler *Dendroica discolor*
Prothonotary Warbler *Protonotaria citrea*
Ptarmigan *Lagopus mutus*
Puerto Rican Flycatcher *Myiarchus antillarum*
Pukeko (= Purple Gallinule) *Porphyrio porphyrio*
Purple Grenadier *Uraeginthus ianthinogaster*
Red-backed Shrike *Lanius collurio*
Red-bellied Thrush *Turdus rufiventris*
Red-billed Firefinch *Lagonosticta senegala*
Red Bishop *Euplectes orix*
Red-breasted Blackbird *Leistes militaris*
Red-breasted Meadowlark *Sturnella loyca*
Red-chested Cuckoo *Cuculus solitarius*
Red-eyed Bulbul *Pycnonotus nigricans*
Red-eyed Vireo *Vireo olivaceus*
Red-gartered Coot *Fulica armillata*
Redhead Duck *Aythya americana*
Red-legged Thrush *Turdus plumbeus*
Red-necked Phalarope *Phalaropus lobatus*
Redpoll *Carduelis flammea*
Redstart *Phoenicurus phoenicurus*
Redthroat *Sericornis brunneus*
Red Wattlebird *Anthochaera carunculata*
Redwing *Turdus iliacus*
Red-winged Blackbird *Agelaius phoeniceus*
Reed Bunting *Emberiza schoeniclus*
Reed Warbler *Acrocephalus scirpaceus*

Resplendent (= Steel Blue) Whydah *Vidua hypocherina*
Robin *Erithacus rubecula*
Rosy-billed Pochard *Netta peposaca*
Rufous-and-white Wren *Thryothorus rufalbus*
Rufous Bush Chat *Cercotrichas galactotes*
Rufous-collared Sparrow *Zonotrichia capensis*
Rufous Hornero *Furnarius rufus*
Rufous-sided Towhee *Pipilo erythrophthalmus*
Sage Thrasher *Oreoscoptes montanus*
Savannah Sparrow *Passerculus sandwichensis*
Scaly-throated Honeyguide *Indicator variegatus*
Scarlet Tanager *Piranga olivacea*
Screaming Cowbird *Molothrus rufoaxillaris*
Sedge Warbler *Acrocephalus schoenobaenus*
Shaft-tailed Whydah *Vidua regia*
Shining Bronze-Cuckoo *Chrysococcyx lucidus*
Shiny Cowbird *Molothrus bonariensis*
Siberian Bluechat *Tarsiger cyanurus*
Siberian Blue Robin *Erithacus cyane*
Siberian Meadow Bunting *Emberiza cioides*
Skylark *Alauda arvensis*
Solitary Vireo *Vireo solitarius*
Sombre Bulbul *Andropadus importunus*
Song Sparrow *Melospiza melodia*
Song Thrush *Turdus philomelos*
Sora Rail *Porzana carolina*
Southwestern Willow Flycatcher *Empidonax traillii extimus*
Sparrowhawk *Accipiter nisus*
Speckled Warbler *Sericornis sagittatus*
Spectacled Weaver *Ploceus ocularis*
Splendid Fairy-wren *Malurus splendens*
Spotless Starling *Sturnus unicolor*
Spotted Flycatcher *Muscicapa striata*
Spotted-backed (= Village) Weaver *Ploceus cucullatus*
Starling *Sturnus vulgaris*

Stonechat *Saxicola torquata*
Straw-tailed Whydah *Vidua fischeri*
Striped Cuckoo *Tapera naevia*
Swallow *Hirundo rustica*
Swamp Sparrow *Melospiza georgiana*
Swift *Apus apus*
Thick-billed Cuckoo *Pachycoccyx audeberti*
Thick-billed Weaver *Amblyospiza albifrons*
Three-spined Stickleback *Gasterosteus aculeatus*
Tickell's Leaf Warbler *Phylloscopus affinis*
Traill's (= Willow) Flycatcher *Empidonax traillii*
Tree Pipit *Anthus trivialis*
Troupial *Icterus icterus*
Veery *Catharus fuscescens*
Village Indigobird *Vidua chalybeata*
Violet-eared Waxbill *Granatina granatina*
Warbling Vireo *Vireo gilvus*
Western Thornbill *Acanthiza inornata*
Wheatear *Oenanthe oenanthe*
Whimbrel *Numenius phaeopus*
Whinchat *Saxicola rubetra*
White-browed Scrubwren *Sericornis frontalis*
White-crowned Koel *Caliechthrus leucolophus*
White-fronted Bee-eater *Merops bullockoides*

White Stork *Ciconia ciconia*
Whitethroat *Sylvia communis*
White-throated Sparrow *Zonotrichia albicollis*
White Wagtail *Motacilla alba alba*
White-winged Chough *Corcorax melanorhamphos*
Willow Flycatcher *Empidonax traillii*
Willow Warbler *Phylloscopus trochilus*
Wood Duck *Aix sponsa*
Wood Thrush *Hylocichla mustelina*
Wood Warbler *Phylloscopus sibilatrix*
Worm-eating Warbler *Helmitheros vermivorus*
Wren *Troglodytes troglodytes*
Yellow-billed Cuckoo *Coccyzus americanus*
Yellow-breasted Chat *Icteria virens*
Yellow-browed Leaf Warbler *Phylloscopus inornatus (= humei)*
Yellowhammer *Emberiza citrinella*
Yellow-hooded Blackbird *Agelaius icterocephalus*
Yellow-rumped Thornbill *Acanthiza chrysorrhoa*
Yellow-shouldered Blackbird *Agelaius xanthomus*
Yellow Wagtail *Motacilla flava*
Yellow Warbler *Dendroica petechia*
Yellow Weaver *Ploceus subaureus*
Yellow-winged Blackbird *Agelaius thilius*
Zebra Finch *Taeniopygia guttata*

References

Acworth, B. (1946) *The Cuckoo and other Bird Mysteries.* Eyre & Spottiswoode, London.

Alderson, G.W., Gibbs, H.L. & Sealy, S.G. (1999) Determining the reproductive behaviour of individual brown-headed cowbirds using microsatellite DNA markers. *Animal Behaviour* 58: 895–905.

Alvarez, F. (1993) Proximity of trees facilitates parasitism by Cuckoos *Cuculus canorus* on Rufous Warblers *Cercotrichas galactotes. Ibis* 135: 331.

Alvarez, F. (1996) Model Cuckoo *Cuculus canorus* eggs accepted by Rufous Bush Chats *Cercotrichas galactotes* during the parasite's absence from the breeding area. *Ibis* 138: 340–342.

Alvarez, F. (1999) Attractive non-mimetic stimuli in Cuckoo *Cuculus canorus* eggs. *Ibis* 141: 142–144.

Alvarez, F., Arias de Reyna, L. & Segura, M. (1976) Experimental brood parasitism of the Magpie *Pica pica. Animal Behaviour* 24: 907–916.

Alves, M.A.S. & Bryant, D.M. (1998) Brood parasitism in the sand martin *Riparia riparia*: evidence for two parasitic strategies in a colonial passerine. *Animal Behaviour* 56: 1323–1331.

Andersson, M. (1984) Brood parasitism within species. In: *Producers and Scroungers: Strategies of Exploitation and Parasitism.* (edited by C.J. Barnard). pp. 195–227. Croom Helm, London.

Andersson, M. (1995) Evolution of reversed sex roles, sexual size dimorphism, and mating systems in coucals (Centropodidae, Aves). *Biological Journal of the Linnean Society* 54: 173–181.

Arcese, P., Smith, J.N.M. & Hatch, M.I. (1996) Nest predation by cowbirds and its consequences for passerine demography. *Proceedings of the National Academy of Sciences USA* 93: 4608–4611.

Arias de Reyna, L. (1998) Coevolution of the Great Spotted Cuckoo and its hosts. In: *Parasitic Birds and Their Hosts* (Ed. by S.I. Rothstein & S.K. Robinson). pp. 129–142. Oxford University Press, Oxford.

Arias de Reyna, L., Recuerda, O., Trujillo, J., Corvillo, M. & Cruz, A. (1987) Territory in the Great Spotted Cuckoo *Clamator glandarius. Journal für Ornithologie* 128: 231–239.

Armstrong, E.A. (1958) *The Folklore of Birds.* New Naturalist; Collins, London.

Arnold, T.W. (1987) Conspecific egg discrimination in American Coots. *Condor* 89: 675–676.

Arnold, T.W., Rohwer, F.C. & Armstrong, T. (1987) Egg viability, nest predation and the adaptive significance of clutch size in prairie ducks. *American Naturalist* 130: 643–653.

Baerends, G.P. & Drent, R.H. (1982) The herring gull and its egg. Part II. The responsiveness to egg features. *Behaviour* 82: 1–416.

Baker, E.C.S. (1913) The evolution of adaptation in parasitic cuckoos' eggs. *Ibis* (1913): 384–398.

Baker, E.C.S. (1923) Cuckoo eggs and evolution. *Proceedings of the Zoological Society of London* 1923: 277–294.

Baker, E.C.S. (1942) *Cuckoo Problems*. Witherby, London.

Baldamus, E. (1892) *Das Leben der Europäischen Kuckucke*. Parey, Berlin.

Baltz, M.E. & Burhans, D.E. (1998) Rejection of artificial parasite eggs by gray kingbirds in the Bahamas. *Condor* 100: 566–568.

Barnard, P. (1989) Territoriality and the determinants of male mating success in the southern African whydahs (*Vidua*). *Ostrich* 60: 103–117.

Barnard, P. (1990) Male tail length, sexual display intensity and female sexual response in a parasitic African finch. *Animal Behaviour* 39: 652–656.

Barnard, P. (1995) Timing of ornament growth, phenotypic variation, and size dimorphism in two promiscuous African whydahs (Ploceidae: *Vidua*). *Biological Journal of the Linnean Society* 55: 129–141.

Barnard, P. & Markus, M.B. (1989) Male copulation frequency and female competition for fertilizations in a promiscuous brood parasite, the Pin-tailed Whydah *Vidua macroura*. *Ibis* 131: 421–425.

Bayliss, M. (1988) Cuckoo X breaks records. *British Trust for Ornithology News* 159: 7.

Beecher, M.D. (1991) Successes and failures of parent-offspring recognition in animals. In: *Kin Recognition* (edited by P.G. Hepper). pp. 94–124. Cambridge University Press, Cambridge.

Bennett, A.T.D. & Cuthill, I.C. (1994) Ultraviolet vision in birds: what is its function? *Vision Research* 34: 1471–1478.

Berthold, P. (1995) Microevolution of migratory behaviour illustrated by the Blackcap *Sylvia atricapilla*. *Bird Study* 42: 89–100.

Bertram, B.C.R. (1992) *The Ostrich Communal Nesting System*. Princeton University Press, Princeton.

Birkhead, T.R. & Møller, A.P. (1992) *Sperm Competition in Birds: Evolutionary Causes and Consequences*. Academic Press, London.

Birkhead, T.R. & Nettleship, D.N. (1984) Alloparental care in the common murre (*Uria aalge*). *Canadian Journal of Zoology* 62: 2121–2124.

Birkhead, T.R., Burke, T., Zann, R., Hunter, F.M. & Krupa, A.P. (1990) Extra-pair paternity and intraspecific brood parasitism in wild zebra finches *Taeniopygia guttata*, revealed by DNA fingerprinting. *Behavioural Ecology and Sociobiology* 27: 315–324.

Blackwall, J. (1824) Observations conducive towards a more complete history of the Cuckoo. *Memoires of the Literary and Philosophical Society of Manchester* 2nd Series, volume iv, 461.

Blaise, M. (1965) Contribution à l'étude du Coucou gris *Cuculus canorus* dans le nord-est de la France. *L'Oiseau et R.F.O.* 35: 87–116.

Bourke, A.F.G. & Franks, N.R. (1991) Alternative adaptations, sympatric speciation and the evolution of parasitic, inquiline ants. *Biological Journal of the Linnean Society* 43: 157–178.

Braa, A.T., Moksnes, A. & Røskaft, E. (1992) Adaptations of bramblings and chaffinches towards parasitism by the common cuckoo. *Animal Behaviour* 43: 67–78.

Braun, B.M. & Hunt, G.L. Jr. (1983) Brood reduction in black-legged kittiwakes. *Auk* 100: 469–476.

Brehm, E. (1869–73) *Dr. Brehm's Ornithology*. In: *Cassells Book of Birds Volume III*. Edited by T.R. Jones, p. 108–109. Cassell, London.

Brewer, A.D. (1995) Cowbird warning. *British Birds* 88: 157.

Briskie, J.V. & Sealy, S.G. (1990) Evolution of short incubation periods in the parasitic cowbirds. *Auk* 107: 789–794.

Briskie, J.V., Sealy, S.G. & Hobson, K.A. (1990) Differential parasitism of least flycatchers and yellow warblers by the brown-headed cowbird. *Behavioural Ecology and Sociobiology* 27: 403–410.

Briskie, J.V., Sealy, S.G. & Hobson, K.A. (1992) Behavioral defenses against avian brood parasitism in sympatric and allopatric host populations. *Evolution* 46: 334–340.

Briskie, J.V., Naugler, C.T. & Leech, S.M. (1994) Begging intensity of nestling birds varies with sibling relatedness. *Proceedings of the Royal Society of London B* 258: 73–78.

Brittingham, M.C. & Temple, S.A. (1983) Have cowbirds caused forest song-birds to decline? *Bioscience* 33: 31–35.

Brockmann, H.J., Grafen, A. & Dawkins, R. (1979) Evolutionarily stable nesting strategy in a digger wasp. *Journal of Theoretical Biology* 77: 473–496.

Brooke, M. de L. & Davies, N.B. (1987) Recent changes in host usage by cuckoos *Cuculus canorus* in Britain. *Journal of Animal Ecology* 56: 873–883.

Brooke, M. de L. & Davies, N.B. (1988) Egg mimicry by cuckoos *Cuculus canorus* in relation to discrimination by hosts. *Nature* 335: 630–632.

Brooke, M. de L. & Davies, N.B. (1989) Provisioning of nestling cuckoos *Cuculus canorus* by reed warbler *Acrocephalus scirpaceus* hosts. *Ibis* 131: 250–256.

Brooke, M. de L. & Davies, N.B. (1991) A failure to demonstrate host imprinting in the cuckoo *Cuculus canorus* and alternative hypotheses for the maintenance of egg mimicry. *Ethology* 89: 154–166.

Brooke, M. de L., Davies, N.B. & Noble, D.G. (1998) Rapid decline of host defences in response to reduced cuckoo parasitism: behavioural flexibility of reed warblers in a changing world. *Proceedings of the Royal Society of London B* 265: 1277–1282.

Brooker, L.C. & Brooker, M.G. (1990) Why are cuckoos host specific? *Oikos* 57: 301–309.

Brooker, L.C. & Brooker, M.G. (1998) Why do Splendid Fairy-wrens always accept cuckoo eggs? *Behavioural Ecology* 9: 420–424.

Brooker, L.C., Brooker, M.G. & Brooker, A.M.H. (1990) An alternative population/genetics model for the evolution of egg mimesis and egg crypsis in cuckoos. *Journal of theoretical Biology* 146: 123–143.

Brooker, M.G. & Brooker, L.C. (1989a) The comparative breeding behaviour of two sympatric cuckoos, Horsfield's Bronze-Cuckoo *Chrysococcyx basalis* and the Shining Bronze-Cuckoo *C. lucidus*, in Western Australia: a new model for the evolution of egg morphology and host specificity in avian brood parasites. *Ibis* 131: 528–547.

Brooker, M.G. & Brooker, L.C. (1989b) Cuckoo hosts in Australia. *Australian Zoological Reviews* 2: 1–67.

Brooker, M.G. & Brooker, L.C. (1991) Eggshell strength in cuckoos and cowbirds. *Ibis* 133: 406–413.

Brooker, M.G. & Brooker, L.C. (1992) Evidence for individual female host specificity in two Australian Bronze-Cuckoos, *Chrysococcyx* spp. *Australian Journal of Zoology* 40: 485–493.

Brooker, M.G. & Brooker, L.C. (1996) Acceptance by the Splendid Fairy-wren of parasitism by Horsfield's Bronze-Cuckoo: further evidence for evolutionary equilibrium in brood parasitism. *Behavioural Ecology* 7: 395–407.

Brooker, M.G., Brooker, L.C. & Rowley, I. (1988) Egg deposition by the Bronze-Cuckoos *Chrysococcyx basalis* and *Ch. lucidus*. *Emu* 88: 107–109.

Brown, C.R. (1984) Laying eggs in a neighbor's nest: benefit and cost of colonial nesting in swallows. *Science* 224: 518–519.

Brown, C.R. & Brown, M.B. (1988) A new form of reproductive parasitism in cliff swallows. *Nature* 331: 66–68.

Brown, C.R. & Brown, M.B. (1989) Behavioural dynamics of intraspecific brood parasitism in colonial cliff swallows. *Animal Behaviour* 37: 777–796.

Brown, C.R. & Brown, M.B. (1991) Selection of high quality host nests by parasitic cliff swallows. *Animal Behaviour* 41: 457–465.

Brown, C.R. & Brown, M.B. (1998) Fitness components associated with alternative reproductive tactics in cliff swallows. *Behavioural Ecology* 9: 158–171.

Brown, K.M. (1998) Proximate and ultimate causes of adoption in ring-billed gulls. *Animal Behaviour* 56: 1529–1543.

Bryant, D.M. & Tatner, P. (1990) Hatching asynchrony, sibling competition and siblicide in nestling birds: studies of swiftlets and bee-eaters. *Animal Behaviour* 39: 657–671.

Bulmer, M.G. (1984) Risk avoidance and nesting strategies. *Journal of theoretical Biology* 106: 529–535.

Burgham, M.C.J. & Picman, J. (1989) Effect of brown-headed cowbirds on the evolution of yellow warbler anti-parasite strategies. *Animal Behaviour* 38: 298–308.

Burton, R.E. (1947) Robins rearing own young and Cuckoo in same nest. *British Birds* 40: 149–150.

Buschinger, A. (1986) Evolution of social parasitism in ants. *Trends in Ecology and Evolution* 1, 155–160.

Catchpole, C.K. & Slater, P.J.B. (1995) *Bird Song: Biological Themes and Variations.* Cambridge University Press, Cambridge.

Chance, E.P. (1922) *The Cuckoo's Secret.* Sidgwick and Jackson, London.

Chance, E.P. (1940) *The Truth about the Cuckoo.* Country Life, London.

Cherry, M.I., Bennett, A.T.D. & Cuthill, I.C. (1998) Matching of eggs of the Red-chested Cuckoo and its hosts: the role of the UV waveband. *Ostrich* 69: 231.

Choudhury, S., Jones, C.S., Black, J.M. & Prop, J. (1993) Adoption of young and intraspecific nest parasitism in Barnacle Geese. *Condor* 95: 860–868.

Cichon, M. (1996) The evolution of brood parasitism: the role of facultative parasitism. *Behavioural Ecology* 7: 137–139.

Clark, K.L. & Robertson, R.J. (1981) Cowbird parasitism and evolution of anti-parasite strategies in the yellow warbler. *Wilson Bulletin* 93: 249–258.

Claudon, A. (1955) Nouvelles observations sur *Cuculus c. canorus* Linné en Alsac. *L'Oiseau et R.F.O.* 25: 44–49.

Clotfelter, E.D. (1998) What cues do brown-headed cowbirds use to locate red-winged blackbird host nests? *Animal Behaviour* 55: 1181–1189.

Collias, E.C. (1993) Inheritance of egg-colour polymorphism in the Village Weaver *Ploceus cucullatus. Auk* 110: 683–692.

Collias, N.E. & Collias, E.C. (1984) *Nest Building and Bird Behaviour,* Princeton University Press.

Craib, J. (1994) Why do Common Cuckoos resemble raptors? *British Birds* 87: 78–79.

Cramp, S. (ed) (1985) *The Birds of the Western Palearctic,* Vol. IV. Oxford University Press, Oxford.

Cruz, A. & Wiley, J.W. (1989) The decline of an adaptation in the absence of a presumed selection pressure. *Evolution* 43: 55–62.

Cruz, A., Manolis, T.D. & Andrews, R.W. (1990) Reproductive interactions of the Shiny Cowbird *Molothrus bonariensis* and the Yellow-hooded Blackbird *Agelaius icterocephalus* in Trinidad. *Ibis* 132: 436–444.

Cruz, A., Manolis, T.H. & Andrews, R.W. (1995) History of Shiny Cowbird *Molothrus bonariensis* brood parasitism in Trinidad and Tobago. *Ibis* 137: 317–321.

Darley, J.A. (1982) Territoriality and mating behaviour of the male Brown-headed Cowbird. *Condor* 84: 15–21.

Darwin, C. (1859) *The Origin of Species.* John Murray, London.

Davies, N.B. (1992) *Dunnock Behaviour and Social Evolution.* Oxford University Press, Oxford.

Davies, N.B. (1999) Cuckoos and cowbirds versus hosts: co-evolutionary lag and equilibrium. *Ostrich* 70: 71–79.

Davies, N.B. & Brooke, M. de L. (1988) Cuckoos versus reed warblers: adaptations and counteradaptations. *Animal Behaviour* 36: 262–284.

Davies, N.B. & Brooke, M. de L. (1989a) An experimental study of co-evolution between the cuckoo *Cuculus canorus* and its hosts. I Host egg discrimination. *Journal of Animal Ecology* 58: 207–224.

Davies, N.B. & Brooke, M. de L. (1989b) An experimental study of co-evolution between the cuckoo *Cuculus canorus* and its hosts. II Host egg markings, chick discrimination and general discussion. *Journal of Animal Ecology* 58: 225–236.

Davies, N.B. & Brooke, M. de L. (1991) Co-evolution of the cuckoo and its hosts. *Scientific American* 264(1): 92–98.

Davies, N.B. & Brooke, M. de L. (1998) Cuckoos versus hosts: experimental evidence for co-evolution. In: *Parasitic Birds and Their Hosts*. pp. 59–79. Edited by S.I. Rothstein & S.K. Robinson. Oxford University Press, Oxford.

Davies, N.B., Bourke, A.F.G. & Brooke, M. de L. (1989) Cuckoos and parasitic ants: interspecific brood parasitism as an evolutionary arms race. *Trends in Ecology and Evolution* 4: 274–278.

Davies, N.B., Brooke, M. de L. & Kacelnik, A. (1996) Recognition errors and probability of parasitism determine whether reed warblers should accept or reject mimetic cuckoo eggs. *Proceedings of the Royal Society of London B* 263: 925–931.

Davies, N.B., Kilner, R.M. & Noble, D.G. (1998) Nestling cuckoos *Cuculus canorus* exploit hosts with begging calls that mimic a brood. *Proceedings of the Royal Society of London B* 265: 673–678.

Davis, D.E. (1942) The phylogeny of social nesting habits in the Crotophaginae. *Quarterly Review of Biology* 17: 115–134.

Dawkins, R. (1976) *The Selfish Gene*. Oxford University Press, Oxford.

Dawkins, R. (1982) *The Extended Phenotype*. W.H. Freeman, Oxford.

Dawkins, R. (1998) *Unweaving the Rainbow*. Allen Lane, The Penguin Press, London.

Dawkins, R. & Krebs, J.R. (1979) Arms races between and within species. *Proceedings of the Royal Society of London, Series B* 205: 489–511.

Dearborn, D.C. (1996) Video documentation of a brown-headed cowbird nestling ejecting an indigo bunting nestling from the nest. *Condor* 98: 645–649.

Dearborn, D.C. (1998) Begging behavior and food acquisition by brown-headed cowbird nestlings. *Behavioural Ecology and Sociobiology* 43: 259–270.

Delnicki, D.E., Bolen, E.G. & Cottam, C. (1976) An unusual clutch of the black-bellied Whistling duck. *Wilson Bulletin* 88: 347–348.

De Naurois, R. (1979) The Emerald Cuckoo of São Tomé and Principe Islands (Gulf of Guinea). *Ostrich* 50: 88–93.

Dewar, D. (1907) An enquiry into the parasitic habits of the Indian Koel. *Journal of the Bombay Natural History Society* 17: 765–782.

Diamond, A.W. (1985) Honeyguide. In *A Dictionary of Birds*, edited by Campbell, B. & Lack, E. T. & A.D. Poyser, Calton.

Dröscher, L. (1988) A study on radio-tracking of the European cuckoo *Cuculus canorus*. *Proceedings of the Int. 100 Do-G. meeting*, 187–193.

Duckworth, J.W. (1991) Responses of breeding Reed Warblers *Acrocephalus scirpaceus* to mounts of Sparrowhawk *Accipiter nisus*, Cuckoo *Cuculus canorus* and Jay *Garrulus glandarius*. *Ibis* 133: 68–74.

Dufty, A.M. Jr. (1982) Movements and activities of radio-tracked brown-headed cowbirds. *Auk* 99: 316–327.

Dunn, E.K. (1985) Cuckoo: Social pattern and behaviour. In: *The Birds of the Western Palearctic*, Volume IV, edited by Cramp, S. pp. 407–412. Oxford University Press, Oxford.

Eadie, J.M. & Fryxell, J.M. (1992) Density dependence, frequency dependence, and alternative nesting strategies in goldeneyes. *American Naturalist* 140: 621–641.

Eadie, J.M., Kehoe, F.P. & Nudds, T.D. (1988) Pre-hatch and post-hatch brood amalgamation in North American Anatidae: a review of hypotheses. *Canadian Journal of Zoology* 66: 1709–1721.

Eadie, J., Sherman, P. & Semel, B. (1998) Conspecific brood parasitism, population dynamics, and the conservation of cavity-nesting birds. In: *Behavioral Ecology and Conservation Biology* (edited by T. Caro). pp. 306–340. Oxford University Press, Oxford.

Eastzer, D., Chu, P.R. & King, A.P. (1980) The young cowbird: average or optimal nestling? *Condor* 82: 417–425.

Elliott, P.F. (1978) Cowbird parasitism in the Kansas tallgrass prairie. *Auk* 95: 161–167.

Elliott, P.F. (1980) Evolution of promiscuity in the brown-headed cowbird. *Condor* 82: 138–141.

Emlen, S.T. & Wrege, P.H. (1986) Forced copulations and intra-specific parasitism: two costs of social living in the white-fronted bee-eater. *Ethology* 71: 2–29.

Evans, P.G.H. (1988) Intraspecific nest parasitism in the European starling *Sturnus vulgaris*. *Animal Behaviour* 36: 1282–1294.

Feare, C.J. (1984) *The Starling*. Oxford University Press, Oxford.

Feare, C.J. (1991) Intraspecific nest parasitism in Starlings *Sturnus vulgaris*: effects of disturbance on laying females. *Ibis* 133: 75–79.

Feare, C.J., Spencer, P.L. & Constantine, D.A.T. (1982) Time of egg laying of Starlings *Sturnus vulgaris*. *Ibis* 124: 174–178.

Field, J. (1992) Intraspecific parasitism as an alternative reproductive tactic in nest-building wasps and bees. *Biological Reviews* 67: 79–126.

Fisher, R.M. (1984) Evolution and host specificity: a study of the invasion success of a specialized bumblebee social parasite. *Canadian Journal of Zoology* 62: 1641–1644.

Fleischer, R.C. (1985) A new technique to identify and assess the dispersion of eggs of individual brood parasites. *Behavioural Ecology and Sociobiology* 17: 91–99.

Fleischer, R.C., Murphy, M.T. & Hunt, L.E. (1985) Clutch size increase and intraspecific brood parasitism in the yellow-billed cuckoo. *Wilson Bulletin* 97: 125–127.

Forslund, P. & Larsson, K. (1995) Intraspecific nest parasitism in the barnacle goose: behavioural tactics of parasites and hosts. *Animal Behaviour* 50: 509–517.

Fraga, R.M. (1979) Differences between nestlings and fledglings of Screaming and Bay-winged Cowbirds. *Wilson Bulletin* 91: 151–154.

Fraga, R.M. (1983) The eggs of the parasitic Screaming Cowbird (*Molothrus rufoaxillaris*) and its hosts, the Bay-winged Cowbird (*Molothrus badius*): Is there evidence for mimicry? *Journal für Ornithologie* 124: 187–193.

Fraga, R.M. (1985) Host-parasite interactions between Chalk-browed Mockingbirds and Shiny Cowbirds. *Ornithological Monographs* 36: 829–844.

Fraga, R.M. (1996) Further evidence of parasitism of Chopi Blackbirds *Gnorimopsar chopi* by the specialised Screaming Cowbird *Molothrus rufoaxillaris*. *Condor* 98: 866–867.

Fraga, R.M. (1998) Interactions of the parasitic Screaming and Shiny Cowbirds (*Molothrus rufoaxillaris* and *M. bonariensis*) with a shared host, the Bay-winged Cowbird (*M. badius*). In: *Parasitic Birds and Their Hosts*. (Ed. by S.I. Rothstein & S.K. Robinson). pp. 173–193. Oxford University Press, Oxford.

Freeman, S. (1988) Egg variability and conspecific nest parasitism in the *Ploceus* weaverbirds. *Ostrich* 59: 49–53.

Freeman, S. & Zink, R.M. (1995) A phylogenetic study of the blackbirds based on variation in mitochondrial DNA restriction sites. *Systematic Biology* 44: 409–420.

Friedmann, H. (1928) The origin of host specificity in the parasitic habit in the Cuculinae. *Auk* 45: 33–38.

Friedmann, H. (1929) *The Cowbirds: A study in the Biology of Social Parasitism*. Charles C. Thomas; Springfield, Illinois.

Friedmann, H. (1960) The parasitic weaverbirds. *Bulletin of the United States National Museum* 223: 1–196.

Friedmann, H. (1963) Host relations of the parasitic cowbirds. *Bulletin of the United States National Museum* 233: 1–276.

Friedmann, H. (1964) The history of our knowledge of avian brood parasitism. *Centaurus* 10: 282–304.

Friedmann, H., Kiff, L.F. & Rothstein, S.I. (1977) A further contribution to knowledge of the host relations of the parasitic cowbirds. *Smithsonian Contributions to Zoology* 235: 1–75.

Fry, C.H. (1974) Vocal mimesis in nestling Greater Honey-guides. *Bulletin of the British Ornithologists' Club* 94: 58–59.

Fry, C.H., Keith, S. & Urban, E.K. (1988) *The Birds of Africa* Volume III. Academic Press, London.

Gärtner, K. (1981) Das Wegnehmen von Wirtsvogeleiern durch den Kuckuck *Cuculus canorus*. *Ornithologische Mitteilungen* 33: 115–131.

Gärtner, K. (1982) Zur Ablehnung von Eiern und Jungen des Kuckucks *Cuculus canorus* durch die Wirtsvögel – Beobachtungen und experimentelle Untersuchungen am Sumpfrohrsänger *Acrocephalus palustris*. *Die Vogelwelt* 103: 201–224.

Gaston, A.J. (1976) Brood parasitism by the Pied Crested Cuckoo *Clamator jacobinus*. *Journal of Animal Ecology* 45: 331–345.

Gehringer, F. (1979) Étude sur le pillage par le coucou *Cuculus canorus* des oeufs de la rousserolle effarvatte. *Nos Oiseaux* 35: 1–16.

Gibbons, D.W. (1986) Brood parasitism and cooperative nesting in the moorhen *Gallinula chloropus*. *Behavioural Ecology and Sociobiology* 19: 221–232.

Gibbs, H.L., Brooke, M. de L. & Davies, N.B. (1996) Analysis of genetic differentiation of host races of the common cuckoo *Cuculus canorus* using mitochondrial and microsatellite DNA variation. *Proceedings of the Royal Society of London B.* 263: 89–96.

Gibbs, H.L., Miller, P., Alderson, G. & Sealy, S.G. (1997) Genetic analysis of brown-headed cowbirds *Molothrus ater* raised by different hosts: data from mtDNA and microsatellite DNA markers. *Molecular Ecology* 6: 189–193.

Gill, B.J. (1982) The Grey Warbler's care of nestlings: a comparison between unparasitised broods and those comprising a Shining Bronze-Cuckoo. *Emu* 82: 177–181.

Gill, B.J. (1983) Brood parasitism by the Shining Cuckoo *Chrysococcyx lucidus* at Kaikoura, New Zealand. *Ibis* 125: 40–55.

Gill, B.J. (1998) Behavior and ecology of the shining cuckoo, *Chrysococcyx lucidus*. In: *Parasitic Birds and Their Hosts* (Ed. by S.I. Rothstein & S.K. Robinson), pp. 143–151. Oxford University Press, Oxford.

Glue, D. & Murray, E. (1984) Cuckoo hosts in Britain. *British Trust for Ornithology News* 134: 5.

Gochfeld, M. (1979) Brood parasite and host coevolution: interactions between Shiny Cowbirds and two species of meadowlarks. *American Naturalist* 113: 855–870.

Godfray, H.C.J. (1995) Signalling of need between parents and young: parent-offspring conflict and sibling rivalry. *American Naturalist* 146: 1–24.

Goguen, C.B. & Mathews, N.E. (1996) Nest desertion by blue-gray gnatcatchers in association with brown-headed cowbird parasitism. *Animal Behaviour* 52: 613–619.

Gorman, M.L. & Milne, H. (1972) Crèche behaviour in the Common Eider *Somateria m. mollissima*. *Ornis Scandinavica* 3: 21–25.

Gowaty, P.A. & Bridges, W.C. (1991) Nest box availability affects extra-pair fertilizations and conspecific nest parasitism in eastern bluebirds *Sialia sialis*. *Animal Behaviour* 41: 661–675.

Grant, P.R. (1986) *Ecology and Evolution of Darwin's Finches*. Princeton University Press.

Graves, J.A. & Whiten, A. (1980) Adoption of strange chicks by herring gulls *Larus argentatus*. *Zeitschrift für Tierpsychologie* 54: 267–278.

Griffith, J.T. & Griffith, J.C. (1999) Cowbird control and the endangered Least Bell's Vireo: a management success story. In: Smith, J.N.M. *et al.* (1999).

Grim, T. & Honza, M. (1997) Differences in parental care of reed warbler *Acrocephalus scirpaceus* to its own nestlings and parasitic cuckoo *Cuculus canorus* chicks. *Folia Zoologica* 46: 135–142.

Grzybowski, J.A. & Pease, C.M. (1999) A model of the dynamics of cowbirds and their host communities. *Auk* 116: 209–222.

Hamer, R. (1970) *A Choice of Anglo-Saxon Verse*. Faber & Faber, London.

Hamilton, W.J. & Hamilton, M.E. (1965) Breeding characteristics of yellow-billed cuckoos in Arizona. *Proceedings of the California Academy of Sciences* 32: 405–432.

Hamilton, W.J. & Orians, G.H. (1965) Evolution of brood parasitism in altricial birds. *Condor* 67: 361–382.

Haney, J.C., Lee, D.S. & Walsh-McGehee, M. (1998) A quantitative analysis of winter distribution and habitats of Kirtlands' Warblers in the Bahamas. *Condor* 100: 201–217.

Hardin, G. (1968) The tragedy of the commons. *Science* 162: 1243–1248.

Harrison, C.J.O. (1968) Egg mimicry in British cuckoos. *Bird Study* 15: 22–28.

Heinsohn, R.G. (1991) Kidnapping and reciprocity in cooperatively breeding white-winged choughs. *Animal Behaviour* 41: 1097–1100.

Hens, P. (1949) Jonge Koekoek (*Cuculus canorus*) doodt een van zijn pleegouders. [Young cuckoo kills one of its fosterers]. *Limosa* 22: 329–330.

Herrick, F.H. (1910) Life and behavior of the cuckoo. *Journal of Experimental Zoology* 9: 169–234.

Hett, W.S. (1936) *Aristotle: Minor Works. On Marvellous Things Heard.* Heinemann, London.

Higuchi, H. (1989) Responses of the Bush Warbler *Cettia diphone* to artificial eggs of *Cuculus* cuckoos in Japan. *Ibis* 131: 94–98.

Higuchi, H. (1998) Host use and egg color in Japanese cuckoos. In: *Parasitic Birds and Their Hosts* (Ed. by S.I. Rothstein & S.K. Robinson), pp. 80–93. Oxford University Press, Oxford.

Higuchi, H. & Sato, S. (1984) An example of character release in host selection and egg colour of cuckoos *Cuculus* spp in Japan. *Ibis* 126: 398–404.

Hill, D.P. & Sealy, S.G. (1994) Desertion of nests parasitised by cowbirds: have Clay-coloured Sparrows evolved an anti-parasite strategy? *Animal Behaviour* 48: 1063–1070.

Hobson, K.A. & Sealy, S.G. (1989) Responses of yellow warblers to the threat of cowbird parasitism. *Animal Behaviour* 38: 510–519.

Hölldobler, B. & Wilson, E.O. (1994) *Journey to the Ants.* Belknap Press, Harvard.

Hosoi, S.A. & Rothstein, S.I. (2000) The enigma of nest desertion: is it really a defense against cowbird parasitism? *Animal Behaviour.* in press.

Hudson, W.H. (1870) Letter on the ornithology of Buenos Ayres. *Proceedings of the Zoological Society of London* (1870): 671–673.

Hudson, W.H. (1874) Notes on the procreant instincts of the three species of *Molothrus* found in Buenos Ayres. *Proceedings of the Zoological Society of London* (1874): 153–174.

Hudson, W.H. (1892) *The Naturalist in La Plata.* London: Chapman & Hall.

Hughes, J.M. (1996) Phylogenetic analysis of the Cuculidae (Aves: Cuculiformes) using behavioral and ecological characters. *Auk* 113: 10–22.

Husby, M. (1986) On the adaptive value of brood reduction in birds: experiments with the Magpie *Pica pica. Journal of Animal Ecology* 55: 75–83.

Immelmann, K. (1965) *Australian Finches in Bush and Aviary.* Angus and Robertson, Sydney.

Immelmann, K., Piltz, A. & Sossinka, R. (1977) Experimentelle Untersuchungen zur Bedeutung der Rachenzeichnungen junger Zebrafinken. *Zeitschrift für Tierpsychologie* 45: 210–218.

Isack, H.A. & Reyer, H.-U. (1989) Honeyguides and honey gatherers: interspecific communication in a symbiotic relationship. *Science* 243: 1343–1346.

Jackson, W.M. (1992) Estimating conspecific nest parasitism in the Northern Masked Weaver based on within-female variability in egg appearance. *Auk* 109: 435–443.

Jackson, W.M. (1993) Causes of conspecific nest parasitism in the Northern Masked Weaver. *Behavioural Ecology and Sociobiology* 32: 119–126.

Jackson, W.M. (1998) Egg discrimination and egg-color variability in the Northern Masked Weaver. In: *Parasitic Birds and Their Hosts* (Edited by S.I. Rothstein & S.K. Robinson), pp. 407–416. Oxford University Press, Oxford.

Jackson, N.H. & Roby, D.D. (1992) Fecundity and egg-laying patterns of captive yearling Brown-headed Cowbirds. *Condor* 94: 585–589.

Jamieson, I.G. (1998) Reproductive skew models and inter-population variation in social structure among cooperatively breeding birds. Proceedings of 22nd International Ornithological Congress. Durban, University of Natal. *Ostrich* 69: 145.

Järvinen, A. (1984) Relationship between the common cuckoo *Cuculus canorus* and its host the redstart *Phoenicurus phoenicurus. Ornis Fennica* 61: 84–88.

Jeffreys, A.J., Wilson, V. & Thein, S.L. (1985) Hypervariable "minisatellite" regions in human DNA. *Nature* 314: 67–73.

Jenner, E. (1788) Observations on the natural history of the Cuckoo. *Philosophical Transactions of the Royal Society, London* 78: 219–237.

Jensen, R.A.C. (1966) Genetics of cuckoo egg polymorphism. *Nature* 209: 827.

Jensen, R.A.C. & Vernon, C.J. (1970) On the biology of the Didric Cuckoo in Southern Africa. *Ostrich* 41: 237–246.

Johnsgard, P.A. (1997) *The Avian Brood Parasites: Deception at the Nest.* Oxford University Press, Oxford.

Jourdain, F.C.R. (1925) A study on parasitism in the cuckoos. *Proceedings of the Zoological Society of London* 1925: 639–667.

Jouventin, P., Barbraud, C. & Rubin, M. (1995) Adoption in the emperor penguin, *Aptenodytes forsteri. Animal Behaviour* 50: 1023–1029.

Kattan, G.H. (1995) Mechanisms of short incubation period in brood-parasitic cowbirds. *Auk* 112: 335–342.

Kattan, G.H. (1997) Shiny Cowbirds follow the "shotgun" strategy of brood parasitism. *Animal Behaviour* 53: 647–654.

Kelly, C. (1987) A model to explore the rate of spread of mimicry and rejection in hypothetical populations of cuckoos and their hosts. *Journal of Theoretical Biology* 125, 283–299.

Kempenaers, B., Pinxten, R. & Eens, M. (1995) Intraspecific brood parasitism in two tit *Parus* species: occurrence and responses to experimental parasitism. *Journal of Avian Biology* 26: 114–120.

Kennedy, E.D., Stouffer, P.C. & Power, H.W. (1989) Postovulatory follicles as a measure of clutch size and brood parasitism in European starlings. *Condor* 91: 471–473.

Kilner, R.M. (1997) Mouth colour is a reliable signal of need in begging canary nestlings. *Proceedings of the Royal Society of London B.* 264: 963–968.

Kilner, R.M. (1999) Family conflicts and the evolution of nestling mouth colour. *Behaviour* 136: 779–804.

Kilner, R.M. & Davies, N.B. (1998) Nestling mouth colour: ecological correlates of a begging signal. *Animal Behaviour* 56: 705–712.

Kilner, R.M. & Davies, N.B. (1999) How selfish is a cuckoo chick? *Animal Behaviour* 58: 797–808.

Kilner, R.M., Noble, D.G. & Davies, N.B. (1999) Signals of need in parent-offspring communication and their exploitation by the common cuckoo. *Nature* 397: 667–672.

King, A.P. (1973) Some factors controlling egg laying in the parasitic cowbird *Molothrus ater. American Zoologist* 13: 1259.

King, A.P. & West, M.J. (1977) Species identification in the North American cowbird: appropriate responses to abnormal song. *Science* 195: 1002–1004.

King, J.R. (1973) Reproductive relationships of the Rufous-collared Sparrow and the Shiny Cowbird. *Auk* 90: 19–34.

Klein, N.K. & Payne, R.B. (1998) Evolutionary associations of brood parasitic finches (*Vidua*) and their host species: analysis of mitochondrial DNA restriction sites. *Evolution* 52: 566–582.

Koenig, W.D., Mumme, R.L., Stanback, M.T. & Pitelka, F.A. (1995) Patterns and consequences of egg destruction among joint-nesting acorn woodpeckers. *Animal Behaviour* 50: 607–621.

Lack, D. (1963) Cuckoo hosts in England. *Bird Study* 10: 185–201.

Lack, D. (1968) *Ecological Adaptations for Breeding in Birds.* Methuen, London.

Lagerström, M. (1983) Kaki, *Cuculus canorus.* In, *Suomen Lintuatlas* edited by Hyytiä, K., Kellomäki, E. & Koistinen, J. pp. 238–239. SLY: n Lintutieto Oy, Helskinki.

Lamba, B.S. (1963) The nidification of some common Indian birds – part I. *Journal of the Bombay Natural History Society* 60: 120–133.

Lamba, B.S. (1966) The egg-laying of the Koel *Eudynamys scolopacea* (Linnaeus). *Journal of the Bombay Natural History Society* 63: 750–751.

Lank, D.B., Rockwell, R.F. & Cooke, F. (1990) Frequency-dependent fitness consequences of intraspecific nest parasitism in snow geese. *Evolution* 44: 1436–1453.

Lank, D.B., Bousfield, M.A., Cooke, F. & Rockwell, R.F. (1991) Why do snow geese adopt eggs? *Behavioural Ecology* 2: 181–187.

Lank, D.B., Cooch, E.G., Rockwell, R.F. & Cooke, F. (1989a) Environmental and demographic correlates of intraspecific nest parasitism in lesser snow geese *Chen caerulescens caerulescens. Journal of Animal Ecology* 58: 29–45.

Lank, D.B., Mineau, P., Rockwell, R.F. & Cooke, F. (1989b) Intraspecific nest parasitism and extra-pair copulation in lesser snow geese. *Animal Behaviour* 37: 74–89.

Lanyon, S.M. (1992) Interspecific brood parasitism in blackbirds (Icterinae): a phylogenetic perspective. *Science* 255: 77–79.

Larsson, K., Tegelström, H. & Forslund, P. (1995) Intraspecific nest parasitism and adoption of young in the barnacle goose: effects on survival and reproductive performance. *Animal Behaviour* 50: 1349–1360.

Lawes, M.J. & Kirkman, S. (1996) Egg recognition and interspecific brood parasitism rates in Red Bishops (Aves: Ploceidae). *Animal Behaviour* 52: 553–563.

Lea, S.E.G. & Kattan, G.H. (1998) Reanalysis gives further support to the "shotgun" model of shiny cowbird parasitism of house wren nests. *Animal Behaviour* 56: 1571–1573.

Lefevre, K., Montgomerie, R. & Gaston, A.J. (1998) Parent-offspring recognition in thick-billed murres (Aves: Alcidae). *Animal Behaviour* 55: 925–938.

Lerkelund, H.E., Moksnes, A., Røskaft, E. & Ringsby, T.H. (1993) An experimental test of optimal clutch size of the Fieldfare, with a discussion on why brood parasites remove eggs when they parasitise a host species. *Ornis Scandinavica* 24: 95–102.

Lessells, C.M. (1986) Brood size in Canada geese: a manipulation experiment. *Journal of Animal Ecology* 55: 669–689.

Leverkühn, P. (1891) *Fremde Eier im Nest: Ein Beitrag zur Biologie der Vögel.* Berlin.

Lichtenstein, G. (1997) Begging behaviour and host exploitation in three species of parasitic cowbirds. *PhD thesis*, University of Cambridge.

Lichtenstein, G. (1998) Parasitism by Shiny Cowbirds of Rufous-bellied Thrushes. *Condor* 100:680–687.

Lichtenstein, G. & Sealy, S.G. (1998) Nestling competition, rather than supernormal stimulus, explains the success of parasitic brown-headed cowbird chicks in yellow warbler nests. *Proceedings of the Royal Society of London B* 265: 249–254.

Lindholm, A.K. (1997) Evolution of host defences against avian brood parasitism. *PhD thesis*, University of Cambridge.

Lindholm, A.K. (1999) Brood parasitism by the cuckoo on patchy reed warbler populations in Britain. *Journal of Animal Ecology* 68: 293–309.

Lindholm, A.K. & Thomas, R.J. (1999) Differences between populations of reed warblers in defences against brood parasitism. *Behaviour.* in press.

Liversidge, R. (1961) Pre-incubation development of *Clamator jacobinus. Ibis* 103: 624.

Liversidge, R. (1970) The biology of the Jacobin Cuckoo *Clamator jacobinus. Ostrich Supplement* 8: 117–137.

Löhrl, H. (1979) Untersuchungen am kuckuck *Cuculus canorus* (Biologie, Ethologie und Morphologie). *Journal für Ornithologie* 120: 139–173.

Lombardo, M.P., Power, H.W., Stouffer, P.C., Romagnano, L.C. & Hoffenberg, A.S. (1989) Egg removal and intraspecific brood parasitism in the European Starling *Sturnus vulgaris. Behavioural Ecology and Sociobiology* 24: 217–223.

Lotem, A. (1993) Learning to recognize nestlings is maladaptive for cuckoo *Cuculus canorus* hosts. *Nature* 362: 743–745.

Lotem, A. & Nakamura, H. (1998) Evolutionary equilibria in avian brood parasitism. In: *Parasitic Birds and their Hosts* (Ed. by S.I. Rothstein & S.K. Robinson). pp. 223–235. Oxford University Press, Oxford.

Lotem, A., Nakamura, H. & Zahavi, A. (1992) Rejection of cuckoo eggs in relation to host age: a possible evolutionary equilibrium. *Behavioural Ecology* 3: 128–132.

Lotem, A., Nakamura, H. & Zahavi, A. (1995) Constraints on egg discrimination and cuckoo-host co-evolution. *Animal Behaviour* 49: 1185–1209.

Lowther, P.E. (1993) Brown-headed Cowbird (*Molothrus ater*). In: The Birds of North America, No. 47 (A. Poole & F. Gill, Eds). Philadelphia: The Academy of Natural Sciences; Washington, D.C.: The American Ornithologists' Union.

Lowther, P.E. (1995) Bronzed Cowbird (*Molothrus aeneus*). In: The Birds of North America, No. 44. (A. Poole & F. Gill, Eds). The Academy of Natural Sciences, Philadelphia, and The American Ornithologists' Union, Washington, D.C.

Lyon, B.E. (1993a) Brood parasitism as a flexible female reproductive tactic in American coots. *Animal Behaviour* 46: 911–928.

Lyon, B.E. (1993b) Tactics of parasitic American coots: host choice and the pattern of egg dispersion among host nests. *Behavioural Ecology and Sociobiology* 33: 87–100.

Lyon, B.E. (1997) Spatial patterns of shiny cowbird brood parasitism on chestnut-capped blackbirds. *Animal Behaviour* 54: 927–939.

Lyon, B.E. (1998) Optimal clutch size and conspecific brood parasitism. *Nature* 392: 380–383.

Lyon, B.E. & Eadie, J.M. (1991) Mode of development and interspecific avian brood parasitism. *Behavioural Ecology* 2: 309–318.

Lyon, B.E., Eadie, J.M. & Hamilton, L.D. (1994) Parental choice selects for ornamental plumage in American coot chicks. *Nature* 371: 240–243.

Macdonald, M.A. (1980) Observations on the Diederik Cuckoo in southern Ghana. *Ostrich* 51: 75–79.

Marchant, S. (1972) Evolution of the genus *Chrysococcyx. Ibis* 114: 219–233.

Marchetti, K. (1992) Costs to host defence and the persistence of parasitic cuckoos. *Proceedings of the Royal Society of London B* 248: 41–45.

Marchetti, K. (2000) Egg rejection in a passerine bird: size does matter. *Animal Behaviour* in press.

Marchetti, K., Nakamura, H. & Gibbs, H.L. (1998) Host-race formation in the Common Cuckoo. *Science* 282: 471–472.

Martínez, J.G., Soler, M. & Soler, J.J. (1996) The effect of Magpie breeding density and synchrony on brood parasitism by Great Spotted Cuckoos. *Condor* 98: 272–278.

Martínez, J.G., Burke, T., Dawson, D., Soler, J.J., Soler, M. & Møller, A.P. (1998a) Microsatellite typing reveals mating patterns in the brood parasitic Great Spotted Cuckoo *Clamator glandarius. Molecular Ecology* 7: 289–297.

Martínez, J.G., Soler, J.J., Soler, M. & Burke, T. (1998b) Spatial patterns of egg laying and multiple parasitism in a brood parasite: a non-territorial system in the great spotted cuckoo (*Clamator glandarius*). *Oecologia* 117: 286–294.

Mason, P. (1986a) Brood parasitism in a host generalist, the Shiny Cowbird: I. The quality of different species as hosts. *Auk* 103: 52–60.

Mason, P. (1986b) Brood parasitism in a host generalist, the Shiny Cowbird: II. Host selection. *Auk* 103: 61–69.

Mason, P. (1987) Pair formation in cowbirds: evidence found for Screaming but not Shiny Cowbirds. *Condor* 89: 349–356.

Mason, P. & Rothstein, S.I. (1986) Coevolution and avian brood parasitism: cowbird eggs show evolutionary response to host discrimination. *Evolution* 40: 1207–1214.

Mason, P. & Rothstein, S.I. (1987) Crypsis versus mimicry and the color of shiny cowbird eggs. *American Naturalist* 130: 161–167.

Massoni, V. & Reboreda, J.C. (1998) Costs of brood parasitism and the lack of defenses on the yellow-winged blackbird – shiny cowbird system. *Behavioural Ecology and Sociobiology* 42: 273–280.

Massoni, V. & Reboreda, J.C. (1999) Egg puncture allows shiny cowbirds to assess host egg development and suitability for parasitism. *Proceedings of the Royal Society of London B.* 266: 1871–1874.

May, R.M. & Robinson, S.K. (1985) Population dynamics of avian brood parasitism. *American Naturalist* 126: 475–494.

May, R.M., Nee, S. & Watts, C. (1991) Could intraspecific brood parasitism cause population cycles? *Acta XX Congressus Internationalis Ornithologici* 1012–1022.

Mayfield, H. (1961) Cowbird parasitism and the population of Kirtland's Warbler. *Evolution* 15: 174–179.

Mayfield, H. (1965) The Brown-headed Cowbird, with old and new hosts. *Living Bird* 4: 13–28.

McBride, H.C.A. (1984) Multiple feeding of a juvenile Cuckoo. *British Birds* 77: 422–423.

McGeen, D.S. & McGeen, J.J. (1968) The cowbirds of Otter Lake. *Wilson Bulletin* 80: 84–93.

McKay, C.R. (1994) Brown-headed Cowbird in Strathclyde: new to Britain and Ireland. *British Birds* 87: 284–288.

McKinney, D.F. (1954) An observation on Redhead parasitism. *Wilson Bulletin* 66: 146–148.

McLean, I.G. & Rhodes, G.I. (1991) Enemy recognition and response in birds. *Current Ornithology* 8: 173–211.

McLean, I.G. & Waas, J.R. (1987) Do cuckoo chicks mimic the begging calls of their hosts? *Animal Behaviour* 35: 1896–1898.

McMaster, D.G. & Sealy, S.G. (1998) Short incubation periods of Brown-headed Cowbirds: how do Cowbird eggs hatch before Yellow Warbler eggs? *Condor* 100: 102–111.

McRae, S.B. (1995) Temporal variation in responses to intraspecific brood parasitism in the moorhen. *Animal Behaviour* 49: 1073–1088.

McRae, S.B. (1996a) Brood parasitism in the Moorhen: brief encounters between parasites and hosts and the significance of an evening laying hour. *Journal of Avian Biology* 27: 311–320.

McRae, S.B. (1996b) Family values: costs and benefits of communal breeding in the moorhen. *Animal Behaviour* 52: 225–245.

McRae, S.B. (1997a) Identifying eggs of conspecific brood parasites in the field: a cautionary note. *Ibis* 139: 701–704.

McRae, S.B. (1997b) A rise in nest predation enhances the frequency of intraspecific brood parasitism in a moorhen population. *Journal of Animal Ecology* 66: 143–153.

McRae, S.B. (1998) Relative reproductive success of female moorhens using conditional strategies of brood parasitism and parental care. *Behavioural Ecology* 9: 93–100.

McRae, S.B. & Burke, T. (1996) Intraspecific brood parasitism in the moorhen: parentage and parasite-host relationships determined by DNA fingerprinting. *Behavioural Ecology and Sociobiology* 38: 115–129.

Mermoz, M.E. & Reboreda, J.C. (1994) Brood parasitism of the Shiny Cowbird, *Molothrus bonariensis*, on the Brown-and-yellow Marshbird, *Pseudoleistes virescens*. *Condor* 96: 716–721.

Mermoz, M.E. & Reboreda, J.C. (1996) New host for a specialised brood parasite, the Screaming Cowbird. *Condor* 98: 630–632.

Mermoz, M.E. & Reboreda, J.C. (1999) Egg-laying behaviour by shiny cowbirds parasitizing brown-and-yellow marshbirds. *Animal Behaviour* 58: 873–882.

Mock, D.W. (1999) Driving parents cuckoo. *Nature* 397: 647–648.

Mock, D.W. & Parker, G.A. (1997) *The Evolution of Sibling Rivalry*. Oxford University Press.

Moksnes, A. (1992) Egg recognition in chaffinches and bramblings. *Animal Behaviour* 44: 993–995.

Moksnes, A. & Røskaft, E. (1987) Cuckoo host interactions in Norwegian mountain areas. *Ornis Scandinavica* 18: 168–172.

Moksnes, A. & Røskaft, E. (1989) Adaptations of meadow pipits to parasitism by the common cuckoo. *Behavioural Ecology and Sociobiology* 24: 25–30.

Moksnes, A. & Røskaft, E. (1992) Responses of some rare cuckoo hosts to mimetic model cuckoo eggs and to foreign conspecific eggs. *Ornis Scandinavica* 23: 17–23.

Moksnes, A. & Røskaft, E. (1995) Egg-morphs and host preference in the common cuckoo *Cuculus canorus*: an analysis of cuckoo and host eggs from European museum collections. *Journal of Zoology* 236: 625–648.

Moksnes, A., Røskaft, E. & Braa, A.T. (1991) Rejection behaviour by Common Cuckoo hosts towards artificial brood parasite eggs. *Auk* 108: 348–354.

Moksnes, A., Røskaft, E. & Korsnes, L. (1993) Rejection of cuckoo *Cuculus canorus* eggs by meadow pipits *Anthus pratensis*. *Behavioural Ecology* 4: 120–127.

Moksnes, A., Røskaft, E. & Tysse, T. (1995) On the evolution of blue cuckoo eggs in Europe. *Journal of Avian Biology* 26: 13–19.

Moksnes, A., Røskaft, E., Braa, A.T., Korsnes, L., Lampe, H.M. & Pedersen, H.Ch. (1991) Behavioural responses of potential hosts towards artificial cuckoo eggs and dummies. *Behaviour* 116: 64–89.

Møller, A.P. (1987) Intraspecific nest parasitism and anti-parasite behaviour in swallows, *Hirundo rustica*. *Animal Behaviour* 35: 247–254.

Molnar, B. (1944) The cuckoo in the Hungarian plain. *Aquila* 51: 100–112.

Montagu, G. (1831) *Ornithological Dictionary of British Birds*, 2nd edition. London.

Moreau, R.E. & Moreau, W.M. (1939) Observations on some East African birds. *Ibis* 14th series 3: 296–323.

Morel, M.-Y. (1973) Contribution à l'étude dynamique de la population de *Lagonosticta senegala* L. (Estrildides) à Richard-Toll (Sénégal). Interrelations avec le parasite *Hypochera chalybeata* Müller (Viduines). *Mémoires du Muséum National d'Histoire Naturelle, serie A, Zoologie* 78: 1–156.

Morse, S.F. & Robinson, S.K. (1999) Nesting success of a neotropical migrant in a multiple-use, forested landscape. *Conservation Biology* 13: 327–337.

Morton, E.S. & Farabaugh, S.M. (1979) Infanticide and other adaptations of the nestling Striped Cuckoo *Tapera naevia. Ibis* 121: 212–213.

Moskát, C. & Fuisz, T.I. (1999) Reactions of Red-backed Shrikes (*Lanius collurio*) to artificial Cuckoo (*Cuculus canorus*) eggs. *Journal of Avian Biology* 30: 175–181.

Mundy, P.J. (1973) Vocal mimicry of their hosts by nestlings of the Great Spotted and Striped Crested Cuckoo. *Ibis* 115: 602–604.

Mundy, P.J. & Cook, A.W. (1977) Observations on the breeding of the Pied Crow and Great Spotted Cuckoo in northern Nigeria. *Ostrich* 48: 72–84.

Munro, J. & Bédard, J. (1977) Gull predation and crèching behaviour in the common eider. *Journal of Animal Ecology* 46: 799–810.

Nakamura, H. (1990) Brood parasitism by the Cuckoo *Cuculus canorus* in Japan and the start of new parasitism on the Azure-winged Magpie *Cyanopica cyana. Japanese Journal of Ornithology* 39: 1–18.

Nakamura, H. & Miyazawa, Y. (1997) Movements, space use and social organisation of radio-tracked common cuckoos during the breeding season in Japan. *Japanese Journal of Ornithology* 46: 23–54.

Nakamura, H., Kubota, S. & Suzuki, R. (1998) Coevolution between the Common Cuckoo and its major hosts in Japan. In: *Parasitic Birds and Their Hosts* (Ed. by S.I. Rothstein & S.K. Robinson), pp. 94–112. Oxford University Press, Oxford.

Nee, S. & May, R.M. (1993) Population-level consequences of conspecific brood parasitism in birds and insects. *Journal of theoretical Biology* 161: 95–109.

Neudorf, D.L. & Sealy, S.G. (1992) Reactions of four passerine species to threats of predation and cowbird parasitism: enemy recognition or generalised responses? *Behaviour* 123: 84–105.

Neudorf, D.L. & Sealy, S.G. (1994) Sunrise nest attentiveness in cowbird hosts. *Condor* 96: 162–169.

Neufeldt, I. (1966) Life history of the Indian Cuckoo *Cuculus micropterus micropterus* Gould in the Soviet Union. *Journal of the Bombay Natural History Society* 63: 399–419.

Neunzig, R. (1929) Zum Brutparasitismus der Viduinen. *Journal für Ornithologie* 77: 1–21.

Newton, A. (1893) *A Dictionary of Birds*. A. & C. Black, London.

Newton, I. (1986) *The Sparrowhawk*. T. & A.D. Poyser, Calton.

Nicolai, J. (1961) Die Stimmen einiger Viduinen. *Journal für Ornithologie* 102: 213–214.

Nicolai, J. (1964) Der Brutparasitismus der Viduinae als ethologisches Problem. *Zeitschrift für Tierpsychologie* 21: 129–204.

Nicolai, J. (1969) Beobachtungen an Paradieswitwen (*Steganura paradisaea* L, *Steganura obtusa* Chapin) und der Strohwitwe (*Tetraenura fischeri* Reichenow) in Ostafrika. *Journal für Ornithologie* 110: 421–447.

Nicolai, J. (1973) Das Lernprogramm in der Gesangsausbildung der Strohwitwe *Tetraenura fischeri* Reichenow. *Zeitschrift für Tierspychologie* 32: 113–138.

Nicolai, J. (1974) Mimicry in parasitic birds. *Scientific American* 231(4): 92–98.

Noble, D.G. (1995) Coevolution and ecology of seven sympatric cuckoo species and their hosts in Namibia. *PhD thesis*, University of Cambridge.

Noble, D.G. & Davies, N.B. (2000) Cuckoo eggs: host egg mimicry or supernormal stimuli? (manuscript).

Noble, D.G., Davies, N.B., Hartley, I.R. & McRae, S.B. (1999) The red gape of the nestling cuckoo *Cuculus canorus* is not a supernormal stimulus for three common hosts. *Behaviour* 136: 759–777.

Nolan, V. Jr. (1978) The ecology and behavior of the Prairie Warbler *Dendroica discolor*. *Ornithological Monographs* 26. American Ornithologists' Union.

Nolan, V. Jr. & Thompson, C.F. (1975) The occurrence and significance of anomalous reproductive activities in two North American non-parasitic cuckoos *Coccyzus* spp. *Ibis* 117: 496–503.

Norman, R.F. & Robertson, R.J. (1975) Nest-searching behaviour in the Brown-headed Cowbird. *Auk* 92: 610–611.

Øien, I.J., Moksnes, A. & Røskaft, E. (1995) Evolution of variation in egg colour and marking pattern in European passerines: adaptations in a coevolutionary arms race with the cuckoo *Cuculus canorus*. *Behavioural Ecology* 6: 166–174.

Øien, I.J., Honza, M., Moksnes, A. & Røskaft, E. (1996) The risk of parasitism in relation to the distance from reed warbler nests to cuckoo perches. *Journal of Animal Ecology* 65: 147–153.

O'Loghlen, A.L. & Rothstein, S.I. (1995) Culturally correct song dialects are correlated with male age and female song preferences in wild populations of Brown-headed Cowbirds. *Behavioural Ecology and Sociobiology* 36: 251–259.

Orians, G.H., Røskaft, E. & Beletsky, L.D. (1989) Do brown-headed cowbirds lay their eggs at random in the nests of red-winged blackbirds? *Wilson Bulletin* 101: 599–605.

Ortega, C.P. (1998) *Cowbirds and Other Brood Parasites*. University of Arizona Press, Tucson.

Ortega, J.C., Ortega, C.P. & Cruz, A. (1993) Does Brown-headed Cowbird egg coloration influence Red-winged Blackbird responses towards nest contents? *Condor* 95: 217–219.

Owen, J.H. (1912) Wrens as foster-parents of the Cuckoo. *British Birds* 6: 91–92.

Owen, J.H. (1933) The cuckoo in the Felsted district. *Report of the Felsted School Science Society* 33: 25–39.

Pagel, M., Møller, A.P. & Pomiankowski, A. (1998) Reduced parasitism by retaliatory cuckoos selects for hosts that rear cuckoo nestlings. *Behavioural Ecology* 9: 566–572.

Patterson, I.J., Gilboa, A. & Tozer, D.J. (1982) Rearing other people's young: brood mixing in the shelduck *Tadorna tadorna*. *Animal Behaviour* 30: 199–202.

Payne, R.B. (1973a) Behavior, mimetic songs and song dialects, and relationships of the parasitic indigobirds (*Vidua*) of Africa. *Ornithological Monographs* 11: 1–333.

Payne, R.B. (1973b) Vocal mimicry of the paradise whydahs (*Vidua*) and response of female whydahs to the songs of their hosts (*Pytilia*) and their mimics. *Animal Behaviour* 21: 762–771.

Payne, R.B. (1973c) Individual laying histories and the clutch size and numbers of eggs of parasitic cuckoos. *Condor* 75: 414–438.

Payne, R.B. (1974) The evolution of clutch size and reproductive rates in parasitic cuckoos. *Evolution* 28: 169–181.

Payne, R.B. (1977a) Clutch size, egg size and the consequences of single versus multiple parasitism in parasitic finches. *Ecology* 58: 500–513.

Payne, R.B. (1977b) The ecology of brood parasitism in birds. *Annual Review of Ecology and Systematics* 8: 1–28.

Payne, R.B. (1983) Bird songs, sexual selection and female mating strategies. In: *Social Behaviour of Female Vertebrates* (edited by S.K. Wasser). pp. 55–90. Academic Press, London.

Payne, R.B. (1997a) Family Cuculidae (Cuckoos). pp. 508–607. In *Handbook of the Birds of the World. Volume 4.* Edited by del Hoyo, J., Elliott, A. & Sargatal, J. Lynx Edicions, Barcelona.

Payne, R.B. (1997b) Avian brood parasitism. In: *Host-Parasite Evolution: General Principles and Avian Models* (edited by D.H. Clayton & J. Moore), pp. 338–369. Oxford University Press, Oxford.

Payne, R.B. (1998) Brood parasitism in birds: strangers in the nest. *BioScience* 48: 377–386.

Payne, R.B. & Groschupf, K.D. (1984) Sexual selection and interspecific competition: a field experiment on territorial behaviour of nonparental finches (*Vidua* spp). *Auk* 101: 140–145.

Payne, R.B. & Payne, K. (1967) Cuckoo hosts in southern Africa. *Ostrich* 38: 135–143.

Payne, R.B. & Payne, K. (1977) Social organisation and mating success in local song populations of Village Indigobirds, *Vidua chalybeata*. *Zeitschrift für Tierpsychologie* 45: 113–173.

Payne, R.B. & Payne, L.L. (1994) Song mimicry and species associations of west African indigobirds *Vidua* with Quail-finch *Ortygospiza atricollis*, Goldbreast *Amandava subflava* and Brown Twinspot *Clytospiza monteiri*. *Ibis* 136: 291–304.

Payne, R.B. & Payne, L.L. (1995) Song mimicry and association of brood-parasitic indigobirds (*Vidua*) with Dybowski's Twinspot (*Eustichospiza dybowskii*). *Auk* 112: 649–658.

Payne, R.B. & Payne, L.L. (1998a) Brood parasitism by cowbirds: risks and effects on reproductive success and survival in indigo buntings. *Behavioural Ecology* 9: 64–73.

Payne, R.B. & Payne, L.L. (1998b) Nestling eviction and vocal begging behaviors in the Australian glossy cuckoos *Chrysococcyx basalis* and *C. lucidus*. In: *Parasitic Birds and Their Hosts*. pp. 152–169. Edited by S.I. Rothstein & S.K. Robinson. Oxford University Press.

Payne, R.B., Payne, L.L. & Rowley, I. (1985) Splendid Wren *Malurus splendens* response to cuckoos: an experimental test of social organisation in a communal bird. *Behaviour* 94: 108–127.

Payne, R.B., Payne, L.L. & Woods, J.L. (1998) Song learning in brood-parasitic indigobirds *Vidua chalybeata*: song mimicry of the host species. *Animal Behaviour* 55: 1537–1553.

Payne, R.B., Payne, L.L. & Woods, J.L. (2000a) Parental care in estrildid finches: experimental tests of a colonization model of *Vidua* brood parasitism. *Animal Behaviour*.

Payne, R.B., Payne, L.L., Woods, J.L. & Sorenson, M.D. (2000b) Imprinting and the origin of parasite-host species associations in brood parasitic indigobirds *Vidua chalybeata*. *Animal Behaviour*.

Payne, R.B., Payne, L.L., Nhlane, M.E.D. & Hustler, K. (1992) Species status and distribution of the parasitic indigo-birds *Vidua* in East and Southern Africa. *Proceedings of the 8th Pan-African Ornithological Congress* 40–52.

Pease, C.M. & Grzybowski, J.A. (1995) Assessing the consequences of brood parasitism and nest predation on seasonal fecundity in passerine birds. *Auk* 112: 343–363.

Peck, A.L. (1970) *Aristotle: Historia Animalium* Vol II. Heinemann, London.

Peer, B.D. & Bollinger, E.K. (1997) Explanations for the infrequent cowbird parasitism on Common Grackles. *Condor* 99: 151–161.

Perrin de Brichambaut, J. (1997) Le comportement parasitaire du coucou gris *Cuculus canorus*: comparaisons régionales, évolution dans le temps. *Alauda* 65: 167–186.

Perrins, C.M. (1967) The short apparent incubation period of the Cuckoo. *British Birds* 60: 51–52.

Petit, L.J. (1991) Adaptive tolerance of cowbird parasitism by prothonotary warblers: a consequence of nest-site limitation? *Animal Behaviour* 41: 425–432.

Petrie, M. & Møller, A.P. (1991) Laying eggs in others' nests: intraspecific brood parasitism in birds. *Trends in Ecology and Evolution* 6: 315–320.

Picman, J. (1989) Mechanisms of increased puncture resistance of eggs of brown-headed cowbirds. *Auk* 106: 577–583.

Picman, J. & Pribil, S. (1997) Is greater eggshell density an alternative mechanism by which parasitic cuckoos increase the strength of their eggs? *Journal für Ornithologie* 138: 531–541.

Pierotti, R. & Murphy, E.C. (1987) Intergenerational conflict in gulls. *Animal Behaviour* 35: 435–444.

Pimm, S.L., Jones, H.L. & Diamond, J. (1988) On the risk of extinction. *American Naturalist* 132: 757–785.

Pinxten, R., Eens, M. & Verheyen, R.F. (1991a) Conspecific nest parasitism in the European Starling. *Ardea* 79: 15–30.

Pinxten, R., Eens, M. & Verheyen, R.F. (1991b) Responses of male starlings to experimental intraspecific brood parasitism. *Animal Behaviour* 42: 1028–1030.

Post, W. & Wiley, J.W. (1977) Reproductive interactions of the shiny cowbird and the yellow-shouldered blackbird. *Condor* 79: 176–184.

Post, W., Nakamura, T.K. & Cruz, A. (1990) Patterns of shiny cowbird parasitism in St. Lucia and southwestern Puerto Rico. *Condor* 92: 461–469.

Powell, A. (1979) Cuckoo in the nest. *Wildfowl News* 81: 15–16.

Power, H.W., Kennedy, E.D., Romagnano, L.C., Lombardo, M.P., Hoffenberg, A.S., Stouffer, P.C. & McGuire, T.R. (1989) The parasitism insurance hypothesis: why starlings leave space for parasitic eggs. *Condor* 91: 753–765.

Pulliam, H.R. (1988) Sources, sinks and population regulation. *American Naturalist* 132: 652–661.

Punnett, R.C. (1933) Inheritance of egg-colour in the 'parasitic' cuckoos. *Nature* 132: 892.

Ralph, C.P. (1975) Life style of *Coccyzus pumilus*, a tropical cuckoo. *Condor* 77: 60–72.

Raven, C.E. (1953) *Natural Religion and Christian Theology*. Cambridge University Press, Cambridge.

Reboreda, J.C., Clayton, N.S. & Kacelnik, A. (1996) Species and sex differences in hippocampus size in parasitic and non-parasitic cowbirds. *Neuroreport* 7: 505–508.

Redondo, T. (1993) Exploitation of host mechanisms for parental care by avian brood parasites. *Etologia* 3: 235–297.

Redondo, T. & Arias de Reyna, L. (1988) Vocal mimicry of hosts by Great Spotted Cuckoo *Clamator glandarius*: further evidence. *Ibis* 130: 540–544.

Redondo, T. & Castro, F. (1992) Signalling of nutritional need by Magpie nestlings. *Ethology* 92: 193–204.

Redondo, T., Tortosa, F.S. & Arias de Reyna, L. (1995) Nest switching and alloparental care in colonial white storks. *Animal Behaviour* 49: 1097–1110.

Reed, H.J. & Freeman, N.H. (1991) Does an absence of gape markings affect survival of leucistic young in the zebra finch? *Bird Behaviour* 9: 58–63.

Reed, R.A. (1968) Studies of the Diederik Cuckoo *Chrysococcyx caprius* in the Transvaal. *Ibis* 110: 321–331.

Rensch, B. (1924) Zur Entstehung der Mimikry der Kuckuckseier. *Journal für Ornithologie* 72: 461–472.

Rensch, B. (1925) Verhalten von Singvögeln bei Aenderung des Geleges. *Ornithologie Monat.* 33: 169–173.

Rey, E. (1892) *Altes und Neues aus dem Haushalte des Kuckucks*. Freese, Leipzig.

Ridley, M. (1993) *Evolution*. Blackwell Science, Oxford.

Robert, M. & Sorci, G. (1999) Rapid increase of host defence against brood parasites in a recently parasitized area: the case of village weavers in Hispaniola. *Proceedings of the Royal Society B.* 266: 941–946.

Robertson, R.J. & Norman, R.F. (1977) The function and evolution of aggressive host behaviour towards the brown-headed cowbird *Molothrus ater*. *Canadian Journal of Zoology* 55: 508–518.

Robinson, S.K. (1988) Foraging ecology and host relationships of Giant Cowbirds in south-eastern Peru. *Wilson Bulletin* 100: 224–235.

Robinson, S.K., Thompson, F.R. III, Donovan, T.M., Whitehead, D.R. & Faaborg, J. (1995a) Regional forest fragmentation and the nesting success of migratory birds. *Science* 267: 1987–1990.

Robinson, S.K., Rothstein, S.I., Brittingham, M.C., Petit, L.J. & Grzybowski, J.A. (1995b) Ecology and behaviour of cowbirds and their impact on host populations. In: *Ecology and Management of Neotropical Migratory Birds*. ed. by T.E. Martin & D.M. Finch. pp. 428–460. Oxford University Press, Oxford.

Rodríguez-Gironés, M.A. & Lotem, A. (1999) How to detect a cuckoo egg: a signal-detection theory model for recognition and learning. *American Naturalist* 153: 633–648.

Rohwer, F.C. & Freeman, S. (1989) The distribution of conspecific nest parasitism in birds. *Canadian Journal of Zoology* 67: 239–253.

Rohwer, S. & Spaw, C.D. (1988) Evolutionary lag versus bill-size constraints: a comparative study of the acceptance of cowbird eggs by old hosts. *Evolutionary Ecology* 2: 27–36.

Romagnano, L., Hoffenberg, A.S. & Power, H.W. (1990) Intraspecific brood parasitism in the European starling. *Wilson Bulletin* 102: 279–291.

Røskaft, E. & Moksnes, A. (1998) Coevolution between brood parasites and their hosts: an optimality theory approach. In: *Parasitic Birds and Their Hosts* (Ed. by S.I. Rothstein & S.K. Robinson). pp. 236–254. Oxford University Press, Oxford.

Røskaft, E., Orians, G.H. & Beletsky, L.D. (1990) Why do Red-winged Blackbirds accept eggs of Brown-headed Cowbirds? *Evolutionary Ecology* 4: 35–42.

Røskaft, E., Rohwer, S. & Spaw, C.D. (1993) Costs of puncture ejection compared with costs of rearing cowbird chicks for Northern Orioles. *Ornis Scandinavica* 24: 28–32.

Rothstein, S.I. (1974) Mechanisms of avian egg recognition: possible learned and innate factors. *Auk* 91: 796–807.

Rothstein, S.I. (1975a) An experimental and teleonomic investigation of avian brood parasitism. *Condor* 77: 250–271.

Rothstein, S.I. (1975b) Evolutionary rates and host defenses against avian brood parasitism. *American Naturalist* 109: 161–176.

Rothstein, S.I. (1975c) Mechanisms of avian egg recognition: do birds know their own eggs? *Animal Behaviour* 23: 268–278.

Rothstein, S.I. (1976) Cowbird parasitism of the cedar waxwing and its evolutionary implications. *Auk* 93: 498–509.

Rothstein, S.I. (1982a) Mechanisms of avian egg recognition: which egg parameters elicit responses by rejecter species? *Behavioural Ecology and Sociobiology* 11: 229–239.

Rothstein, S.I. (1982b) Successes and failures in avian egg and nestling recognition with comments on the utility of optimality reasoning. *American Zoologist* 22: 547–560.

Rothstein, S.I. (1986) A test of optimality: egg recognition in the Eastern Phoebe. *Animal Behaviour* 34: 1109–1119.

Rothstein, S.I. (1990) A model system for coevolution: avian brood parasitism. *Annual Review of Ecology and Systematics* 21: 481–508.

Rothstein, S.I. (1992) Brood parasitism, the importance of experiments and host defences of avifaunas on different continents. *Proceedings of the Seventh Pan-African Ornithology Congress*: 521–535.

Rothstein, S.I. (1993) An experimental test of the Hamilton-Orians hypothesis for the origin of avian brood parasitism. *Condor* 95: 1000–1005.

Rothstein, S.I. (1994) The cowbirds' invasion of the far west: history, causes and consequences experienced by host species. *Studies in Avian Biology* 15: 301–315.

Rothstein, S.I. & Cook, T.L. (1999) Cowbird management, host population regulation and efforts to save endangered species. In: Smith, J.N.M. *et al.* (1999).

Rothstein, S.I. & Fleischer, R.C. (1987) Vocal dialects and their possible relation to honest status signalling in the Brown-headed Cowbird. *Condor* 89: 1–23.

Rothstein, S.I. & Robinson, S.K. (eds) (1998) *Parasitic Birds and Their Hosts: Studies in Coevolution.* Oxford University Press, Oxford.

Rothstein, S.I., Farmer, C. & Verner, J. (1999) Cowbird vocalisations: an overview and the use of playbacks to enhance Cowbird detectability. In: Smith, J.N.M. *et al.* (1999).

Rothstein, S.I., Patten, M.A. & Fleischer, R.C. (MS) Phylogeny, specialization and parasite-host coevolution.

Rothstein, S.I., Verner, J. & Stevens, E. (1984) Radio-tracking confirms a unique diurnal pattern of spatial occurrence in the parasitic brown-headed cowbird. *Ecology* 65: 77–88.

Rowan, M.K. (1983) *The Doves, Parrots, Louries and Cuckoos of Southern Africa.* Croom Helm, London.

Rowley, I. & Russell, E. (1990) Splendid Fairy-wrens: demonstrating the importance of longevity. In: *Cooperative Breeding in Birds.* Edited by P.B. Stacey & W.D. Koenig. pp. 3–30. Cambridge University Press, Cambridge.

Safriel, U.N. (1975) On the significance of clutch size in nidifugous birds. *Ecology* 56: 703–708.

Sandell, M.I. & Diemer, M. (1999) Intraspecific brood parasitism: a strategy for floating females in the European starling. *Animal Behaviour* 57: 197–202.

Sato, T. (1986) A brood parasitic catfish of mouthbrooding cichlid fishes in Lake Tanganyika. *Nature* 323: 58–59.

Sayler, R.D. (1996) Behavioural interactions among brood parasites with precocial young: canvasbacks and redheads on the Delta marsh. *Condor* 98: 801–809.

Scott, D.M. (1977) Cowbird parasitism on the gray catbird at London, Ontario. *Auk* 94: 18–27.

Scott, D.M. (1991) The time of day of egg laying by the brown-headed cowbird and other icterines. *Canadian Journal of Zoology* 69: 2093–2099.

Scott, D.M. & Ankney, C.D. (1983) The laying cycle of brown-headed cowbirds: passerine chickens? *Auk* 100: 583–592.

Scott, D.M., Weatherhead, P.J. & Ankney, C.D. (1992) Egg-eating by female Brown-headed Cowbirds. *Condor* 94: 579–584.

Sealy, S.G. (1992) Removal of Yellow Warbler eggs in association with cowbird parasitism. *Condor* 94: 40–54.

Sealy, S.G. (1996) Evolution of host defences against brood parasitism: implications of puncture-ejection by a small passerine. *Auk* 113: 346–355.

Sealy, S.G. & Bazin, R.C. (1995) Low frequency of observed cowbird parasitism on eastern kingbirds: host rejection, effective host defence or parasite avoidance? *Behavioural Ecology* 6: 140–145.

Sealy, S.G., Neudorf, D.L. & Hill, D.P. (1995) Rapid laying by Brown-headed Cowbirds *Molothrus ater* and other parasitic birds. *Ibis* 137: 76–84.

Seel, D.C. (1973) Egg-laying in the Cuckoo. *British Birds* 66: 528–535.

Seel, D.C. (1977) Migration of the northwestern European population of the Cuckoo, *Cuculus canorus*, as shown by ringing. *Ibis* 119: 309–322.

Seel, D.C. & Davis, P.R.K. (1981) Cuckoos reared by unusual hosts in Britain. *Bird Study* 28: 242–243.

Semel, B. & Sherman, P.W. (1986) Dynamics of nest parasitism in wood ducks. *Auk* 103: 813–816.

Semel, B., Sherman, P.W. & Byers, S.M. (1988) Effects of brood parasitism and nest-box placement on wood duck breeding ecology. *Condor* 90: 920–930.

Shaw, P. (1984) The social behaviour of the Pin-tailed Whydah *Vidua macroura* in northern Ghana. *Ibis* 126: 463–473.

Sherry, D., Forbes, M.R.L., Khurgel, M. & Ivy, G.O. (1993) Females have larger hippocampuses than males in the brood-parasitic brown-headed cowbird. *Proceedings of the National Academy of Sciences USA* 90: 7839–7843.

Sibley, C.G. & Ahlquist, J.E. (1990) *Phylogeny and Classification of Birds: A Study in Molecular Evolution.* Yale University Press, New Haven.

Simons, L.S. & Martin, T.E. (1990) Food limitation of avian reproduction: an experiment with the cactus wren. *Ecology* 71: 869–876.

Skagen, S.K. (1988) Asynchronous hatching and food limitation: a test of Lack's hypothesis. *Auk* 105: 78–88.

Skead, D.M. (1975) Ecological studies of four estrildines in the central Transvaal. *Ostrich* (supplement) 11: 1–55.

Slagsvold, T. (1998) On the origin and rarity of interspecific nest parasitism in birds. *American Naturalist* 152: 264–272.

Smith, J.N.M. & Arcese, P. (1994) Brown-headed Cowbirds and an island population of Song Sparrows: a 16-year study. *Condor* 96: 916–934.

Smith, J.N.M., Arcese, P. & McLean, I.G. (1984) Age, experience and enemy recognition by wild song sparrows. *Behavioural Ecology and Sociobiology* 14: 101–106.

Smith, J.N.M., Cook, T.L., Rothstein, S.I., Robinson, S.K. & Sealy, S.G. (eds) (1999) *The*

Ecology and Management of Cowbirds: Studies in the Conservation of North American Passerine Birds. University of Texas Press, Austin.

Smith, N.G. (1968) The advantage of being parasitised. *Nature* 219: 690–694.

Soler, J.J. & Møller, A.P. (1996) A comparative analysis of the evolution of variation in appearance of eggs of European passerines in relation to brood parasitism. *Behavioural Ecology* 7: 89–94.

Soler, J.J., Soler, M., Møller, A.P. & Martínez, J.G. (1995) Does the Great Spotted Cuckoo choose Magpie hosts according to their parenting ability? *Behavioural Ecology and Sociobiology* 36: 201–206.

Soler, J.J., Sorci, G., Soler, M. & Møller, A.P. (1999) Change in host rejection behavior mediated by the predatory behavior of its brood parasite. *Behavioural Ecology.* 10: 275–280.

Soler, M. (1990) Relationships between the Great Spotted Cuckoo *Clamator glandarius* and its corvid hosts in a recently colonized area. *Ornis Scandinavica* 21: 212–223.

Soler, M. & Møller, A.P. (1990) Duration of sympatry and coevolution between the Great Spotted Cuckoo and its Magpie host. *Nature* 343: 748–750.

Soler, M. & Soler, J.J. (1991) Growth and development of Great Spotted Cuckoos and their Magpie hosts. *Condor* 93: 49–54.

Soler, M., Palomino, J.J. & Martínez, J.G. (1994a) Activity, survival, independence and migration of fledgling Great Spotted Cuckoos. *Condor* 96: 802–805.

Soler, M., Soler, J.J., Martínez, J.G. & Møller, A.P. (1994b) Micro-evolutionary change in host response to a brood parasite. *Behavioural Ecology and Sociobiology* 35: 295–301.

Soler, M., Martínez, J.G., Soler, J.J. & Møller, A.P. (1995a) Preferential allocation of food by Magpies *Pica pica* to Great Spotted Cuckoo *Clamator glandarius* chicks. *Behavioural Ecology and Sociobiology* 37: 7–13.

Soler, M., Soler, J.J., Martínez, J.G. & Møller, A.P. (1995b) Chick recognition and acceptance: a weakness in Magpies exploited by the parasitic Great Spotted Cuckoo. *Behavioural Ecology and Sociobiology* 37: 243–248.

Soler, M., Soler, J.J., Martínez, J.G. & Møller, A.P. (1995c) Magpie host manipulation by Great Spotted Cuckoos: evidence for an avian Mafia? *Evolution* 49: 770–775.

Soler, M., Martínez, J.G. & Soler, J.J. (1996) Effects of brood parasitism by the Great Spotted Cuckoo on the breeding success of the Magpie host: an experimental study. *Ardeola* 43: 87–96.

Soler, M., Soler, J.J. & Martínez, J.G. (1997) Great Spotted Cuckoos improve their reproductive success by damaging Magpie host eggs. *Animal Behaviour* 54: 1227–1233.

Soler, M., Soler, J.J., Martínez, J.G., Pérez-Contreras, T. & Møller, A.P. (1998) Micro-evolutionary change and population dyanamics of a brood parasite and its primary host: the intermittent arms race hypothesis. *Oecologia* 117: 381–390.

Sorenson, M.D. (1991) The functional significance of parasitic egg laying and typical nesting in redhead ducks: an analysis of individual behaviour. *Animal Behaviour* 42: 771–796.

Sorenson, M.D. (1993) Parasitic egg laying in Canvasbacks: frequency, success, and individual behaviour. *Auk* 110: 57–69.

Sorenson, M.D. (1995) Evidence of conspecific nest parasitism and egg discrimination in the Sora. *Condor* 97: 819–821.

Sorenson, M.D. (1997) Effects of intra- and interspecific brood parasitism on a precocial host, the canvasback, *Aythya valisineria. Behavioural Ecology* 8: 153–161.

Sorenson, M.D. (1998) Patterns of parasitic egg laying and typical nesting in redhead and canvasback ducks. In: *Parasitic Birds and Their Hosts.* (Edited by S.I. Rothstein & S.K. Robinson). pp. 357–375. Oxford University Press, Oxford.

Sorenson, M.D. & Payne, R.B. (1998) A single origin of brood parasitism in African finches. (Proceedings of the 22nd International Ornithological Congress, Durban). *Ostrich* 69: 208.

Southern, H.N. (1954) Mimicry in cuckoos' eggs. In *Evolution as a Process.* Edited by J.S. Huxley, A.C. Hardy & E.B. Ford. pp. 219–232. Allen & Unwin, London.

Soyfer, V.N. (1994) *Lysenko and the Tragedy of Soviet Science.* Rutgers University Press, New Brunswick, N.J.

Spaw, C.D. & Rohwer, S. (1987) A comparative study of eggshell thickness in cowbirds and other passerines. *Condor* 89: 307–318.

Spencer, O.R. (1943) Nesting habits of the black-billed cuckoo. *Wilson Bulletin* 55: 11–22.

Steyn, P. (1973) Some notes on the breeding biology of the Striped Cuckoo. *Ostrich* 44: 163–169.

Steyn, P. & Howells, W.W. (1975) Supplementary notes on the breeding biology of the Striped Cuckoo. *Ostrich* 46: 258–260.

Stokke, B.G., Moksnes, A., Røskaft, E., Rudolfsen, G. & Honza, M. (1999) Rejection of artificial cuckoo (*Cuculus canorus*) eggs in relation to variation in egg appearance among reed warblers (*Acrocephalus scirpaceus*). *Proceedings of the Royal Society of London B* 266: 1483–1488.

Stouffer, P.C. & Power, H.W. (1991) Brood parasitism by starlings experimentally forced to desert their nests. *Animal Behaviour* 41: 537–539.

Stouffer, P.C., Kennedy, E.D. & Power, H.W. (1987) Recognition and removal of intraspecific parasite eggs by starlings. *Animal Behaviour* 35: 1583–1584.

Swynnerton, C.F.M. (1918) Rejections by birds of eggs unlike their own: with remarks on some of the cuckoo problems. *Ibis* Tenth Series 6: 127–154.

Sykes, P.W. & Clench, M.H. (1998) Winter habitat of Kirtland's Warbler: an endangered Nearctic/Neotropical migrant. *Wilson Bulletin* 110: 244–261.

Taborsky, M. (1994) Sneakers, satellites, and helpers: parasitic and cooperative behavior in fish reproduction. *Advances in the Study of Behavior* 23: 1–100.

Takasu, F. (1998a) Why do all host species not show defense against avian brood parasitism: evolutionary lag or equilibrium? *American Naturalist* 151: 193–205.

Takasu, F. (1998b) Modelling the arms race in avian brood parasitism. *Evolutionary Ecology* 12: 969–987.

Takasu, F., Kawasaki, K., Nakamura, H., Cohen, J.E. & Shigesada, N. (1993) Modeling the population dynamics of a cuckoo-host association and the evolution of host defences. *American Naturalist* 142: 819–839.

Tallamy, D.W. & Horton, L.A. (1990) Costs and benefits of the egg-dumping alternative in *Gargaphia* lace bugs (Hemiptera: Tingidae). *Animal Behaviour* 39: 352–359.

Teather, K.L. & Robertson, R.J. (1986) Pair bonds and factors influencing the diversity of mating systems in brown-headed cowbirds. *Condor* 88: 63–69.

ten Cate, C. & Bateson, P.P.G. (1989) Sexual imprinting and a preference for 'supernormal' partners in Japanese quail. *Animal Behaviour* 38: 356–358.

Terborgh, J. (1989) *Where Have All The Birds Gone?* Princeton University Press, Princeton.

Teuschl, Y., Taborsky, B. & Taborsky, M. (1998) How do cuckoos find their hosts? The role of habitat imprinting. *Animal Behaviour* 56: 1425–1433.

Thompson, F.R. III. (1994) Temporal and spatial patterns of breeding Brown-headed Cowbirds in the midwestern United States. *Auk* 111: 979–990.

Topsell, E. (1614) *The Fowles of Heauen or History of Birdes.* Edited by T.P. Harrison & F.D. Hoeniger (1972), University of Texas Press, Austin.

Trine, C.L. (1998) Wood Thrush population sinks and implications for the scale of regional conservation strategies. *Conservation Biology* 12: 576–585.

Trivers, R.L. (1974) Parent-offspring conflict. *American Zoologist* 14: 249–264.

Tschanz, B. (1968) Trottellummen (*Uria aalge aalge* Pont.). *Zeitschrift für Tierpsychologie* 4: 1–103.

van Valen, L. (1973) A new evolutionary law. *Evolutionary Theory* 1: 1–30.

Varga, F. (1994) *Cuckoo Observations Around the Source of River Zagyva.* Published by Ferenc Varga, Uniprint Nyomda, kft.

Vehrencamp, S.L., Bowen, B.S. & Koford, R.R. (1986) Breeding roles and pairing patterns within communal groups of groove-billed anis. *Animal Behaviour* 34: 347–366.

Vernon, C.J. (1964) The breeding of the Cuckoo Weaver *Anomalospiza imberbis* in southern Rhodesia. *Ostrich* 35: 260–263.

Victoria, J.K. (1972) Clutch characteristics and egg discriminative ability of the African Village Weaverbird *Ploceus cucullatus*. *Ibis* 114: 367–376.

von Haartman, L. (1981) Coevolution of the cuckoo *Cuculus canorus* and a regular cuckoo host. *Ornis Fennica* 58: 1–10.

Walkinshaw, L.H. (1949) Twenty-five eggs apparently laid by a cowbird. *Wilson Bulletin* 61: 82–85.

Wallace, A.R. (1889) *Darwinism: An Exposition of the Theory of Natural Selection with some of its Applications.* Macmillan, London.

Ward, D. & Smith, J.N.M. (1998) Morphological differentiation of Brown-headed Cowbirds in the Okanagen Valley, British Columbia. *Condor* 100: 1–7.

Ward, D., Lindholm, A.K. & Smith, J.N.M. (1996) Multiple parasitism of the red-winged blackbird: further experimental evidence of evolutionary lag in a common host of the brown-headed cowbird. *Auk* 113: 408–413.

Weatherhead, P.J. (1989) Sex ratios, host-specific reproductive success and impact of brown-headed cowbirds. *Auk* 106: 358–366.

Webster, M.S. (1994) Interspecific brood parasitism of Montezuma Oropendolas by Giant Cowbirds: parasitism or mutualism? *Condor* 96: 794–798.

Weigmann, C. & Lamprecht, J. (1991) Intraspecific nest parasitism in bar-headed geese *Anser indicus. Animal Behaviour* 41: 677–688.

Weller, M.W. (1959) Parasitic egg laying in the redhead *Aythya americana* and other North American Anatidae. *Ecological Monographs* 29: 333–365.

Weller, M.W. (1968) The breeding biology of the parasitic black-headed duck. *Living Bird* 7: 169–208.

West, M.J. & King, A.P. (1985) Social guidance of vocal learning by female Cowbirds: validating its functional significance. *Zeitschrift für Tierpsychologie* 70: 225–235.

West-Eberhard, M.J. (1986) Alternative adaptations, speciation, and phylogeny (A Review). *Proceedings of the National Academy of Sciences,* U.S.A. 83: 1388–1392.

White, G. (1789) *The Natural History of Selborne.* Edited by R. Mabey (1977), Penguin, Harmondsworth.

Whitfield, M.J. (1999) Results of a Brown-headed Cowbird control program for the southwestern Willow Flycatcher. In: Smith J.N.M. *et al.* (1999).

Wiley, J.W. (1985) Shiny cowbird parasitism in two avian communities in Puerto Rico. *Condor* 87: 165–176.

Wiley, J.W. (1988) Host selection by the shiny cowbird. *Condor* 90: 289–303.

Wiley, J.W., Post, W. & Cruz, A. (1991) Conservation of the yellow-shouldered blackbird *Agelaius xanthomus,* an endangered West Indian species. *Biological Conservation* 55: 119–138.

Williams, T.D. (1994) Adoption in a precocial species, the lesser snow goose: intergenerational conflict, altruism or a mutually beneficial strategy? *Animal Behaviour* 47: 101–107.

Wilson, E.O. (1971) *The Insect Societies.* Belknap Press, Harvard.

Wood, D.R. & Bollinger, E.K. (1997) Egg removal by Brown-headed Cowbirds: a field test of the host incubation efficiency hypothesis. *Condor* 99: 851–857.

Woodward, P.W. (1983) Behavioural ecology of fledgling brown-headed cowbirds and their hosts. *Condor* 85: 151–163.

Wyllie, I. (1981) *The Cuckoo.* Batsford, London.

Yamagishi, S. & Fujioka, M. (1986) Heavy brood parasitism by the Common Cuckoo *Cuculus canorus* on the Azure-winged Magpie *Cyanopica cyana. Tori* 34: 91–96.

Yamauchi, A. (1993) Theory of intraspecific nest parasitism in birds. *Animal Behaviour* 46: 335–345.

Yamauchi, A. (1995) Theory of evolution of nest parasitism in birds. *American Naturalist* 145: 434–456.

Yokel, D.A. (1986) Monogamy and brood parasitism: an unlikely pair. *Animal Behaviour* 34: 1348–1358.

Yokel, D.A. & Rothstein, S.I. (1991) The basis for female choice in an avian brood parasite. *Behavioural Ecology and Sociobiology* 29: 39–45.

Yom-Tov, Y. (1980) Intraspecific nest parasitism in birds. *Biological Reviews* 55: 93–108.

Yom-Tov, Y., Dunnet, G.M. & Anderson, A. (1974) Intraspecific nest parasitism in the Starling *Sturnus vulgaris. Ibis* 116: 87–90.

Zahavi, A. (1979) Parasitism and nest predation in parasitic cuckoos. *American Naturalist* 13: 157–159.

Zahavi, A. & Zahavi, A. (1997) *The Handicap Principle.* Oxford University Press, Oxford.

Zann, R.A. (1996) *The Zebra Finch.* Oxford University Press.

Zuñiga, J.M. & Redondo, T. (1992) No evidence for variable duration of sympatry between the Great Spotted Cuckoo and its Magpie host. *Nature* 359: 410–411.

Index

Other books in the series

THE ATLAS OF BREEDING BIRDS IN BRITAIN AND IRELAND compiled by J.T.R. Sharrock

FLIGHT INDENTIFICATION OF EUROPEAN RAPTORS compiled by R.F. Porter, I. Willis, S. Christensen and B.P. Nielsen

THE BIRDWATCHERS DICTIONARY by Peter Weaver

ESTUARY BIRDS OF BRITAIN AND IRELAND by A.J. Prater

OWLS OF EUROPE by Heimo Mikkola

THE BEE-EATERS by C.H. Fry

BIRDS IN SCOTLAND by Valerie M. Thom

GULLS: a guide to identification by P.J. Grant

WADERS: their breeding, haunts and watchers by Desmond and Maimie Nethersole-Thompson

THE SKUAS by Robert W. Furness

BIRDS OF THE MIDDLE EAST AND NORTH AFRICA by P.A.D. Hollom, R.F. Porter, S. Christensen and I. Willis

THE SPARROWS by J. Denis Summers-Smith

BIRDS AND BERRIES by Barbara and David Snow

WEATHER AND BIRD BEHAVIOUR Second Edition by Norman Elkins

RARE BIRDS IN BRITAIN AND IRELAND by J.N. Dymond, P.A. Fraser and S.J.M. Gantlett

THE KESTREL by Andrew Village

POPULATION ECOLOGY OF RAPTORS by Ian Newton

MAN AND WILDFOWL by Janet Kear

BIRDS BY NIGHT by Graham Martin

BIRDS AND FORESTRY by Mark Avery and Roderick Leslie

RED DATA BIRDS IN BRITAIN by L.A. Batten, C.J. Bibby, P. Clement, G.D. Elliott and R.F. Porter

THE RUFF by Johan G. van Rhijn

THE MAGPIES by T. R. Birkhead

BIRDS OF THE STRAIT OF GIBRALTAR by Clive Finlayson

IN SEARCH OF SPARROWS by J. Denis Summers-Smith

THE PIED FLYCATCHER by Arne Lundberg and Rauno V. Alatalo

THE ANCIENT MURRELET by Anthony J. Gaston

THE PINYON JAY by John M. Marzluff and Russell P. Balda

GREAT AUK ISLANDS: a field biologist in the Arctic by Tim Birkhead

THE PEREGRINE FALCON Second Edition by Derek Ratcliffe

A DICTIONARY OF BIRDS by Bruce Campbell and Elizabeth Lack

THE NEW ATLAS OF BREEDING BIRDS IN BRITAIN AND IRELAND: 1988-1991 compiled by D. W. Gibbons, J.B. Reid and R.A. Chapman

THE DIPPERS by Stephanie Tyler and Stephen Ormerod

THE HISTORICAL ATLAS OF BREEDING BIRDS IN BRITAIN AND IRELAND 1875-1900 by Simon Holloway

RARE BIRDS DAY BY DAY by Steve Dudley, Tim Benton, Peter Fraser and John Ryan

FIELD GUIDE TO THE BIRDS OF THE MIDDLE EAST by R. F. Porter, S. Christensen and P. Schiermacker-Hansen